Contents

	Introduction	vii
	Acknowledgements	ix
Chapter 1.	Higher Education Prior to 1960	1
Chapter 2.	New Ideas at the Department of Education	25
Chapter 3.	A Tale of Two Committees	41
Chapter 4.	Limerick Wants a University	65
Chapter 5.	A System Takes Shape 1968-74	79
Chapter 6.	The Universities Mark Time	96
Chapter 7.	Binary or Comprehensive?	113
Chapter 8.	1977-1980 – A Period of Consolidation	136
Chapter 9.	The Universities Come in from the Cold	184
Chapter 10.	'The Centre Cannot Hold'	211
Chapter 11.	Some International Comparisons	247
Chapter 12.	A New Agenda?	268
	Appendices	282
	Bibliography	287

Introduction

The number of students in higher education in the Republic of Ireland grew by more than a factor of six between 1964 and 1997, from 18,000 to over 112,000. The prospects still are for further growth. Thirty years ago the state had what by European standards was a small élite system of higher education based mainly on five university colleges. A generation later it has a diversified and well-developed provision of mass higher education with greater participation rates among eighteen year olds than many comparable European countries, including Britain.

The rapid growth in higher education partly explains why the Republic of Ireland currently has the fastest growing economy in the European Union. The increased provision has positioned the Irish state well for an age where information and developed brainpower have become key ingredients for any modern society wishing to achieve economic growth and wealth creation. Ireland has reached this position by a mixture of planning and luck.

In the 1960s the Irish state almost accidentally entered into a social engineering project which built up technological and vocational education outside the universities. This project received new life in the 1980s when supported by the state's Industrial Development Authority. The Authority transformed the situation by involving the universities, which in turn began to adapt themselves to meet the state's manpower requirements. The strong position in which Ireland found itself at the turn of the century was partly due to deliberate planning; it was also due to accidents of history and the political process, and to strong personalities. Irish higher education is not a pure designer project and it does not have a tidy history.

Major expansion in higher education is a phenomenon of developed countries in the second half of the twentieth century. In other countries it has given rise to a thriving body of research and analysis on the history and process of these developments, and on the outcomes and social effects of mass higher education. While research into Irish education has expanded very significantly over the past twenty-five years as evidenced, for example, in *Irish Educational Studies*, the work of the Educational

Studies Association of Ireland and the volume of postgraduate studies, relatively little attention has been devoted to the rapidly growing sector of higher education. Elsewhere this growth has spawned a veritable academic industry. Perhaps in time the same will happen in Ireland.

In the evolution of Irish higher education over the period since the 1960s the most significant development has been the growth from almost nothing of a large system of vocational and technological education outside the universities. The author spent much of the 1970s and 1980s working with the Higher Education Authority and the National Council for Educational Awards. He was in a position to observe the new system grow from small beginnings to become a very sizeable and influential part of Irish higher education.

While this study draws on archival and hitherto unpublished material, the author has predominantly used the available material – official publications, Oireachtas (Irish parliamentary) reports, national and local newspapers and existing literature on Irish education – to interpret the ebb and flow of Irish higher education since the early 1960s. This has been supplemented by a small number of interviews. Individuals were selected for interview primarily to cover the period to 1973 (prior to the author's first working in the area of third-level administration when he had not the same vantage point for the unfolding of events) and where it seemed necessary to put on record salient and undocumented detail about events prior to that period.

The period from the mid 1960s to the end of the twentieth century will almost certainly come to be seen as a watershed in higher education in Ireland. Many of the institutions founded in that period will survive and grow, and are likely to play an increasingly important part in the lives of Irish citizens. This is a study of how they originated, how they developed and why.

Acknowledgements

This book has grown out of a doctorate thesis and I owe a debt of gratitude to many people who assisted me in the period when both were in preparation.

My thesis supervisor, Professor Valentine Rice, and the Department of Higher Education and Educational Research at Trinity College Dublin provided a welcoming, tolerant and supportive home for a student with an unpredictable work schedule and a consequent irregular commitment to the task in hand.

I am grateful to the staffs of the libraries at Trinity College Dublin, University College Dublin, National University of Ireland Galway and the National Library of Ireland, and the staff of the National Archives, for their courtesy and assistance. I am in debt for support beyond the call of duty to Pattie Punch at the library of the University of Limerick, Margaret Purcell, librarian of the National Council for Educational Awards, and above all to Mary Prendergast and her staff in the library of the Institute of Public Administration.

I have had an enormous number of helpers on this journey. I am grateful to numerous individuals in government departments, state organisations, third-level colleges and professional bodies for relevant information and assistance. Former colleagues at the National Council for Educational Awards and the Higher Education Authority have been most helpful in supplying information on a variety of points. In a more fundamental way I am indebted to many of them for stimulation, argument and discussion over many years; that more than anything else has inspired this study.

I am especially grateful to John Hayden, Eddie O'Donnell, Dermot Finan, Peter Fuller and Professor John Coolahan who read the manuscript and made many valuable observations and suggestions. Needless to say they bear no responsibility for any remaining shortcomings.

The manuscript was typed by Linda Finnerty at thesis stage and subsequently reworked by Jackie O'Neill. It is doubtful whether anybody else could have coped with this author's hieroglyphics and certainly not with such efficiency and good humour.

Tony McNamara has been a most helpful and understanding

publisher. In thanking him I would add my sincere gratitude to his colleagues Jim Power, Tom Turley and Eileen Kelly.

Most of all my wife, Marian, and our three children, Johnny, Barbara and Philippa, have over a very long time provided the unseen support and encouragement and the welcome distractions without which this project would never have been completed. My debt to them is beyond repayment.

CHAPTER 1

Higher Education Prior to 1960

The beginnings

The university is one of the most important legacies which the modern world has inherited from medieval Europe. Initially universities were not specifically founded as such but evolved spontaneously over a period of time. They first crystallised in Paris and Bologna in the twelfth century. From about 1245 onwards most universities were specifically founded by popes, emperors or secular rulers. By 1300 there were fifteen to twenty universities functioning in Europe and by 1500 about seventy.[1]

One of the ways in which Ireland diverged from the general pattern of European development can be seen in the failure to establish a university. A bull of establishment of a university in Dublin was received from Pope John XXII in 1320, and while there is evidence of a building, a constitution based on the Oxford model, and the conferring of degrees, the university failed. Attempts to establish a university in Drogheda in 1465 and a university in Dublin in 1475 both failed, as did a further attempt in Dublin in 1568.[2] The Anglo-Norman settlement of Ireland failed to achieve a centre of culture comparable to other centres throughout Europe. Success was to come with the Tudor settlement and the foundation of Trinity College.

Trinity College formally came into existence on 3 March 1592 when it was granted a royal charter by Queen Elizabeth I. The charter refers to the college as *Mater Universitatis* (mother of a university), but all efforts made subsequently to extend the university to include more colleges failed, and it has remained a university, the University of Dublin, with one college. The college opened in 1594 with a small number of students. Only eighty-nine students were admitted in the first fifteen years. Student numbers rose from 65 in 1613 to 340 in 1680, 472 in 1704, 583 in 1774 and 993 in 1792.[3] By 1824 this had risen to 2000, but it declined thereafter and it was not until the late 1960s that the student body again exceeded this level.

The original curriculum was modelled on Cambridge. Until the 1830s there was one course for the degree of Bachelor of Arts which embraced classics, mathematics, a little science and some philosophy and ethics. An honours level was only introduced into the basic course in 1834. The idea of a common curriculum remained at Trinity College until modern times. It was only in 1953 that logic ceased to be compulsory for all TCD students, and until the 1960s students had to graduate in arts before graduating in a professional discipline.[4]

For virtually all of its existence Trinity College has been a self-governing academic community. The 1592 charter was amended a number of times, the most comprehensive amendment being the letters patent of 1911 which transferred and vested basic legislative authority in the Board of Trinity College. The Board is composed mainly of the senior fellows and elected representatives of the junior fellows and professors. The 1997 Universities Act brought the possibility of outside representation for the first time.[5] The University Senate, dating from the eighteenth century, confers the degrees of the university, while the University Council established by the letters patent of 1874 is responsible for all academic functions of the university.

In the early years there were no prescribed religious tests for entry or office holding. From 1637 fellows and faculty had to take holy orders, and a series of tests and oaths made it impossible on grounds of conscience for Catholics to attend or graduate from the college. Over a long period Trinity College became an institution to provide an educated clergy for the Protestant established church, and was the mainstay of the social, political and religious values of the ruling Anglican élite.[6]

From 1793 Catholics and non-conformists could enter Trinity College and obtain degrees, though professorships, fellowships and scholarships remained confined to Anglicans. An Act of 1873 abolished religious tests for all posts except those in the Divinity School.[7] In 1873, and again in 1907, Trinity College successfully resisted all attempts at removing the University of Dublin from the control of Trinity College, so that the college never became a university for the majority of the people of Ireland in the period prior to the establishment of the state in 1922.

The 'university question' of the nineteenth century

The absence of higher education for Catholics and non-conformists was to be an area of conflict from the end of the eighteenth to the beginning of the twentieth century. The introduction of the penal laws in the eighteenth century and the absence of any suitable education in Ireland forced Catholics to go to colleges in mainland Europe.[8] Irish colleges were established in a number of continental cities (most notably Rome, Paris and Salamanca). By 1792 the French Revolution had closed most of the continental colleges, and concessions to Irish Catholics had become a necessity.[9]

In 1795 the government agreed to give direct funding for the establishment of a Catholic college at Maynooth. Further financial support for the college came in 1845 and 1869. While lay students attended in the early years, from 1817 Maynooth was the national seminary for the education of Catholic priests until 1966. In 1896 the college was constituted a pontifical university,[10] and in 1909 St Patrick's College Maynooth became the first recognised college of the National University of Ireland.

In the 1840s a more ambitious attempt was to provide higher education for the Catholic and Presbyterian laity. The Academical Institutions (Ireland) Act 1845 provided for the setting up of three Queen's Colleges at Belfast, Cork and Galway.[11] The colleges were to be non-denominational and non-residential, with a curriculum which had the utilitarian flavour of the newly-established London University. The underlying reality was that the use of state funds for a purely Catholic university was politically unacceptable to both Protestant and British public opinion generally. The three colleges opened in 1849. The Queen's University in Ireland was incorporated by charter in 1850 and was to act as the examining and degree-awarding body for the colleges until 1879. While the initial Catholic reaction to the Queen's Colleges was mixed,[12] by the early 1850s it had hardened under the leadership of the new Archbishop of Armagh, Paul Cullen. A number of papal rescripts as well as the Synod of Thurles in 1850 forbade priests to hold any office in the colleges and advised the laity to avoid them.[13] The Pope urged the hierarchy to set up a Catholic university on the lines of the Belgian model established in Louvain in 1835, and funding was organised in Ireland, England and the United States.

In November 1851 John Henry Newman was invited to become rector of the Catholic University, a post he filled until November 1858.[14] The university was formally established in 1854, but despite Newman's grand design for a great Catholic university, Ireland in the post-famine years was not ready for such a liberal vision. From the fifteen students admitted on the opening day of the university, numbers peaked at 299 in 1863.[15] Because the university had no charter to award degrees, and also because it was unendowed and largely relied on annual church gate collections for financing, the student body was mainly confined to students of ample means, many of whom were from abroad.[16] The one successful component of the Catholic university was its medical school.[17] This opened in 1855 and by the end of 1856 most of the medical lecturers had achieved recognition from one of the medical licensing bodies, the Royal College of Surgeons. The college also developed a successful teaching relationship with a number of hospitals.[18] The number of students in the school reached 100 by 1860, 200 by 1893, and by 1900 was the largest of the country's six medical schools.

The rest of the university went into decline from the mid 1860s onwards and by 1879 there were about six students to occupy the ten professors.[19] In 1882 the bishops remodelled the Catholic University to consist of a group of Catholic institutions. The main university house in St Stephen's Green – Newmans's St Patrick's – became officially known as University College.[20] In November 1883 the management of University College was entrusted by the bishops to the Jesuit order, and Father William Delany SJ became president. The year 1883 was effectively the end of the Catholic University, although it was never formally wound up.[21]

During the period from 1845 to 1908 the Queen's Colleges developed with varying fortunes. Their initial growth had been slow because they had been established during the aftermath of the great famine. Having had an average of about 400 students per annum in the 1870s, Queen's College Belfast declined from a level of 566 students in 1881-82 to 359 in 1898-99. From about 300 students in 1879-80 Queen's College Cork had declined to 175 by the end of the century. Queen's College Galway was always struggling for numbers. It peaked at 201 students in 1882-83, but had declined to 70 by 1907-08.[22] The lack of secondary schools, the superior attraction of Trinity College Dublin, and the condemnation of the Colleges by the Catholic church hindered growth. These factors caused least problems for the Belfast College, which was in general harmony with its religious and cultural milieu.

In the Queen's Colleges, as in the Catholic University, the most popular and successful faculty by far was medicine. Medical students outnumbered all others in the three colleges as a whole from 1867-68 onwards. At Cork they had a small majority over arts students from as early as 1854-55.[23] Law, civil engineering and agriculture attracted very small numbers, while science was a subset of the arts faculties.

Because neither the Queen's Colleges nor the Catholic University successfully resolved the question of university education for Catholics, the problem continued to be debated through the 1860s and 1870s. Eventually in 1879 a compromise solution for Catholic grievances emerged in the form of the Royal University of Ireland which replaced the Queen's University. The Royal University of Ireland was an examining and degree-awarding body which provided for twenty-six fellowships evenly divided between Catholics and Protestants. The holders were to be examiners in the university and professors in teaching institutions approved by the university senate. All the Catholic fellows were concentrated in University College (the Jesuit-run successor to the Catholic University),[24] with the remainder divided between the three Queen's Colleges and Magee College, a Presbyterian Theological College in Derry.

The judgement of history on the Royal University of Ireland has been largely negative.[25] It nevertheless provided the foundations of what in the next century was to become the largest university institution in Ireland, University College Dublin (UCD), it gave previously lacking degree status to students at Magee College, and at Cecilia Street and University College it maintained a high standard for both pass and honours degrees, [26] and its wide and progressive curriculum helped to develop the secondary school system, which in turn provided the student body necessary for university growth.

The most important contribution of the Royal University was that it opened university education to women. The university's charter, modelled on that of the University of London, allowed for this. Women presented themselves for the first matriculation examination of the Royal University in 1882 and twenty-five passed. Of these, nine eventually sat a BA examination in 1884.[27] Queen's College Cork began admitting women students to arts lectures in 1886 and Queen's College Galway did likewise in 1888. Cecilia Street Medical School accepted women students from 1896. When women failed to gain entrance to University College, both the Dominican and Loreto orders opened colleges which provided courses for the university's examinations, as did the multi-denominational Alexandra College.[28] When the National University of Ireland came to be established in 1909 the admission of women students had ceased to be a matter of any controversy.

The Royal University was unlikely to provide a long-term settlement. From the 1880s through to 1908 there was an ongoing campaign for more equitable treatment for Catholics in the sphere of higher education. Royal commissions on higher education were established in 1901 and 1906 and a final solution eventually emerged with the Irish Universities Act 1908. The Act abolished the Royal University of Ireland and established instead the Queen's University Belfast and a new National University of Ireland (NUI), a federal university comprising the Queen's Colleges in Cork and Galway, now called University College Cork and University College Galway, together with University College Dublin, formed out of University College and Cecilia Street Medical School. This new constitutional arrangement was to survive intact for almost ninety years. Trinity College was content to be left untouched, and the Catholic hierarchy was satisfied that the prevailing ethos of the NUI colleges would be Catholic.[29]

Higher education outside the universities

While the nineteenth century saw the playing out and resolution of the question of university education for Catholics and Non-Conformists, a great deal of what eventually became part of higher education had been developing through that century outside the universities, both under the auspices of the state and of various professional and cultural groups.

The development of Trinity College Medical School and the Royal College of Physicians in the seventeenth century saw the introduction of what would nowadays be regarded as professional medical education. The growth of medical education was to be very slow until the nineteenth century.[30] Those two schools taught medicine only; no special provision was made for surgery. Surgeons were trained through a process of apprenticeship, with no diploma to attest to qualification. Surgeons were grouped with barbers in the Guild of Barber Surgeons, established by a royal charter of Henry VI in 1446. The Guild remained the sole legally recognised body representing the science and art of surgery in Ireland until the foundation by charter of the Royal College of Surgeons in Ireland (RCSI) in 1784.

The College of Surgeons obtained its first premises in 1789. Its professorship of surgery, first established in 1785, appears to have been the first in either Britain or Ireland. By 1835 there were 300 students at the college, compared to 200 medical students at

Trinity College.[31] Between 1804 and 1889 seventeen small privately owned medical schools flourished in Dublin, and two in Cork. They could not award degrees themselves, but they prepared students for the various examinations of the licensing bodies (particularly the College of Surgeons) and their courses and lectures were recognised by the bodies. The two largest and longest-lasting, the Ledwich School (dating from 1809) and the Carmichael School (originating in 1812), were absorbed into the Royal College of Surgeons in Ireland in 1889.[32]

A significant group in the development of the medical profession was the apothecaries, the forerunners of the modern pharmacists. This profession began to develop in an organised form in Dublin from early in the seventeenth century, and acquired a charter in 1745 which gave apothecaries general superintendence over their profession. An act of 1791 established the Apothecaries Hall, which for many years had a monopoly on the importation and distribution of drugs and the licensing of retail outlets. The Hall also developed its own medical school.[33]

A division between those apothecaries who wished to act only as dispensers, as distinct from medical men, saw the establishment of the Pharmaceutical Society to further the interests of pharmacy and chemistry.[34] The Society received statutory recognition in 1875 with powers to regulate the practice of pharmacy in Ireland. From as early as 1879 it ran part-time courses which continued until the introduction of a two-year full-time course in 1952.

Before 1859 many practising dentists were self-taught and did not even have a general education. The first dental hospital opened in 1876, and in 1878 the Royal College of Surgeons instituted a licence in dental surgery, the first dental qualification in Ireland. Also in 1878 the Dental Practitioners Act was passed, making compulsory the education and registration of dentists.[35] While both Trinity College and the National University introduced degrees in dentistry, for most of the early years of the twentieth century the majority of dental students continued to attend RCSI.

The first hospital training programme for nurses was organised in the Adelaide Hospital in 1858.[36] Nursing took on more formality in the opening years of the twentieth century, but it was to be well into the second half of the century before nursing studies came to be regarded as part of higher education.

Irish medicine developed greatly in the nineteenth century. Hospitals were built and clinical teaching of students developed.[37] Medical education and practice was regularised. Dublin was a leading centre of world medicine and a number of medical teachers – Graves, Stokes, Corrigan, Colles and Jacob – made original contributions to the study of disease. Women were first admitted to the medical register in 1876 and RCSI opened its school to women in 1885. By the turn of the century medical undergraduates formed the majority in all university colleges except Trinity.[38] Medicine continued to occupy a central place in university education for the first half of the twentieth century. The only medical school to develop outside the university framework was the Royal College of Surgeons, which was to grow successfully as a private institution.

Over the centuries two classes of lawyer, barrister and solicitor, came into existence in Ireland.[39] Barristers were entitled to plead in court, they were the senior branch of the profession and all judges were appointed from their ranks. A charter of 1792 made the Benchers of the Honorable Society of King's Inns, an unincorporated association dating from 1539, the regulators of the legal profession. Until the 1860s the basic qualification for the call to the Bar was the keeping of terms at the Inns, which was demonstrated by attending a specified number of dinners. Examinations were introduced in 1864, and lectures in 1872.

Attorneys and solicitors, who acted in legal proceedings preparatory to court hearings and in legal matters not involving litigation, formed a law society in 1830. Examinations were introduced for solicitors in 1860 and legislation in 1866 and 1898 allowed solicitors increased control over their profession. The shape of the modern legal profession is recognisable at the end of the nineteenth century. While the Bar had predominantly graduate entry from the 1850s at least, in the early 1900s only ten per cent of solicitors were graduates. A significant part of educational provision for law developed outside the universities, and law was to remain a cinderella subject within the universities well into the twentieth century, with most senior academic positions filled on a part-time basis.

Commercial education only began to develop in the twentieth century. In the 1870s the Royal Dublin Society (RDS) initiated a project of holding annual examinations in the elementary branches of education with a view to granting certificates to deserving candidates for appointment to banks and other commercial establishments.[40] Accountancy was the only discipline in what would now be referred to as business studies to achieve any level of development in the nineteenth century.

In May 1888 the Institute of Chartered Accountants in Ireland (ICAI) was established by charter.[41] It introduced a system of training under articles, and from 1891 offered limited membership to those qualifying by examination. ICAI ensured that its students received proper training in professional offices, but it did not begin to concern itself with lectures or education facilities for its students until after the Second World War, so that for most of the period from 1888 onwards tuition relied on English or Scottish correspondence colleges.[42]

Unlike medicine and law, accountancy continued to be organised on an all-Ireland basis after partition in 1922. ICAI, by straddling the border, remained part of the British profession, while two London-based bodies, the Association of Certified and Corporate Accountants (ACCA) and the Institute of Cost and Works Accountants (subsequently to become CIMA, the Chartered Institute of Management Accountants) proceeded to grow sizeable Irish memberships throughout the twentieth century. Accountancy was an economic sector in which Britain and Ireland were to remain one labour market.[43]

Accountancy was slower than other disciplines to achieve university recognition, with the first chair being established in UCD in 1963. While commerce faculties existed in the NUI colleges from their inception, it was not until the 1970s that the universities began to develop business schools as such, and that other disciplines such as marketing and personnel management began to flourish.

In most major industrial countries technical education grew up as a response to the development of manufacturing. Because Ireland was not industrialised, there was little provision for technical education. The Royal Dublin Society was a pioneer of early technical education with its own lectures, professors and a library.[44] It also developed a museum of industry which was taken over by the state in 1854, and which in 1867 became the Royal College of Science for Ireland.[45] The college had four faculties of mining, agriculture, engineering and manufactures. Its student body was small and in the period to 1900 mostly came from outside Ireland. In 1900 the college came under the newly established Department of Agriculture and Technical Instruction, and in the period to 1926 student numbers increased to levels between 80 and 120 per annum.[46] In 1926 the college was absorbed into University College Dublin, having had relatively little impact on Irish society.

For much of the nineteenth century engineers in Ireland acquired their knowledge and skill from their private study, their practical work, and the advice of their seniors.[47] Higher technical education effectively began with the creation of the chair of civil engineering at Trinity College in 1842. The Queen's Colleges provided for engineering but attracted significant numbers only at Cork.[48] The Royal University retained an examining function in engineering. Another source of engineering education was the Institution of Civil Engineers of Ireland founded in 1835.[49] Students could qualify as professional engineers through the Institution, but only a handful did so. Engineering began to experience significant development in the twentieth century within the NUI colleges. Because most of its initial provision was in universities, engineering developed overwhelmingly as a graduate profession, and consequently had none of the status problems which characterised the discipline in Britain.[50]

The Royal Institute of Architects in Ireland was founded in 1839, but only began to develop a system of professional education in the twentieth century, with its own board of architectural education and its own examination system from 1921 onwards. Prior to that, architecture operated on an apprenticeship system. In the twentieth century professional education for architecture was to develop at University College Dublin and the College of Technology, Bolton Street.[51]

The most important industry in Ireland for many centuries was agriculture, but it was one to which higher education made minimal contribution. The main source of new ideas was the Royal Dublin Society with its botanic gardens, professorships, library, lectures and shows. With the setting up of the national school system in the 1830s an attempt was made to teach the elements of agriculture to all rural students as part of the primary curriculum. Because there was no second-level teaching of agriculture, there was no potential student body for any university course in agriculture.

Agriculture was provided, but quickly petered out, at the Queen's Colleges in Cork and Galway, and at the Royal College of Science in Ireland.[52] The latter's faculty was resurrected early in the twentieth century when the college came under the newly founded Department of Agriculture and Technical Instruction.[53] That department was also to lay the groundwork for the development of technical education and, to a lesser extent, agricultural education, the benefits of which would only be felt later in the twentieth century.[54] Agriculture finally came to be developed as a subject within the National University, and in 1924 higher agricultural education was rationalised with the establishment of the Faculty of General Agriculture at UCD and the Faculty of Dairy Science at UCC.[55]

As early as 1800 the Royal Dublin Society had resolved to establish a public veterinary school. Eventually in 1895 a charter was granted to the Society to establish the Royal Veterinary College of Ireland. It opened in 1900, and in 1913 was taken over by the Department of Agriculture and Technical Instruction. It was affiliated to the Royal College of Veterinary Surgeons, and its courses and examinations were as prescribed by the Royal College, a situation which lasted until 1954. In 1946 the National University of Ireland established a faculty of veterinary medicine in UCD, TCD followed suit in 1954, and legislation was introduced in Ireland to make the UCD and TCD degrees registrable qualifications in the Republic of Ireland.[56]

The Royal Dublin Society also made a major contribution to the development of the arts in Ireland. Art education in Ireland grew out of schools sponsored by the Society (known from 1731 to 1820 as the Dublin Society). From 1746 the Society provided for the education of youths at two centres in Dublin out of which grew three schools of drawing, and a school controlled by the Society. These schools collectively established state-sponsored art education in Ireland, and effectively all visual art education in Ireland has been state-sponsored ever since.[57]

In the middle years of the nineteenth century a new centralised and state-controlled art education regime began to be devised and imposed throughout the United Kingdom. Schools of design supported by the state developed in Cork, Belfast, Waterford, Limerick, Derry and Clonmel.[58] With the establishment of the Department of Agriculture and Technical Instruction in 1900 a policy was pursued of amalgamating art schools with technical schools.

The Dublin college, owned by the RDS, was an exception. By 1849 it was located in Kildare Street, came under civil service control at the Department of Science and Art in South Kensington in 1854, and came out from under the RDS altogether in 1877. In 1900 it came under the Department of Agriculture and Technical Instruction (DATI), and passed to the newly-formed Department of Education in 1924. The school (which became the National College of Art in 1930) was administered directly by the

Department of Education until the early 1970s, a regime that was both unhappy and ineffective.[59] The reconstitution of the college and its establishment on a statutory basis was finally achieved in 1971, and in that decade both the National College of Art and Design and art education formally took their place in Irish higher education.

Up to the middle of the nineteenth century music training was exclusively in the hands of private tutors. In 1848 the Irish Academy of Music was founded, the Cork School of Music opened in 1878, and the Dublin Municipal School of Music was opened in 1888.[60] While degrees in music had been conferred regularly by the University of Dublin in the second half of the nineteenth century, courses were not provided. Music was introduced to Queen's College in Belfast in 1902, to Cork in 1906, and to UCD in 1913. The number of degree students was very small. Popular and folk music did not figure in higher education provision.

One of the earliest and most significant areas of higher education to develop outside the universities was teacher training. Following the introduction of primary education in 1831, the Commissioners of National Education set up model schools and a training college in Marlborough Street in Dublin. These were the first schools in the United Kingdom to be established by the state.[61] After 1850 Catholic clerical managers were forbidden to recruit teachers from model schools, or from the central training college, to schools under their control.

In the 1870s the Catholic Archbishop of Dublin supported the establishment of two colleges for Catholic student teachers, one for men, St Patrick's College Drumcondra, established by the Vincentan order in 1875, and the other for women established in 1877 by the Sisters of Mercy and eventually located at Carysfort Park, Blackrock. After considerable pressure the government agreed to give state support to denominational training colleges in 1883. In 1884 the Church of Ireland Training College for men and women was affiliated to the Board of Commissioners for National Education, and further Catholic colleges were founded in Waterford, Belfast and Limerick. By the turn of the century more than half of all principal and assistant teachers had received one or two years' training.[62] Teacher training colleges (to be restyled colleges of education in the 1960s) came to attract a high calibre of student, and the large colleges in Dublin and Limerick came to be significant third-level institutions in their own right, a status rarely enjoyed by their counterparts in Britain and continental Europe.

Teacher education at second level developed in the twentieth century.[63] For secondary schools this was undertaken by universities via the one year Higher Diploma in Education for graduates. With the development of technical and vocational schools,[64] the Department of Education set up colleges for teachers of domestic economy, rural and general science, woodwork and building, and metalwork. Other teaching positions were filled by graduates, and second-level teaching came to provide the major outlet for arts graduates in the twentieth century.

Higher education in the twentieth century

The most significant achievement of the legislation setting up the National University of Ireland and Queen's University Belfast in 1908 was the provision of a framework which would last virtually unchanged for the rest of the century. In that sense it has to be judged a success.

The failure to achieve one university to cater for all of Ireland in the shape of the 1908 settlement of the university question has been seen as the harbinger of the political development of Ireland in the following decade.[65] The first major battle to be fought in the Senate of the new National University was over making the Irish language a compulsory subject for matriculation. Pressure from the Gaelic League, particularly on those nationalist politicians occupying positions on the governing structures of the new university, was effective. The proposal was accepted and Irish became compulsory. NUI was well on the way to becoming the university for nationalist Ireland, [66] as Queen's was to become the university for unionist Ulster. Graduates and faculty of NUI, especially UCD, and graduates of the old University College, most notably Pádraig Pearse, Éamon de Valera, Thomas McDonagh and Eoin MacNeill, were to the fore in the independence struggle of the years 1916 to 1922, and in the formation of the new state.

At one level the universities played a central and significant role in the new state after 1922. The graduates of the National University and the University of Dublin elected members to the Dáil (the lower house of the Irish parliament) until 1937, and to the Seanad (the upper house of the Irish parliament, more generally known by its English title of 'Senate') thereafter. Academics such as MacNeill, Michael Hayes, Patrick McGilligan and John Marcus O'Sullivan occupied positions in government, while University College Galway was singled out in 1929 as an institution that would assist in the national project of reviving the Irish language. Nevertheless the universities did not prosper in the early years of independent Ireland. Apart from state grants and student fees, the NUI colleges had few other financial endowments. Universities were financed, not by the Department of Education, but by the Department of Finance whose parsimony was legendary.

In terms of size UCD quickly came to outpace every other college. In 1909 it had 458 undergraduates, just slightly larger than UCC.[67] In 1926 it had 1,100 students having acquired the buildings and student body of the College of Science. It had topped 2,000 by 1934 and 3,000 a decade later, by which stage it had easily overtaken Trinity College to constitute the largest university institution in the state. It exceeded 4,000 students in 1954-55 and 5,000 by 1959. At that stage it was double the size of Trinity College and UCC, and five times that of UCG.[68] It had also developed the largest university schools in medicine, science and engineering, and was the specialist college in agriculture and architecture. Unlike the other NUI colleges, it was national rather than regional in the composition of its student body with a comprehensive intake from all over the country.[69]

UCD's influence was to be diminished by the fashion in which it became something of a victim of the civil war. The college came to be associated with Cumann na nGaedheal and its successor, Fine Gael, with four professors, filling positions as cabinet ministers in the early government of the Free State.[70] The republican side, as represented by Fianna Fáil, had no comparable involvement with universities with the exception of Éamon de Valera, who succeeded Archbishop Walsh as Chancellor of the National University of Ireland in 1921, a position he held until his death in 1975. While de Valera appears to have maintained even-handedness as chairman of the NUI Senate,[71] UCD (and by extension the universities in general) was not especially popular with many of his more populist supporters.[72]

For the first twenty-five years of the new state's existence Trinity College retained an aloofness from the mainstream of Irish political and social life, viewed essentially by officialdom as a private institution catering for a largely Protestant minority of the population.[73] Having depended for almost a generation on fees and investment income,[74] in 1946 it made a case to the government for a state grant.[75] A grant of £35,000 was forthcoming in 1947, and Trinity College was to figure in state support for universities thereafter. Until the late 1960s a sizeable part of the Trinity student body came from outside the state,[76] but with the removal of the episcopal ban on Catholics attending the College in 1970, Trinity came very quickly into the mainstream of university life in Ireland. There was a deeply ironic twist in the fact that the College was to be initially rescued from its exile in the 1940s by a Fianna Fáil government. Trinity College can arguably be viewed as one of the very few direct beneficiaries of the Irish civil war. [77]

One of the features of the National University (and one which Trinity College was to track eventually) was a very strong vocational emphasis. In the early years of the twentieth century the universities (apart from Trinity College) were primarily medical schools. When UCD opened in 1909, over 55 per cent of its 458 undergraduates were reading medicine, and medicine remained the largest faculty until 1922-23.[78] Thirty-six per cent of full-time university students in NUI colleges in 1938-39 were in medicine, a figure which was close to half at UCC. Inevitably much of the early science teaching was concerned with servicing NUI medical schools.

Science students in NUI rose from 6.7 per cent (344) in 1938-39, to 13.3 per cent in 1958. Engineers made up 9.3 per cent of the student body in 1938, but had declined to 7.4 per cent by 1958, reflecting a lack of investment in the period after the Second World War. Commerce was not a growth area in the early years while, apart from Trinity College, the university law schools did not develop until the 1970s. In the NUI colleges arts did not loom large, as evidenced in Table 1.

TABLE 1: Arts students in selected years as percentage of student body [79]

Year	UCC	UCD	UCG	TCD
1938-39	14.7	27.6	22.9	44.0
1948-49	31.1	33.6	22.7	51.3
1953-54	31.5	35.8	26.0	48.2
1958-59	35.0	35.6	27.2	50.7

Only in Trinity College, where almost all students took an arts degree before proceeding to a vocational primary degree, did arts students come anywhere close to half of the student body. In the

NUI colleges there was a significant vocational function to arts faculties, in that a very sizeable proportion of graduates went on to teaching. During the 1960s and 1970s the arts bias of Irish universities came under considerable attack. The evidence would suggest that this was based on a false perception; there was a very strong vocational component to university education, especially in the colleges of the National University.

Higher vocational education did not begin in vocational colleges until the late 1940s and early 1950s. Following the enactment of the Vocational Education Act 1930 the City of Dublin Vocational Education Committee became responsible for the existing technical institutes in Dublin, located at Kevin Street, Bolton Street, Chatham Row, and Parnell Square, as well as the Institute at Rathmines.[80] In 1941 a new college was opened in Cathal Brugha Street to train domestic economy teachers and to provide education and training for the Irish hotel and catering industry. In the early part of the century the Dublin colleges, together with colleges in Cork and Limerick, had developed a sizeable programme of technical courses, provided on a part-time basis. Some of these were for apprentices and out of these grew some specialised technician post-apprenticeship courses.

The first full-time certificate courses of the late 1940s and early 1950s were geared primarily towards helping students to prepare for the membership examinations of professional bodies in accountancy, architecture and engineering, and the external examinations of London University. By 1960 this still accounted for a very small portion of full-time provision in what would have been classified as higher education, and there was little to suggest that it was likely to become a major area of growth.

By the mid-1950s a problem which could no longer be ignored as the NUI colleges, especially UCD, grew in size, was accommodation. The original building project for UCD at Earlsfort Terrace was less than half-completed when finance dried up in 1919, and in essence there had been no capital investment in the NUI colleges for over a generation.

Eventually in September 1957 the Minister for Education established a commission to enquire into the accommodation of the constituent colleges of the National University of Ireland. The commission reported in May 1959. It supported the move to a new campus at Belfield in the case of UCD and a 200 per cent increase on its existing accommodation. Increases of 60 per cent in the case of UCC and 130 per cent in the case of UCG were also recommended.[81] In March 1960 the Dáil agreed in principle to the transfer of UCD to Belfield.

The commission also recommended the appointment of a University Development Committee, which would assist in co-ordinating the building projects of the universities, would be a useful liaison between colleges and government, and in time could perhaps advise on long-term plans for development and policies of co-ordination.[82]

A difficulty was that the Department of Education had only inherited university funding from the Department of Finance in the late 1950s and it had no tradition of policy-making for higher education, and hence no policy. A year later it decided to establish another commission with the same chairman, the High Court Justice, Cearbhall Ó Dálaigh. A commission of nine people to look at university buildings was succeeded by one comprising twenty-eight individuals to look at the entire gamut of higher education. This group might have been expected to provide the missing blueprint for higher education in Ireland. Events were to prove otherwise.

Notes

1 A most useful summary of the origins of the medieval university is to be found in Cobban, A. B. (1992), 'Universities 1100-1500' in B. R. Clark and G. Neave (eds.), *The Encyclopaedia of Higher Education*, vol. 2, Oxford: Pergamon Press, pp. 1245-1251.

2 McGrath, F. (1979), *Education in Ancient and Medieval Ireland*, Dublin: Studies, pp. 216-223.

3 Luce, J. V. (1992), *Trinity College Dublin: The First 400 Years*, Dublin: Trinity College Dublin Press, pp. 2-12. Trinity College has been more extensively researched and written about than any other Irish institution of higher education. In terms of printed works it was estimated in the late 1980s that there were at least 4,500 relevant items, excluding articles in periodicals and routine tourist guides to Dublin. For a summary of the relevant material, see Benson, C. (1991), 'Trinity College: A Bibliographical Essay' in C. H. Holland (ed.), *Trinity College Dublin and the Idea of a University*, Dublin: Trinity College Dublin Press, pp. 357-371.

4 Luce, p. 156. Luce comments that it was only in 1978 that specialisation finally triumphed over the medieval concept of a common curriculum in the liberal arts. See also McElligott, T. J. (1966), *Education in Ireland*, Dublin: Institute of Public Administration, p. 133.

5 The college had been granted a large measure of autonomy under its original charter, but this had been greatly curtailed by the letters patent of Charles I in 1637. The 1911 King's Letter gave TCD a massive ability to regulate its own affairs by ordinance. There was no provision for outside representation on the

Board of Trinity College Dublin until the passing of the 1997 Universities Act. The Trinity College Dublin and the University of Dublin Bill 1997, a private bill to allow changes to the structure and composition of the Board of Trinity College, was still working its way through the Oireachtas in summer 2000.

6 A celibacy rule for fellows existed until the 1830s. Most of the thirty-five provosts of Trinity College in the period prior to the 1920s were in holy orders. The Irish Universities Act of 1873 (Fawcett's Act) did away with the obligation for fellows of Trinity College to be in holy orders. At one stage in the eighteenth century two thirds of the students graduating were destined for holy orders. Cullen, L. M. (1983), *The Emergence of Modern Ireland 1600- 1900*, Dublin: Gill and Macmillan, p. 129.

7 Luce, p. 98.

8 Irish Catholics were so deprived of education at home that the question of higher education had never arisen. See Gwynn, D. (1948), *O'Connell, Davis and the Colleges Bill*, Cork: Cork University Press, p. 28. Gwynn notes, that in addition to continental colleges, the Jesuit college at Stonyhurst in Lancashire had also provided for the sons of wealthy Irish Catholics. There was an attempt to found a university in Kilkenny, taking advantage of the brief reign of King James II. In 1685 James Phelan, Bishop of Ossory, had established a school in Kilkenny. While James II was spending the winter of 1689-90 in the town he was petitioned to hand over the old Kilkenny College and its endowments as a site for the school. He granted a charter which designated it as a university, the Royal College of St Canice, with authority to teach and confer degrees in all arts and sciences. The Royal College lasted from 21 February to 21 July 1690. See Leonard, J. (1996), *A University for Kilkenny: Plans for a Royal College in the Seventeenth Century*, Dún Laoghaire: St Canice's Press, especially pp. 22-45.

9 Irish students were also to be found in sizeable numbers at Nantes, Bordeaux and Antwerp. See Corish, P. J. (1995), *Maynooth College 1795-1995*, Dublin: Gill and Macmillan, pp. 1-25. By 1690 it is reckoned that there were up to thirty Irish colleges throughout the continent of Europe. Also O'Connor, R. F. (1981), 'The Growing Demand for Catholic Education in the Eighteenth Century leading to the Establishment of St Patrick's, Maynooth 1795', *Irish Educational Studies*, vol. 1, pp. 216-307.

10 The College had looked for pontifical university degrees in theology about fifty years previously, but was blocked by Archbishop Paul Cullen, who wished to set up a faculty of theology in the Catholic University in Dublin. See Corish, P. J. (1985), *The Irish Catholic Experience: A Historical Survey*, Dublin: Gill and Macmillan, p. 200. Also Corish, *Maynooth*, p. 240.

11 For a description of the issues involved in the establishment and early development of the Queens' Colleges see Moody, T.W. and Beckett, J.C. (1959), *Queen's Belfast 1845-1949 : The History of a University*, London: Faber and Faber, pp. 1-83; Murphy J.A. (1995), *The College: A History of Queen's/University College Cork 1845-1995*, Cork: Cork University Press, pp. 1-21; McGrath, F. (1951), *Newman's University: Idea and Reality*, Dublin: Browne and Nolan, pp. 43-83; Coolahan, J. (1981), *Irish Education: Its History and Structure*, Dublin: Institute of Public Administration, pp. 113- 117; Morrissey, T. J. (1983), *Towards a National University: William Delany S.J. 1835-1924*, Dublin: Wolfhound Press, pp. 38-48.

12 Daniel O'Connell, for example, was strongly opposed. See McDonagh, O. (1991), *O'Connell: The Life of Daniel O'Connell 1775-1847*, London: Weidenfeld and Nicholson, pp. 543-545. Archbishop MacHale of Tuam was claiming a positive equality of rights for Catholics such as the older generation of bishops had never contemplated. Where they had striven to remove restrictions, MacHale was demanding the full rights and privileges of the governing caste. See Gwynn, *O'Connell*, p. 38.

13 Larkin, E. (1980), *The Making of the Roman Catholic Church in Ireland 1850-1860*, Chapel Hill: The University of North Carolina Press, pp. 28-39. The prohibition on the day was carried by only two votes, as was the proposal to issue a synodal letter warning the laity of the dangers posed by the colleges.

14 There is considerable doubt as to when exactly Newman resigned his position, see McGrath, *Newman's University*, pp. 469-489. History records that his major contribution in Dublin was the expression of his celebrated views on the nature of university education set forth in his *Discourses on University Education* (some of which were delivered in the form of public lectures in Dublin in 1852).

15. There were 91 students in the arts and science faculties, 108 in the medical school and 100 in evening classes. In the period from 1854 to 1879 the grand total of full-time students – excluding evening, affiliated and medical students – was 521, or an average yearly intake of about twenty. McCartney, D. (1999), *UCD A National Idea: the History of University College Dublin*, Dublin: Gill and Macmillan, p. 8.

16. Meenan, F.O.C. (1987), *Cecilia Street: The Catholic University School of Medicine 1855-1931*, Dublin: Gill and Macmillan, p. 8. Lee observed that 'much of the £190,000 spent was contributed by the Catholic poor, fleeced to subsidise the education of middle-class Catholics,' Lee, J. (1973), *The Modernisation of Irish Society 1848-1918*, Dublin: Gill and Macmillan, p. 31. The annual total raised varied from £4,000 to £9,000 and rarely met the running costs (McCartney, *UCD*, p. 15).

17 McRedmond, L. (1990), *Thrown Among Strangers: John Henry Newman in Ireland*, Dublin: Veritas, p. 116. Meenan, *Cecilia Street*, pp. 18-19.

18 For the relationship between the school and one of its teaching hospitals, see Meenan, F.O.C. (1994), *St Vincent's Hospital 1834-1994: An Historical and Social Portrait*, Dublin: Gill and Macmillan, pp. 33-37.

19 Fathers of the Society of Jesus (1930), *A Page of Irish History: Story of University College, Dublin 1883-1909*, Dublin: Talbot Press, pp. 8, 49.

20 The colleges of the remodelled university were St Patrick's, Maynooth, the University College (St Stephen's Green), the Cecilia Street School of Medicine, Blackrock College, Holy Cross College, Clonliffe, St Patrick's College, Carlow, St Kieran's College, Kilkenny, the Carmelite College, Terenure, and the Jesuits' St Ignatius College, which never developed after the order took over University College, see Morrissey, *William Delany*, p. 72.

21 Commission on Higher Education (1967), *Report*, Dublin: Government Publications Office, p. 5; McGrath, *Newman's University*, p. 491. McCartney noted that the Catholic University had never been abolished, that it survived, and still survives (though more as a legal fiction), in the person of its rector, the Archbishop of Dublin, and in the trustees of the Catholic University Medical School, which awards prizes to students in UCD. McCartney, *UCD*, p. 145.

22 For QCB figures, Moody and Beckett, p. 305. For UCC, Murphy, *the College*, pp. 109, 152. For QCG, the figures are taken from Ó hEocha, C. (1984), 'The Queen's College at Galway – Some Memories' in D Ó Cearbhaill (ed.), *Galway: Town and Gown 1484-1984*, Dublin: Gill and Macmillan, pp. 177, 180-181.

23 Belfast was slowest to reach this position, but medical students outnumbered all others from 1870 onwards. The numbers in the medical school in Galway dropped dramatically from 1882 apparently as a result of the replacement of the Queen's University by the Royal University. The numbers, mainly from the north of Ireland, remained small until the establishment of UCG in 1908. Murray, J. P. (1999), 'Medicine' in T. Foley (ed.), *From Queen's College to National University: Essays on the Academic History of QCG/UCG/NUI Galway*, Dublin: Four Courts Press, p. 149.

24 This arrangement was to operate for the lifetime of the Royal University, but the decision to concentrate all the fellowships in University College gave rise to considerable friction among the interested Catholic parties, see Morrissey, *William Delany*, pp. 88-112.

25 The Commission on Higher Education rejected the concept of a council for academic awards because it was too reminiscent of the failed concept of the Royal University (*Commission Report*, p. 133). McGrath observed that "the establishment of the Royal University was usually regarded as a retrograde step academically, since it constituted a purely examining machine as the central institution" (McGrath, *Newman's University*, p. 493). For F.S.L. Lyons "...the heart does not instinctively warm to a university which is at bottom no more than a board of examiners." Lyons, F.S.L. (1974), *Ireland since the Famine*, London: Collins/Fortana, pp. 93-98.

26 Moody and Beckett, p. 297; Murphy, *The College*, p. 121. See also Meenan, *Cecilia Street*, p. 52. During the lifetime of the Royal University, approximately 40 per cent of Cecilia Street students took its courses, while 60 per cent sat for the Diploma of the Royal Colleges which were perceived as less exacting. Financial considerations (the degree being one year longer than the diploma) also played a part in student choice.

27 Breathnach, E (1981), *A History of the Movement for Womens' Higher Education in Dublin 1860-1912*, Dublin: University College Dublin, unpublished MA thesis, p. 60. This is a most comprehensive study of the admission of women to higher education in Ireland. The issue is also discussed at length in McCartney, *UCD*, pp. 72-84.

28 See Morrissey, *William Delany*, pp. 279-284. Also O'Driscoll, F. (1985), 'Archbishop Walsh and St Mary's University College, 1893-1908,' *Irish Educational Studies*, vol. 5, no. 2, pp. 283-301. For a summary of higher education facilities available to women students in Britain in the 1890s, see Breathnach, *Womens' Higher Education*, p. 95. Trinity College Dublin did not admit women until 1904, see Luce, *The First 400 Years*, pp. 117-121. See also Parkes, S. M. (1996), 'Higher Education 1793-1908' in W. E. Vaughan (ed.), *A New History of Ireland, vol. vi, Ireland under the Union II 1870-1921*, Oxford: Clarendon Press, p. 561.

29 Commission on Higher Education Report, pp. 5-8; McElligott, *Education in Ireland*, pp. 138-145; Coolahan, *Irish Education*, pp. 116-121, 122-124; Murphy, *the College*, pp. 160-163; Lyons, *Ireland since the Famine*, pp. 93- 98.

30 Widdess, J. D. H. (1967), *The Royal College of Surgeons in Ireland and its Medical School 1784-1966*, Edinburgh: E&S Livingston, p. 9. For consideration of the related history of the Trinity College Medical School and the Royal College of Physicians in Ireland, see Fleetwood, J. F. (1983), *The History of Medicine in Ireland*, Dublin: The Skellig Press, pp. 32-47.

31 Widdess, p. 79.

32 For the private medical schools, see Fleetwood, pp. 191-206; Widdess, pp. 95-101; Meenan, *Cecilia Street*, p. 4.

33 When this school closed in the 1850s, the premises in Cecilia Street were acquired by John Henry Newman and became the forerunner of the UCD medical school.

34 Commission on Higher Education, *Submission on Pharmaceutical Education from the Pharmaceutical Society of Ireland.* Commission Papers, TCD Manucripts Library, File no. 7143, Folder 11.

35 The only diploma in dentistry which had previously been established in Britain and Ireland was that of the English College of Surgeons in 1860. For discussion of dental education, see Widdess, pp. 92-94. Also *Commission Papers*, TCD Manuscripts Library, File no. 7143, Folder 18.

36 Scanlan, P. (1991), *The Irish Nurse – A Study of Nursing in Ireland: History and Education 1718-1981*, Manorhamilton: Drumlin Publications, p. 58.

37 Up to the end of the 1820s it was possible for medical students to qualify without ever examining a patient. See Meenan, *St Vincent's Hospital*, p. 32.

38 Not all of these were absorbed by the Irish economy. Emigration among Irish doctors emerged as a pattern in the nineteenth century. Meenan noted that many of the Cecilia Street graduates went abroad, some joining the army medical services as assistant surgeons (Meenan, *Cecilia Street*, p. 37).

39 The definitive study of the origins of the Irish legal profession is Hogan, D. (1986), *The Legal Profession in Ireland 1789-1922*, Dublin: Incorporated Law Society of Ireland.

40 Meenan, J. and Clarke, D. (1981), *The Royal Dublin Society 1731-1981*, Dublin: Gill and Macmillan, p. 36.

41 Robinson, H. W. (1983), *A History of Accountants in Ireland*, Dublin: Institute of Chartered Accountants in Ireland, pp. 6-11. Also O'Regan, P. and Murphy, B. (1999), *Professionalisation in a Political Context: The origin and development of the accountancy profession in Ireland 1884-1914* (paper delivered to Irish Accounting and Finance Association, UCC, May 1999).

42 At the end of the twentieth century these still provided assistance to a small minority of Irish students studying for the examinations of the Chartered Institute of Management Accountants and the Association of Chartered Certified Accountants.

43 ICAI had the majority of its members in Northern Ireland until after the Second World War. See Quin, T. (1988) 'A centenarian renders his account' in D. Rowe (ed.), *The Irish Chartered Accountant: Centenary Essays 1888- 1988*, Dublin: Gill and Macmillan, p. 64.

44 The landed class which had directed the Society for over a century had enjoyed considerable influence and financial support under the eighteenth century Irish parliament. This began to change with the growth of strong centralised bureaucracies in London and Dublin from the 1830s onwards. For an insight

into the Society's decline, see Jarrell, R. A. (1983), 'The Department of Science and Art and Control of Irish Science 1853-1905,' *Irish Historical Studies*, vol. 23, no. 92, pp. 330-347, especially pp. 334-339.

45 For a succinct history of the College, see Kelham, B. B. (1967), 'The Royal College of Science for Ireland (1867-1926)', *Studies*, vol. 56, pp. 297-309. This article also provides background on how the Royal Dublin Society lost its sway over scientific education from the 1850s onwards.

46 With the growth in numbers after 1900 the necessity for new accommodation led to the design of a new building in Merrion Street, which was completed in 1911. The College of Science buildings had by the end of the century become the government buildings of the Irish state.

47 de Courcy, J. W. (1985), *A History of Engineering in Ireland*, Dublin: Institution of Engineers of Ireland.

48 Murphy, *The College*, p. 78; Moody and Beckett, p. 141.

49 The Institution was founded as the Civil Engineers' Society of Ireland in 1835, but adopted the title of Institution of Civil Engineers in Ireland in 1844. The original body embraced civil engineers, military engineers and architects. Under its 1844 by-laws architects were no longer eligible for membership, see Griffith, J. P. (1887), 'Presidential Address,' *Transactions of the Institution of Civil Engineers of Ireland*, vol. xix, pp. 34-36.

50 Raftery, P. (1968), ibid., vol. 94, p. v. Also Hogan, M.A. (1961), ibid., vol. 87, pp. 91, 115.

51 Graby, J. (1989), *150 Years of Architects in Ireland: The Royal Institute of the Architects of Ireland 1839-1989*, Dublin: RIAI and Eblana Editions, pp. 16-18, 24-25, 30-31; Rothery, S. (1991), *Ireland and the New Architecture 1900- 1940*, Dublin: Lilliput Press, p. 62.

52 Murphy, *The College*, p. 76; Moody and Beckett, p. 146. Murphy suggests that academic agricultural courses were theoretical and dilettantish, and at best availed of by small numbers of prospective estate managers in the shape of sons of gentry and large farmers.

53 Hoctor, D. (1971), *The Department's Story – A History of the Department of Agriculture*, Dublin: Institute of Public Administration, p. 58.

54 For an assessment of that Department's contribution, see Akenson, D. H. (1996), 'Pre-university Education 1870-1921,' in Vaughan, *Ireland under the Union 1870-1921*, pp. 529-532.

55 Albert Agricultural College (1938), *Centenary Souvenir 1838-1938*, pp. 113-114.

56 McGeady, P. A. (1981). 'The Irish Veterinary College,' in Meenan and Clarke, *Royal Dublin Society*, pp. 132-141. Also *Papers of Commission on Higher Education*, TCD Manuscripts Library File 7143, Folder 17. Veterinary education at university level was concentrated at University College Dublin in 1977.

57 Turpin, J. (1995), *A school of art in Dublin since the Eighteenth Century: A History of the National College of Art and Design*, Dublin: Gill and Macmillan, pp. 55, 75.

58 Barrett, C. and Sheehy, J. (1996), 'Visual Arts and Society 1850-1900' in Vaughan, *Ireland under the Union*, pp. 444-448.

59 Turpin, especially pp. 415-538.

60 Fleischmann, A. (1996), 'Music and Society 1850-1921' in Vaughan, *Ireland under the Union*, pp. 500-522.

61 This was a very important precedent. It made it easier for the state to make further initiatives in the 1840s in setting up the Queen's Colleges and the schools of design, and to set up the Royal College of Science for Ireland in the 1860s.

62 Coolahan, *Irish Education*, pp. 5-6, 32; McElligott, *Education in Ireland*, pp. 7-8.

63 Coolahan, p. 102; McElligott, pp. 86-87.

64 For an overview of technical education in Ireland see McMillan, N. (ed.), (2000), *Prometheus's Fire: A History of Scientific and Technological Education in Ireland*, Carlow: Tyndall Publications. See also Duff, T., Hegarty, J. and Hussey, M. (2000), *The Story of the Dublin Institute of Technology*, Dublin: Blackhall Publishing, pp. 3-11.

65 A seminal article on the topic is Moody, T. W. (1958) 'The Irish University Question of the Nineteenth Century,' *History*, vol. 43, pp. 90-109. See also Parkes, *Higher Education 1793-1908*. For background to the 1908 Act, see McCartney, UCD, pp. 31-42.

66 For the controversy, see Morrissey, *William Delany*, pp. 321-343. Also Ó Cuiv, B. (1996) 'Irish Language and Literature' in Vaughan, *Ireland under the Union*, p. 407. McCartney observes that the nationalist UCD representatives on the NUI Senate were responsible for imposing the so-called compulsory Irish matriculation in the face of strong opposition from some Cork and Galway senators, McCartney, *UCD*, p. 40.

67 National University of Ireland (1932), *Handbook 1908-1932*, Dublin: Sign of the Three Candles, p. 109.

68 *Commission on Higher Education Papers*, TCD Manuscripts Library, Folder 9.

69 See, for example, *Report of the Commission on Accommodation Needs of the Constituent Colleges of the National University of Ireland (1959)*, Dublin: Stationery Office, p. 55. Even from the time of the debate and discussion on the 1908 Act, UCD was regarded as a national institution. For example, the county councillors elected to the UCD governing body came from a national panel, whereas to UCC and UCG it was from a provincial panel, McCartney, *UCD*, p. 39.

70 During the Civil War and subsequently, the consistent policy of the President of UCD, Denis Coffey, had been to insulate the college from the turmoil as far as possible. Although Chancellor of the University, de Valera was virtually forbidden to enter UCD. What should have been a temporary expedient was to harden into settled practice to the loss of the college. See Meenan, J. (1990), *George O'Brien: A Biographical Memoir*, Dublin: Gill and Macmillan, p. 149.

71 McCartney regards the judicious impartiality of de Valera as Chancellor as having preserved the National University 'from becoming a political plaything between rival factions', McCartney, D. (1983), *The National University of Ireland and Éamon de Valera*, Dublin: The University Press of Ireland, p. 37.

72 In 1960 a future Minister for Education, Donogh O'Malley, put down a motion at the Fianna Fáil parliamentary party urging action against the 'UCD junta'. Horgan, J. (1997), *Seán Lemass: the Enigmatic Patriot*, Dublin: Gill and Macmillan, p. 297. The President of UCD at the time was Michael Tierney, a son-in-law of Eoin MacNeill, a former Dáil Deputy, senator and backroom activist in both Cumann na nGaedheal and Fine Gael. (Lemass himself did not appear to be an unqualified admirer of UCD. ibid., p. 295).

73 For a cameo of Trinity College Dublin as an isolated unionist enclave in post-independence southern Ireland, see McDowell, R. B. (1997), *Crisis and Decline: The Fate of the Southern Unionists*, Dublin: Lilliput Press, pp. 197- 211. Also Luce, *The First 400 Years*, pp. 146-147. Lydon, J. (1991), 'The silent sister: Trinity College and Catholic Ireland' in Holland, *The Idea of a University*, pp. 42-43. A future Provost, F.S.L. Lyons, observed that in the generation before the Treaty, Trinity College made practically every mistake it could make, and that the crude and ignorant jibes of Mahaffy (eventually to become a Provost of Trinity) and others at the renaissance of Irish culture aroused a deep resentment, for which Lyons felt it was still paying in the 1960s, Lyons, F.S.L. (1967) in F. McManus (ed.), *The Years of the Great Test*, Cork: Mercier Press, p. 97. See also Dempsey, P. (2000), 'Trinity College and the New Political Order' in M. Cronin and J. M. Regan (eds.), *The Politics of Independence 1922-49*, Basingstoke: Macmillan Press, pp. 217-231. Dempsey argues that TCD's ghetto status predated 1922, and indeed 1800.

74 Vaughan, W.E. (1991), 'Paying for the Christmas Dinner: the College's Income and Expenditure,' in Holland, *The Idea of a University*, pp. 60-62. As late as 1958-59 as much as 22.8 per cent of TCD's income came from investments. The comparable NUI figures were: UCC – 5.5 per cent, UCD – 2.2 per cent, UCG – 5.1 per cent (Commission on Higher Education Papers, TCD Manuscripts Library, Folder 9).

75 The original approach was made to the Taoiseach, Mr de Valera, in a letter sent by the Provost, E. H. Alton, and the Registrar, K. C. Bailey, on 8 November 1946. The government decision was taken on 21 February 1947. (National Archives, Department of Taoiseach. File S13962/A). In November 1948 the College requested the government to increase the annual grant from £35,000 to £61,000 and also requested a non-recurrent grant of £75,000. In November 1949 the College requested an increase from £35,000 to £75,000 (National Archives, Department of Taoiseach. File S13962/B1).

76 In 1962-63, 46.4 per cent (1,374) of all TCD students were from outside Ireland (*Commission on Higher Education Report*, p. 790).

77 There was a very considerable difference in the language and tone of discussions between Trinity College and Eamon de Valera when Fianna Fáil were in office and when the College was dealing with the Inter-Party Government of 1948-51 led by John A. Costello. (National Archives, Department of Taoiseach, File S13962 B/2).

78 McCartney, *UCD*, p. 49.

79 These figures have been compiled by the author from figures supplied to the Commission on Higher Education by the colleges. There is some discrepancy between the figures as shown here and those contained in the report of the Commission.

80 Dublin Institute of Technology (1996), *Self-Evaluation Study: Review of Quality Assurance Procedures in Dublin Institute of Technology, Appendix A – Historical Profile of Dublin Institute of Technology*.

81 *Commission on Accommodation Needs*, pp. 44-45, 86-87, 122. The Belfield project is dealt with authoritatively in McCartney, *UCD*, pp. 227-279.

82 *Commission on Accommodation Needs*, p. 128.

Chapter 2

New Ideas at the Department of Education

The publication in November 1958 of the report, *Economic Development*, prepared by Dr T. K. Whitaker, Secretary of the Department of Finance, is widely viewed as a watershed in the economic history of the state.[1] With minor exceptions the arguments in his report were reproduced in the First Programme for Economic Expansion which the government laid before the Oireachtas in November 1958.[2] The programme and the report were published at a time of acute economic depression. Against that background the programme set out a comprehensive plan for the whole economy for the period from 1958 to 1963 aimed at achieving a growth rate of 2 per cent. The programme also heralded a switch in economic policy from protection to free trade and export-led growth. The main elements of the policy were: a) the attraction of foreign investment; b) the lifting of controls on foreign ownership of firms and profit repatriation; c) the introduction of capital and other grants to new and expanding firms; and d) corporation profits tax concessions to exporting (and later to all manufacturing) firms.[3] The programme was essentially a recognition that the industrial structure, which had been buttressed by protection and tariff walls from 1932 onwards, could provide neither the jobs nor the incomes necessary to meet the aspirations of the population.

The programme's growth target of 2 per cent per annum proved in the event to be too modest. In the five-year period covered by the Programme the volume of Gross National Product rose by over 4 per cent per annum. The government launched the Second Programme for Economic Expansion in 1963 to cover the period from 1964 to 1970. This was a far more detailed and elaborate exercise than its predecessor. The target for economic growth was set at 4 per cent per annum. However, because of unfavourable economic conditions and a heavy deficit in the balance of payments, the Second Programme was officially abandoned in 1967.[4] A third programme to cover the period from 1969 to 1972 was published in 1969. This produced a new emphasis on full employment but very little was heard of it after its publication. The growth rate achieved in the period from 1961 to 1973 averaged 4.1 per cent per annum, and between 1963 and 1973 manufacturing employment rose at an average annual rate of 1.7 per cent, about three times the OECD average. Economic growth was faster and more sustained than in any previous period in Irish history. Living standards rose by over 50 per cent. By 1971 the population had grown by over 100,000 from the low base of 1961 to the highest level recorded in the history of the state.[5]

The extent to which these programmes and economic planning in general contributed to the economic prosperity of the 1960s has been a matter of debate. The verdict of economists has tended to the view that the whole planning exercise was seriously flawed from a methodological point of view.[6] It has been argued that it was the policies, particularly in relation to foreign trade and investment, which caused the economy to take off, and that the economic programmes were mere accompaniments charting the economy's course.[7] Despite this professional scepticism a popular view persists that the programmes made an important contribution to Irish society. Part of their significance lay in the fact that for the first time there was a state commitment to a comprehensive and rational plan for the economy as a whole. What many commentators see as the most important feature of the exercise of economic planning was that it gave a sense of direction and a psychological boost to politicians, to those involved in public administration and to the general public.[8]

Economic planning and the education sector

At a formal level the programmes had relatively little impact on the education sector and very little to say about the role of education in economic development. There was virtually no reference to education in either the First Programme or Dr Whitaker's study, apart from the specialised subject of agricultural education.[9] The Whitaker study did contain praise for the vocational education system as being more flexible than either the primary or secondary systems, and as having a missionary enthusiasm about its work. The absence of any reference to education and the failure of either Dr Whitaker's report or the First Programme to offer any guidance on general educational matters appear to have been the subject of criticism at various fora where the two documents were discussed.[10]

These criticisms apparently were taken on board and the Second Programme contained a chapter on education. The increased production, which was regarded as a major aim of the programme, was seen as providing the resources for educational improvement. 'Better education will support and stimulate continued economic expansion. Even the economic returns from investment in education and training are likely to be as high in the long run as those from investment in physical capital', observed the programme's authors. The chapter on education saw economic growth as increasingly dependent on the application of the results of scientific research and development to the practical problems of production. Growth required not merely the training of the required calibre of technicians and technologists, but 'the expansion of educational facilities as a whole to ensure the greatest possible use of talent at all levels of ability'. The chapter repeated the content of proposals on technical education issued in May 1963 by the Minister for Education, Dr Hillery, and stated that the general aim of government policy was to ensure that industry, by defining its needs and co-operating in the measures required to meet them, would make full use of the vocational schools to develop a skilled labour force. It also noted that liaison between industry and the vocational education authorities had not been very extensive.[11] Educational issues did not figure at all in the Third Programme.

Taken together the three programmes did not have much of importance to say about education. Even the Second Programme contained nothing new or original, although the acceptance by the Minister for Finance of the need for educational development was regarded as of some significance.[12] While the programmes themselves may have had little direct influence on what was happening in the Department of Education, they were a significant indicator of the changes in the environment of public administration which characterised the 1960s. No government department was immune from that influence. It is widely accepted that the change in policy heralded by the First Programme was largely brought about by the increased influence of Seán Lemass, who succeeded Éamon de Valera as Taoiseach in June 1959. He is credited with having supported Whitaker in emphasising the necessity for rational economic and social planning, and he was keen to see government departments taking a more interventionist role in this process.[13] While such a role had been part neither of the brief nor the self-image of the Department of Education since its inception in 1924, by the early 1960s there were individual civil servants in that Department who were beginning to view matters differently.

Prior to the 1960s there was no conscious or serious attempt to link the school system with the economy or the demands of the labour market. The objectives of education as set out in the Constitution – the moral, intellectual, physical, spiritual and social education of children – would have been accepted by ministers and officials in the Department of Education.[14] The great bulk of children in the education system were in schools which directly or indirectly came under the control of the churches. Officials in the Department of Education accordingly worked at one of the most sensitive intersections between church and state.[15] In addition the Department had as part of its brief a major role in promoting the restoration of the Irish language.[16] A Department saddled with the herculean task of restoring the language, while acting simultaneously as a major stakeholder between God and Caesar, was in post-independence Ireland more likely to display caution than a sense of adventure.

The self-concept of the Minister for Education (and, by inference, of many of his officials) tended to be modest, and received perhaps its most famous articulation in 1956 in the words of the then minister, Richard Mulcahy. 'I regard the position as minister in the department of Education', he told the Dáil, 'as that of a kind of dungaree man, the plumber who will make the satisfactory connections and streamline the forces and potentialities of the educational workers and educational management in this country. He will take the knock out of the pipes and will link up everything'.[17]

Ironically Mulcahy's 'dungaree man' speech was made at a time when personnel changes at senior level in the Department were bringing into positions of influence a number of officials who disagreed with the view implicit in the Mulcahy speech that the Minister had no function in the making of policy.[18] These officials emerged into prominence at a time when the Department of Education began to have experience of a new calibre of minister. In the decade between 1958 and 1968 there were five holders of the position of Minister for Education – Jack Lynch, Patrick Hillery, George Colley, Donogh O'Malley and Brian Lenihan. All of them, with the exception of Lynch, were brought into the cabinet by Lemass. They belonged to the first post-independence generation of Fianna Fáil politicians and, together with Charles Haughey and Neil Blaney, were to be the ministers most associated with the economic take-off of the 1960s and the changing of the guard within Fianna Fáil.[19] A succession of younger ministers meant that the Department of Education had at the helm men who were in tune with the major thrust of government policy during the Lemass years, a policy that saw the establishment of new procedures for economic and social decision-making.

Observers are largely unanimous in holding the view that the policy changes in the late 1950s and early 1960s saw a fundamental shift in attitude among government ministers. Economic considerations and arguments generally came to dominate political discourse. One economist has described it as political nationalism being replaced by materialism as the dominant theme of political debate. Another observed that around 1963 there occurred within education a general change in emphasis, away from purely educational and language revival questions towards the social and economic dimensions.[20] A celebrated article in the Autumn 1968 edition of *Studies* by Seán O'Connor, then an Assistant Secretary in the Department of Education, merely confirmed the increasingly obvious fact that economic considerations predominated in the decision-making of the Department.[21]

From 1958 onwards then there existed sufficient indigenous influences on the Department of Education, which on their own would have gone a long way to bringing that Department and its officials towards approaching their brief from the viewpoint of the economist. As it happened, there also existed an extraneous, but parallel, influence which was, if anything, more potent. This was the Organisation for Economic Co-operation and Development (OECD).

The Department of Education and the Organisation for Economic Co-operation and Development

On 16 April 1948 a Committee for European Economic Co-operation (CEEC) met in Paris and adopted a constitution establishing a permanent organisation of sixteen participating countries, known as the Organisation for European Economic Co-operation (OEEC). This organisation, together with the Economic Co-operation Agency (ECA), a body created by the US government, had joint responsibility for the supervision of the European Recovery Programme, a plan for large-scale US aid for economic re-organisation in Europe (popularly known as Marshall Aid after the US Secretary of State who organised it).

Ireland was closely associated with OEEC from its inception. It was a signatory of the European Co-operation Agreement in Paris in April 1948 and ratified the agreement in June 1948. Of the $5 billion of Marshall Aid, Ireland received $146.2 million. The then Minister for External Affairs, Seán McBride, was a vice-president of the OEEC Council of Ministers and played a key role in negotiating with ECA on behalf of the sixteen countries involved.[22] Initially OEEC was primarily occupied with questions of trade and trade payments, but in the early and mid-1950s it turned its attention increasingly to co-operation in other areas of economic activity such as industry, agriculture, energy, tourism, productivity and manpower.

By the time the Department of Education began its association with it, OEEC had begun to emphasise the link between investment in education and economic progress.[23] By the late 1950s most European countries had successfully completed their post-war economic recovery and were engaged in a policy of economic growth. Such a policy implied not only a rise in capital investment, but a higher rate of technical innovation and the ability to exploit it industrially. In turn this called for an increased supply of scientific, technical and other qualified manpower with a consequent adaptation of the educational system.

In 1958 OEEC established a Committee for Scientific and Technical Personnel. In 1959 Ireland was one of the subjects of a programme of reviews of national policies for science and education. The first Irish review was devoted to the teaching of science in schools and colleges. At the suggestion of the Irish authorities, a second review of education in Ireland was devoted to technical education and economic development, with special emphasis on the position of the technician. The Committee for Scientific and Technical Personnel in turn established a Study Group in the Economics of Education. While the economists in the study group were by no means unanimous in positing a link between increased investment in education and economic growth, OEEC itself began to manifest such a belief.[24]

In the late 1950s OEEC had run a Mediterranean Regional Project (MRP) to work out proposals for the long-term programming of resources into education. Following its experiment in Southern Europe it was keen to spread the techniques it had evolved into an examination of the more advanced countries in Northern and Western Europe. In October 1961 a policy conference on 'Economic Growth and Investment in Education' was held in Washington, and as a by-product the conference was used to find two countries outside the Mediterranean region which would volunteer to conduct a national survey of their entire educational system. It would appear that most representatives baulked at the idea of exposing their country's shortcomings to the world's gaze and only the Irish, and subsequently the Austrian, delegation agreed to recommend the project to its government.[25] The Minister, Dr Hillery, sought and obtained the government's approval to set up, in co-operation with the re-christened OECD, an expert team to survey Irish education and report on its findings. The team began its work in 1962 and reported in 1965. Both its existence and its labours are regarded as landmarks.[26]

Investment in education

The main findings of the survey related to manpower, participation and the use of resources. The terms of reference of the survey team did not preclude it from examining third-level education. In the introductory chapter the third-level system was described, and the report dealt with forecasts of pupil enrolments at third-level, projected requirements and supply of third-level teachers, cost projections, university student entrants, university student output, participation, and the financing of third-level education.[27] The existence of the Commission on Higher Education appears to have reduced the attention which the survey team might otherwise have given to third-level education. The report noted that projections for third-level enrolments had to be considered tentative pending the report of the Commission. It is significant also that, while the report made a detailed study of the use of resources in national, secondary and vocational schools, no such exercise was conducted with regard to third-level.[28]

That the report of the survey team was of major importance is widely accepted.[29] A retired Secretary of the Department of Education could contend that such advances in education as were made in subsequent years might not have taken place at all were it not for the publication of the report. At an earlier period, when head of the Development Unit set up within the Department of Education as a result of the report, he had written that it had 'signposted the direction of educational reform and, by high-lighting our deficiencies, offered a challenge that could not be ignored'.[30] Donogh O'Malley as Minister for Education had observed that it had been 'a guideline and basic document for us to work on for the future'.[31]

Ironically the survey team in its report made modest claims for its own activity. It saw its limited task as 'the prosaic one of examining those resources which are indispensable to any system of education'. It did not regard it as its function to say what the objectives of the educational system should be, or what priority or weight should be given to particular objectives. Its role rather was an ancillary one, to supply an adequate base of information for effective decisions and policies. Years afterwards the director, Professor Patrick Lynch, continued to stress that the survey team made only one recommendation (with regard to the establishment of a development unit in the Department of Education), and that the study was concerned with the efficiency of the system rather than with policy recommendations.[32] Nevertheless, while eschewing recommendations, the survey team in effect provided an agenda and assisted *inter alia* in reorienting educational policy towards a concern with the labour market needs of a developing economy.[33] While the *Investment in Education* report may have had the most powerful impact of any of the OECD-supported exercises, its major impact was at first and second level. The report which was to have most influence on higher education was to be an earlier report on the training of technicians.

The position of technical education

With the removal in the late 1950s of the protectionist policies which had operated in the state since 1932, foreign capital came to be courted actively, and foreign industry, with developed technical and financial resources and established connections with world markets, began to be attracted to the country. With them came a growing awareness of modern technology. This in turn was to affect the education system, and particularly technical education.

Technical education was and still is provided under the framework of the Vocational Education Act 1930. The Act distinguished between two elements, continuation education and technical education. Continuation education was seen to 'continue and supplement education provided in elementary schools and to include general and practical training in preparation for employment in trades etc., and also general and practical training for the improvement of young persons in the early stages of employment'.[34] Technical education was seen as having two main purposes, training young people for entry to particular employments and improving the skills of those already employed. Continuation and technical education were normally conducted within the same building, the vocational school. The social perception and esteem of vocational schools was in general not very high.[35] The vocational schools were widely viewed as being 'there for the pupils unable to get to secondary schools and those others who were filling in time till the statutory obligation of school attendance no longer applied'.[36] Against such a background the status of technical education was problematic. As the area of education most amenable to direct influence and direction from the Minister for Education, it was also most likely to figure initially, if the Department of Education became interested in taking a more interventionist role in the implementation of wider state policy.

The period in office of Jack Lynch as Minister for Education from March 1957 to June 1959 brought the first stirrings of a new initiative.[37] During that time there was pressure from within the Vocational Teachers' Association for the extension of vocational education to eighteen years of age, with entry to third-level technological education possible at the completion of a vocational school course.[38] During the period of office of Mr Lynch's successor, Dr Patrick Hillery, technical education in the broadest sense became a matter of focus. During his first year in office he told the Dáil that the production of a surplus of graduates, especially science graduates, was a calculated risk that had to be taken if one were to believe that the country had a future. In the same speech he identified the education of technicians as an area in which the country was weak, and indicated that he saw an improvement in this area as the function of vocational schools.[39] This was the first occasion on which the Minister is recorded as having raised the question of the training of technicians. A new avenue was about to open.

The technician question

At one level it is surprising that the issue of technicians should have been raised by the Department of Education with OECD in the early 1960s. Technicians were not a burning topic of national debate. A shortage of technicians was not a problem about which industrial representative bodies were lobbying government. When OECD examiners visited Ireland in 1962, they claimed to have found a widespread interest in the technician problem, but no general agreement on, or understanding of, the technician's precise role and function. One of the examiners, Dr Werner Rasmussen, Denmark's Director and Commissioner of Technical Education, observed that there seemed to be no common language among the people interviewed, even though they all spoke English.[40] This should not have been a surprise. The concept of a technician was unfamiliar in a society which was industrially underdeveloped. The notion of technician education was unfamiliar also, because Ireland had a system of technical education and training derived largely from Britain. One of the main characteristics of that system, a nineteenth century legacy, was the principle whereby training for industry was based almost entirely on craft apprenticeship. Industries which had grown up within that tradition, and with the trade union practices that accompanied it, were not ideally equipped or motivated to specify their demand for technicians to the educational authorities.

In advance of the visit by the examiners OECD and the Department of Education undertook a joint survey of the tasks, responsibilities, recruitment and training of technicians in a number of Irish firms.[41] This survey faced major problems. First it had the difficulty of fitting accepted definitions of the technician to the Irish industrial scene. As the OECD report noted, doubt concerning the validity of the title 'technician' was bound to arise frequently in the then-existing stage of Irish industrialisation, and was due to such factors as the absence of a nationally accepted technician diploma, the preponderance of consumer and intermediate goods industries whose scientific and technical functions were less clearly defined than in the capital goods industries, and the fact that management was often not conversant with technical and scientific issues.[42] Secondly the survey found difficulties in choosing appropriate firms. Because of the short time available for the work, the survey had to be limited in size.

No clear pattern of shortages emerged. A number of firms complained of the lack of a pool of trained technicians, but their demands were very spasmodic. There was no steady demand for even a small number of technicians in any one industry. Few firms seemed disposed to co-operate with vocational education committees to organise training which would help to remedy the absence of such a pool. An accompanying background paper, prepared for the examiners, concluded that one of the major problems with Irish technical education lay in obtaining the support of industry for the establishment of courses. It also reached tentative conclusions on the modification of existing courses, the required output of technicians and the establishment of a technician council. It further suggested that the uncertainties of industry might be remedied by the establishment of a council charged with responsibility for the training and qualifications of technicians.[43]

The joint preparatory exercise between the Department of Education and OECD succeeded in laying bare the paucity of statistical data and the difficulty surrounding any projections of the demand and need for technicians. The examiners in their report were conscious that their remarks about the need for an expansion in technical training, as well as changes in its form, were not based on any firm projections but on 'informed guesses' from experts in the field.[44] They concluded that a determined attempt should be made to improve the coverage of manpower surveys of existing demand for technical personnel, and also observed that the assembly and collation of statistical data should not be a matter for *ad hoc* investigation, but should be a permanent part of the work of the educational authorities.

The examiners considered that any curriculum of advanced technical education should be based on mathematics and the physical sciences. To ensure that entrants to colleges of technology had reached this level, they should have followed a specially devised course, on the completion of which they would be awarded a technical school leaving certificate recognised nationally. The other recommendations of the examiners related to the establishment of a national committee to deal with course structures, entry requirements, curriculum design and industrial experience appropriate to technicians, co-operation between the universities and the colleges of technology, responsibility for the financing of technical and technological training, and the form it should take.[45]

The examiners visited Ireland for a week in September 1962, and in a procedure developed by OECD, an Irish delegation, headed by the Minister and the Secretary of the Department of Education, visited Paris in January 1963 for the 'confrontation meeting' structured around the country review of Ireland.[46] Four months later in a press conference on 20 May 1963, the minister announced his proposed initiative with regard to technician education and training. The initiative was to centre around Regional Technical Colleges. The minister also announced the inauguration of a technical schools leaving certificate.

The report of the OECD examiners was published in 1964. Unlike *Investment in Education* in the following year, it provoked little public discussion (except in a small segment of the engineering profession). Its main message was that economic advance required the development of technical manpower, and that in any such development a place had to be found for technician education, regardless of whether local industry signalled a demand for it. The report and its findings might have been expected to disappear without trace. Initially that was what happened. There was no follow-up to the report for some years. However, the seeds in time were to fall on unexpectedly fertile ground. That outcome could not have been predicted in 1964.

Notes

1 See, for example, Lyons, *Ireland Since the Famine*, pp. 628-631; Fanning, J. R. (1990), 'The Genesis of Economic Development,' in J. F. McCarthy (ed.), *Planning Ireland's Future: The Legacy of T. K. Whitaker*, Dublin: Glendale Press, pp. 74-76.

2 *Economic Development,* (1958), Dublin: Stationery Office; *Programme for Economic Expansion,* (1958), Dublin: Stationery Office. For background and context, see Fanning, J.R. (1978), *The Irish Department of Finance 1922-58,* Dublin: Institute of Public Administration, pp. 461-519; also McCarthy, J. F. (1990), 'Whitaker and the 1958 Plan for Economic Development,' in McCarthy, *Planning Ireland's Future*, pp. 11-63; also Horgan, *Lemass*, pp. 174-180.

3 For a summary of the Plan, see Lyons, *Ireland since the Famine*, pp. 628 *et seq.* Also Fitzpatrick, J. and Kelly, J. (1985), *Perspectives on Irish Industry,* Dublin: Irish Management Institute, pp. xvii-xix.

4 *Second Programme for Economic Expansion,* (1963), Dublin: Stationery Office. Lyons, *Ireland since the Famine*, p. 632. Also Walsh, B. M. (1979), 'Economic Growth and Development', in J.J. Lee (ed.), *Ireland 1945-70,* Dublin: Gill and Macmillan, pp. 35-36.

5 Nolan, S. (1984), 'Economic Growth' in J.W. O'Hagan (ed.), *The Economy of Ireland – Policy and Performance,* Dublin: Irish Management Institute, p. 216; Kennedy, K. A. (1992) , 'The Context of Economic Development' in J.H. Goldthorpe and C.T. Whelan (eds.), *The Development of Industrial Society in Ireland,* Oxford: Oxford University Press, pp. 6-12; Walsh, *Economic Growth and Development,* p. 33.

6 For a succinct survey of the role of economic planning in Ireland, see Bradley, J. (1994), 'The Legacy of Economic Development: The Irish Economy 1960-1987', reproduced in C. Ó Grada (ed.), *The Economic Development of Ireland Since 1870,* vol. II, Aldershot: Edward Elgar Publishing Ltd., pp. 128-160.

7 Neary, P. (1984), 'The Failure of Economic Nationalism', *The Crane Bag,* vol. 8, no. 1, pp. 68-76.

8 Murphy, J.A. (1975), *Ireland in the Twentieth Century,* Dublin: Gill and Macmillan, p. 143. Also Walsh, *Economic Growth*, p. 36. Also Kennedy, K. A.

and Dowling, B. R. (1975), *Economic Growth in Ireland – The Experience since 1947,* Dublin: Gill and Macmillan, pp. 253-254.

9 *First Programme*, pp. 23-24.

10 FitzGerald, G. (1969), 'Grey, White and Blue' in B. Chubb and P. Lynch (eds.), *Economic Development – Planning,* Dublin: Institute of Public Administration, pp. 125-126.

11 *Second Programme*, Part I, p. 13. Part II, pp. 193, 205. Dr Hillery's proposals and their significance are dealt with in Chapter 3 below.

12 O'Connor, S. (1986), *A Troubled Sky – Reflections on the Irish Educational Scene 1957-68,* Dublin: Educational Research Centre, St. Patrick's College, p. 87.

13 There is significant evidence that Lamass and Whitaker diverged considerably in their basic beliefs. See Bew, P. and Patterson, H. (1992), *Sean Lemass and the Making of Modern Ireland 1945-66,* Dublin: Gill and Macmillan, p. 194; Lee, J. J. 'Seán Lemass' in Lee, *Ireland 1945-70,* pp. 16-26; Walsh, D. (1986), *The Party: Inside Fianna Fáil,* Dublin: Gill and Macmillan, pp. 71-75.

14 *Bunreacht na hÉireann (Constitution of Ireland),* (1937), Article 42.1. For a discussion of the performance of the Department of Education and successive ministers as policy-makers, see Ó Buachalla, S. (1988), *Education Policy in Twentieth Century Ireland,* Dublin: Wolfhound Press, pp. 250-291.

15 Ó Buachalla, S. (1985), 'Church and State in Irish Education in this Century', *European Journal of Education,* vol. 20, no. 4, pp. 351-359, Whyte J. H. (1980), *Church and State in Modern Ireland 1923-1979,* Dublin: Gill and Macmillan, pp. 16-21, 337-343, 350, 389-395; Ó Buachalla, *Education Policy,* pp. 36-48, 49-84, 137-168, 205-249, 320-325.

16 This was a sensitive political mission whose importance was hinted at in Dr Hillery's revealing comment in the Dail in 1964 that there were two parts to the job of Minister for Education, one being the Irish language and the other the Department of Education. *Dáil Debates,* vol. 210, col. 284 (27 May 1964). For an overview of the relationship between the Department of Education and the Irish language, see Ó Buachalla, *Education Policy,* pp. 58-60, 254-258, 341-356; Hindley, R. (1990), *The Death of the Irish Language,* London: Routledge, pp. 36-42.

17 *Dáil Debates,* vol. 159, col. 1494 (19 July 1956).

18 O'Connor, *A Troubled Sky,* p. 3.

19 Horgan, *Seán Lemass,* pp. 293-301. Walsh, *The Party,* p. 82; Lee, *Seán Lemass,* p. 24. For a detailed assessment of the policy contribution of these ministers, see Ó Buachalla, *Education Policy,* pp. 278-290.

20 Neary, *Failure of Nationalism,* p. 70. Sheehan, J. 'Education and Society in Ireland 1945-70' in Lee, *Ireland 1945-70,* p. 63. Ó Buachalla marks 1957 as a crucial year of transition, *Education Policy,* p. 50. Professor Desmond Williams (writing in 1953) dated the interest in economic debate as arising in 1948 and observed that politicians had adopted 'economics' after the declaration of the Republic in 1949, quoted in Fanning, R. (1984), 'Economists and Governments: Ireland 1922-52' in A. E. Murphy (ed.), *Economists and the Irish Economy from the Eighteenth Century to the Present Day,* Dublin: Irish Academic Press, p. 138.

21 O'Connor, S. (1968), 'Post Primary Education: Now and in the Future', *Studies* vol. 57, pp. 233-251. Also Randles, E. (1975), *Post Primary Education in Ireland: 1957-70,* Dublin: Veritas Publications, p. 311.

22 For a general summary of the early development of OEEC and Irish involvement, see Maher, D.J. (1986), *The Tortuous Path – The Course of Ireland's Entry into the EEC 1948-73,* Dublin: Institute of Public Administration, pp. 24-28; Fanning, *Department of Finance*, pp. 407-434; Murphy, *Ireland in the Twentieth Century*, p. 123. For the impact of the Marshall Plan on Ireland, see Whelan, B. (2000), *Ireland and the Marshall Plan 1947-1957*, Dublin: Four Courts Press. For extra background see Walker, M. (1993), *The Cold War,* London: Fourth Estate, pp. 50-56; Calvocoressi, p. (1991), *World Politics since 1945*, London: Longman. The Organisation for European Economic Co-operation (OEEC) existed from April 1948 until December 1960, when the Organisation for Economic Co-operation and Development (OECD) was set up under a convention signed by the OEEC member countries and by Canada and USA.

23 Friis, H. (1964), 'Preface', in S. E. Harris (ed.), *Economic Aspects of Higher Education,* Paris: Organisation for Economic Co-operation and Development, p. 7. See also Vaizey, J., (n.d.) 'Introduction', *The Residual Factor and Economic Growth – Study Group in the Economics of Education,* Paris: Organisation for Economic Co-operation and Development, pp. 9-10.

24 Kaldor, N. 'Comment on Mr Ingvar Svennilson's paper,' *Residual Factor – Study Group*, p. 143; Vaizey, J. 'Towards a New Political Economy, or Some Problems of Some Aspects of Economies in the light of 'Human Resources' Problems', ibid., p. 201. Friis, *Preface*, p. 7.

25 O'Connor, *A Troubled Sky*, p. 63. The Washington conference was a landmark in a number of ways. Professor Guy Neave observes that the so-called 'residual theory', which attributed economic growth to that residual from industrial and commercial investment which is investment in education, 'was launched upon the world at the OECD Washington Conference of 1961'. Neave, G. (1982), 'On the Edge of the Abyss: An Overview of Recent Developments in European Higher Education', *European Journal of Education*, vol. 17, no. 2, p. 125.

26 For a valuable discussion of the influence of this report, of the role of OECD, and the growth in influence of economics as an approach to questions of education, see O'Sullivan, D. (1992), 'Cultural Strangers and Educational Change: The OECD Report *Investment in Education* and Irish Education Policy', *Journal of Education Policy*, vol. 7, no. 3, pp. 445-469.

27 *Investment in Education*, (1965), Dublin: Stationery Office, pp. 15-17, 45-48, 71-75, 97-100, 126-128, 141, 172-173, 311. The Report also contained a significant discussion on the position of technician education.

28 Seán O'Connor maintained that the survey team did not enquire into third-level because of the existence of the Commission on Higher Education. (O'Connor, *A Troubled Sky*, p. 113). The Commission secretariat did supply data to the *Investment in Education* Survey Team (Report, pp. 45, 74). The Commission was offered the services of OECD experts to survey science and technology. The offer was declined, as the Commission wanted them as agents of the Commission (*Commission Minutes*, pp. 215-217).

29 See Lyons, *Ireland Since the Famine*, pp. 652-654; Brown, T. (1982) *Ireland: A Social and Cultural History 1922-79,* London: Fontana Paperbacks, pp. 249-251; Coolahan, *Irish Education*, pp. 165-168; Clancy, P. (1988), *Who Goes to College? A Second National Survey of Participation in Higher Education*, Dublin: Higher

Education Authority, p. 9; O'Connor, *A Troubled Sky*, pp. 110-121; Ó Buachalla, *Education Policy*, p. 72; Ó Buachalla, S. (1984), 'Policy and Structural Development in Higher Education', *European Journal of Education*, vol. 19, no. 2, p. 165. For a critique of the long-term effects of the Report on the secondary school curriculum, see Lynch, K. (1992), 'Education and the Paid Labour Market', *Irish Educational Studies*, vol. 11, pp. 13-33.

30 O'Connor, *A Troubled Sky*, p. 121; O'Connor, *Studies*, p. 233.

31 *Dáil Debates*, vol. 225, col. 1854 (6 December 1966).

32 *Investment in Education*, p. xxxiii. Patrick Lynch, *Irish Times* (Letters Column), 6 January 1988. Also Interview in *Education Forum*, Radio One, Radio Telefís Éireann, 5 January 1989.

33 Clancy, *Who goes to College?*, p. 9. A further example of how economic analysis provided new paradigms for educational thinking, in this case courtesy of American health economist, Professor A. Dale Tussing, is analysed in O'Sullivan, D., (1992) 'Shaping Educational Debate: a case study and an interpretation', *Economic and Social Review*, vol. 23, no. 4, pp. 423-438.

34 Vocational Education Act 1930, s. 3. For general background to the Act and the establishment of the VEC system, see Ó Buachalla, *Education Policy*, pp. 62-64, 223-225, 268-269.

35 Coolahan, *Irish Education*, pp. 102-103.

36 O'Connor, *A Troubled Sky*, p. 4.

37 *Dáil Debates*, vol. 161, col. 702 (2 May 1957).

38 Randles, *Post Primary Education*, p. 28.

39 *Dáil Debates*, vol. 180, cols. 936-949 (23 March 1960).

40 Review of National Policies for Science and Education (1964), *Training of Technicians in Ireland*, Paris: OECD, p. 100. The second OECD examiner on the team was Alan Peacock, Professor of Economics, University of York.

41 The background papers were prepared by John O'Donnell, Professor of Chemical Engineering, University College Dublin. Professor O'Donnell had been one of a number of active members of the engineers' professional body writing about technician issues in the early 1960s. See O'Donnell, J. P. (1962), 'Manpower for Industry', *Engineers Journal*, vol. 15, pp. 242-246. For an overview of initiatives taken in relation to technicians and technician education in the 1960s, see Collins, L. (1975), 'The Technician', *Engineers Journal*, pp. 14-18. Within the Department of Education Dr Hillery had established a study committee on technicians in Irish industry as early as September 1961. It spent much of its time discussing the lack of demand from industry for fully trained technicians and the lack of estimates of future requirements. It never eventually got around to carrying out proposals to make surveys of the technician needs of particular sections of Irish industry (*OECD, Training of Technicians*, pp. 31-35, 37, 83).

42 OECD, *Training of Technicians*, p. 37. There is no single universally applicable definition of the term technician. However, the 1969 report of the UK Committee on Technician Courses and Examinations (the Hazelgrave Report) adopted the following description: 'Technicians and other technical support staff occupy a position between that of the qualified scientist, engineer or technologist on the one hand, and the skilled foreman or craftsman or operative on the other. Their education and specialised skills enable them to exercise

technical judgement. By this is meant an understanding, by reference to general principles, of the reasons for and the purposes of their work, rather than a reliance solely on established practices or accumulated skills'. National Advisory Council on Education for Industry and Commerce, (1969), *Report of the Committee on Technician Courses and Examinations,* London: HMSO, p. 3. See also Ó Maolcatha, N. (1986), 'The Role of the Technician in Economic Development', in R. J. A. Bradley (ed.), *Proceedings of NCEA/UNESCO International Symposium on Technician Training and Education,* Dublin: NCEA pp. 3-5. Also Collins, *The Technician,* pp. 14-16. For a recent definition see *Standards and Routes to Registration – SARTOR (1997),* London: Engineering Council.

43 OECD, *Training of Technicians,* p. 42. The Engineers' Association had recommended the setting up of a national council to recognise training courses for technicians to the Commission on Higher Education (*Engineers' Journal,* vol. 18, 1965, p. 232). The Irish Committee of the Institute of Mechanical Engineers had recommended *inter alia* an increase in the supply of engineering technicians with a recognised diploma (*Commission Minutes,* p. 132).

44 OECD, *Training of Technicians,* p. 86.

45 ibid, pp. 90-92, 110-112.

46 For background on the preparation of the report and the Paris meeting, see O'Donnell, J.P. (1963), 'Paris 'Confrontation' Meeting on Irish Education: How the OECD Report was Prepared', *Engineers' Journal,* vol. 16, pp. 216-219. O'Donnell was critical of some of the shortcomings of the report. He saw the technical schools leaving certificate as introducing a new rigidity.

CHAPTER 3

A Tale of Two Committees

Two committees were to influence the shape of Irish higher education in the 1960s. The first was the Commission on Higher Education and the second was the Steering Committee on Technical Education.

The Commission on Higher Education

At the time of the establishment of the Commission in 1960, higher education had not long been the responsibility of the Department of Education. In parallel with the British tradition, where universities were funded (via the University Grants Committee) through the Treasury, Irish universities had been funded through the Department of Finance. The funding was transferred to the Department of Education in the mid-1950s.[1] Higher education had not been a traditional area of concern of the Department of Education and it did not fit neatly into the organisation and management of that Department. There was the additional difficulty that the administrative staff dealing with higher education, virtually without exception, were not university graduates and accordingly did not have direct experience of higher education.[2] There was therefore no tradition of policy-making with regard to the sector.

As noted previously, in 1958 the Minister for Education, Jack Lynch, established the Commission on Accommodation Needs of the Constituent Colleges of the National University of Ireland. This group reported within eighteen months.[3] The main issue of concern to the government was the question of whether to support the decision of the UCD authorities to relocate the college at Belfield. In addition to its recommendations on issues of accommodation, the Commission suggested the establishment of a University Development Committee to advise on long-term plans for development and co-ordination. Mr Lynch's successor, Dr Patrick Hillery, and his Department concluded that there were so many pressing problems in higher education that there was urgent need for a commission which would examine and make recommendations on a variety of important matters.[4]

The first public indication that a commission on higher education was contemplated came from Dr Hillery in the Dáil on 23 March 1960. Among the items which he saw as requiring consideration were access and entry requirements, the allocation of grants according to needs, the need to establish another university college or an additional constituent college of the National University of Ireland, the possible establishment of a University Development Committee (as recommended by the Commission on Accommodation Needs), the functions of higher technical schools and the avoidance of duplication of public expenditure on professional courses in universities and such schools. Significantly the Minister spoke also of a missing rung in the educational ladder 'inasmuch as there is no official channel for the talented and determined vocational education student to proceed via the National University to a degree in his own subject.'[5]

The Commission's purpose and remit

The Commission was set up in October 1960.[6] Under its terms of reference it was to inquire into and make recommendations in relation to university, professional, technological and higher education generally, with special reference to the general organisation and administration of education at these levels, the nature and extent of the provision to be made, the machinery for the making of appointments in university colleges and the provision of courses of higher education through Irish.[7] These terms of reference were very wide. There was no single issue on which the Commission was being asked to focus. Rather it had freedom to review all aspects of higher education in a fashion never previously attempted in the history of the state.

The Commission was chaired by the Chief Justice, Cearbhall Ó Dálaigh, and had twenty-eight members. Seven of the group were current or former university academics (two being from outside the state). The others represented a wide spectrum of ecclesiastical, educational, civil service, research, commercial state-sponsored body, and Irish language interests and experience. There was only one representative of technological higher education.[8] In the group there was one engineer and one individual from private business. There was no economist or statistician from within the state, nor was there any representation of those involved in teacher education or educational studies at third level. The absence of such representation made it less likely that the Commission would be fully attuned to changes and developments taking place concurrently within Irish education and within higher education abroad. Although the group was large, it was to prove to be deficient in key areas.

The Commission sat for over six years and did not complete even its interim report until February 1967. By contrast the influential Robbins Report, which had a brief similar to that of the Commission and which was to influence the development of British higher education in a major way for a fifteen-year period, was appointed by Treasury minute in February 1961 and signed its report in September 1963.[9] The long delay and the absence of any interim report did not help the standing of the Commission's report when it eventually arrived.[10] Once the Commission had been appointed, both the Minister, Dr Hillery, and his successor, George Colley, declined to issue statements of policy in answer to Dáil questions relating to higher education. From as early as April 1962 the Minister for Education was being asked how long it was anticipated the Commission would take to report.[11] This pressure was to be kept up over a four-and-a-half year period, particularly by deputies from the Limerick constituencies who considered that Limerick's case for a university was being long-fingered.[12]

The exasperation felt in some quarters because of the delay was most dramatically illustrated by an extraordinary outburst during an estimates speech in November 1966 from no less a person than the Parliamentary Secretary to the Taoiseach (and Government Chief Whip), Deputy Michael Carty. He called for the abolition of the Commission if it did not report promptly, suggested that its recommendations would be invalidated by the passage of years, and hinted that the Commission had threatened to resign if the Minister made any reference to proposals for university education. He suggested that, if there was any truth in the latter rumour, his advice to the Minister would be to 'let them resign and be damned to them'.[13] Deputy Carty's comments were disowned within days by the Taoiseach, Mr Lynch, following the threatened resignation of the chairman of the Commission.[14] Significantly the opposition parties in the Dáil made no attempt to have Mr Carty censured in any way. He was merely echoing their sentiments in a more forceful manner. Such a prelude was not an encouraging augury for the standing of the final report or the seriousness with which its proposals would be greeted by the Minister, Donogh O'Malley.

Assumptions of the Commission

In its report and in setting out the basic problems to be solved, the Commission did not attempt to address in any explicit or thematic fashion the goals of higher education. In its own words it generally interpreted its terms of reference as applying to that level of education for which in Ireland the Leaving Certificate of the Department of Education, or university matriculation, or equivalents, were normal entry requirements. 'In practice we dealt with institutions rather than levels or kinds of education'.[15]

The Commission did have its own understanding of higher education. The report felt that indiscriminate demands had been made in the past on Irish universities. These demands and the colleges' acceptance of them were seen to denote an absence of any clear view of what a university might reasonably be expected to concern itself with. The university was not a professional academy, nor a congregation of such academies, existing only to provide a training for the several professions. Neither was it a universal provider of all forms of higher education nor a mere purveyor of academic labels. It was seen as: a) a place for the study and communication of basic knowledge; b) the repository of the highest standards in teaching and scholarship; c) conserving accumulated knowledge and passing it on to successive generations of students; d) re-examining that knowledge and re-stating it in the light of new scholarship, and e) adding to existing knowledge and advancing it beyond its present frontiers. These were seen as the purposes to which the university had to relate its functions, and the obligations that the university had to be permitted to keep uppermost, regardless of what other requests for professional and technical education fell upon it.

The report argued further that the functions of institutions of higher education, especially universities, as centres of learning, scholarship and liberal education should not be allowed to become overwhelmed by the claims made upon them to provide the country with its requirements of skilled manpower.[16] Likewise the value of higher education for the community did not merely consist of the content of expert knowledge needed by a modern society. Irrespective of service to these needs, higher education had to be looked upon as a good in itself, an intrinsic asset conferring a particular benefit on the country as well as on the individual.

Arguably the strongest critique of the Commission's shortcomings came in one of its many minority reports, that of Professor C.F. Carter, Professor of Political Economy at Manchester University and subsequently first Vice-Chancellor of the University of Lancaster.[17] It was his belief that the Commission's analysis of the role of the university was inadequate and confused, and had led to a view of its functions which, if used as a guide to action, would strengthen the harmful tendency to remoteness from everyday life which is always present in an institution of higher learning. He totally disagreed with the Commission's statement that 'the university is a place for the study and communication of basic knowledge', which in its context could only mean that the growth of applied studies in universities should be inhibited. Carter argued that the statement was historically untrue, since important traditional branches of study, such as medicine and law, had always been essentially practical and vocational. The suggestion that another institution might give students 'a specific preparation for livelihood that the university, with its broader obligation to scholarship, could not properly be asked to undertake' seemed to him, as a generalisation, total nonsense.

The commissioners' view of a university was not totally eccentric. Three dominant models or classifications have characterised the historical development of European universities over the past two centuries.[18] The first of these, the German or 'research model', is concerned primarily with research activities, a model which became very influential through the way in which it was adapted in the United States.[19] The second is the British or 'personality model' which had a strong interest in the personality development of students. The function of 'character formation' or 'liberal education' played a more important role in English than in other university systems. Its most celebrated exponent was John Henry Newman.[20] The third model is the French or 'professional training model'. If one accepts that none of these are pure models and that universities in Germany, Britain and France contain elements of all three, one could say that the Commission's primary emphasis for the Irish university was on the first or German model, with a strong emphasis also on the second or British model, and with the professional training model as the weakest of these three. By the time the Commission came to report, it was to a Department of Education whose preference among the three models would have been the reverse. It is conceivable that the Department might have accepted this approach to higher education at the time the Commission was established in 1960. By

1967 however, after many years of exposure to ideas prevalent within OECD, it was no longer prepared to subscribe to such a non-utilitarian view of higher education.

Clark Kerr, American academic and former President of the University of California at Berkeley, has outlined six major purposes which he saw as the standard official statement by nations about their systems of higher education.[21] These are i) transmission of a common culture; ii) contributions to the development of individual students; iii) contributions to research and scholarship; iv) extension of greater equality of opportunity; v) advancement of human capability to meet labour market needs; and vi) public service in its many forms to society. The emphasis in the Commission's report was on the first three of these. It had less concern with the latter three, and indeed was almost totally silent on the issue of equality of opportunity. Those to whom it was reporting in the first place, the Minister and his Department, would by 1967 have put the emphasis strongly on the last, rather than on the first, three.

Report of the Commission

Given the approach of the Commission many of its principal recommendations inevitably centred around institutions. It recommended a number of new ones – new colleges, a permanent Commission for Higher Education, a Council of Irish Universities, a National College of Agricultural and Veterinary Sciences, a Technological Authority and a number of individual colleges to be established in place of a disbanded National University of Ireland.

In terms of non-university higher technological and vocational education its most important recommendations were the New Colleges and the Technological Authority. Two new colleges, envisaged as working to the standard of a pass degree in arts, science and commerce, were seen as helping to meet the growing demand for higher education in a way suitable to the country's educational needs, as relieving the universities of any obligation to meet the whole of the growing demand for higher education, and as creating institutions which would become centres of intellectual and cultural life in their regions. It was recommended that they be established in Dublin and Limerick, while others were envisaged for the South-East and the North-West.[22]

The Technological Authority was intended to have the functions of technological education and training, research and service, and information, including testing and standards. The Commission considered that, on the whole, technological training was not provided in the Irish system of higher education, and it seemed best that responsibility for technological education and training should be linked with the general responsibility for the development and promotion of technology in the country. [23] The commissioners acknowledged that there was a shortage of trained technicians in industry, and that this deficiency had to be remedied if industrial development was not to be seriously retarded. The services of trained technicians could be used to maximum advantage only if the industrial processes in which they were engaged had been developed on sound technological principles. They concluded that the need for trained technicians must be given due recognition in the allocation of resources, and that the development of technology and technological training lay at the basis of industrial growth. Neither the New Colleges nor the concept of a Technological Authority enjoyed unanimous support on the Commission, [24] and they were among the many major recommendations which were never to be implemented.

Impact of the Commission's report

Discussion of the details of the Commission's interim report was overshadowed by a statement from the Minister for Education, Donogh O'Malley, on 18 April 1967 that, contrary to what had been recommended by the Commission, he proposed to merge Trinity College Dublin and University College Dublin into one university.[25] This was to generate an often heated debate which continued sporadically for almost five years until the Higher Education Authority's publication of a report on university reorganisation in June 1972. That report effectively put an end to the proposal to merge the two colleges.[26]

Of its thirty-seven principal recommendations[27] only a minority were implemented. Of those that were implemented the most important was the establishment in August 1968 of an *ad hoc* Higher Education Authority with functions akin to those which the report envisaged for a permanent Commission for Higher Education.[28] Outcomes which were in accordance with the Commission's recommendations were that no additional university was established in the short term, none of the existing medical schools was closed and the period of training for national teachers was extended to three years, although the colleges of education were not to be associated with the proposed New Colleges. A minimum standard for entry to university, equivalent to a pass in the Leaving Certificate with honours in two subjects, was introduced. A higher education grants scheme was introduced by statute in 1968,[29] but the recommended parallel loans scheme was never established. University presidents subsequently were appointed for a limited term. The National College of Art was given a new constitution,[30] the training of military cadets was associated with university studies at University College Galway, and the Irish Folklore Commission was established as an institute within University College Dublin. Education as a subject of study and research came to be developed within the universities.[31] Student bodies were given greater recognition in the reorganisation of student life, and the Commission's recommendations that a large-scale programme of hostels for students was not practicable, until other more pressing needs of higher education had been satisfied, became a matter of policy within the newly-established Higher Education Authority. At least thirteen areas can be identified where the Commission's recommendations can be shown, or at least argued, to have had an influence.

Most of the major recommendations of the Commission were never implemented. The legislation governing the National University of Ireland remained in place for another generation (although virtually every Minister for Education from Donogh O'Malley to Niamh Bhreathnach subsequently announced proposals to change it).[32] The constitution of TCD was not restated by act of the Oireachtas. New university governing authorities with a majority of members elected by academic staffs were not created. The appointments system for academic staff was not changed fundamentally, staff/student ratios in universities did not improve in the manner envisaged,[33] university degree courses did not move to a minimum of four years, the separate research institutes and the universities did not establish closer relationships, no statutory Council of Irish Universities was established, the New Colleges did not come into existence, nor did the National College for Agricultural and Veterinary Sciences, nor the Technological Authority, nor the special schemes intended to ensure a supply of Irish-speaking university staff of high academic calibre. Numerous other lesser recommendations of the Commission were likewise ignored.

The majority of the recommendations required action by the state. By the time the report of the Commission came to be published, the Department of Education was already well on the way to developing an agenda of its own for higher education that was both independent of, and unlike that of, the Commission. Some indication of how the report was viewed at the Department of Education can be gleaned from the comments of a then Assistant Secretary, Seán O'Connor. He found many of the report's proposals deeply disappointing. Although conceding that there were many good and sensible recommendations in the report, his overall impression was that the Commission was determined to protect the universities at all costs and to make them even more élite than, in his opinion, they already were. He viewed the New Colleges as a device to preserve the high standards of the university in face of the danger the Commission saw from the growing demand for higher education. As a consequence teacher training, because of its concerns with techniques as well as fundamental principles, and technical and technological training, for similar reasons, had to be accommodated outside the universities.[34]

The delay in producing the report was bound to damage its ultimate authority in many ways. For example, the Commission's enquiries in the matter of technician training were made during the first hearings of oral evidence in 1961.[35] Had they been conducted at a later period it is conceivable that they might have been more sensitive to the growing demand for an educational initiative with regard to the education and training of technicians. The fact that in the seven-year period the Department of Education had come to develop its own agenda was calculated to lessen the likelihood of many of the report's recommendations being implemented. Apart from these two factors, there were other major weaknesses in the report that prevented its having much impact. In the first place no fewer than twelve of the twenty-seven members who signed the report submitted reservations.[36] Nor were the reservations confined to minor points. Seven of the signatories penned reservations on the National College of Agricultural and Veterinary Sciences, six had reservations on the New Colleges, three with regard to the Technological Authority and three on the proposals for developing university studies through Irish. Other topics on which reservations were entered included the advisability of retaining two universities in Dublin, university governance, teacher education, higher medical education and the four-year minimum for degree study. The fact that almost one-tenth of the entire report was taken up with reservations on central issues was virtually guaranteed to undermine its authority.

What was particularly significant was the view, criticised by Professor Carter as noted above, that the university's commitment should be to the study and communication of basic knowledge rather than specific preparation for livelihoods. O'Connor refers to it in relation to teacher training and to technical and technological education.[37] The same distinctions were drawn in relation to law, architecture, business and administrative studies and social sciences.[38] Basic knowledge and scholarship were seen as the concerns of the university, while professional and technical studies were the concern of professional bodies or educational institutions of another kind. At the time this was being written the Department of Education was groping its way towards a major intervention in Irish higher education. The report with which it was presented portrayed the universities as aloof entities whose scholarship and standards required preservation and protection. There was little in the report to suggest that the universities had any role as catalysts for a growing economy, or that they could be relied upon to provide responses to the economic and social demands which the Department of Education, and successive ministers, had felt for some years that they should be addressing. On the contrary the report provided strong arguments for setting up an alternative provision which would cater for some of these perceived demands and help in the construction of Dr Hillery's missing educational rung.

Regional Technical Colleges

The issue which was responsible initially for bringing the Department of Education into an interventionist role in higher education was the regional technical colleges. Ironically, as originally conceived, these colleges had no function in third-level or higher education. They were first mooted by the Minister for Education, Dr Hillery, at a press conference on 20 May 1963 in the course of a statement on post-primary education. The main initiative announced there was a proposal to establish comprehensive schools, but the minister also stated that it was his intention to establish a Technical Schools Leaving Certificate, and concomitantly to arrange for the provision of a limited number of technological colleges with regional status in which the courses for that Certificate would be provided.[39]

In the Dáil in February 1964 the minister explained that this certificate would be a means by which a student could proceed to a higher technological course, whether in a higher technological college or a university. This extra technical course was to be provided mainly in new regional technical colleges of which ten were envisaged. Earlier, in reply to questions, the minister had indicated that the main role of the colleges was to provide courses for a) the Technical Schools Leaving Certificate, b) apprentice training and c) higher level technician training. It was envisaged that particular colleges would cater on a nationwide basis for the various specialised occupations concerned. Technician courses in food processing, for instance, would be confined to one college or at most two. The minister added that planning with regard to sites, building, financing, syllabuses, staffing and organisation was proceeding as rapidly as possible.[40]

Initial progress with regard to the provision of regional technical colleges was slow. In May 1964 Dr Hillery announced in the estimates debate for the Department of Education that plans were in hand to provide a college in Carlow which it was intended would be the first to open. At the same time he announced that a first draft of the programme for the Technical Schools Leaving Certificate had been prepared and had been sent for comment to the Irish Vocational Education Association and the Vocational Teacher's Association.[41] Three years were to elapse before the concept of a Technical Schools Leaving Certificate was finally abandoned,[42] but the protracted discussion on it, and the difficulty in reaching decisions on the future of second-level education in vocational schools, were among the factors leading to the delay in establishing the regional technical colleges.

Dr Hillery left the Department of Education in April 1965 and was succeeded by George Colley. In June 1965 Mr Colley told the Dáil that building plans were in train for four colleges, planning for site acquisition was under way for three others, and that responsibility for liaison with the vocational education committees concerned had been assigned to a senior inspector in the Department of Education.[43] Little further progress on regional technical colleges took place during Mr Colley's fifteen-month tenure of office and this was apparently a matter of some concern to him. Mr Colley was replaced as Minister for Education in July 1966 by Donogh O'Malley and the question of these colleges became a matter of priority for him. Within less than three months he had established the Steering Committee on Technical Education.[44]

The Steering Committee on Technical Education

The Committee was established in September 1966 and its terms of reference were to advise the minister generally on technical education. Side by side with the Committee the minister appointed a consortium of architects, engineers and quantity surveyors to supervise the erection of the colleges.[45] The Steering Committee was asked, on behalf of the minister, to provide the consortium with a brief for the colleges. This necessitated the Committee preparing outline curricula for each projected course. The Committee was also asked, in preparing its brief, to consider all matters relevant to such a task and to ensure as far as possible that its brief harmonised with any future thinking on third-level technical education.[46] At the same time the members were informed that it had already been decided to build eight regional technical colleges at Cork, Limerick, Waterford, Galway, Sligo, Dundalk, Athlone and Carlow, and their advice was asked on the need for a ninth college at Letterkenny.

The Steering Committee had eight members and was chaired by Noel Mulcahy, Senior Management Specialist at the Irish Management Institute. Significantly, half of the group were engineers, as was the secretary, Jeremiah Sheehan, then an inspector in the Department of Education. This, of course, was also the minister's profession. Only two of the eight had direct involvement with the education system: John O'Donnell, Professor of Chemical Engineering at UCD and Charles McCarthy, General Secretary of the Vocational Teachers' Association.[47] The Committee was serviced from within the Technical Instruction Branch of the Department, but it also had the services of a statistician, William Hyland, and the Assistant Secretary of the Development Branch, Seán O'Connor. While the report of the Committee does not indicate that O'Connor was a major contributor, the minister had been advised by his predecessor, George Colley, that O'Connor's involvement was necessary if the project was to be expedited.[48] O'Connor sat in on all meetings of the Committee and appears to have played a crucial role in it.[49] The Committee completed its report in April 1967, but a report embodying a preliminary brief was made available to the Department in January 1967.[50] The setting up of the consortium almost simultaneously with the establishment of the Committee put strong pressure on the latter to hasten its report and left it very little time to consider all the implications of its assignment, as it duly noted. Its task was not helped by the fact that the Department was not in a position to provide it with the supporting services necessary for an undertaking of that kind.

Report of the Steering Committee

The Committee's report was succinct. It concluded that Irish people generally had not had the opportunity to become technically skilled and that this had left a serious gap in the stock of knowledge and skills necessary for the development of productive enterprise. If the demand for needed skills did not arise naturally, it had to be stimulated artificially, and regional technical colleges were seen as providing one of the answers to this problem. Another way of stimulating demand was to ensure that due recognition was given to the various courses available in the colleges. Accordingly the Committee recommended the establishment of a National Council for Educational Awards with responsibility for the standard of entry and qualification, syllabuses and courses, the award of certificates and diplomas and the negotiation of reciprocal recognition with other countries.[51]

The Committee viewed the main long-term function of the colleges as educating for trade and industry over a broad spectrum of occupations ranging from craft to professional level, notably in engineering and science but also in commercial, linguistic and other specialties. In the short term the colleges were seen as concerned with filling gaps in the industrial manpower structure, particularly in the technician area. For planning purposes it was assumed that the colleges would provide a) senior cycle post-primary courses leading to the Leaving Certificate, b) Junior and Senior Trade Certificate courses on day or block release for apprentices, c) courses for technician qualifications at various levels, d) courses leading to higher technician qualifications or, in some cases, to professional level, and e) adult education courses, including retraining courses provided by agreement with the newly-formed AnCO.[52] The Committee provided detailed projections of student numbers and costs for the first four categories.[53]

The Committee recommended that the minister proceed with all eight regional technical colleges as soon as possible. A number of its recommendations were concerned with the building brief, the phasing of the building programme and the establishment of a

Building Project Unit within the Department.[54] Its recommendations also dealt with the internal organisation of the colleges, and the recruitment and training of the supervisory staff. It was recommended that the Galway college should be designated as the main centre for hotel and catering courses outside Dublin, and that a local technical college, as distinct from a full regional technical college, should be provided in Letterkenny. This latter recommendation was not accepted by the government and a college with full regional status was established, an outcome not unrelated to the presence in the cabinet of the very influential Minister for Agriculture, Neil Blaney.[55] In examining the role which these colleges should play in each region, the Committee went on to consider the desirability of education being administered regionally and recommended the establishment of Regional Education Councils having accountability for all education in each of the regions. While nothing came of this proposal, it was to rear its head again in 1973, 1985, and in the White Paper of 1995.[56] It was also to be a bone of contention between the Department of Education and the Irish Vocational Education Association.[57]

The Committee found severe problems arising from the sparseness of information on which adequate projections of the likely demand for places in regional technical colleges, and of demand by industry and other sectors for the graduates of the colleges, could be based. Already existing reports and discussions relating to technical education at sub-professional level were considered inconclusive, because the demand for technical personnel by industry was insufficiently specific to determine the education and training requirements in any detail. The Committee emphasised that educational and economic planning were not realistic without a continuing system of manpower supply and demand forecasting, and considered the problem so acute that it advised the minister to examine the possibility of inviting an outside consultancy or research organisation to conduct feasibility surveys to evaluate the implications of providing forecasts of demand for places in, and products of, the colleges.[58] An outside consultancy was subsequently engaged to make these investigations, but the project broke down because of the inadequacy of the statistical information available.[59] Subsequent attempts at manpower forecasting in 1969 and 1979[60] were to become the responsibility of the Department of Labour rather than the Department of Education.

The Steering Committee and the Commission on Higher Education

Having been enjoined to ensure that its brief would harmonise with any future thinking on third-level technician education, the Committee also considered relevant aspects of the Report of the Commission on Higher Education. At the time only the summary of the Commission's report was to hand. The Committee saw itself as being in agreement with the Commission in the role it envisaged for the colleges, in that the prospective courses concentrated mainly on technician and craft apprentice education together with senior cycle secondary work. On the question of the New Colleges the Committee did not agree with the Commission's views either on the entry standards appropriate to new third-level institutions or on the levels of academic qualifications which they should award. It believed that an undesirable dichotomy in higher education would be created by establishing admission norms in those institutions inferior to those of the universities. It also dissented from the suggestion that the level of attainment in such institutions should be limited to pass degree standard. It concluded that no arbitrary limits should be set to their achievements, the sole criterion being one of merit. Otherwise there would be artificial disadvantages in terms of the calibre of staff and students and a disincentive both to the development of new courses and facilities and the improvement of existing ones. The Committee was also opposed to any suggestion that secondary teacher training should be provided mainly in the universities, whereas other post-primary teachers would be catered for by a co-operative arrangement between New Colleges, institutions of higher vocational education and the teacher training colleges. It considered that any new schemes of teacher training should promote equality of standards of qualification rather than maintain differentials.

The Committee was particularly interested in the recommendations of the Commission that a New College be established in Limerick. It saw the New College (or whatever other third-level institution might be decided upon) and the Regional Technical College as complementary components of a single major educational complex on one site providing courses in arts, science, commercial and technical studies up to graduate level, although the two colleges of which it would consist could retain their separate identities and be separately administered. It suggested that provision might also be made for the training of teachers.[61]

What was eventually decided upon for Limerick was a National Institute for Higher Education. This was quite different from the concept of the New College as set out by the Commission. It was also different from what was recommended by the Steering Committee in that no Regional Technical College was established there.[62] The Limerick site eventually acquired an institution providing a range of courses to graduate level as suggested by the Steering Committee and, in time and on the same complex, an institution providing for the training of teachers. The eventual decision on third-level provision in Limerick approximated more closely to the recommendations of the Committee than to those of the Commission. Additionally the ethos of the Limerick college reflected the concern with technology and technical education of the Steering Committee rather than the general cultural concern which characterised the proposals of the Commission.

The Steering Committee did not explicitly disagree with the concept of the New College. Nevertheless its dissent on the question of teacher education, and on entry standards and levels of academic qualifications, implied that it did not favour the concept. It had elsewhere recommended the establishment of a National Council for Educational Awards which, at the highest levels, would discharge functions similar to those of the Council for National Academic Awards in Britain, in other words with power to award degrees.[63] The Commission had considered the option of having existing non-university institutions brought under a single academic authority which would lay down curricula, approve courses, conduct or supervise examinations and award qualifications.[64] It saw several objections to such an arrangement. It considered that it was part of the history of Irish education that a scheme of a similar kind, that of the Royal University of Ireland, was rejected sixty years previously as unsuitable for, and inimical to, the educational needs of the country. It saw such an arrangement as providing for an examination and a qualification but not an integrated education, and as lacking the focus which the New College could give to intellectual and cultural life in the region which it served. It also saw it as creating a dichotomy between the institution that would provide the training and the authority that would prescribe the courses and conduct or supervise the examinations, thereby emphasising that the acquisition of a qualification is the end towards which education is directed rather than towards the training of the intellect and the formation of personality. On this, as on other issues, it was the view of the

Committee rather than the Commission that was to be more influential.

The influence of the Steering Committee report

The establishment of the Steering Committee as late as 1966 to determine the role of the regional technical colleges has been described by one critic as a blatant example of the procedure of 'putting the cart before the horse' which typified much of the reorganisation of Irish post-primary education in the 1960s. The same critic, commenting on the report's recommendation that the minister initiate surveys to forecast the demand for places in the colleges and for their products, also observed that one would have expected that these two important questions would have been asked and answered before the decision was taken to set up the colleges.[65] These criticisms are valid, but they assume that the formulation and execution of policy is a predominantly rational and constant progression. The formulation and execution of policy with regard to the regional technical colleges certainly followed no such linear progression. They were first conceived of as part of a major state initiative within post-primary education in Ireland. The announcement of May 1963 was both a major innovation and a significant intervention by the then minister, Dr Hillery. At the time it was seen in the Department as an intervention carrying a good deal of risk.[66] Having undertaken such an intervention, there was within the Department a sense of commitment to following through with the project, which continued despite changes of minister.

The regional technical colleges project was intimately bound up with the plan to introduce a Technical Schools Leaving Certificate. For reasons not explored here the idea of such a certificate was eventually abandoned. Nevertheless the concept of a regional technical college assumed its own life. It became a matter of considerable interest to politicians, some of whom were keen to ensure that these colleges were located within their regions or constituencies.[67] Little progress was achieved with the idea in the period from 1963 to 1966 because of the difficulty of grappling with changes sought or proposed within the vocational education system.

What the Steering Committee provided was a rationale for the colleges which made them largely independent of changes at second-level within the vocational education system. The rationale was entirely consistent with the role set out for the colleges by the Minister for Education in February 1964.[68] The Committee also was able to draw on the two OECD reports, *Training of Technicians in Ireland* and *Investment in Education*. Both of these had pointed to the necessity for much greater activity in providing education for technicians. With such weighty outside support the Committee was on strong ground in recommending an initiative, even if it could not accurately quantify the level of demand for places or for the student output. While there might have been an element of an act of faith in what was being proposed, few would have questioned that good works were involved.

There can be no doubt about the influence of the Steering Committee report. Its conclusions were largely adopted as policy. In setting out to the Dáil the functions of the colleges and the courses of study to be undertaken, both Donogh O'Malley and his successor, Brian Lenihan,[69] drew almost verbatim on the Committee's report. That within a few years the colleges began to diverge from the Steering Committee blueprint cannot be put down to a lack of enthusiasm for the conclusions reached by it, but rather to other pressures which will be examined later.

The Steering Committee and third-level education

The Steering Committee did not envisage that, particularly in their early years, the regional technical colleges would become institutions catering primarily for third-level education. In its report it provided detailed projections of the student population in the colleges in 1972 (assuming that the colleges would open in 1969) and global projections for 1975.[70] Its projections for 1972 are contained in Table 2.

From the figures it is clear that the Committee projected that in 1972 only 20 per cent of the output and just over 28 per cent of the stock of students in the colleges would be at technician, higher technician and professional level. Because the projections were largely made for the building consortium's brief, no figures were included for part-time evening students, but there was nothing in the Committee's report to suggest that part-time provision in the colleges was to be geared primarily towards courses at the higher level. The Committee envisaged that between 31 per cent and 32 per cent of both student output and stock would be at Senior Cycle or Advanced Senior Cycle level, and that 48 per cent of output and 40 per cent of stock in 1972 would comprise apprentices. On the face of it there was no evidence that the Committee was planning a major initiative in third-level education, or committing any impropriety by trespassing on the territory of the Commission on Higher Education.

TABLE 2: Steering Committee Projections of Student Output and Stock at RTCs in 1972.

Course Category	Output	Stock
Senior Cycle	2115	4230
Advanced Senior Cycle	640	640
Craft Apprentice	1800	3600
Distributive Craft Apprentice	700	940
Hotel and Catering	1705	1705
Technician	1260	2200
Higher Technician	375	1500
Professional	110	660
Total	*8605	*15485

*The totals are incorrect but are recorded as in Appendix II of the Steering Committee's Report. They should read 8705 and 15475 respectively.

The Commission itself had seen institutions of vocational education as coming only partially within its purview and as being the most suitable institutions in which to provide higher technician training.[71] The Steering Committee could not reasonably have foreseen that pressure both from the private secondary schools and from second-level vocational schools would within a relatively short time reduce, and eventually remove, the provision of senior cycle courses from the colleges altogether. Nor in 1967 could it have anticipated that An Comhairle Oiliuna (AnCO), the Industrial Training Authority, would transform and reduce the role of the education system in the training and education of apprentices. Both of these developments were instrumental in forcing regional technical colleges into becoming institutions increasingly concerned with third-level education. Not only was it not anticipated that the colleges would evolve in this way so quickly, but the development when it came was a matter of concern to some of the officials in the Department of Education.[72]

While the Steering Committee may not have appeared to be cutting across the area of concern of the Commission, it was in time to prove that it had done so. Once the government had committed itself to the concept of the Regional Technical College as defined by the Steering Committee, it was less likely to encourage a parallel development of the New College as envisaged by the Commission. When it also endorsed the Committee's concept of a National Council for Educational Awards it was choosing to adopt its view that the progress of the colleges should not be deterred by any artificial limitation on either the scope or the level of their educational achievements.[73] With its recommendations on Regional Technical Colleges, special treatment for Limerick and a National Council for Educational Awards, the Steering Committee had provided a framework for third-level education which would prove more attractive to the new brand of thinking in the Department of Education than anything contained in the Report of the Commission on Higher Education.

Notes

1 It was suggested in a Dáil debate by Deputy Professor John O'Dovovan that the Universities and Colleges Vote was moved to the Department of Education by the then Minister for Finance to avoid uproar over the size of a grant to Trinity College *(Dáil Debates*, vol. 254, col. 1490 – 15th June 1971). The issue that seems to have brought the matter to a head was UCD's proposed move to Belfield.

> At the meeting of the government held on 15 June 1956, the Minister for Education referred, in connection with a proposal for the transfer of University College Dublin to a new site at Belfield, to the difficulties involved in the existing situation in which he is the Minister responsible for university education, while the vote for Universities and Colleges is accounted for by the office of the Minister for Finance. The Minister for Finance also expressed the view that this situation is anomalous. It was agreed that the matter would be considered by the Taoiseach, the Minister for Education and the Attorney General.

(National Archives, Department of the Taoiseach, File S 140108). The changeover took place shortly afterwards. See also McCartney, *UCD*, pp. 240-260.

2 Graduate recruitment to the Department of Education was largely confined to the inspectorate (*Dáil Debates*,. vol. 200, col. 37, 10 March 1963).

3 *Commission on Accommodation Needs*, p. 123. The Commission had the same Chairman, Cearbhall Ó Dálaigh, and the same Secretary, Séamus Ó Cathail, as its successor body, the Commission on Higher Education. It had eight members apart from the Chairman, and in its eighteen months' existence it also produced three interim reports, on each of the three constituent colleges of the National University of Ireland.

4 *Memorandum from Dr T. Ó Raifeartaigh, Secretary, Department of Education to Secretary, Department of Finance, 3 February 1960*, National Archives,

Department of Taoiseach, File 16289. The idea of having a commission to look at higher education appears to have been mooted in the Department of Finance seven or eight years previously (National Archives, Department of Taoiseach, File 13809B).

5 *Dáil Debates*, vol. 180, cols. 948-952, 1506 (31 March 1960).

6 ibid., vol 186, col. 947 (23 February 1961). The Commission held its inaugural meeting on 8 November 1960. Its fifty-ninth and final plenary meeting was held on 13/14 October 1967.

7 ibid., vol. 194, col. 1541 (10 April 1962); *Commission Summary*, p. 1. At the initial meeting of the Commission on 8 November 1960 the Minister, Dr Hillery, told the members that he had thrown open the terms of reference as widely as possible, and that the only limit to their recommendations was the Constitution of the country and, in particular, the rights and obligations laid down in Article 42. (See Speech by Dr P. J. Hillery, *Commission Minutes*, pp. 1-4; TCD Manuscripts Library, File 7121).

8 This was Martin J. Cranley, Principal, College of Technology, Kevin Street, Dublin. At an early stage in the Commission's life he left the education sector, having been appointed Director of the Institute for Industrial Research and Standards.

9 United Kingdom, Committee on Higher Education appointed by the Prime Minister under the Chairmanship of Lord Robbins 1961-63, *Report*, (London: HMSO, 1963).

10 Ironically the likelihood of this happening was predicted by a Limerick Fine Gael deputy, John Carew, when Dr Hillery first suggested a commission to the Dáil (*Dáil Debates*, vol. 180, col. 1483 – 31 March 1960).

11 ibid., vol. 194, col. 1541 (10 April 1962). The speed at which the Commission operated was exceptionally slow. Six months into its work the Chairman referred to the Commission as 'scraping the ground'. He saw them at that stage as holding preliminary meetings on issues that might arise in the oral evidence (*Commission Minutes*, p. 151). As early as February 1961, one of the members, Bishop Philibin, had foreseen a problem in this area and had unsuccessfully raised the question of some of Justice Ó Dálaigh's judicial duties being taken from him so that he could devote more time to the work of the Commission (*Commission Minutes*, p. 36). While decisions on capital spending were made during the period in which the Commission sat (for example, the new Science Building at UCC. Cabinet Minutes 13 July 1965, National Archives, *Department of Taoiseach*, File S 13258C), the crucial delay was in the area of policy formulation. The issue arose in early 1963 as to whether the Commission should communicate some of its initial conclusions informally. The Chairman at that point reiterated his view that the Commission could only convey its views to responsible quarters by way of a formal report and that, in the meantime, the institutions of higher education had the right to proceed in the normal way with any proposals for new developments, and the Commission could not properly intervene in these matters. (*Commission Minutes*, p. 1078).

12 *Dáil Debates*, vol. 217, col. 567 (6 July 1965); vol. 220, cols. 681-682 (2 February 1966); vol. 221, col. 1282 (9 March 1966).

13 *Dáil Debates*, vol. 225, cols. 2019-2020 (30 November 1966).

14 The Chairman wrote to the Taoiseach indicating that, in the absence of a public

statement disassociating the government and the Minister from Mr Carty's statement, he was tendering his resignation as Chairman of the Commission. He was telephoned very quickly by the Taoiseach who indicated that the government would make clear its desire for the Commission to continue its work, and the fact that there was no truth in the suggestions that members of the Commission had threatened to resign if the Minister for Education were to proceed with plans of his own. Such a statement was issued (*Commission Minutes*, pp. 2098-2099, 16/17 December 1966, TCD Manuscripts Library, File 7130). See also *Dáil Debates*, vol. 226, col. 96 (6 December 1966).

15 *Commission Summary*, p. 2. It should be observed that the term 'higher education' was still relatively new. It has been noted that in Britain until the 1960s 'higher education' meant the universities, although the phrase was not in common use. It was not until the appointment of the Robbins Committee in February 1961 to 'review the pattern of full-time higher education in Britain' that a concept of higher education embracing sectors other than the universities became widespread currency. Silver, H. (1990), *A Higher Education: The Council for National Academic Awards and British Higher Education 1964-89*, Basingstoke: The Falmer Press, p. 7.

16 *Commission Report*, pp. 118-122.

17 ibid., pp. 889-890.

18 Gellert, C. (1993) 'Structures and Functional Differentiation: Remarks on Changing Paradigms of Tertiary Education in Europe', in C. Gellert (ed.), *Higher Education in Europe*, London: Jessica Kingsley Publishers, pp. 237-243.

19 According to Rau, the German 'research model' was exemplified by the Humboldtian concept of a university whose core was a) autonomy, b) unity of knowledge and research, c) unity of all knowledge, d) education through academic knowledge and e) scholarly life in solitude and liberty. See Rau, E. (1993) 'Inertia and Resistance to Change of the Humboldtian University' in Gellert, *Higher Education in Europe*, pp. 37-38.

20 Gellert would see Newman as one of the main influences on this approach to higher education. For Newman, research and *wissenschaft* were not necessarily attributes of university life but could be pursued in academies outside. In the French model Gellert would see the elite activities associated with universities being performed by the *grandes écoles*, while much of the major research activity would happen outside the universities in research institutes.

21 Kerr, C. et al. (1979), *12 Systems of Higher Education: 6 Decisive Issues*, New York: International Council for Educational Development, pp. 1-11. Also Kerr, C. (1987), 'A Critical Age in the University World: Accumulated Heritage versus Modern Imperatives', *European Journal of Education*, vol. 22, no. 2, p. 185. Kerr was chairman of the Carnegie Commission of Inquiry into US higher education in the 1960s.

22 *Commission Report*, p. 127.

23 ibid., pp. 180-184.

24 ibid., pp. 864, 899, 908, 932, 937.

25 *Dáil Debates*, vol. 227, cols. 2181-2193 (20 April 1967). See also Organisation for Economic Co-operation and Development (1969), *Reviews of National Policies for Education: Ireland*, Paris: OECD, pp. 131-138. The Minister's announcement was made shortly after receiving the interim report and some

time before the final report was likely to be ready. This greatly angered many members of the Commission. Professor Theo Moody, a member of the Commission, thought that they had been treated disgracefully, that it was clear in retrospect that the Minister had already made up his mind in December 1966 (the time of the Carty incident) and that the Commission had been deceived. The Chairman felt that it had obviously been the Minister's objective to ensure that the views of the Commission did not have any public airing until his own particular proposal had been launched. He felt that his whole purpose had been to get a glimpse of the Commission's final recommendations to see if they afforded him any support for what he had already decided to do. (*Commission Minutes*, pp. 2333-2335, 5 May 1967, TCD Manuscripts Library, File 7130).

26 Higher Education Authority (1972), *Report on University Reorganisation,* Dublin: Stationery Office.

27 As defined by the Commission itself, *Commission Report*, pp. 855-858. Also *Commission Summary*, pp. 94-97.

28 *Irish Times*, 17 August 1968; *Dáil Debates*, vol. 236, col. 1783 (31 October 1968).

29 Local Authorities (Higher Education Grants) Act 1968 (Number 24 of 1968).

30 An Coláiste Ealaíne is Deartha Act 1971 (Number 28 of 1971).

31 Coolahan, J. (1989), 'The Fortunes of Education as a Subject of Study and Research in Ireland', *Irish Educational Studies*, vol. 1, pp. 1-34.

32 For example in 1967 and in 1974. Legislation was finally passed in 1997.

33 Higher Education Authority (1974), *Progress Report 1974,* Dublin: Higher Education Authority, p. 84. Also Higher Education Authority (1985), *General Report 1974-1984*, Dublin: Higher Education Authority, p. 28.

34 O'Connor, *A Troubled Sky,* p. 173.

35 *Commission Report*, p. 393.

36 ibid., pp. 863-944.

37 O'Connor, *A Troubled Sky*, p. 173.

38 *Commission Report*, pp. 311-312, 323-324, 331, 335.

39 OECD, *Ireland: Review 1969*, pp. 119-126. Also Horgan, *Lemass*, pp. 293-295.

40 *Dáil Debates*, vol. 207, cols. 379, 505-506 (5 February 1964).

41 ibid., vol. 209, col. 1534 (8 May 1964).

42 Randles, *Post-Primary Education*, p. 279.

43 *Dáil Debates*, vol. 216, col. 964 (16 June 1965).

44 Steering Committee on Technical Educational, (1969), *Report to the Minister for Education on Regional Technical Colleges,* Dublin: Stationery Office, Prl. 371.

45 *Dáil Debates*, vol. 225, col, 1878 (30 November 1966).

46 *Steering Committee*, pp. 5, 28.

47 ibid., p. 2.

48 On the question of Colley's concern about the slow progress with the colleges in the mid 1960s and his desire to have O'Connor involved in the Steering Committee, the author's source is a conversation with O'Connor in February 1986.

49 Ó Maolcatha, *Role of the Technician*, p. 11.

50 *Steering Committee*, p. 6. See also *Dáil Debates*, vol. 226, col. 103 (6 December 1966).

51 *Steering Committee*, pp. 7-8.

52 ibid., pp. 11-12.
53 ibid., pp. 44-47.
54 ibid., pp. 39-40.
55 *Dáil Debates*, vol. 232, col. 470 (6 February 1968).
56 *Steering Committee* p. 30; *Dáil Debates*. vol. 266, col. 1230-34 (27 June 1973); vol. 268, cols. 366-367, 407-409 (23 October 1973); vol. 269, cols. 1140-41 (6 December 1973); O'Connor, *A Troubled Sky*, p. 157; Green Paper (1985), *Partners in Education – Serving Community Needs*, Dublin: Stationery Office, pp 9-19. The issue continued into the 1990s. The *Programme for a Partnership Government* of January 1993 re-opened the issue. The Minister for Education issued a position paper on regional education councils in March 1994 and the topic merited an entire chapter in the 1995 White Paper. See Department of Education (1995), *Charting our Education Future: White Paper on Education*, Dublin: Stationery Office, pp. 165-180.
57 It also inspired an unusually direct parliamentary attack on civil servants, in this case in the Department of Education (*Dáil Debates*, vol. 237, cols. 1482-85, 28 November 1968).
58 *Steering Committee*, pp 8-9, 41.
59 O'Connor, *A Troubled Sky*, pp. 176-177.
60 *Dáil Debates*, vol. 2, col. 139 (4 November 1969); vol. 311, col. 1433 (15 February 1979).
61 *Steering Committee*, pp. 26-28.
62 Third-level work developed in three of the schools run by City of Limerick VEC (Building, Commerce, and Art). Three students from the School of Building were among the first group of students to be awarded a National Certificate in Engineering by NCEA in 1972. The schools appear to have become part of Limerick Technical College in the mid 1970s. This multi-campus college was to be re-named Limerick College of Art, Commerce and Technology (COACT) in 1980. The College then became Limerick Regional Technical College under the Regional Technical Colleges Act 1992, and Limerick Institute of Technology in 1998.
63 ibid., p. 8. The Steering Committee was the first body to recommend explicitly the establishment of an institution akin to the Council for National Academic Awards.
64 *Commission Report*, pp. 133-134.
65 Randles, *Post Primary Education*, pp. 233, 273.
66 This point was emphasised to the author by Sean O'Connor in conversation, February 1986.
67 *Dáil Debates*, vol. 202, col. 1372 (14 May 1963); vol. 210, col. 28 (26 May 1964).
68 ibid., vol. 207, cols. 505-506 (6 February 1964).
69 ibid., vol. 232, cols 470-471 (6 February 1968); vol. 238, cols. 1708-1709 (26 February 1969).
70 *Steering Committee*, p. 44.
71 *Commission Report*, p. 402.
72 Conversation with Seán O'Connor, February 1986.
73 *Steering Committee*, p. 11.

CHAPTER 4

Limerick Wants a University

Limerick missed out on a university in the 1840s.[1] Although it had lobbied for inclusion, Belfast, Cork and Galway were chosen as the locations of the three Queen's Colleges. While the draft legislation showed some indecision as to the choice between Limerick or Galway, the decision in favour of Galway had been taken by September 1845.[2] In post-famine Ireland the Galway college did not prosper and limped along as part of the Queen's University from 1850 to 1881, and as a 'stand-alone' college preparing students for the examinations of the Royal University of Ireland from 1881 to 1908. In 1909 it evolved into University College Galway, one of the three constituent colleges of the National University of Ireland.

The issue of a university college for Limerick arose indirectly at the time of the establishment of the National University of Ireland. Mungret College had opened as a diocesan seminary in 1880 and was taken over by the Jesuits in 1882.[3] From then until 1908 it prepared students for the examinations of the Royal University with significant success. An attempt was made by the Jesuit authorities to achieve recognised college status (similar to that obtained by St. Patrick's College, Maynooth) under the 1908 Act, but there appears to have been no significant lobby for Mungret within the Limerick region, and the last degree students from Mungret presented themselves for a BA degree of the National University of Ireland in 1912.[4]

The issue of a university for Limerick arose briefly in the mid-1930s with a number of resolutions passed by local authorities and teachers unions in Limerick city and county calling for the establishment of a constituent college of NUI in Limerick.[5] The issue was revived by Limerick Chamber of Commerce in September 1944. A report commissioned by it was discussed at a public meeting in March 1946, when it was decided to send a deputation to meet the Taoiseach and the Minister for Education to press claims for a university.[6] The Taoiseach, Mr de Valera, was also Chancellor of the National University of Ireland and a man with native roots in County Limerick. He was not enthusiastic about the idea. He intimated to the Limerick group that no useful purpose would be served by meeting with them, that the establishment of further colleges would affect the interests of the existing institutions, and suggested that the Limerick group contact the authorities of University College Cork to see if a satisfactory scheme could be worked out with them. Nothing ensued.[7]

The next initiative was to bear fruit. In 1957 the Mayor of Limerick, Alderman Ted Russell TD, invited representatives of secondary schools in or near Limerick city to a meeting to consider ways and means of providing facilities for university education in the city. The City Council set up a sub-committee (the 'Mayor's Committee') to look at the issue in November 1957. Its report considered various options such as an independent university, recognised college status within NUI, a joint relationship such as existed between Magee College and Trinity College (with first and second years of a degree programme taken at the junior college), and the possibility of having the first university year in arts, science and commerce taught in recognised secondary schools. The report eventually opted for NUI constituent college status and in November 1959 Limerick Corporation called on the government to establish an NUI constituent college in Limerick. Similar resolutions were passed by Limerick County Council and all neighbouring county councils.

In the meantime another group had been established which would come to have more persistence and muscle than any previous lobby for Limerick. The Limerick University Project Committee was established on 29 October 1959.[8] It was instigated by a number of past pupils unions in the Limerick area, and it was intended to aid the Mayor's Committee and continue its work by explaining the demands for university education in Limerick. The Committee had representatives from teaching, law, architecture, engineering and accountancy, and also included commercial and agricultural interests. It formed sub-committees for statistics, finance and publicity. In May 1960 representatives of the Committee met with Dr Hillery, the Minister for Education. At that point Dr Hillery had announced that he was establishing the Commission on Higher Education and he told the group that the question of a university for Limerick was one that would be considered by the Commission.[9]

The Committee made its written submission to the Commission early in 1961, and was interviewed by it in October 1961. Thereafter the Commission was lobbied consistently by the Project

Committee and by various other bodies from the mid-west region, such as trade unions, chambers of commerce, local authorities, National Farmers Association, guilds of Muintir na Tíre, vocational education committees and co-operatives.[10] Lobbying of government also continued during that period. During the life of the Commission the one group to keep consistent pressure for a speedy report was that pressing for a university for Limerick. As noted previously, from as early as 1962 the Minister for Education was put under pressure from Limerick deputies, who considered that the Limerick case was being long-fingered. Limerick Corporation passed a further motion in December 1963 to the effect that Limerick needed a university and that a constituent college of NUI should be set up in the city without delay.[11] In January 1966 (when the Commission was already sitting for over five years) the City Council called on the Minister for Education to ensure that the Commissioners' report should become available at the earliest possible date.[12]

When the report of the Commission finally arrived in 1967, the Minister for Education was none other than one of the two Fianna Fáil deputies for Limerick East, Donogh O'Malley. There was no indication from the Dáil record over many years that he had offered full support to either the Project Committee or the campaign for a university for Limerick. In February 1963 at a function in Limerick, he was quoted as having forecast 'that it would be a surprise if there were a university in Limerick even by the time the children of the present children now studying for the Leaving Certificate were grown up'.[13] The Commission's report concluded that Limerick should not have an university, but one of two 'New Colleges.'[14] On the publication of the summary of the commissioner's report the Project Committee had initially welcomed the proposal for a 'New College' in Limerick.[15] It subsequently told the Minister that the 'New College' would only be acceptable on three conditions: a) that honours degrees would be available, b) that the College would have the same entry standards as the universities and c) that the title 'New College' would become 'University College.'[16] Any lingering enthusiasm for the New College concept subsequently waned when it became increasingly clear that it was likely to be stillborn.[17]

Donogh O'Malley died suddenly in March 1968 at the age of forty-eight. Ironically, while he himself may have offered little tangible support to the university campaign, his death had the effect of opening up the issue. Not for the first time in political life a by-election elevated a local issue to the national agenda. During the by-election campaign, his successor, Brian Lenihan, indicated that detailed consideration and the results of his own examinations so far seemed to indicate that there was substance in Limerick's claim for a university.[18] For the first time a Minister for Education was expressing support, when such had not been forthcoming from either de Valera or O'Malley. This helped to galvanise the Project Committee which kept the pressure on the minister. By the following November a special meeting of the Committee was contemplating a constitutional action against the government under Article 42 of Bunreacht na hÉireann for failing to meet the Limerick case for a university.[19] What happened during 1968, and especially in the nine-month period after Donogh O'Malley's death, was that political pressure for a decision with regard to Limerick's claim for a university forced the government to take certain decisions with major and far-reaching policy implications.

In February 1968 Donogh O'Malley, in one of his last Dáil appearances, referred to the proposal to locate one of the nine regional technical colleges in Limerick.[20] In one of his first contributions as minister, Brian Lenihan told the Senate in June 1968 that he envisaged UCC, UCD, UCG, and probably a university in Limerick, growing in size with the diffusion of the university population around the country.[21] By October he was giving a different signal. During an estimates debate it was put to him that what was intended for Limerick was a Regional Technical College. He replied that what the government wanted to do was to establish a 'tier of education post-Leaving Certificate and not yet full university'.[22] Whether this would apply to all regional technical colleges or just to the college at Limerick was not fully clear. In closing the debate on the estimates some weeks later he agreed with Deputy Barry Desmond that there had been new thinking with regard to regional technical colleges. Whereas his predecessor had defined a technical college as a place catering for second-level education and a college of technology as one catering for third-level,[23] he spoke of a liason between second and third-level education tending to merge into a new type of education which would be post second-level and not yet third-level.[24] In short the Minister and the Department were still in the process of trying to formulate a new policy for the provision of higher or third-level education, and as a result they were experiencing difficulty in deciding on the form of third-level provision for Limerick.

The increasing political pressure eventually told, and on 11 December 1968 Mr Lenihan announced that the government had decided to build 'a third-level education institution in Limerick' and had asked the Higher Education Authority to recommend on how it might fit into the framework of higher education.[25] A new national policy for higher education was being crafted partially by the requirements of the mid-west region.

The Higher Education Authority, to which the problem was referred, was a new body. It had been established on an *ad hoc* basis in July 1968.[26] The Authority had an advisory role in relation to all of higher education. The first project assigned to it was to advise the Minister on the nature and form of legislation required to implement the government decisions on higher education, with particular reference to the proposal to merge TCD and UCD. The Limerick question was the second major political problem to be diverted in the Authority's direction.

HEA reported within three months. Before addressing the Limerick question it first devoted its attention briefly to the question of an awards body. It was satisfied that there was an established demand for further and more advanced technological, and other specialised, third-level courses. It was also satisfied that there should be formal recognition on a national basis for such courses, and saw the solution in the establishment of a Council for National Awards with powers to grant certificates, diplomas and degrees.[27]

Turning to the question of the provision of third-level facilities at Limerick, it argued that, if provision were being made for the coming decade only, there would be a case for the closing of an existing university institution rather than founding a new one. Like the Commission it concluded that there was no national need for another university college. It saw the country as lacking a new, and increasingly important, form of higher education with the application of scientific knowledge and method as its primary purpose. The Authority argued that technological education in Ireland had not yet found its proper level, that its content required further upgrading and that the scope of its operations needed to be extended. It felt that it would be a departure from the *raison d'etre* of institutions of technology for them to conform to the methods and requirements of a university, particularly as they had to cater not only for students of degree calibre, but for many others engaged in a variety of disciplines leading to other than strictly academic qualifications.[28]

Like the Steering Committee, the HEA looked to Britain for a model and saw the Council for National Academic Awards and the polytechnics as having come to form a strong and distinctive sector complementary to the universities. In the pattern of that development it saw a solution to the general Irish demand and need, but more especially to the problems of Limerick and its area. It saw the Limerick college as carrying the prestige of degree-earning courses of various kinds with an extensive provision on a scale, and in a manner, not open to universities, as offering sandwich courses for employed people and providing for areas of study not fully covered in existing institutions. It also saw the Limerick college as especially suited to the provision of courses of the type with which the Council for National Awards would be concerned.

The Higher Education Authority report was to lay down the guidelines for how the Limerick college would develop. On the surface it provided the minister with practical assistance and advice in grappling with a politically complex decision. In reality it had done far more. It effectively articulated the rationale for what would come to be called the 'binary system' within Irish higher education. The real significance was that a body largely composed of university academics provided the Department of Education with the arguments for why it should develop a new system of technological education outside the universities. Viewed in that light the first report to emanate from the Higher Education Authority was a seminal document, as important as the Steering Committee report and of greater significance in the long term than the report of the Commission.

Within a month of receiving the report the minister, Mr Lenihan, indicated that he had accepted the broad basis of the Authority's approach and would shortly be taking steps to appoint a director and establish a planning board for the Limerick Institute.[29] He was not prepared to concede the title of university to the Limerick institution and suggested that nomenclature was irrelevant. What mattered was that courses of degree status would be provided in the Institute. Even before the Authority had reported, he had taken to referring to the proposed institute as a polytechnic-type institution.[30] His successor, Pádraig Faulkner, persisted with the view that the Limerick institute should not have the title of university. 'By not calling it a university we were setting up something which could be developed in a new way, and in our view and in the Department's view, would fill a vacuum in Irish education,' he told the Senate.[31] The title of National Institute for Higher Education appears to have been settled upon by usage at some stage in the early months of 1971. While the decision to set up an institution which was not a university fell short of what the Limerick University Project Committee had looked for, the Committee gave a guarded welcome to the Higher Education Authority proposals in May 1969.[32] When the planning board for the new institution came to be set up in February 1970, two of the LUPC members, Margaret Lyddy, the honorary secretary, and James Lyons, were included among the seven members, thus helping to assist the acceptance of the new institute in the region. Some time later it was decided not to proceed with a regional technical college in Limerick.[33] The position of Director of the Institute was advertised in June 1969 and Dr Edward Walsh was appointed to the position in November 1969, taking up duty on 1 January 1970.[34]

In setting out the functions of the new institution shortly after he had received HEA's recommendations, Brian Lenihan had stated that it would be geared to the regional and national requirements of business, technology, administration and teacher training.[35] The education provided was intended to amalgamate both technician and technological teacher training and a university-type education of degree category.[36] The Steering Committee had suggested the possibility of providing for teacher training in its report, and it was eventually decided to locate a college of teacher education, specialising in the first instance in physical education, but later encompassing other areas, such as rural science, woodwork and metalwork, on the same campus as the National Institute but entirely independent of it. [37] The Limerick college from the beginning acquired the role of flagship of a new approach to technological education. According to Seán O'Connor, the Development Branch in the Department of Education had been promoting the concept of an institution of high prestige to top the technical area. Unlike the universities, the institution would be limited in function to the technological areas of learning.[38] This line was maintained by Pádraig Faulkner during his four-year term at the Department of Education. The Limerick college came to have a symbolic role in the new approach to technical and technological education which the minister and his Department were intent on implementing.[39]

A Planning Board was established to oversee the building of the Institute and to make specific proposals for courses of instruction, staff, equipment, library and other facilities.[40] By August 1970 it had submitted a draft constitution for the Institute to the Minister, and it also indicated that it was eager to commence courses even before the buildings had been completed.[41] The balance of degree and non-degree course provision was a matter of some contention. Brian Lenihan had anticipated originally that about a quarter of the students would be taking degree courses, while the remainder would be following courses leading to certificates and diplomas. Like so much else that was to follow throughout the subsequent decades, this was a complete under-estimate of the demand and the outcome. Less than two years later, and some eighteen months before the Institute opened, the director, Dr Walsh, indicated that from the start diploma and degree programmes would be offered and that initially the student body would be divided equally between the diploma and degree programmes.[42] In this Dr Walsh was already at odds with the minister and his Department, and some months later Mr Faulkner questioned the wisdom and practicability of the Institute's embarking on degree courses from the outset.[43]

Higher education in Limerick briefly returned to the fray of political controversy in early summer 1971. Detailed proposals with regard to courses and staffing were the subject of discussions between the Planning Board and a Higher Education Authority working-party from November 1970. The Planning Board intended the courses to run from September 1971. The Authority's advice to the minister was that the degree courses proposed were not themselves in keeping with the type of programme the Authority wished for the Institute.[44] The minister, in accepting the Authority's advice, told the Dáil that the establishment of the Institute was authorised on the clear basis that it would be primarily a technological institute, while catering for a significant element of the humanities. The HEA had recommended that it would not be possible to provide and equip laboratory workshops in time for commencement in 1971, and accordingly that it would not be possible to mount courses of a technical type by that date. The minister set his face against first-year classes in arts and commerce for which laboratory work was not required. The Limerick Institute was intended to be seen clearly as an institution of technology, and it would have been too compromising to commence operations on a piecemeal basis or give ambiguous signals as to purpose and status by commencing with courses in commerce and arts. Accordingly the opening was postponed by one year.

There were other reasons for this decision. One was that the Department was having difficulty in deciding on the composition and shape of a National Council for Educational Awards. It was quite determined that this body would make all awards at the Limerick Institute, and the fact that it had not yet been established was almost certainly a factor in the decision to delay an opening in Limerick. There was also a suggestion aired publicly at the time that the decision may have been influenced by the fact that detailed plans were not ready in time for a visit by a party from the World Bank.[45]

The decision to postpone opening caused the minister and the Higher Education Authority to come under attack at a public meeting in Limerick, and local authorities in the region called for the Institute to open its doors in 1971.[46] This was to prove to be the only occasion of public confrontation between the Planning Board and the minister. The minister's decision stood. Some three months later agreement was reached between the minister and the Institute, and it was accepted that initially the Institute would have degree programmes in applied electronics, business, secretarial science and European Studies.[47] A programme in applied science was agreed at a later date, and these constituted the five discipline areas on offer to the first students, and those for which the first senior academic staff were appointed in February 1972.[48]

There were 1,000 applicants for the 113 places offered for the courses commencing in September 1972, of which 67 were on degree programmes. The Institute was officially opened by the Taoiseach, Jack Lynch, on 27 September 1972.[49] The Planning Board continued in existence until 1975, and from the opening of the Institute increasingly took on the function of a board of management, with considerable autonomy on matters such as entry requirements and admissions.[50] A further 129 students were admitted in 1973 and 242 in 1974.

From the time he assumed the position of director, Dr Edward Walsh was to prove a very forceful and forthright personality, and over a period of two-and-a-half decades was destined to become a controversial figure both in his championing of his own institution and his attacks, not only on the existing system of higher education, but on Irish education generally.[51] His first public address, given within a month of taking up his appointment, gave a foretaste of what would follow. Speaking to the local committee of the Irish Management Institute, he outlined the new educational approaches he envisaged for the Limerick institution. Apart from having a continuing education centre, he spoke of the Institute delivering associate degree programmes (along the lines developed in community colleges in the United States in the 1960s) and meeting the educational requirements of those who did not have the qualifications for entry to the bachelor degree. He went on to criticise the pursuit of knowledge for its own sake as a misplaced luxury, and spoke critically of the universities as finishing schools where too many of Ireland's better young men and women were selected for emigration, thanks to an almost non-existent career guidance system and ill-suited university curricula.[52]

Dr Walsh had spent some eight years in the United States prior to taking up his position in Limerick and, in identifying innovative approaches for the new institution before it opened, he was bringing to bear influences from North America that in the early 1970s were mostly novel to Irish higher education. The Institute was the first in Ireland to adopt the modular approach to course design throughout its programmes, and Dr Walsh had signalled this at the beginning of the planning process.[53] Another innovation of which he also spoke at an early stage was that of students' completing their courses within specific industries.[54] From its opening, industrial placement (or co-operative education, as it was called by the Institute) was a component part of all full-time programmes, and students spent up to one quarter of their time off the campus in placements related to what they were studying.

Dr Walsh quickly came to the fore as an advocate of greater emphasis on the education of technologists.[55] The development of technological education became something of a mission with which the Institute was to be identified and his vision for Limerick was expressed as that of Ireland's MIT (Massachusetts Institute of Technology).[56] In this he was furthering what had become the policy of the Department of Education, and was promoting the role for the Limerick Institute that had been envisaged for it originally by the Higher Education Authority. Dr Walsh was also going with the flow and was able to articulate and give shape to some of the objectives of key decision-makers at a national level. This was a wave which Dr Walsh was to ride very successfully for many years. There was, nevertheless, another strand which was quite at odds with this.

There remained in the Limerick region a residual desire for a university. This had no support within the Department of Education or the Higher Education Authority, among the university authorities, or indeed virtually anywhere else in Irish education. Dr Walsh was to prove that, not alone could he live with such a potentially conflicting force, but could actually harness it. At no time was the issue of a university for Limerick off the agenda for very long. Those who, against all the odds, continued to hope that the Institute would have the status and the title of a university received a substantial boost in October 1973. When the Minister for Education, Richard Burke, was being presented with the Institute's Twenty Year Development Plan, he announced that Limerick would eventually have a university. He indicated shortly afterwards that he was not thinking about the immediate future, but about a development that might come within a decade.[57] The embers had not been extinguished.

Dr Walsh was only thirty-one when he was appointed to the position of Director of the Limerick college. He had left Ireland shortly after graduating in engineering from University College Cork in 1959. In age terms he was a generation younger than many of the senior figures in Irish higher education such as, for example, those sitting on the Higher Education Authority. He had a missionary belief in the importance of technology and technical education, which would have appealed to the senior officials in the Department of Education who effectively had appointed him. They had a similar mission at that time. In addition he had a very critical and outspoken opinion of the shortcomings of the Irish university system, which would also have appealed to the same officials at that period. His style was diametrically different from that prevailing in the somewhat staid upper echelons of Irish higher education at the end of the 1960s. Dr Walsh in contrast exhibited a brashness which verged on the naïve. Given that he was a complete stranger to the scene, it is conceivable that the relevant senior personnel in the Department of Education may have thought that such a young man, who shared many of their views, was malleable. If they ever entertained that hope, it is certain that it would not have taken them very long before they concluded that they had recruited the wrong man.

Notes

1 The series of committees, and attempts to achieve an institution of university status in Limerick, are set out very usefully in Kearney, P. J. (1975), *Towards a University: A Historical Account of the Campaigns to have a University Established in Limerick with Particular Reference to the Period 1838-1947,* NUI Galway Library (unpublished MA thesis). The opening section of this chapter relies heavily on Kearney's study.

2 Kearney, *Towards a University,* pp. 40, 51. For background to the debate on the relative merits of Limerick and Galway, see Mitchell J. (1998), 'Queen's College Galway 1845-1858: From Site to Structure,' *Journal of the Galway Archaeological and Historical Society,* vol. 50, pp. 49-57.

3 From 1882 to 1888 it was run as the diocesan seminary for Limerick diocese. From 1888 onwards it operated as a Catholic secondary school, also incorporating an apostolic school preparing students for the early stages of study for the priesthood. The fact that it provided for Intermediate Certificate appears to have hampered its claim for university recognition on the passing of the National University of Ireland legislation . Effectively it had retained the status of a secondary school.

4 This appears to have been part of a temporary transition measure to accommodate Mungret students who had matriculated in the Royal University. There was opposition from within UCC to the existence of another university institution in Munster.

5 Curiously this initiative appears to have risen from within a Fianna Fáil cumann in Newmarket-on-Fergus, County Clare (Kearney, p. 70).

6 National Archives, Department of Taoiseach, File 16735A. Also Kearney, p. 85.

7 Kearney, pp. 86-91. Alfred O'Rahilly, President of UCC, once the issue of constituent college status was not pursued, appears to have been quite helpful. He told a public meeting in Limerick on 11 December 1946 that the basic position was that NUI did not want any amendment to its charter.

8 Limerick University Project Committee (1961*), Submission to Commission on Higher Education,* p. 2; Kearney, pp. 101-104.

9 Kearney, p. 105. One of the members of the Project Committee, An Bráthair S.S. de Faoite, Principal, Limerick CBS, was appointed to the Commission.

10 *Commission Minutes,* pp. 37, 62, 71, 178, 206, 217, 939, 1117, 1164, 2187.

11 National Archives, Department of Taoiseach, Files 16735A and 16735B.

12 Kearney, pp. 107-108. At about the same time the Project Committee wrote to the Taoiseach, Seán Lemass, asking the government to decide in principle to establish a university in Limerick without waiting for the report of the Commission (National Archives, Department of Taoiseach, File 16735B).

13 *Limerick Weekly Echo,* 9 February 1963. Just over a month later, speaking to the Limerick Industrial Committee, which was discussing proposals for a regional school of advanced technical education in the city, he said that the establishment of technical colleges outside Dublin had to be undertaken without delay. The desirable pattern of provision appeared to be a foundation base of craft courses for apprentices, a number of technician courses appropriate to the needs of the region, and some technological courses to tap the local source of talent (*Irish Press,* 25 March 1963). This has remarkable echoes of the Steering Committee on Technical Education four years in advance of that group's report.

14 See chapter 3.
15 *Irish Independent*, 23 March 1967.
16 Kearney, p. 108.
17 Heney, M. (1968), 'Limerick's Case for a University', *Irish Times*, 23-24 December 1968.
18 *Irish Independent*, 22 May 1968.
19 ibid., 14 November 1968.
20 *Dáil Debates*, vol. 232, col. 470 (6 February 1968).
21 *Seanad Debates*, vol. 65, col. 604 (20 June 1968).
22 *Dáil Debates*, vol. 236, col. 1825 (31 October 1968).
23 ibid., vol. 232, col. 765 (8 February 1968).
24 ibid., vol. 237, col. 1691 (3 December 1968). It is clear from the departmental file that in the latter part of 1968 neither the Department nor the Minister were clear on the concept, and that the Limerick institute was envisaged as performing some of the functions subsequently discharged by NCEA (National Archives, Memo from Brian Lenihan, Department of Taoiseach, File 16735B).
25 *Irish Times*, 12 December 1968. Also *Dáil Debates*, vol. 238, col. 572 (6 December 1968), col. 522 (6 February 1969). Mr Lenihan's problems were compounded by the fact that his statement of 11 December was premature, and was issued by mistake (National Archives, File 16735B).
26 The circumstances of its establishment are discussed below in chapter 6.
27 Higher Education Authority (1969), *A Council for National Awards and a College of Higher Education at Limerick*, Dublin: Higher Education Authority, p. 5.
28 ibid., pp. 9-10.
29 *Dáil Debates*, vol. 239, col. 1784 (17 April 1969).
30 *Irish Times*, 24 January 1969. What was significant here was that the Minister had already begun referring to the new Limerick institution as a college of technology, and it was also clear that this institute was going to be something bigger than a regional technical college.
31 *Seanad Debates*, vol. 71, col. 1236 (17 November 1971).
32 Kearney, p. 113.
33 *Dáil Debates*, vol. 248, col. 1925 (23 July 1970).
34 ibid., vol. 241, col. 947 (17 July 1969); vol. 242, cols. 2159-2160 (27 November 1969); *Irish Independent*, 15 July 1969; *Sunday Independent*, 11 January 1970.
35 *Dáil Debates*, vol. 239, col. 1553 (16 April 1969).
36 ibid., col. 1786 (17 April 1969).
37 *Dáil Debates*, vol. 240, col. 411 (1 May 1969); vol. 248, col. 1926 (23 July 1970); vol. 259, col. 1569 (15 March 1972); vol. 268, cols. 401-404 (23 October 1973). The college opened on an adjoining campus in 1972 as the National College of Physical Education, and was retitled Thomond College of Education in 1976. It was absorbed into the University of Limerick in 1992.
38 O'Connor, *A Troubled Sky*, p. 174.
39 Apart from the symbolic elements, and the role of Limerick in supporting a wider departmental and ministerial agenda, there were pragmatic reasons for this approach. Michael O'Kennedy, who was Parliamentary Secretary at the Department from 1970 to early 1973, hinted that this approach was recommended as one likely to find favour in securing financial assistance from the World Bank. *Dáil Debates*, vol. 290, cols. 145-146 (27 April 1976).

40 *Irish Times*, 28 February 1970. The Board was chaired by the Institute's Director, Dr Edward Walsh. The other members were Philip Hilliard (a Killarney businessman), James Lyons (a Limerick solicitor), Margaret Lyddy (a Limerick housewife and Honorary Secretary of the University Project Committee), Dr Finbarr O'Callaghan (Assistant Chief Inspector, Department of Education), Dr Declan O'Keeffe (Professor of Civil Engineering, UCG), and Paul Quigley (General Manager, Shannon Free Airport Development Company). The Secretary was Anne Sadlier. The Higher Education Authority was not represented, but from early in 1971, James F. Dukes, the Authority's Secretary, began to attend Planning Board meetings and continued to do so for over a year.

41 *Irish Independent*, 20 June 1970. Also *Irish Times*, 28 September 1970.

42 *Limerick Chronicle*, 23 January 1971.

43 *Irish Times*, 15 May 1971; *Cork Examiner*, 15 May 1971.

44 *Dáil Debates*, vol. 253, cols. 1955-1958 (19 May 1971).

45 *Irish Times*, 26 May 1971.

46 *Dáil Debates*, vol. 253, cols. 1955-1961 (19 May 1971); vol. 254, col. 1910 (17 June 1971); *Irish Independent*, 23 July 1971.

47 *Irish Independent*, 2 October 1971.

48 *Irish Times*, 23 February 1972.

49 *Irish Press*, 28 September 1972.

50 *Dáil Debates*, vol. 264, col. 254 (29 November 1972).

51 See, for example, *Dáil Debates*, vol. 256, col. 1179 (4 November 1971). Also *Limerick Leader*, 17 October 1971.

52 *Limerick Leader*, 28 January 1970; *Irish Times*, 29 January 1970.

53 *Irish Times*, 5 October 1971.

54 *Irish Independent*, 13 March 1970.

55 *Irish Times*, 23 March 1970.

56 *Education Times*, 18 October 1973.

57 *Irish Independent*, 16 October 1973; *Irish Times*, 16 October 1973; *Dáil Debates*, vol. 268, col. 1255 (6 November 1973); vol. 269, col. 1158 (6 December 1973).

Chapter 5

A System Takes Shape 1968-74

The 1960s witnessed rapid expansion in student numbers and significant reorganisation of higher education systems in many of the developed countries of Europe and North America.[1] By the early 1960s it was becoming clear that Ireland was conforming to the pattern of substantial growth in student numbers in institutions of higher education evident in mainland Europe, though not at that stage in Britain.[2]

In the academic year 1965-66, there were 20,698 students in full-time higher education in the state.[3] The bulk of these were accounted for by the university institutions – Trinity College, UCD, UCC, UCG and St Patrick's College Maynooth,[4] 15,441 students in all. Teacher training accounted for 1,732 students. Vocational and technological education, comprising the third-level work of the VECs in Dublin and Cork, accounted for 1,007 students. The remaining 2,508 students were in a variety of institutions such as the Royal College of Surgeons in Ireland, the National College of Art and a number of seminaries run by religious orders and congregations, who in the late 1960s still accounted for a significant number of third-level students.[5]

Although there was an expansion in demand, there was still relatively little capital investment in higher education by the state, and effectively decision-making was long-fingered while the Commission sat.[6] Shortly after the presentation of its interim report, the minister expressed his intention to merge the two Dublin university institutions. How this affected university development is set out in the following chapter. A major decision with regard to the future shape of higher education was, as has been seen, brought about by the response to demands from the Limerick region. Another, and arguably the most important, development in higher education also got under way in the late 1960s. It did so almost by stealth, if not indeed by accident.

Regional Technical Colleges

It has already been seen that, when they were first mooted in 1963, the regional technical colleges were envisaged as initiatives in second-level education. By 1967 with the Report of the Steering Committee it was clear that some of their work would be at third-level. In February 1968 Donogh O'Malley confirmed to the Dáil that a sum of £7,000,000 had been made available to meet the cost of building the colleges, and that it had also been decided that the cost would be met directly from central funds, with none of the costs to be borne by local rates, as would customarily be the case with schools built for a vocational education committee.[7] But where did they fit in the system?

The functions envisaged for the colleges by the minister involved education for trade and industry over a broad spectrum of occupations ranging from craft to professional level, notably in engineering and science, but also in commercial, linguistic, catering, art and design and other specialities.[8] This was identical to what had been formulated by the Steering Committee.[9] The same formula was repeated by Mr O'Malley's successor, Brian Lenihan, with regard to the Athlone college in February 1969[10] and by his successor, Pádraig Faulkner, in December 1969 with regard to the colleges in general.[11]

As already explained, when initially conceived in 1963 their work was envisaged as being entirely at second-level. The Steering Committee had recommended that some of their work would be of a third-level nature. Because the Committee's report was not published for almost two years, Donogh O'Malley, in drawing on it to outline the functions of the colleges, found himself having to define explicitly the functions of vocational schools, technical colleges and colleges of technology.[12] Having drawn a sharp distinction between a technical college, essentially a second-level institution, and a college of technology, offering courses at third-level, he added that it was difficult to insist on such sharp distinctions in the case of Regional Technical Colleges, as they would be providing higher technician and commercial education, as well as courses regarded as appropriate to a technical college.

Some months later Brian Lenihan appeared to regard these colleges as operating at a higher level, when he bracketed them with the colleges of technology in Dublin as a network having its own field of higher education in technological subjects related to the industrial requirements of a particular region. As an example, he cited a proposed advanced faculty of food technology at the Carlow college which would be related to the needs of Erin Foods and the requirements of the Sugar Company.[13] In the following December he was referring to the Carlow college as an appropriate centre for a degree programme in food technology.[14] In spite of Mr Lenihan's musings on his ambitious plans for the development of the colleges as centres of higher education, the general perception of the colleges in late 1968 was that they were to be second-level institutions.[15]

It was planned to open the colleges in 1969. Because the buildings were not completed, only a small number of courses could be run. In the autumn of 1969 fifty pupils were enrolled in Athlone, forty-seven in Carlow, ninety-two in Dundalk and ninety-six in Waterford. Both Athlone and Dundalk enrolled Leaving Certificate students, while the bulk of the remaining students were enrolled in apprentice courses. A number of other students were enrolled at nearby vocational schools pending transfer to the Regional Technical Colleges as facilities became available.[16] The opening of the colleges in Carlow and Athlone gave rise to publicly expressed fears that they would compete with existing schools, and that their existence might eventually lead to a concentration of senior cycle courses, particularly those which required capital investment in laboratories, in the regional technical colleges.[17] The minister, Mr Faulkner, insisted that there were no grounds for such fears. The Fine Gael education spokesman, Garret FitzGerald, continued to raise them. In the Dáil he referred to concern that the colleges were not developing in the way intended. He spoke of reports that they were not attracting the kind or level of students that had been expected, and that they were moving out of their intended sphere to compete with local secondary schools. While expressing himself as being in favour of integration between the secondary and vocational sectors of education, he did not think it helpful that colleges of technology, established to provide technician courses, were being turned into secondary schools.[18]

Dr FitzGerald was echoing the fears of the authorities of second-level schools, both secondary and vocational, that the regional technical colleges with facilities far in advance of the normal second-level school would be a major counter-attraction to local schools. The validity of his argument about the purpose and function of the regional technical colleges was open to question, given the diverse functions envisaged for them by the Steering Committee. However second-level school authorities in, for example, Carlow could have been excused for being concerned at having to compete for Leaving Certificate students with a college which was envisaged by the former minister as having resources sufficient to provide a faculty of advanced food technology to cater for Erin Foods and the Sugar Company. Some years later, when he had left office, Pádraig Faulkner admitted that he had recognised that there would be ill-feeling among post-primary schools because of the availability of Leaving Certificate in the regional technical colleges. Nevertheless he felt it necessary that it should be available both as an incentive, and as part of the effort to raise the status of technical schools, and also to help the regional technical colleges build up numbers in their early years. He saw it merely as a concession and, to meet the objections of the second-level schools, decided that the facility would be available for only five years, after which the colleges would become purely third-level institutions.[19]

One feature of the regional technical colleges that did not conform to the Steering Committee blueprint was the arrangement for their management. It will be recalled that the Steering Committee had felt very strongly that the colleges should be seen as involving a new concept operating under new institutional arrangements, helping to develop a fresh image for technical education. With that in mind it went on to recommend the establishment of Regional Education Councils.[20] Whatever about the feasibility of such councils at that juncture, with all the attendant problems of jurisdiction over the private secondary schools, a fresh image for technical education appeared to imply that the colleges should not be governed by the provisions of the Vocational Education Act 1930. In his estimates speech of February 1968, Donogh O'Malley envisaged the colleges being run by a regional board on which local industrial interests, the vocational education committees and the Minister for Education would have representation.[21] The intention was to emphasise the regional character of the colleges, whereas VEC schemes were organised on a county basis. In October 1968 Brian Lenihan carried the matter further. He explained that there would be a college council for each college. The council would be composed of representatives of the local authorities, industry, the trade unions, teachers' associations, the Roman Catholic bishop of the diocese and the Department of Education. The day-to-day management was to be conducted by a small management committee, subject to the authority of the college council.[22]

This proposal was already a subject of debate within the vocational education committee system. In August 1968 a circular had been issued to all chief executive officers of VECs setting out the proposed arrangements for college councils and management committees, and indicating that the latter would be composed of five members nominated by the Irish Vocational Education Association, the Association of Chief Executive Officers, the Federated Union of Employers, the Irish Congress of Trade Unions and the Department of Education.[23] The Department representative was to act as chairman. When the circular came to be considered by the County Carlow VEC, it declined to submit any nomination for the college council at the Regional Technical College. Instead it passed a motion declaring that it found the constitution of the college council and the board of management repugnant to the 1930 Act and called on the Minister to bring the administration of the colleges more into line with that Act. It also instructed the chief executive officer to contact the Irish Vocational Education Association with a view to raising the matter with the minister.[24]

The Association, the umbrella body for vocational educational committees, took up the issue. As a lobby the Association had considerable muscle. At this time it was strengthening its lobbying powers under the presidency of Jack McCann, an Independent councillor from County Offaly. Vocational education committees were one of the relatively few areas retaining some modicum of power in the sphere of local government. As such, many Dáil deputies, ministers included, had cut their political teeth on these committees and many of them remained as members after their election to the Dáil. The activists in the Association tended to be drawn from all parts of the political spectrum, and often included government backbenchers. In the case of the Carlow resolution, for example, the proposer was a Fianna Fáil county councillor and the seconder a Fianna Fáil deputy. A minister could ignore an interest group of that nature at his peril.

In this instance the stakes were very high as far as the Association was concerned. Normally its lobbying was conducted discreetly at the Department of Education in Marlborough Street, but on this occasion the pressure was also applied in the Dáil. The spokesman was the Fine Gael Deputy, Gerry L'Estrange, who, in the debate on the Estimates, launched a wide-ranging diatribe which focused particularly on the civil service, which he described as trying to abrogate the rights of parents and public representatives.[25] He appealed to the minister to change his mind. When Mr Lenihan came to reply to the debate, he emphasised that no formal decisions had been taken with regard to the operation of the boards of management.[26] Two months later he announced, in answer to a Dáil question, that the colleges would be managed by a board of management appointed in accordance with Section 21 (2) of the Vocational Education Act 1930. The matter had been decided, and unlike many others, it did not surface again in any serious fashion for many years.

Although the colleges were henceforth to have a board of management which was formally a sub-committee of the local vocational education committee, they were funded directly by the Department of Education by means of an earmarked grant channelled through the VEC.[27] In the years from 1969 to 1974 the amounts of recurrent state grants to the colleges were as follows: 1969-70: £130,000; 1970-71: £376,000; 1971-72: £552,000; 1972-73: £860,000; 1973-74: £1,309,000; 1974: £1,455,000.[28]

The first five of the regional technical colleges, Athlone, Carlow, Dundalk, Sligo and Waterford, commenced full operation in the autumn of 1970. For the first year the third-level students did not have access to state support, as the higher education grants scheme did not apply to the courses being run by the colleges. By the following year the Department had prepared a specimen scheme for Vocational Education Committee scholarships.[29] The majority of VECs conformed to the specimen scheme, but some submitted schemes which were designed to exclude pupils from secondary schools from availing of the scholarships. While the scholarship schemes operated by the committees were subject to ministerial sanction, the minister had no power under the 1930 Act to impose a scholarship scheme on any committee. In the circumstances the minister, Mr Faulkner, and his officials could only advise all committees that it was the minister's desire that the scholarship schemes should be open to all holders of the Leaving Certificate. The value of the scholarships was equated with higher education grants, with the same means test applying.

Pádraig Faulkner felt that the limited number of VEC scholarships would maintain what he saw as the continued imbalance between university courses and technical and technological courses.[30] He accordingly decided that there should be a sufficient number available to all committees to widen the scope of the scholarship scheme in order to include all Leaving Certificate subjects and offer freedom of choice to all post-primary students to pursue third-level courses in the regional technical colleges. About 300 VEC scholarships were awarded in 1971-72 and 1972-73 at a cost of £164,056 and £207,699 respectively.[31] It was left to Faulkner's successor, Richard Burke, to augment the scheme. A further £120,000 was added to the estimates for 1973-74 to bring the number of scholarships available to 1,200. The value of the scholarships was kept in line with the higher education grants scheme, but unlike that scheme, the scholarships were competitive and were to remain so.[32] Table 3 shows the growth in student numbers at Regional Technical Colleges from 1970 to 1974.[33]

TABLE 3: Growth in student numbers at Regional Technical Colleges 1970-74.

	Second-Level	Third-Level	Total
1970-71	278	194	472
1971-72	529	590	1119
1972-73	560	1214	1774
1973-74	526	1600	2126

The Steering Committee in 1967 did not see any final fixed pattern of courses in the colleges.[34] This view was reiterated by Ministers O'Malley, Lenihan and Faulkner in the period between 1968 and 1970, though there came to be an increasing emphasis on work at technician and higher technician level.[35] All of the five regional technical colleges which become operational in the autumn of 1970 offered full-time certificate courses in the areas of science, engineering and business studies. These courses were designed to run over two years. Because most staff were not recruited until shortly before the colleges opened, the original syllabuses were designed by teams consisting of heads of schools from the Regional Technical Colleges and the VEC third-level colleges in Dublin and Cork, supervised by senior inspectors in the Department of Education.[36]

Fifty-one students completed the two-year courses in the five colleges in 1972, twenty of them in business studies, seventeen in science and nine in engineering.[37] The students received national awards from the National Council for Educational Awards (NCEA) which had been set up a short time previously. In 1973 their number had increased to 275 in six colleges (Letterkenny having opened in 1971) and in 1974 to 402 in seven colleges (Galway having opened in 1972). In 1973 eighteen students had completed national diplomas in five of the colleges, and this number had increased to 123 from ten courses by 1974.[38] All of the ten diploma courses were in different specialist areas, but this did not presage a concentration of specialised diplomas in individual colleges.

While the development of courses at technician and higher technician level absorbed a major part of the effort of regional technical colleges in the period up to 1974, by no means all of their third-level work was confined to courses validated by NCEA. A number of the colleges ran courses preparing students for the examinations of professional bodies, and, for example, the colleges in Waterford, Sligo and Athlone had full-time courses leading to the examinations of professional accountancy bodies. Students on these courses did not sit for NCEA-monitored examinations.

The number of regional technological colleges rose to eight in the autumn of 1974 with the opening of the regional technical college at Bishopstown in Cork. While the college opened on a greenfield site, it was not an entirely new institution. Effectively the third-level component of the existing Crawford Municipal Technical Institute moved into the new RTC. Ironically it experienced more teething problems than the other RTCs. Its school and departmental structure differed from the other regional technical colleges and the transition to the new campus brought industrial relations problems which took some years to sort out. There was nonetheless a new network of eight colleges which had the contours of a national system. The body which provided the cement for that system was the National Council for Educational Awards.

The National Council for Educational Awards

The 1964 OECD report on the *Training of Technicians in Ireland* was the first to suggest a council charged with national responsibility for the training and qualifications of technicians.[39] Among the functions envisaged for it was the awarding of national technician diplomas. As already noted, the Commission on Higher Education was opposed to the idea of non-university institutions being brought under a single external academic authority with responsibility for the approval of courses and the awarding of qualifications.[40] It noted suggestions that there was need for a national system of awards which would define the status of the technician, and requested Cumann na nInnealtóirí (one of the forerunners of the Institution of Engineers of Ireland) to furnish an outline scheme for a national council which would determine the standards and other aspects of technician training and would award a qualification.[41] The Commission made no recommendation with regard to such a body, although it did not appear to be opposed to it. The Steering Committee on Technical Education took up the idea of a technician awards body, but went further and suggested that it should be a body along the lines of the Council for National Academic Awards in Britain.[42]

In December 1968, Brian Lenihan gave the first public clue that he was toying with the NCEA concept when he spoke in the Dáil about having an institute of technology which would co-ordinate the work in the courses at the various regional technical colleges.[43] Shortly afterwards he met with the Higher Education Authority in the course of referring to it the question of a third-level institution for Limerick. At that meeting the idea of a National Council for Educational Awards was put to him by one of the members, Hugh de Lacy, with the suggestion that it could provide the mechanism for the award of degrees at the Limerick college.[44] Concurrently with its deliberations on the Limerick question the Authority established a sub-group to consider the question of an awards body and shortly afterwards submitted recommendations to the minister both on the Council for National Awards and the Limerick question within the one report.[45] It was quite clearly envisaged both by the Authority in its report, and subsequently by the minister, that the Council would be the body responsible for awards at the new Limerick institute.[46] While recommending that the Council be established, the Authority deferred a definitive recommendation on the nature of the constitution under which it should operate until it had had an opportunity of consulting the university authorities and the Irish Federation of University Teachers, particularly on the question of the award of degrees by the Council.[47] The process of consultation was lengthy and the main item of concern at all times seems to have been the question of ensuring that NCEA degrees were comparable with those of the universities.[48] The considerable delay in deciding on the terms of reference and constitution of the Council was, as already noted, one of the factors leading to the postponement of the opening of the Limerick Institute in 1971.

The *ad hoc* Council was established in March 1972 and held its first meeting at the Department of Education on 11 April.[49] It was appointed for a period of three years or until such time as a statutory Council was established. It consisted of a Chairman,

J.C. Nagle, a former Secretary of the Department of Agriculture, and twenty-two members appointed by the minister in a personal rather than a representative capacity. Of these, seven held academic posts in Irish universities, six had positions in Irish higher education institutions other than universities, three were involved in post-primary education and six were drawn from the fields of agriculture, commerce, industry and public administration. The first acting director was Jack McGlone, a senior inspector in the Department of Education.[50] The first director of the Council, Pádraig MacDiarmada, Examinations Officer at University College Galway, took up the position in December 1973.[51]

From the earliest stages much of the detailed work of evaluation and assessment of course arrangements and standards of student attainment was referred by the Council to specialist boards of studies. Four were established to handle a) Physical and Biological Sciences and Mathematics, b) Architecture, Construction and Engineering, c) Business Studies and Commerce and d) General Studies and Education. The boards of studies in turn appointed panels, comprising board members and others having the expertise necessary to carry out the assessment of specialised areas. The Council also appointed extern examiners to monitor student performance in the terminal examinations. By 1974 about 250 people were involved in the work of the boards of studies and the panels of assessors.[52] The boards, panels and groups of extern examiners were in many ways unique in Irish education in the extent to which they involved individuals from outside the sphere of education in the detailed assessment and evaluation of courses. The boards dealing with business studies and with engineering, architecture and construction studies had a majority of members who were not attached to educational institutions and the same applied to a number of the specialist panels.[53]

Three broad categories of award were envisaged: a National Certificate to be awarded after the equivalent of two years of full-time study; a National Diploma to be awarded either after a further year of specialised study or on completion of a three-year course; and a degree which would require the equivalent of four years of full-time study. The requirement of four years for a degree applied to all disciplines, regardless of the fact that many university courses in arts, commerce and science required only three years.

Because of the limited time available before students were due to complete courses in June 1972, there was considerable difficulty in carrying out the necessary assessments and evaluation. The

Department of Education attached considerable importance to the first group of successful students from the regional technical colleges being the recipients of NCEA awards, and accordingly the Council gave temporary recognition to the certificate courses being offered in science, engineering and business studies in the five regional technical colleges involved. As noted, the syllabuses had been prepared by Department of Education committees before the RTC programmes got under way. The examination papers set in the colleges were moderated by extern examiners who also monitored the marking of the scripts. Broadly similar arrangements were to apply in the following year.[54] Although the Department had envisaged common syllabuses and examinations, particularly at certificate level, this was successfully resisted by the regional technical colleges. [55]

During the academic year 1973-74 the Council established a procedure of course validation which was to become its norm. Colleges were asked to submit programmes of study according to a set format. These in turn were examined by panels of assessors who made one or more visits to the college for discussions with staff and students and for an inspection of the facilities.[56] When approved, courses normally had recognition for a period varying between three and five years. In the early years course approval was often a lengthy process, because many of the staff had been recruited from business and industry rather than teaching, and as a result the role, not only of assessors, but of extern examiners became one of advisors and consultants on curriculum development.

Although the terms of reference of the Council did allow it to discharge the function of an examining body, it did not see its role as devising courses, issuing syllabuses or setting examinations. From the outset it effectively became a matter of principle that the initiative on all these matters was to rest with individual colleges, the Council's role being to validate their proposals and monitor their implementation.

At the end of 1974, 141 submissions had been received by the Council from thirty institutions. Of these, eighteen were at degree level and forty-eight at National Diploma.[57] In 1972, 93 awards were made, 486 in 1973 and 850 in 1974, a total of 1,429 in all. Of these, over three quarters were in engineering and science, with over 56 per cent (806 awards in all) being in the area of engineering and construction studies.[58] Over the three years slightly more than four out of every five awards had been at the level of National Certificate, though in 1974 the Council awarded its first degrees to four students who had completed their degree programme in physical education at St Mary's College, Twickenham. The status and standing of these degrees was soon to be tested.

The City of Dublin Vocational Education Committee

In the years prior to 1968 the development of non-university education in technological disciplines had occurred largely within the colleges of the City of Dublin Vocational Education Committee.[59] Third-level work was mainly concentrated in the Colleges of Technology at Bolton Street and Kevin Street and the College of Commerce, Rathmines. Between them in the academic year 1969-70 they had over 11,000 students. Of these 4,960 were third-level students,[60] composed of 2,983 at Rathmines, 993 at Bolton Street and 984 at Kevin Street. The majority of the students took their courses by part-time study, but even allowing for this, it was reckoned that there was the equivalent of over 2,000 full-time third-level students in the three colleges. While the colleges, particularly Bolton Street, provided a considerable amount of teaching for a variety of courses in the apprentice area, over 60 per cent of the work of these colleges was of a third-level nature catering for technicians, technologists and students preparing for the examinations of professional bodies in accountancy and other commercial areas.

While many of the courses were geared to the examinations of professional bodies, a number, in areas such as architecture, engineering and business studies, were designed by the individual colleges and were subsequently recognised by professional bodies for exemption purposes.[61] College diplomas were awarded at the end of the study period. The VEC reckoned that, in 1968-69, 385 students at Bolton Street and 106 students at Kevin Street were studying to degree level, while a small number from Kevin Street sat the external degree examinations for the Bachelor of Science at London University.[62] In some cases students who had completed the diplomas in engineering and architecture were recognised as having reached such a standard that they were admitted to study for a master's degree in Irish universities.[63]

With such growth and development the Committee found itself with an accommodation problem, so that by the late 1960s applicants for some courses in the colleges were unable to secure entry.[64] A planning committee of the VEC submitted a report (subsequently known as the 'Ballymun Project') which proposed to bring together higher technician, technological, higher commercial and management departments from the three colleges into one campus.[65] In July 1968 Brian Lenihan had indicated that there would be a new institution at Ballymun.[66] In February 1969, following a discussion with the Committee, he referred the Ballymun proposals to the Higher Education Authority. The VEC submitted the proposals to HEA in June 1969, and after over a year's study by a specialist working party, the Authority adopted the report on the Ballymun project in December 1970.[67]

The HEA accepted that there was an urgent need for additional third-level facilities in Dublin, largely in the technician area, and that many of the educational objectives of the proposed development would be defeated if the required additional facilities were not provided substantially on a single site. Where the Committee had proposed 4,000 student places, HEA recommended 3,320. The HEA report adopted the proposal that the third-level activity in Rathmines and Bolton Street should be transferred to Ballymun, and that Kevin Street be confined to third-level courses in the area of applied biological science. The report also recommended rationalisation of architectural education, with one national school of architecture located in UCD. It further recommended a governing structure for Ballymun which, while containing substantial VEC representation, would be independent of the Committee and financed by HEA.[68] The recommendation with regard to the governing structure angered the City of Dublin VEC.[69] As with the Steering Committee it again raised the issue of the role of VECs in third-level education, and this was so unwelcome that the minister and the Department temporarily delayed publication of the Authority's report.[70] Four years after the HEA had completed its report, and over six years after Mr Lenihan had promised a complex in Ballymun, no decision had been taken on it. In late 1974 the Ballymun project was one more casualty of the indecision surrounding the future of higher education in Dublin.

The indecision also affected the relationship of the City of Dublin VEC colleges with the National Council for Educational Awards. The Committee had long experience of technician education, and its teaching staff, in many ways, constituted the greatest resource in terms of expertise and experience in that field within the state. In a memorandum to the Commission on Higher

Education it had recommended that appropriate machinery – on the lines of professional bodies, preferably, and perhaps under their sponsorship – should be devised to establish and maintain standards for technician education and training. It suggested the setting up of an industrial education council which would establish education committees for different industries, co-ordinate standards, and award qualifications or recognise existing qualifications.[71] On the establishment of the National Council for Educational Awards, the Dublin colleges remained aloof from the Council. They were well represented on NCEA boards of studies and as assessors and externs[72] but, with the exception of Bolton Street and Cathal Brugha Street, NCEA awards were not sought for students taking technician courses. Had the Dublin colleges sought degree recognition from the *ad hoc* National Council for Educational Awards in its first two years of existence and been more enthusiastic supporters of that body, it is possible that the decisions announced on 16 December 1974 might have been substantially different.

No decision was likely to be reached on the future structure of the Dublin colleges independently of decisions on the future of the two university colleges in Dublin. When the decisions were eventually announced, Dublin VEC was to discover that, just as it had lost ground relative to the rest of the country in the six years during which the alternative system was developed between 1968 and 1974, it was scheduled to lose further ground under the proposals and decisions of December 1974. It was not just the VEC which was to be the loser. The real losers would be the potential students from the Dublin area who for many years were destined to miss out on education provision as compared to their contemporaries in the rest of the country.

Notes

1 Kerr, *12 Systems of Higher Education,* p.168, Table 2. See also Clancy, P. (1995), *Access to College: Patterns of Continuity and Change*, Dublin: Higher Education Authority, p. 20.

2 *Commission Report,* p. 75, Table 56.

3 An Roinn Oideachais, *Tuarascáil Staitistiúil,* 1965-66, Table 2.

4 Although St Patrick's College, Maynooth, was a recognised, and not a constituent college of the National University of Ireland, it was always classified by the Department of Education as being of university status and was so treated by the Commission and in all other statistical returns.

5 There were, for example, 3,195 male clerical students (excluding novices of

religious orders) in 1965-66. Of these 1,545 were students for the diocesan priesthood, 404 were from missionary societies and 1,246 from religious orders. The figure of 3,195 already showed a decline from a peak of 3,409 in 1961-62, and it was to fall to 1,890 by 1970-71. Newman, J., Ward, C., and Ryan, L. (1971), *A Survey of Vocations in Ireland*, Dublin: Research and Development Unit, p.7, Tables 4 and 5. Students in religious establishments ceased to be a significant factor in the numbers of higher education students categorised as 'other' from the early 1970s onwards.

6 The delay in the Commission's deliberations did not totally paralyse capital expenditure. The first phase of the UCD development, the science building, was opened in 1964, while the go-ahead for the science block at UCC was given in 1965 (Cabinet Minutes, 13 July 1965, National Archives, Department of Taoiseach, File S13258C).

7 *Dáil Debates*, vol. 232, col. 470 (6 February 1968).

8 ibid., col. 471.

9 Steering Committee Report.

10 *Dáil Debates*, vol. 238, cols. 1708-1709 (26 February 1969).

11 ibid., vol. 243, col. 475 (4 December 1969).

12 ibid., vol. 232, col. 765 (8 February 1968).

13 ibid., vol. 236, cols. 922-923 (11 July 1968).

14 ibid., vol. 237, col. 2081 (5 December 1968).

15 *Irish Times*, 14 December 1968.

16 *Dáil Debates*, vol. 238, col. 1934 (18 December 1969).

17 ibid., col. 1937.

18 ibid., vol. 244, col. 2167 (5 March 1970).

19 ibid., vol. 268, col. 557 (24 October 1973).

20 *Steering Committee*, pp. 29-30.

21 *Dáil Debates*, vol. 232, col. 471 (6 February 1968).

22 ibid., vol. 236, col. 1781 (31 October 1968); vol. 237, col. 1565 (28 November 1968).

23 ibid., vol. 237, col. 1481 (28 November 1968).

24 ibid., col. 1484.

25 ibid., cols. 1481-1485.

26 ibid., col. 2088 (5 December 1968).

27 From the beginning of the financial year 1969-70 the Book of Estimates recorded the funds voted for Regional Technical Colleges under a separate subhead within the Vote for Vocational Education.

28 The figures are taken from the Books of Estimates for the period. At the end of 1974 the commencement of the financial year was changed from April to January and hence the 1974 figure covers a nine-month period.

29 *Dáil Debates*, vol. 268, col. 558 (24 October 1973).

30 ibid.

31 ibid., cols. 389, 558.

32 ibid., col. 1253 (6 November 1973).

33 The figures are derived form the editions of *Tuarascáil Staitistiúil (Statistical Report)* issued by the Department of Education (An Roinn Oideachais) and covering the years in question.

34 *Steering Committee*, p. 11.

35 *Dáil Debates*, vol. 232, col. 471 (6 February 1968); vol. 236, col. 922 (11 July 1968); vol. 237, col. 2081 (5 December 1968); vol. 238, col. 1709 (26 February 1969); vol. 245, col. 1319 (15 April 1970).

36 Interview with Jack McGlone, Assistant Chief Inspector, Department of Education and first Acting Director, National Council for Educational Awards, 1972-73 (Dublin, December 1987).

37 NCEA, *First Annual Report*, p. 32. The only one of the Regional Technical Colleges (subsequently Institutes of Technology) so far to produce a record of its early years is Galway, see O'Hara, B. (1993), *Regional Technical College Galway: The First 21 Years*, Galway: Research and Consultancy Unit, Regional Technical College.

38 NCEA, *Second Annual Report*, pp. 41-44.

39 OECD, *Training of Technicians*, pp. 42, 90.

40 *Commission Report*, pp. 133-134.

41 ibid., p. 393.

42 *Steering Committee*, pp. 8, 41.

43 *Dáil Debates*, vol. 236, col. 2081 (5 December 1968).

44 This point was confirmed in interviews with James F. Dukes, Professor J.N.R. Grainger and Hugh de Lacy. All stated that the initiative for the establishment of an awards body at this time came from the Higher Education Authority rather than from the Department of Education. Both Dukes and Grainger stressed that the initial suggestion was made by de Lacy.

45 HEA, *A Council for National Awards*, p. 6.

46 ibid., p. 11. Also *Dáil Debates*, vol. 238, col. 1710 (26 February 1969).

47 HEA, *A Council for National Awards*, p. 6. Also Higher Education Authority, *First Report*, Dublin: Stationery Office, 1969, pp. 31, 37-38.

48 HEA, *A Council for National Awards*, p. 6; *Dáil Debates*, vol. 252, col. 1733 (31 March 1971).

49 NCEA, *First Annual Report*, p. 7. Also J. McGlone, interview, December 1987.

50 NCEA, *First Annual Report*, p. 9.

51 NCEA, *Second Report*, p. 50.

52 ibid., p. 5.

53 ibid., pp. 24-25, 28-36.

54 ibid., p. 12.

55 J. McGlone, interview, December 1987. The resistance appears to have been to common examinations particularly.

56 NCEA, *First Annual Report*, p. 13.

57 NCEA, *Second Report*, p. 5.

58 These figures are derived from the first two reports of the Council. There are minor discrepancies with regard to the published figures for 1974.

59 See Duff, Hegarty and Hussey, pp. 13-28. There was also some third-level work carried on by VEC colleges in Cork and Limerick.

60 These figures are calculated from data contained in Higher Education Authority (1972), *Report on the Ballymun Project*, Dublin: Stationery Office, pp. 12-26.

61 *Commission Report*, pp. 177-178, 326, 382-386.

62 *Dáil Debates*, vol. 238, cols. 1070-1071 (18 February 1969).

63 ibid. Also Luce, *The First 400 Years*, p. 194.

64 HEA, *Report on Ballymun Project*, p. 10.

65 ibid., p. 68. Duff, Hegarty and Hussey, pp. 28-33.
66 *Dáil Debates*, vol. 236, col. 922 (11 July 1968).
67 HEA, *Report on Ballymun Project*, p. 1.
68 ibid., pp. 61-64.
69 Interview with Hugh de Lacy, former Principal, College of Technology, Kevin Street, Dublin and member of Higher Education Authority, 1968-1982 (Dublin, January 1988).
70 Professor J.N.R. Grainger, interview, December 1987.
71 *Commission Report*, pp. 391-392.
72 NCEA, *First Annual Report*. Also NCEA, *Second Report*.

CHAPTER 6

The Universities Mark Time

While the Department of Education busied itself in building up a new system of colleges and technological education between 1968 and 1974, the universities were largely forced to mark time. They were not a priority for state investment, there was an abortive attempt to merge the two university institutions in Dublin, the Higher Education Authority was established *inter alia* as a buffer between the Department and the universities, and a new policy and ethos began to develop in relation to technological education. The universities in some quarters came to be regarded as a brake on economic development.

The merger proposal

The Presentation and Summary of Report from the Commission on Higher Education was made available to the Minister for Education, Donogh O'Malley, in March 1967.[1] On 18 April he announced that he intended to dissolve the National University of Ireland and in the ensuing reorganisation merge Trinity College Dublin and University College Dublin within one university.[2] The Commission had recommended that UCD, UCC and UCG should be established by Act of the Oireachtas as independent universities to replace the NUI.[3] Only one of the Commission's members, Lieutenant-General M.J. Costello, entered a reservation on this point.[4] He alone had recommended the merger of the two colleges. The members of the Commission viewed their recommendations on the two Dublin colleges as of primary importance and concluded that Trinity College and University College Dublin could not be amalgamated successfully. [5]

O'Malley's proposal was unexpected, although the issue of merger appears to have been discussed within the Department of Education during the 1960s.[6] The question of the merger of the two colleges had surfaced in 1960 at the time of the proposal to transfer University College Dublin to the Belfield site. At that point the Minister for Education, Dr Patrick Hillery, had affirmed that it was his duty as Minister for Education 'to respect with the most scrupulous care the consciences of our citizens, both of those of the majority and minority religions', and he intimated that he did not accept the idea of merger.[7] Significantly in the same debate, Donogh O'Malley, at that time a government backbencher, stated that he favoured such an amalgamation[8] The announcement of April 1967 was an indication that he had not changed his mind. His main argument was the necessity to avoid duplicating scarce resources, although he also spoke at length of the desirability of merging two historical traditions. His statement indicated that he had first put a proposal to the government on rationalising the university position in Dublin in December 1966, and that he had government authorisation for the announcement.[9] It has been queried whether the announcement was authorised by the government as a whole,[10] but there can be little doubt that his statement was prepared by senior officials of the Department of Education and that there was support at that level for the idea, if not the timing, of the merger proposal.[11]

In contrast to his success with the introduction of a scheme for free post-primary education which he had announced in a similarly unexpected and flamboyant fashion in September 1966, Mr O'Malley found progress very slow with regard to the shaping of his planned new university in Dublin. He admitted as much in the Dáil shortly before his death in March 1968.[12]

He had attempted to achieve progress in the matter. In the summer of 1967 the retiring Secretary of the Department of Education, Dr Tarlach Ó Raifeartaigh, and the principal officer with responsibility *inter alia* for the Higher Education vote, James F. Dukes, were assigned the task of devising a merger plan that would be viable. In September 1967 Dr Ó Raifeartaigh was appointed special advisor on higher education to the minister, and from then until July 1968 he and Mr Dukes were in constant contact and negotiation with both Trinity College and University College Dublin.[13]

On Donogh O'Malley's death the issue was taken up by the new Minister for Education, Brian Lenihan. On 6 July 1968 he issued a statement on behalf of the government, the major part of which outlined 'decisions' with regard to the most suitable allocation of faculties and departments in the reconstituted University of Dublin.[14] The following month the Higher Education Authority was established with tasks which included advising the minister 'on the nature and form of the legislation which would be required in order to implement the Government's decisions on higher education as contained in the recent announcements'.[15]

By the time the Authority was established it had become clear to many, including the HEA members, that university opinion generally was opposed to the concept of a single university in Dublin. The Authority was asked by representatives of NUI whether it would be prepared to consider an alternative solution. It informed them that it would give the fullest consideration to any agreed alternative scheme put forward by the National University and Trinity College which would provide for the degree of rationalisation and co-ordination sought by the government.[16] Eventually in April 1970 the two university institutions submitted a joint set of proposals, usually referred to as the NUI/TCD Agreement.[17] HEA proceeded to examine and compare the government proposals and the NUI/TCD Agreement for their educational merits, financial implications and relative workability. In December 1971 the Authority presented its *Report on University Reorganisation* to the minister, Pádraig Faulkner. It recommended that there be two separate universities in Dublin linked by a statutory Conjoint Board.[18] Effectively the idea of merger died once the Higher Education Authority advised against it, but formally the government decision stood until the Fianna Fáil administration went out of office in March 1973. Indeed it can be said to have been abandoned formally only with the publication of the decisions of the coalition government in December 1974.

The proposal to merge Trinity College and University College Dublin was an important background matter during the formative period of the new system of higher vocational and technological education. It was a matter of major concern and preoccupation of the newly-formed Higher Education Authority for the first three years of that body's existence. For an even longer period it was a preoccupation of senior university administrators and also of concerned academic staff.[19] In the process the universities were losers in the battle for resources. When in April 1970 the government came to provide only £15 million of the minimum of £24 million which HEA had argued was essential to tackle the chronic problems of university accommodation, an *Irish Times* editorial spoke of the academics as having failed to educate their constituents, the public, as to why the universities' financial needs should be met, and having failed to relate their institutions to the society which supported them.[20] The same editorial referred to the way in which the merger proposal had absorbed and wasted academic energies.

While never perhaps intended as such, the merger proposal operated as a major diversion which postponed decision-making on the university colleges and put the universities and their administrators in a defensive and adversarial role *vis a vis* the government. The government had been committed very publicly by Donogh O'Malley to merge the two Dublin colleges. It did not succeed in doing so and no government welcomes having to admit failure on an issue on which it has taken a stand so publicly. From 1967 onwards the government put in train its own initiatives with regard to an alternative system of higher education. It is arguable that the ability of the universities to influence the direction of the new institutions was substantially weakened by the fact that over a period of five years a sizeable section of the university community was dedicated to reversing a major decision of government. Where it may have wished to oppose or modify aspects of government policy with regard to non-university third-level education, its bargaining power was diminished by the merger debate.

The Higher Education Authority

The merger proposal and the decision to reconstitute the Cork and Galway colleges as independent universities was the first response to issues addressed in the report of the Commission on Higher Education. The establishment of the Higher Education Authority was the second. The Commission had recommended the establishment of a statutory permanent Commission for Higher Education which would be the financial authority for the system, would assist in implementing its own report and would keep the problems of higher education under continuous review. It was envisaged as consisting of nine members appointed by the government and reporting directly to the Taoiseach.[21] Winding up on the estimates for his Department in February 1968, Donogh O'Malley indicated that, as 'part of a frontal assault on our higher education problem', he was considering the Commission's proposal and envisaged a commission or authority, akin to the University Grants Committee in Britain, which would be charged with the co-ordination of the financial needs of the universities and of 'other elements of the higher education spectrum, possibly including the technological colleges or a section of them'.[22] Four months later, during the debate on the Local Authorities (Higher Education Grants) Bill, his successor, Brian Lenihan, told the

Senate that he would shortly be announcing proposals for the creation of a Higher Education Authority which would supervise all aspects of higher education, with power to allocate funds, decide on where facilities should be located and ensure a uniform system of salary, promotion and staff transfer.[23]

On 6 July Mr Lenihan, in the course of an announcement dealing mainly with the provision of higher education in Dublin, stated that the government had accepted the recommendation of the Commission on Higher Education that a permanent authority be established to deal with the financial and organisational problems of higher education.[24] The following week he told the Dáil that he planned to rationalise higher education under the supervision of the Higher Education Authority and spoke of the colleges of technology and the nine regional technical colleges having their own field of higher education in technological subjects which could be administered in an overall capacity by the Authority.[25]

On 15 August 1968 the government announced the functions, terms of reference and membership of the new *ad hoc* Authority.[26] Its role was advisory and was focused on existing provision of higher education, the elimination of unnecessary duplication, budgets and financial allocations to institutions of higher education, and problems associated with gradings, appointments, tenure, salary, superannuation and mobility of university staff. It was also its function to maintain a continual review of the country's needs in higher education and to advise on higher education matters referred to it by the minister and other bodies. As an interim assignment it was requested to advise the minister on the nature and form of the legislation required to implement the recently announced government decisions on higher education.

The interim assignment was that which engaged most public attention. For many months the Authority was viewed by outsiders as having primarily the task of producing a detailed plan for the Dublin merger.[27] The interim assignment was also seen by many university staff in this light. The Commission on Higher Education had recommended that none of the membership of a body such as HEA should be drawn from institutions coming under its scope. It felt that the dual function of acting on behalf of both the institutions and the community could most suitably be exercised by a body whose members were not committed to institutional interests and whose decisions could clearly be seen to be disinterested.[28] This was not the approach adopted in setting up the Authority either in its *ad hoc* or in its statutory incarnations. Of the fifteen members of the first *ad hoc* Authority, six were drawn from the university colleges, one from St Patrick's College Maynooth, and one from a College of Technology in Dublin.[29] On its establishment there was very strong criticism of the university academics, particularly those from University College Dublin, who had agreed to act on the Authority.[30] Even as late as 1971 a Professor in University College Dublin, John O'Donovan, used the privilege of a Dáil debate to refer to the academics who had accepted membership of the Authority as 'quislings'.[31]

Such indeed were the misgivings surrounding the establishment of the Authority that Mr Lenihan, in addressing the members at their first meeting, stressed that the Authority was to be 'in no way an executive arm of the government or of any department of state, but was to be an autonomous body and would function as such pending the introduction of formal legislation'.[32] He also informed the members that their terms of reference were not immutable and invited recommendations from the membership as to the appropriate amendments which might be desirable when legislation came to be drafted. Following its first meeting, the Authority issued a statement highlighting the minister's references to its independence and declaring that, as an autonomous body, it would, before making recommendations, take a view of the opinions of the government, the university institutions and of other institutions of higher education.

The Authority statement also indicated that the minister, at its request, had made clear that he had not asked the members to commit themselves to such future decisions on higher education as the government might take. The minister, on the contrary, had envisaged the Authority contributing to the shaping of decisions, with its terms of reference widened 'to enable it to consider such matters as the place of technological colleges and teacher training colleges in the system of higher education'.[33] The minister's statement was made at the insistence of the members of the Authority, and they also insisted that the statement be given publicity. While it was of crucial importance to the university members on the Authority, it appears to have been argued for just as strongly by those from outside the field of education. Effectively the Authority members were setting down the conditions under which they would serve.[34] At its first meeting, therefore, the Authority established an important point and staked out an area of independence. In its *ad hoc* phase, that independence was to be most clearly demonstrated by its recommendation that the merger of the two Dublin university colleges was not practicable.

In its first year the issue which was borne in on the Authority as transcending all else was the accommodation crisis in the universities. So large did it loom that in its first report the Authority highlighted it to the extent of giving it priority over the account of its own proceedings.[35] The Authority's conclusion was that, if reasonable and indeed minimal standards of accommodation were to be attained, the capital cost over the following six years would not be less than a forecast figure of £24 million. Not much more than one half of that sum was agreed to by the government.[36] It was clear that in its early years the Authority, in arguing the case for university expansion, was going to be at a disadvantage in an area where the Department had its own interests and commitments to a building programme for the regional technical colleges and the new Limerick institution.

During its *ad hoc* phase the Authority produced three further major reports on the questions of teacher education,[37] university reorganisation[38] and the Ballymun project proposed by the City of Dublin Vocational Education Committee.[39] In its *Report on Teacher Education*, submitted to the Minister for Education, the Authority recommended the establishment of a body to be styled An Foras Oideachais, with general functions in relation to the education and training of teachers and the promotion of their professional interests.[40] It also recommended that the primary teachers' training course be extended from two to three years duration, leading to the degree of Bachelor of Educational Science from the National Council for Educational Awards.[41] Significantly the Authority was here arguing for a development which would have greatly strengthened the binary system (a concept which is explained at some length in the next chapter). It was also an act of faith in the proposed National Council for Educational Awards. In so recommending, the Authority was running contrary not only to the feelings of most teachers, and more especially the teachers' unions, but also to previous ministerial commitments.

Two years previously Brian Lenihan had undertaken to integrate the teacher training colleges within the university system, with the students working to degree level.[42] The Authority's recommendations were strongly criticised by the Fine Gael spokesman on education, Garret FitzGerald.[43] The minister, Pádraig Faulkner, disagreed with FitzGerald's approach and suggested it could adversely influence the status of degrees from the National Council.[44] It later emerged that Faulkner had always favoured a university degree for primary teachers.[45] As minister he asked for comments on the Authority's report from those closely associated with colleges of education and other interested parties. Almost without exception they wanted a university degree.[46] It was eventually left to Faulkner's successor, Richard Burke, to take the decision to link the colleges of education with the universities.[47] On this matter the Authority had produced a recommendation which caused political difficulties for the minister and helped postpone decision-making for some years. On the other hand it had been consistent in trying to protect the status of the as yet unborn Council for National Awards whose establishment it had recommended a year previously.

The Authority became a statutory body in May 1972.[48] The Bill to establish it was published in late 1970 and first debated in February 1971.[49] In the debate on the Bill the minister, Pádraig Faulkner, indicated that he viewed the Authority as the link between his department and the institutions of higher education,[50] and as a separate organisation set up for the specific purpose of giving independent advice to the minister. It was seen as dealing mainly with financial and administrative matters, and with academic questions only to the extent that they impinged on these matters.[51] In the Dáil the minister accepted amendments which added to the general functions of the Authority those of promoting the attainment of equality of opportunity in higher education,[52] and of promoting the democratisation of the structure of higher education.[53]

The most contentious discussions in the debates on the Higher Education Authority Bill centred around four matters. Firstly the Authority was not to be given any power over the designation of additional bodies as institutions of higher education and this was seen as a retention of important powers by the Department. Secondly the principle of money being earmarked by a government department was seen as going against the whole concept of the bill. Garret FitzGerald, in particular, objected to the publication in the Book of Estimates of the annual grant to each college funded by the Authority. This he regarded as 'looking behind a grant-in-aid' and an unacceptable erosion of the Authority's autonomy.[54] Further inroads on that autonomy were seen in the requirement for ministerial approval for staff numbers and appointments, and in the fact that the chairman was appointed by the government on the recommendation of the minister and could be removed from office by the government.[55] Both Deputies FitzGerald and Thornley were inclined to the view that, in the period between the establishment of the *ad hoc* Authority and the publication of the Bill, the autonomy originally envisaged for it had been gradually reduced.[56]

The concern of the opposition spokesman does not appear to have been shared by the members of the Authority. The Authority had been shown the Bill in its entirety before its publication. During the debates the secretary, James Dukes, not only briefed the minister but, as he was at that stage still a civil servant on secondment, sat with him in the Dáil.[57]

In the two and a half years which followed the statutory establishment of the Authority its primary concern became the executive operations relating to the funding of university colleges and a small number of designated institutions. This is reflected in its first *Progress Report* of March 1974 which had less material relating to matters of general policy than any previous Authority publication.[58] Once it had executive tasks and money to dispense, it was to be expected that much of its energy would be devoted initially to establishing procedures and to making the case for greater resources for the bodies which it funded. The transition was not, in fact, as dramatic as it might have been. Although in the first five years of its existence the Authority was purely an advisory body, the material for the Book of Estimates dealing with universities continued to be prepared by Mr Dukes, as he had been doing since the Higher Education vote had been transferred from the Department of Finance some years previously. Informally the Authority had had executive powers since its inception.[59] The Authority did not ignore non-university education, and among its early initiatives as a statutory body was a visit to each of the new regional technical colleges conducted by its Liaison Committee.[60]

In the period from mid-1972 to the end of 1974 the Authority was increasingly identified with university education. That indeed was how some would have preferred it to be, as was made clear by Senator Professor Quinlan of University College Cork in the Senate debate on the HEA Bill.[61] That point had worried David Thornley in the Dáil when he questioned the minister as to whether there might be two categories of institutions, those with which the Authority would traditionally be dealing, and those with which the minister could deal. Mr Faulkner replied that this would be the factual situation at the beginning.[62] By 1974 the Authority found itself in the ironic position that, having helped to bring about an alternative system of higher education, it was now largely excluded from decision-making in that thriving and developing sector of non-university higher education, and was forced into the role of fighting the unpopular case of the university institutions whose purported defects were sometimes claimed to have made the alternative system necessary.

A technological ethos

Apart from the difficulties arising from being at odds with successive ministers over the reorganisation of university education in Dublin, there was a further disadvantage under which universities came to labour from the late 1960s onwards. The Department of Education and individual ministers had come to believe strongly in the importance of technology and technological education, and came to acquire the conviction, given explicit expression in the later 1970s by John Wilson, as Minister for Education, that there was a technological ethos with which university interference was undesirable.[63] It has been illustrated that from the early 1960s the Department of Education, under the influence of OECD, had worked on the assumption that manufacturing and industrial expansion required a pool of trained personnel and that these people required to be educated technically and technologically.[64] For this to happen, technical education required upgrading and the education system also needed to devote special attention to providing for a largely non-existent intermediate layer of technicians which would be crucial to Irish industrial expansion.[65] Since second-level education was strongly influenced by the requirements for entry to third-level education, it was also felt that an enhanced status for technical and technological education was also desirable, preferably through a new educational institution.[66]

While the necessary planning for an initiative with regard to technician education was being put in train, an emphasis came to be placed on educational provision for technology. The approach of the Commission on Higher Education and the earliest recommendations of the Higher Education Authority were central to this new emphasis.[67] Both the Commission and the Authority, though for different reasons, had recommended that universities were not the appropriate location for the development of technological education. The Department of Education concurred with that view.[68] There were initially three grounds for that opinion. Firstly it was held that universities were concerned with fundamental and theoretical studies, whereas technology was concerned with the applied and the practical.[69] Secondly there was a perceived academic bias within Irish education at both second and third level. While not solely responsible for this, the universities were major contributors and could scarcely be expected to provide the counterbalance to this bias.[70] Finally the concept of autonomy was central to the functioning of Irish universities and accordingly they could not be expected to give due regard to governmental programmes, even where these required an increased emphasis on technological education.[71]

This last point was reiterated by both Pádraig Faulkner and Michael O'Kennedy in recalling their own period at the Department of Education. Faulkner was convinced that Ireland had sufficient universities and the Limerick institute was intended to provide a balance between academic and technological education.[72] Michael O'Kennedy observed that the concept of university autonomy entailed universities deciding on course content and duration, and on student intake, and that Ireland had new needs that could not be serviced by autonomous universities.[73]

These arguments eventually provided the grounds for establishing an alternative system of higher education, modelled largely on that of Britain with an awards body responsible for academic validation nationally, but also, and unlike the British model, with one teaching institution (NIHE Limerick) which was to be a flagship for the new approach and the new emphasis on technical and technological education.

The universities as such had always had their critics in the Dáil and Senate. In the 1960s and 1970s there were, for example, individuals such as Deputy Martin Corry,[74] Deputy Jack McQuillan,[75] Dr Noel Browne (whose particular target was UCD),[76] Deputy Joseph Leneghan,[77] Senator Tómas Ó Maoláin,[78] Deputy James Tunney and Deputy Eugene Timmons.[79] Deputy Tunney was to serve as Parliamentary Secretary, and subsequently Minister of State, at the Department of Education for the period from 1977 to 1981, and as a backbencher he had been a persistent critic of what he saw as the abuse of university autonomy and the lack of democracy within the universities.[80]

What was also significant was that from 1970 onwards the consensus that steps needed to be taken to build up technical education, and overcome the bias towards the academic, was not confined to backbench deputies but was reflected by those who were themselves university personnel, or represented the universities in the Senate. In 1970, as Fine Gael spokesman on education, Dr Garret FitzGerald observed that Ireland had an academic educational sector which was very large in relation to its numbers and had an esteem beyond that normally granted in other countries to academic, as compared to vocational, education. He did not think that Ireland had the outlets for so many academically trained people and that the over-supply was an encouragement to emigration.[81] Senator Professor James Dooge saw a major problem not merely with the training of technicians, but in the social status they enjoyed. He also thought that the ratio of academic to vocational education graduates was out of line, mainly because too few technicians were being trained.[82]

This type of consensus continued throughout the 1970s. Speaking on the debate on the Local Authorities (Higher Education Grants) Bill in 1978, the independent Senator, Professor John A. Murphy, thought that everybody would agree that the country desperately needed a considerable diversion of students from the traditional academic area to the non-university technological sector.[83] In the same debate one of the senators elected by the graduates of the National University of Ireland, Gemma Hussey, welcomed as a side effect of the Bill the greater impetus to a very badly needed raising of status and interest in technology and in the technology courses offered by non-university institutions.[84] In the same debate Senator Professor Richard Conroy of the Royal College of Surgeons in Ireland referred to the excessively traditional Irish universities with their heavy emphasis on arts subjects and nowhere near sufficient support or emphasis on science and technology.[85] Senator Noel Mulcahy, who had chaired the Steering Committee in 1966, suggested that more of the available money should go towards technical training rather than to arts faculties, and suggested that the minister might consider differential support for students, presumably to make arts faculties less attractive.[86]

In 1979, speaking on the debate on the National Council for Educational Awards Bill, the Chancellor of the National University of Ireland, Senator T.K. Whitaker, observed that there was probably still in Ireland much too great an emphasis on purely academic education and that there was need to do more to upgrade the status of vocational and technical education.[87] In the same debate Senator Augustine Martin, then a lecturer and subsequently a Professor of English at University College Dublin, referred to the obsession with university education as the only acceptable form of third-level education.[88] Throughout the period, backbenchers of different parties had reiterated these arguments and opinions.[89] By any standards this was a formidable consensus, and by the late 1970s it was not confined to ministers or officials of the Department of Education, nor to populist backbenchers.

Over the period there were relatively few Dáil deputies or senators who offered dissent from the prevailing consensus. The first to raise a query was Dr David Thornley, the Labour Party spokesman on education, as early as 1971. His view was that higher education went through cycles of fashion, and that the current prevailing fashion was the technological, and he warned that one could never be absolutely certain that at any one time a major running-down of one area of teaching and a major expansion of another was wise.[90] Both as a backbencher and as minister, John Wilson was of the view that there was a lack of balance where there was not a liberal arts foundation to technical and technological education.[91] In 1973, in one of his few recorded contributions to a debate on the topic of education, a future Taoiseach, Charles J. Haughey, went against the conventional wisdom in observing that education was not, and should not be, the key to economic growth.[92]

The temptation to attack the perceived academic and arts bias in the universities was not, of course, confined to the Dáil or Senate. The kind of consensus which was expressed in the Houses of the Oireachtas was echoed elsewhere, and during the 1970s there were many attacks on the academic bias and the alleged predomination of the arts and humanities, most notably by the Director of the National Institute for Higher Education, Dr Edward Walsh,[93] and the Director-General of the Confederation of Irish Industry, Liam Connellan.[94]

Conclusion

By the beginning of the academic year 1974-75 the contours of a binary system of higher education were not only evident but appeared to be well-established. Within the previous four years a National Institute for Higher Education, a National College of Physical Education and eight Regional Technical Colleges had opened their doors. A National Council for Educational Awards had been established with responsibility for the maintenance of educational standards at these institutions, and the remit of the Council was broad enough to allow it to assess standards and make awards at a variety of other institutions which did not have organisational or academic links with the two existing universities. A Higher Education Authority had also been established in that period. While its advisory role extended to all aspects of third-level education, its funding and executive functions were confined almost exclusively to the universities.[95] The newer institutions were all funded directly by the Department of Education.

Decisions on the reorganisation of the Irish universities and the provision for higher education in Dublin had been exercising the minds of ministers and officials in the Department of Education for some years and the issues were undoubtedly overdue for resolution. While these issues posed difficult problems, possibly requiring some radical initiatives, it appeared unlikely that they would call into question the desirability of having a binary system. The gradual and relatively uncontroversial evolution of such a binary system was nevertheless abruptly halted on the morning of 16 December 1974.

Notes

1 *Dáil Debates*, vol. 227, col. 753 (15 March 1967).

2 ibid., vol. 227, cols. 2181-2193 (20 April 1967). See also OECD (1969), *Ireland: Review*, pp. 131-138. There has been little detailed study of the merger proposal in the thirty years since it was first mooted. The most useful background accounts are contained in Luce, *The First 400 Years*, pp. 181-198, and McCartney, *UCD*, pp. 314-341.

3 *Commission Summary*, p. 94.

4 *Commission Report*, pp. 891-896.

5 Andrews, C.S. (1982), *Man of No Property*, Cork: Mercier Press, pp. 295-296. The central importance of this issue was emphasised by the Secretary to the Commission, Séamus Ó Cathail, in an interview with the author, December 1987.

6 Interview with James F. Dukes, former Secretary, Higher Education Authority, (Dublin, November 1987).

7 *Dáil Debates*, vol. 180, cols. 939-940 (23 March 1960).

8 ibid., col 970 (23 March 1960).

9 OECD, *Ireland: Review 1969*, pp. 134-135.

10 Andrews, *Man of No Property*, p. 295.

11 O'Connor, *A Troubled Sky*, p. 203.

12 *Dáil Debates*, vol. 232, cols. 783-789 (8 February 1968).

13 J. F. Dukes, interview.

14 HEA, *University Reorganisation*, Appendix II, pp. 77-82.

15 *Dáil Debates*, vol. 236, cols. 1783-1784 (31 October 1968). Also, HEA, *University Reorganisation*, p. 4.
16 ibid.
17 ibid., pp. 83-92.
18 ibid, p. 59.
19 The Irish Federation of University Teachers held many sessions on the matters related to university reorganisation during the period. See, for example, Irish Federation of University Teachers (1974) *University Education in Ireland: Report of a Seminar, November 1973*, Dublin: IFUT.
20 *Irish Times*, 29 April 1970.
21 *Commission Report*, pp. 477-485.
22 *Dáil Debates*, vol. 232, cols. 783-784 (8 February 1968).
23 *Seanad Debates*, vol. 65, col. 604 (20 June 1968).
24 HEA, *University Reorganisation*, p. 77. In the same statement the minister announced the establishment of a Conference of Irish Universities to deal principally with academic problems common to all university institutions.
25 *Dáil Debates*, vol. 236, cols 922-930 (11 July 1968).
26 HEA, *First Report*, pp. 26-27; *Dáil Debates*, vol. 236, cols. 1783-1784 (31 October 1968).
27 *Irish Independent*, editorial, 14 December 1968.
28 *Commission Report*, p. 482.
29 A number of the others were drawn from the business world.
30 *Irish Times*, 19 August 1968. (The hostility openly expressed by faculty members at University College Dublin does not appear to have existed to any similar extent in Trinity College Dublin. This was the view of Professor J.N.R. Grainger, Professor of Zoology and Comparative Anatomy, Trinity College Dublin and a member of the first *ad hoc* Authority, as expressed in an interview with the author, Dublin, December 1987).
31 *Dáil Debates*, vol. 252, col. 1983 (1 April 1971).
32 HEA, *First Report*, p. 27, pp. 54-57.
33 ibid., p. 28.
34 J.F. Dukes, interview.
35 HEA, *First Report*, pp. 10-11.
36 *Irish Times*, 15 April 1970.
37 Higher Education Authority (1970), *Report on Teacher Education*, Dublin: Stationery Office.
38 HEA, *University Reorganisation*.
39 Higher Education Authority, *Report on the Ballymun Project*.
40 HEA, *Teacher Education*, pp. 9-12.
41 ibid., pp. 13-15.
42 *Dáil Debates*, vol. 235, col. 1250 (19 June 1968). Also col. 558 (5 June 1968).
43 ibid., vol. 251, col. 1066 (10 February 1971). Also vol. 252, cols. 1707-1711 (31 March 1971).
44 ibid., vol. 252, col. 1733 (31 March 1971).
45 ibid., vol. 268, col. 549 (24 October 1973).
46 ibid., col. 417 (23 October 1973).
47 *An Muínteoir Náisiúnta*, May 1973.
48 HEA, *Progress Report*, p. 1.

49 *Dáil Debates*, vol. 251, col. 1035 (10 February 1971).
50 ibid., col. 1037.
51 ibid., col. 1144.
52 ibid., vol. 252, col. 302 (3 March 1971).
53 ibid., col. 289.
54 ibid., col. 2110 (1 April 1971).
55 ibid., vol. 254, col. 1519 (15 June 1971).
56 ibid., vol. 253, col. 146 (20 April 1971); vol. 252, col. 265 (3 March 1971); col. 2007 (1 April 1971).
57 J.F. Dukes, interview.
58 HEA, *Progress Report.*
59 J.F. Dukes, interview.
60 HEA, *Progress Report*, pp. 57-61.
61 *Seanad Debates*, vol. 70, col. 765 (30 June 1971).
62 *Dáil Debates*, vol. 252, col. 264 (3 March 1971).
63 ibid., vol. 311, col. 1245 (14 February 1979).
64 OECD, *Training of Technicians*, p. 13.
65 *Dáil Debates*, vol. 268, cols. 535-561 (24 October 1973).
66 O'Connor, *A Troubled Sky*, p. 174.
67 *Commission Report*, pp. 183-188. Also HEA, *A Council for National Awards*, pp. 9-13.
68 *Dáil Debates*, vol. 239, col. 1784 (17 April 1969).
69 HEA, *A Council for National Awards*, p. 9.
70 *Dáil Debates*, vol. 290, cols. 326-334 (28 April 1976).
71 ibid., cols. 140-146 (27 April 1976).
72 ibid., vol. 290, col. 140 (27 April 1976).
73 ibid., col. 329.
74 ibid., vol. 180, col. 1487 (31 March 1960).
75 ibid., cols. 1451-1452.
76 ibid., cols. 1378-1383. Also vol. 181, cols. 311-320 (28 April 1960).
77 ibid., vol. 245, col. 168 (21 April 1970).
78 *Seanad Debates*, vol. 71, col. 1270 (17 November 1971).
79 *Dáil Debates*, vol. 295, col. 1591 (16 February 1977). Deputies McQuillan and Browne were members of the Labour party. Deputies Corry, Leneghan, Tunney and Timmons and Senator Ó Maolain were all members of Fianna Fáil.
80 ibid., vol. 259, cols. 138-142 (22 February 1972); vol. 267, col. 941 (12 July 1973); vol. 268, cols. 976-978 (31 October 1973).
81 ibid., vol. 245, col. 1415 (16 April 1970).
82 *Seanad Debates*, vol. 70, col. 934 (1 July 1971).
83 ibid., vol. 90, col. 271 (22 November 1978).
84 ibid., col. 290.
85 ibid., col. 276.
86 ibid., col. 346 (29 November 1978). At the time he chaired the Steering Committee in 1966-67 Noel Mulcahy (Noel Ó Maolcatha) was a senior management specialist at the Irish Management Institute (IMI). He was subsequently Deputy Director-General of IMI. In the period 1975-76 he was Acting Chairman of the National Council for Educational Awards. He was nominated to the Senate by the Taoiseach, Jack Lynch, in 1977 and remained a

Senator until 1981. In 1983 he was appointed Dean of the College of Engineering and Science at the National Institute for Higher Education, Limerick. He was Vice-President of the University of Limerick from 1991 to 1996.

87 ibid., vol. 93, col. 171 (14 November 1979).

88 ibid., col. 173.

89 *Dáil Debates*, vol. 245, col. 1674 (21 April 1970); vol. 251, cols. 1123, 1129 (10 February 1971); vol. 259, col. 814 (22 February 1972).

90 ibid., vol. 252, col. 262 (3 March 1971); col. 2007 (1 April 1971).

91 ibid, vol. 268, col. 428 (23 October 1973); vol. 313, col. 1576 (26 April 1979).

92 ibid., vol. 268, col. 1039 (31 October 1973).

93 ibid., vol. 256, col. 1179 (4 November 1971); Walsh, E. (1974), 'The University Situation in Ireland Today,' *University Education in Ireland,* (IFUT), pp. 48-51; Walsh, E. (1977), 'Education, Technology and Society,' *STEM*, pp. 19-26; Walsh, E. (1980), 'Science, Technology and Education,' *Ireland in the Year 2000: Proceedings of a Colloquy,* Dublin: An Foras Forbartha, pp. 21-32.

94 Connellan, L. (1980), 'Trends to the Year 2000 – The Industrial Sector,' *Ireland in the Year 2000,* pp. 71-75.

95 The authority's executive functions also extended to the Royal College of Surgeons in Ireland and to the College of Pharmacy.

CHAPTER 7

Binary or Comprehensive?

When the coalition government headed by Liam Cosgrave assumed office in March 1973 the post of Minister for Education was allotted to Richard Burke. He inherited much unfinished business in third-level education. Issues relating to university reorganisation, the future of higher education in Dublin and the statutory arrangements to be made for the National Institute for Higher Education Limerick, and the National Council for Educational Awards were among the most important. That most of these problems were interdependent and had to be tackled simultaneously would not have been a general view.

An unexpected upheaval

No statement by the minister during 1973 and 1974 gave any indication that a radical reorganisation of the structure of higher education was contemplated. For that reason a government announcement of 16 December 1974 came as a major surprise.[1] The statement detailed some of the history of the problem issues of university organisation. It briefly contrasted the advantages and disadvantages of a binary and a comprehensive system of higher education and stated that the government had decided 'to initiate the establishment of the structures necessary to secure a comprehensive system of higher education in Ireland'. Having stated that legislation would be introduced to give effect to this decision, the minister went on to announce eighteen individual proposals.

The proposals or decisions (they were referred to as both in the statement) contained unexpected elements in relation to the universities. The National University of Ireland was to remain, but would only comprise University College Cork and University College Galway. A new university was to be constituted from University College Dublin. St Patrick's College Maynooth had the option of becoming a constituent college of any one of the three universities in the state. The document had finally buried the merger proposals of Donogh O'Malley. It also announced the establishment of a conjoint board to co-ordinate the two Dublin universities, and spelt out the envisaged redistribution of university faculties in Dublin. It proposed the establishment of a conference of Irish universities and provided for the statutory recognition of theology as a university discipline.

Degree powers were to be withdrawn from the National Council for Educational Awards, and it was to be restructured as the Council for Technological Education, which would plan and co-ordinate courses, and validate and award non-degree third-level qualifications in the two NIHEs at Dublin and Limerick, and in the regional technical colleges.

A second National Institute for Higher Education was announced in the document. It was to be established in Dublin and to be a recognised college of one of the Dublin universities, with the capacity to evolve into a constituent college of that university or become an autonomous degree-awarding institution. The Limerick Institute was to become a recognised college of the new truncated National University of Ireland with the same scope for evolution to constituent college or autonomous status. New funding arrangements were announced for many of the institutions. The regional technical colleges were to continue to be funded, through the Vocational Educational Committees, by the Department of Education, but in consultation with the Council for Technological Education.

The government statement ran to ten pages.[2] Given the radical and unexpected nature of the proposed upheaval, it was somewhat surprising that what were expressed as decisions had not been preceded, or accompanied by, some detailed explanation. The minister conceded as much and declared that it was his intention to publish a more detailed statement later. For some time afterwards he declined to elaborate on a number of issues on the grounds that he would prefer to await the production of a comprehensive publication.[3] In the event no such document was ever published and the contents of the statement of 16 December 1974 were to be the expression of what the government hoped to achieve in higher education during its period of office.

Reaction to the statement was almost uniformly negative. There were a small number of exceptions.[4] Ironically in the light of subsequent events, the most notable was the Director of the National Institute for Higher Education Limerick, Dr Edward Walsh. He welcomed the proposals which, if implemented, would tend to reduce the gulf between the sciences and the humanities, encourage student mobility between the traditional systems and lead to a more efficient use of national educational resources. The fact that the government should decide to establish a second NIHE was considered as a tribute to the pioneering work of the Limerick Institute.[5]

The initial lack of enthusiasm and outright opposition must have made it clear from the outset to Mr Burke that his task of introducing a comprehensive system was going to be uphill. Even the normally cautious Higher Education Authority through its chairman, Dr Ó Raifeartaigh, immediately let it be known that it had had 'no part whatsoever in the drawing up of the Minister's proposal'.[6] The Chairman added that HEA had issued its own views through its previous reports and had always thought that these proposals were the best solution to the problem.

The responses from Trinity College, University College Cork and University College Galway were less than welcoming. Trinity College, in particular, felt itself under threat. The provost, Dr F.S.L. Lyons, declared that those portions of the announcement which related to TCD were quite unacceptable.[7] Some months later he outlined in detail the grounds for the College's opposition to the proposals, the general effect of which would be to cut it off from direct contact with the main areas of agricultural, technological and commercial development in the country during the years ahead.[8] The Irish Federation of University Teachers was also critical of the proposals and particularly concerned about their effect on the autonomy of universities.[9]

If the universities were in the main unhappy with the proposals, the third-level sector outside the universities was even more opposed. In spite of Dr Walsh's initial welcome, the Planning Board of NIHE was soon to issue a statement which, while welcoming the broad outlines of the minister's plan, criticised the proposed designation of NIHE as a recognised college of the National University of Ireland. The Board argued that, given the conditions currently applicable to a recognised college in the NUI system, designation would hinder development taking place on the Limerick campus, and would prevent it playing its appropriate part in a comprehensive system. It urged instead that NIHE should be established from the outset as a constituent college of NUI, or alternatively as an autonomous degree-awarding institution.[10] This statement from the Planning Board marked the beginning of what was to become a most acrimonious and unpleasant relationship, and the strongest of many conflicts between the minister and a third-level institution.

Within days of the announcement of the proposals, a statement from the principals and staff of the eight regional technical colleges expressed their concern.[11] It spoke of the development of technical colleges being sacrificed, while the long established vested interests in third-level education were being appeased. The constitution of the replacement for NCEA was strongly criticised as being seriously damaging to applied science and technology. As was to be expected the City of Dublin Vocational Education Committee was unenthusiastic at what had happened its own proposals for the Ballymun complex. The chairman of the Committee, Patrick Donegan, strongly attacked the plans, and warned that the Committee would oppose them as far as possible.[12] Concerted opposition from the City of Dublin VEC did not augur well for the success of Mr Burke's scheme. The Committee chairman, Mr Donegan, was an active and influential member of the Labour Party, and the VEC in the city of Dublin was controlled by Labour and Fine Gael colleagues of the coalition ministers.

The one major body which kept its own counsel in the immediate aftermath of the announcement was the National Council for Educational Awards. The proposals had major implications for its future and its function within higher education. It was losing degree-awarding powers, but instead it was to have planning and co-ordination functions, as well as its validating role in the non-university sector.[13] The Council, having no prior warning of what was to befall it, obtained a meeting with the minister on the day following the announcement. After the meeting the minister was reported to have confirmed that the validation of all NCEA awards would be fully honoured and safeguarded.[14]

The Union of Students in Ireland opposed the proposals from the time of their announcement, and was to be their most vocal critic throughout the following two and a half years. On balance the initial media comment was generally supportive of the minister's proposals, with the *Irish Independent* and the *Evening Herald* being the most favourably disposed.[15] It was clear from the first day that the minister and his colleagues had stirred a hornet's nest and that he was going to have a difficult battle. Most of the established interests in higher education were being confronted. What then were the minister and his government colleagues hoping to achieve and what ideas lay behind this onslaught on the *status quo?*

The argument

The minister's statement set out the conviction that the fundamental problem centred on 'whether to continue and to develop the existing binary system or to initiate the establishment of a fully comprehensive system of higher education'. Even to those working within higher education in Ireland at the time the terms 'binary' and, more particularly, 'comprehensive' system were not an established part of normal vocabulary. To those who had followed educational debates in Britain from the mid-1960s onwards the notion of a binary system would have been familiar. Neither then nor later was the idea of a comprehensive system of higher education to become familiar in Ireland.[16]

The concept of the binary system, which was an administrative rather than an educational construct, was first set out in 1965 by the then UK Secretary of State for Education and Science, Anthony Crosland.[17] In the binary system he identified on the one hand an autonomous sector comprising the universities and the then emergent colleges of advanced technology, and on the other the public sector, comprising the leading technical colleges, colleges of art and colleges of technology. Crosland offered a number of reasons for his preference for a binary policy. The ever-increasing need and demand for vocational, professional and industrially-based courses could not be fully met by the universities. It required a separate sector with a different tradition and outlook. It was desirable also that a substantial part of higher education be under social control and directly responsive to social needs. As mixed communities of full-time and part-time staff and students, public sector colleges were expected to have closer and more direct links with industry, business and the professions, and to be interested in applying knowledge to the solution of problems.

In the speech at Woolwich in 1965 setting out the concept, Crosland added that the government accepted this dual system as fundamentally the right one, with each sector making its own distinctive contribution to the whole. This government infinitely prefered it to the alternative concept of a unitary system, hierarchically arranged on the 'ladder' principle with the universities at the top and other institutions down below. Such a system was be characterised by a continuous rat-race to reach the first or university division, a constant pressure on those below to ape the universities above, and a certain inevitable failure to achieve the diversity in higher education which contemporary society needs.

These sentiments would have had a resonance among those taking decisions on higher education in Ireland in the period prior to 1974. The minister and the government were now committed to abandoning this approach.

The main apologist for the proposed new comprehensive system was the Minister for Industry and Commerce, Justin Keating. He argued that a unitary or comprehensive system was necessary to abolish the 'distinctions between these dirty finger-nail, not quite respectable, technological subjects and other subjects' and to recognise that technology had come of age and was worth its place at the pinnacle of academic life. He wished Ballymun 'to be a college of a university with the same pay, same buildings, same staff-student ratios, same technicians, same playing fields, same society for students mixed-in with other students on a basis of equality, not any sort of second-class institution'. He warned that the binary system perpetuated injustice, inequality, and a division between culture and non-culture. Keating was also prepared to appeal to nationalist sentiments. He observed that OECD had characterised the binary system as uniquely British, and he questioned why any society would wish to emulate the scientific, cultural, technological and educational performance of the United Kingdom.[18]

A second articulate supporter of the proposed comprehensive model was the Minister for Foreign Affairs, Dr Garret FitzGerald. His arguments were somewhat more pragmatic than Keating's. Referring to the claims for university independence, he said that, if they were all met, there would be a proliferation of universities unparalleled in Europe. Ireland, with a university for every 400,000 people, a larger ratio than Britain or even Sweden, would become the laughing stock of Europe. As he saw it, the main problems of higher education were the imbalance between the academic and the technical, the fact that too many students were aspiring to university status and the lack of co-ordination in Dublin. The comprehensive system was designed to solve the problem arising from the lack of mobility between the universities and the other colleges, and to put all the colleges on a par.[19] He argued that to retain the binary system was to contemplate condemning the technological sector to being perpetually under-financed and discriminated against.

It was generally believed that Keating and FitzGerald had been the key figures in the cabinet committee which was responsible for the December 1974 document.[20] Both of them defended the proposals at length in the Dáil, and Keating defended them publicly at other fora. Neither Keating's nor FitzGerald's arguments ever sparked off a public debate. Had they been contained in a White Paper, it is possible that a debate on them might have taken place.

When no comprehensive statement or White Paper followed the December announcement, the terms of reference and the argument, as defined by the minister, became structural and managerial. Mr Burke was taking on the administrators of most of third-level education. Since there was no wider rationale to which to appeal nor any grand vision around which public opinion or the media could be rallied, he was committed to tackling them in the realm of structures and management reorganisation, on the low rather than on the high ground. There had already been seven years of trench warfare between ministers and the two Dublin universities since Mr O'Malley first announced the merger proposals. Now the Cosgrave government was opting for even more elaborate trench warfare on different terrain and with a much larger and angrier group of adversaries.

In the absence of a White Paper the government's rationale was not clearly spelled out. Apart for the interventions of Keating and FitzGerald, the reasoning had to be inferred. It appeared to be implied that the only degree worth having was from a university, and that the technical colleges needed the respectability of the universities.[21] The proposed constitution of the Council for Technological Education suggested that it might be intended that the regional technical colleges should become branches of the two National Institutes for Higher Education. Such would have been a major role change for those colleges. The entire exercise also begged the question of what function the Higher Education Authority was to have within higher education. It had been set up to act *inter alia* as the advisor to government on an area in which the Department of Education had no tradition of policy-making. In this instance, a cabinet sub-committee took it on itself to invent a new policy on higher education and to have it accepted by cabinet. The policy arguably was not that of the Minister for Education. Almost certainly his officials would have had difficulty in speedily drafting a White Paper to articulate such an unfamiliar, and perhaps unpalatable, approach. The minister also had very little machinery to hand to implement the new policy. At the press conference announcing the decision, when questioned about the O'Malley merger proposals, Mr Burke observed that it was always more difficult to implement than to announce.[22] He could scarcely have uttered a more painfully accurate prophecy of what was to be his own fate over the following two years.

Implementing the proposals

The minister was soon on the defensive. The attack in the Dáil began as soon as the House resumed after the Christmas recess.[23] This was to set a pattern whereby the Minister was to be harried on these issues by the opposition for the remainder of his term in office.

While many groups and deputations clamoured for the minister's attention in the opening weeks of 1975, the first issue to which he had to address himself was the future of NCEA. The Council had not conferred any degrees before the abolition of its degree powers was announced. Ironically it was about to have its first degree conferring. In 1970, the year preceding the opening of the National College of Physical Education, Irish students had gone to St Mary's College of Physical Education Twickenham on Irish government scholarships. In summer 1974 NCEA examination board meetings had been held in Twickenham,[24] and it was envisaged that the successful students would be the Council's first graduates.

Apart from the Twickenham graduates, there was a further problem in that the first entrants to the National College of Physical Education were due to graduate in the following summer and, if they were not to receive NCEA degrees, alternative arrangements were required as a matter of extreme urgency. The Department of Education approached one of the university colleges with a view to its conferring the degrees on the students of the National College. The approach was unsuccessful. Accordingly on 18 February 1975 the minister met with the NCEA Council and empowered it to award degrees in physical education to successful NCPE students. He also stated that the government had agreed to empower NCEA to award degrees in respect of degree-level courses which were already under way and which the universities were found not to be in a position to validate. He added that the power to award degrees would remain with the Council until the universities were prepared to undertake such validation.[25]

On 21 March, on the basis of advice from a number of quarters, the minister announced that he was going to allow the Council to retain its name rather than assume the title of Council for Technological Education. Three days later a Bachelor of Arts degree was conferred on four of the students of St Mary's College Twickenham at the NCEA headquarters.[26] This was an inauspicious start for the minister. He was not merely forced to reverse the decision on a new title for NCEA, but was also compelled to allow it to begin to operate as a degree-awarding body, at least for an interim period.

The next problem facing him was the appointment of governing bodies for the two National Institutes. This was not as straightforward a process as might have been expected. Some of those approached to become members of the governing bodies, especially in the case of the new institute in Dublin, were apparently reluctant to agree initially, and the process of selection was unpopular with some of the nominating bodies. It took the Minister almost six months to convene the new governing bodies. Nor did his problems with them end there. The governing body of the Dublin institute put off the election of a chairman at its first meeting on the grounds that the members did not know each other. When they reconvened one month later, the Chairman of the City of Dublin VEC, Patrick Donegan, was elected to the chair.[27] Given that Mr Donegan had been implacably and publicly opposed to the establishment of the Institute from the beginning, this was a further guarantee to the minister that the establishment of the National Institute for Higher Education Dublin would not be a smooth process.

Meanwhile there was taking place in Dublin an initiative which had not been envisaged in the December 1974 proposals, but which was prompted by, and drew its inherent logic from, them. As already noted, Trinity College Dublin had not merely opposed the proposals, but had seen them as having very serious and adverse consequences for it. Of particular concern to the College was the proposal that TCD should have a faculty of engineering science without capital investment.

For about six years previously the College had had an arrangement whereby electrical engineering students at Kevin Street College of Technology, and mechanical and production engineering students at Bolton Street, had been accepted on postgraduate courses at TCD. By the end of 1974 some fifty engineering degree-holders of the two VEC colleges had been admitted as postgraduate students. Given the threat to the future of engineering education at TCD, a closer link with the Dublin

VEC colleges made strategic sense. The City of Dublin VEC had submitted an application for degree recognition for the relevant courses to NCEA. The announcement that the colleges of teacher education were to receive their degrees from the universities seems to have been a factor in giving Dublin VEC second thoughts about pursuing NCEA recognition, and the decisions of December 1974 were apparently seen by the VEC as a way of pursuing alternatives. The VEC chairman, Mr Donegan, wrote to TCD asking the College to provide a short-term solution to its problems. Trinity College moved quickly. By 28 May 1975 it was in a position to advise NCEA of its decision to award degrees for both courses concerned. The provost spoke of the Board of Trinity College regarding the arrangement as a temporary measure, and suggested that ultimately the decision as to how long it would continue would lie with the governing body of the proposed NIHE.[28]

The first conferring of degrees on students of the two VEC colleges took place in December 1975. By then the Irish Management Institute, the Froebel College of Education and the Christian Brothers Teacher Training College had made a formal application for an association with TCD for the purpose of degree awards. The minister indicated at an early stage that he was not opposed to the development and saw it as being of the kind outlined in the government document.[29]

The link between Trinity College and the VEC colleges was opposed by the Union of Students in Ireland. The Fianna Fáil spokesman, John Wilson, was also opposed to the development. He declared that he would approve of TCD sharing facilities and co-operating on research with the colleges of technology, but not on its awarding degrees, which he felt should be done by NCEA.[30] He was to discover in time that, even as Minister for Education, he could not reverse the process.

Problems in Limerick and Galway

While the minister had managed in the short term to defuse potential problems relating to the awarding of degrees to the students of the National College of Physical Education, a much bigger problem was on the horizon in Limerick. The first intake to the National Institute for Higher Education was due to graduate in 1976, and it was clear that decisions on the awarding body could not be left with impunity till the eleventh hour as in the case of NCPE. While the *ad hoc* NCEA and NCPE (which from 1971 to

1976 had no governing body and was administered directly by the Department of Education) might be amenable and co-operative in their dealings with the minister, there was clearly no such guarantee that the same would apply in the case of NIHE. Here the stakes were much higher. Limerick's claim for a university, Mr Burke's near-espousal of that case in October 1973, and the Institute's own ambitions in that regard were the backdrop. Here too was an institution with increasingly strong local roots, which had locked horns with the minister's predecessor, and had shown considerable skill in successfully lining up political and other opposition to unwelcome ministerial interventions.

Given the Planning Board's objections to the government proposals, the minister could not expect to make progress until a governing body had been appointed. Some months after it was installed, NIHE applied to the National University of Ireland for recognised college status.[31] If NIHE's application was grudging, it was also unwelcome to the university colleges, who were themselves in conflict with the minister and objected to having the additional chore of course validation foisted on them without any additional resources being supplied by the minister.[32] Inevitably it was only a matter of time before the students began to mobilise. A week of protest against alleged government silence on the question of the degrees to be awarded to NIHE students was arranged for 4 November 1975, to coincide with the conferring of degrees by NCEA on graduates of the neighbouring National College of Physical Education.[33]

The governing body of NIHE decided to mark the first anniversary of the government's decision with a press release advising it that the recognised college relationship within NUI was not a feasible solution, and that the time-consuming and expensive recognition exercise was unlikely to lead to a solution satisfactory to NIHE. It saw the five degree programmes operating at NIHE as differing significantly in content, structure and aim from those offered at UCC and elsewhere in NUI.[34]

NIHE's forebodings were borne out when a highly critical and controversial UCC report to NUI became available, a situation exacerbated when the report was leaked to a newspaper. The report had referred to its grave concern at the overall level of academic qualifications among NIHE staff, some of whom did not appear to qualify for recognised lecturer status within NUI. It recommended that only some of the courses be recognised by NUI for full degree status, and it was especially critical of the administrative systems degree, while also criticising examinations generally for shallowness in subject treatment and lenient marking. The reaction of the director, Dr Walsh, to the report was angry. He claimed not to be surprised by the UCC report, as NIHE had set out to establish standards different from the traditional universities and based on the requirements of business, industry and employers. He added that NIHE was not set up to look for academic approval from the traditional universities and that, if it had, it would have gone about its business in a different way.[35]

The relationship between NIHE and UCC became most unhappy.[36] Shortly after the leaking of the UCC report the minister met a deputation of TDs and students and told them that it would have to be accepted that degrees at NIHE would be awarded by NUI. In March the Senate of the National University of Ireland declared NIHE a recognised college and made provision for the institution of the degrees of Bachelor of Technology and Bachelor of Commercial Studies which were to be awarded to NIHE students. No provision was made for honours degrees. The NUI Senate also recognised four of the five proposed degree programmes, stipulating additional study in the European Studies programmes, but refusing to approve the administrative science degree.[37]

Mr Burke's problems with the NIHE governing body did not end with formal recognition by NUI. Within weeks he had to issue an ultimatum to it following complaints that the Institute was dragging its heels over the conditions of approval set down by NUI, and was refusing to submit documents as requested by UCC. The governing body, following an emergency meeting, decided to comply with the NUI request. At this point the final year students decided not to complete the NUI matriculation forms and burnt them outside the NUI offices in Dublin. This was followed by a one day strike.[38]

Soon afterwards UCC set up a working party to consider the question of how honours degrees could be awarded to NIHE students. The students eventually furnished matriculation forms to NUI, and NUI degrees were awarded at NIHE in the autumn of 1976, though not conferred for another year. In an attempt to improve relations between NUI and NIHE, responsibility for supervision and validation was transferred from UCC to UCG in the summer of 1976.[39] After over eighteen months of effort and acrimony the minister had finally succeeded in bringing about a shotgun marriage between two very reluctant partners. As will be seen, the marriage did not long survive its consummation.

While NCEA as a body was always most co-operative with the minister, even here he found progress slow. It took the minister until early January 1976 to arrange the membership of the new Council.[40] It had its first meeting on 11 February 1976. Its degree powers had been removed, but it had acquired powers of planning and co-ordination. By the time the minister had come to establish the new NCEA, the main opposition party, Fianna Fáil, had made it a matter of policy that it would restore its degree powers and organised a two-day debate in Dáil Eireann calling on the minister to establish NCEA as the degree-awarding authority in 'third-level non-university education'.[41]

It appears to have been the minister's intention that, having acted as a degree-awarding body for physical education students in 1975, NCEA should award no further degrees. There was one further area of difficulty, a course in hotel and catering management at Galway regional technical college. Under the terms of the minister's statement of 18 February 1975 NCEA was expected to continue its consideration of the degree submission for that course, and it granted degree recognition at its meeting of 15 July 1975. Many of the members of the NCEA Council and some of the colleges associated with it were anxious to see NCEA retain its degree powers. In a memorandum which it submitted to the minister in January 1975 outlining its proposals for the functions of the restructured NCEA, the Council suggested an arrangement whereby joint validation of degrees by the universities and NCEA would be possible. The idea was again mooted by the acting chairman, Noel Ó Maolcatha, at the conferring of students at NCPE in November 1975.[42]

The Galway degree issue lay largely dormant for some months, although raised a number of times in the Dáil. In early June 1976 four students sat the final examinations at the end of their four-year course of study. The legend at the top of at least one of the examination papers indicated that it was part of the final examination for a BA degree in Hotel and Catering Management.[43] The paper did not, of course, indicate by whom the degree would be awarded. It could not do so. Over the summer University College Galway was invited to become involved in consideration of the programme with a view to the awarding of a degree. It was made clear that this was likely to be a protracted process. Eventually NCEA decided to award a diploma to the four students, but the students refused to accept the award at conferring. The principal, Mr J G Corr, referred to their having being recipients of 'naked injustice'.[44] The matter dragged on until Mr Burke's successor, Peter Barry, on 7 March 1977 permitted NCEA to award degrees to the four successful students. The degrees were conferred on 9 May 1977.[45] To what extent Mr Barry's action represented an abandonment of the government's policy on degree awards was never made clear. It was soon to become an academic question, as the coalition government was voted out of office shortly afterwards in the general election of June 1977. Stripping NCEA of its degree powers had not proved as easy as might have been anticipated.

Before being appointed EEC Commissioner in November 1976 Mr Burke had taken some other initiatives in implementation of the government's policy. In October 1976 Dr Daniel O'Hare, Principal of Waterford Regional Technical College, was appointed the first Director of the National Institute for Higher Education Dublin.[46] Almost as his last act as Minister for Education in November 1976, Mr Burke established a Working Party on Higher Education in Dublin, chaired by Dr Tom Walsh, Chairman of NCEA. The main tasks of the seven-member working party were to make proposals for the apportionment of academic activity as between NIHE and the existing City of Dublin VEC colleges, to distribute VEC courses and to make proposals regarding the apportionment of buildings, the transfer of staff and the governing structures of a new VEC institution and the relationship with its NIHE counterpart. The working party reported to the new minister, Peter Barry, within a month in December 1976.[47]

During 1975 and 1976 most of Mr Burke's energies in relation to third-level education were devoted to the myriad problems affecting non-university higher education to which his own government's proposals had given rise. Relatively little time was spent in attempting to bring about the changes envisaged in the university sector. Rationalisation as between UCD and TCD did take place within the faculties of dentistry, pharmacy and veterinary medicine,[48] and in August 1976 the minister announced that UCC, UCG and St Patrick's College, Maynooth, were to become separate universities and that the National University of Ireland was to be dissolved.[49] In so deciding the minister was abandoning some of the main arguments for the entire December 1974 package as expounded by Dr FitzGerald, but Mr Burke's change of mind was very welcome in the three colleges concerned, and signalled the end of an eighteen month period of hostility in the case of both UCC and UCG. Once this decision had been taken, the minister was in a position to consider the question of draft legislation to give effect to the government's plans for a comprehensive (as distinct from a binary) system of higher education. He established a Working Party on Higher Education which had its first meeting in the offices of the Higher Education Authority on 21 September 1976.

The Higher Education Legislation Working Party

In a statement on 23 September 1976 announcing the setting up of a working party the minister spoke of the considerable body of government decisions requiring legislative enactment.[50] To speed the process he had asked the Higher Education Authority to set up with him a joint working party to draft the heads of an education act. The minister chaired the group which consisted of an assistant secretary in the Department of Education, the chairman and secretary of the Higher Education Authority and five individuals from the university colleges.[51] The minister stated that the members of the working party were not there in a representative capacity, but were requested to serve because of their experience in college administration. It was envisaged that the working party's membership could be extended if necessary.

The method chosen by the minister to speed up the drafting process was quite unusual. That the minister resorted to it reflected not so much the undoubted absence of a tradition of legislative activity within his own Department, as the lack of a tradition of policy-making in relation to universities and the absence of any precedents within the Department. The major legislation on universities, the Irish Universities Act 1908 and its associated charters, had pre-dated the founding of the state. Despite its obvious limits the device chosen by the minister was effective, and it produced the heads of a very comprehensive Bill within a few weeks. While the members may not have been there in a representative capacity, the presence of senior university administrators in the group was almost guaranteed to reduce the number of problems the minister might have from the university sector, and from those in universities who feared the potential for state intrusion and encroachment upon university autonomy. On the other hand the absence of any member from the other bodies whose legislative future was under consideration was equally guaranteed to provoke controversy, and it duly did so.[52]

The working party met on ten separate days. It had just two meetings with outside groups, one representing the National Council for Educational Awards and the second the National Institute for Higher Education Limerick. At no stage was there any indication that there would be a widening of the membership. Two of the institutions, Thomond College of Education and NIHE Dublin, had their relevant sections drafted without any consultation.[53]

In the later meetings of the working party it was clear to its members that there might be foundation to the rumours that the minister was shortly to depart as Irish EEC Commissioner in Brussels, and the announcement to that effect of 26 November came as no great surprise. By the time Mr Burke resigned as minister the group had prepared a draft with the heads of the entire Bill as envisaged by the minister. It had one final meeting with Mr Burke's successor, Peter Barry, early in January 1977. A more comprehensive discussion of the draft heads was to have taken place in February 1977, but never occurred. Mr Barry did not abandon the idea of introducing legislation, and in the time-honoured optimism of Irish government ministers in such matters he told the Dáil in May 1977 that the legislation was nearly ready.[54]

The outline of the Bill as drafted by the working party contained eleven sections. Four new universities were to be established – the National University Dublin, the University of Cork, the University of Galway and the University of Maynooth. Some changes to the statutes of Trinity College were envisaged to bring its governing structures into line with the other universities. The heads provided for the appointment of commissioners to make statutes for the new universities, pending the election of their first governing bodies (or Councils as it was intended that they should be called). The commissioners were also to arrange for the winding up of the National University of Ireland. Provision was made for the establishment of a joint Universities Council responsible for setting minimum matriculation requirements and criteria and procedures for the recognition of courses in non-university institutions. Provision was made for the establishment of a Joint Clinical Medical Board of the National University Dublin and Dublin University (Trinity College), for the amendment (unspecified) of the charter of the Royal College of Surgeons in Ireland and for the funding of theology by the Higher Education Authority.

The final four sections dealt with the two National Institutes for Higher Education, the National Council for Educational Awards and Thomond College of Education. The provisions for the non-university colleges were virtually identical to those proposed by the minister. In what was clearly a very contentious political area the members of the working party were prepared to bow to the minister's wishes.[55] It was not their area of competence and, in any case, the minister, or his successor, would have to carry the responsibility of piloting any such legislation through the Oireachtas. The lengthiest discussions took place at the early meetings of the working party and concerned the governing structures of the universities. A number of models were looked at, and charters of British universities drawn up in different periods of the twentieth century were examined. For the most part only British models were examined, for the very simple reason that documentation relating to such arrangements in other countries appeared to have been available neither at HEA nor the Department of Education. Once these matters had been largely agreed the working party made very considerable progress. This was a reflection of the minister's desire to complete the task quickly.

In retrospect Mr Burke's convening of the working party can be viewed as a gallant effort to have some tangible achievement after a gruelling two years of attempting to change the system of higher education radically. Had his Bill been drafted and passed through the Oireachtas in any way recognisably similar to what his working party had drafted, he would indeed have achieved a major restructuring. The reality was that, given the stage at which the group was convened, there was never the remotest prospect of such comprehensive legislation being passed in the lifetime of the Dáil. This would have applied even if Mr Burke had never been appointed commissioner. Had he been minister in the early months of 1977, it is questionable whether draft legislation, as comprehensive as envisaged, could have emerged from the Parliamentary Draftsman's Office before a June election in 1977. The extent to which he appreciated this is unclear.

The long-term effects

Although as a result of the government's proposals parts of the higher education sector went through a period of very considerable turmoil during the period from 1975 to 1977, very little of consequence was achieved and there were few long-term effects. There were in retrospect two major outcomes. The first was that Trinity College allied itself with the City of Dublin Vocational Education Committee (CDVEC) and also entered into an association with a number of other third-level colleges. The second was the establishment of the National Institute for Higher Education Dublin.[56]

It is doubtful if Trinity College would have developed such extensive links with CDVEC, were it not for the threats implied in the Burke proposals. In the long term these threats never materialised, the only faculty which the college lost was veterinary medicine, and it in turn became the only college in Dublin with schools of dentistry and pharmacy. Initially it was thought that the link with CDVEC would not outlive the establishment of NIHE Dublin, because it was assumed that that body would take over the third-level work of the Committee. That did not happen. NIHE was, in time, to develop as an entity totally separate from CDVEC, which in turn continued its degree work in association with Trinity College Dublin. Once it had developed this relationship, the VEC did not look to NCEA for validation of its degree programmes when that body had its degree powers restored.[57] That served to weaken the position of NCEA.

The two years of controversy and uncertainty were to prove damaging to NCEA in the long term. What was attempted in the period under discussion was a radical change of state policy, and NCEA was the cockpit in and through which much of the change was to be mediated. What should have been primarily an academic and a standards body became embroiled in political street-fighting concerning its survival and function. Once it entered that arena NCEA became quite effective at fighting its own political battles, and the decision by the Fianna Fáil government in 1977 to restore its degree powers could have been viewed as a major political coup for NCEA. There was a price. Reversion to the status of a quality assurance institution with few wider political ambitions was not easily achieved after the heady experience of a period of successful political infighting. Over time this was to present NCEA with problems of credibility and acceptability both among its own associated institutions and in the wider world of higher education.

The cabinet sub-committee which was responsible for drawing up the proposals, which eventually emerged on 16 December 1974, was arguably the strongest group of five for such a task that could ever have been drawn from any cabinet in the history of the state. Garret FitzGerald and Justin Keating had years of experience of university teaching, administration and politics, the experience of Conor Cruise O'Brien as an academic spanned three continents, Mark Clinton had been a university administrator before entering politics, and indeed the minister himself was the only member of the group who had never been on a university payroll. How then could they have been responsible for such an apparent fiasco and for an initiative which was destined to sink virtually without trace?[58] There are a number of potential explanations.

First they were in retrospect too ambitious. What was attempted was too radical to be achieved in the life of a single government, especially one which failed to be re-elected. Had the cabinet sub-committee come up with these proposals early in its first year of office, say by the summer of 1973, and had Mr Burke had four years to work on them, it is just possible that he would have seen them on to the statute book. It is interesting to observe that, in spite of the uphill task facing him from January 1975 onwards, by August 1976 Mr Burke had modified the proposals sufficiently to make them broadly acceptable to the universities, and he had also forced many of the more unpalatable aspects on NIHE Limerick, NCEA and the regional technical colleges. Moreover he had the heads of a very comprehensive bill in initial draft form by the time he resigned to become EEC Commissioner. Undoubtedly there would have been aspects of the draft legislation that would have caused difficulty,[59] but the biggest problem would have been getting such a comprehensive bill initially through the Parliamentary Draftsman's Office, and then through both houses of the Oireachtas. Given the late start to the initiative, it would have happened only if the government had been re-elected in 1977.

Secondly the forces ranged against change in the non-university sector were far greater than either the cabinet committee or the minister may have realised. A new set of institutions had come into place in the form of NIHE Limerick, the RTCs and NCEA. They had already put down political roots and had acquired considerable lobbying skills. As already noted, they also had a rationale for their existence. Changing their entire framework from the top down in the fashion attempted was more easily said than done. In addition the ideas that served to underpin the comprehensive approach were not ones to which the new institutions were naturally responsive. The comprehensive approach gave a prominence to university values, but these key institutions had recently been established to perform functions which it was believed that universities could not be expected to undertake. The Burke proposals served to suggest that a university degree was the only kind worth having. Although there was little or no explicit theory underpinning its development, there was already *de facto* a binary system in operation. Overturning it from above in the Irish political context would always be difficult, and so it proved.

Subsequent events were to show that those who were sceptical of the long-term viability of the binary approach were justified. It proved to be quite a fragile concept when attacked from within, as NIHE Limerick was to demonstrate a decade later. The Limerick institute was eventually to persuade a Fianna Fáil administration that a university degree and university status were the only kind worth having. In the mid-1970s this was an idea whose time had not yet come.

Notes

1 The author worked at the time with the Higher Education Authority and can recall that the contents of the announcement came as a surprise to both the Authority and its secretariat.

2 Government Information Service (1974), *Statement by the Minister for Education, Mr Richard Burke TD when announcing on Monday December 16, 1974, the Government Proposals in relation to Higher Education.*

3 *Irish Times*, 13 January 1975.

4 A statement from UCD welcomed the decision to grant independence to the college. The Executive Committee of St Patrick's College Maynooth welcomed the initiation of a comprehensive system of higher education and the proposal to make statutory provision for theology as a university discipline. There was also a qualified expression of support from the Principal of Sligo Regional Technical College, Dr Con Power, and a welcome in principle from the standing committee of the Association of Vocational Education Colleges.

5 *Irish Times*, 17 December 1974, 18 December 1974.

6 ibid., 18 December 1974.

7 ibid., 17 December 1974. TCD was not, of course, alone in the university sector in its opposition. The governing body of UCC, while welcoming the retention of the Cork Dental School and the recognition granted to theology, had great reservations about the proposals. A statement from UCG indicated its disappointment, similar to that of UCC, at not being established as an independent university.

8 ibid., 14 March 1975.

9 ibid., 23 December 1974, 25 January 1975.

10 *Irish Press*, 27 January 1975.

11 *Irish Independent*, 19 December 1974.

12 ibid., 22 December 1974.

13 The way in which many NCEA Council members and most of its staff learnt of the government proposals has a place in educational folklore. It appears that,

during a conference on an aspect of curriculum development organised by NCEA at a Dublin hotel, a principal of a regional technical college arrived with an early edition of an evening newspaper and proclaimed that 'ye are all abolished'!

14 *Irish Times*, 18 December 1974.

15 For a survey on how the media handled the announcement, see *Education Times*, 26 December 1974.

16 The most useful background on the development of comprehensive universities is to be found in Teichler, U (1988), *Changing Patterns of the Higher Education System: The Experience of Three Decades*, London: Jessica Kingsley Publications, pp. 38-43. Also Neusel, A. and Teichler, U. (1983) 'Comprehensive Universities – History, Implementation, Process and Prospects' in H. Hermanns, U. Teichler and H. Wasser (eds.), *The Compleat University: Break from Tradition in Germany, Sweden and the USA*, Cambridge, Mass: Schenkman Publishing Company Inc., pp. 175-196.

17 The text of Crosland's speech is reproduced in Pratt. J. and Burgess. T. (1974), *The Polytechnics: A Report,* London: Pitman Publishing, pp. 203-207. The word 'binary' to describe the system was first used, not by Crosland, but by his predecessor, Sir Edward Boyle.

18 *Dáil Debates*, vol. 278, cols. 331-336 (12 February 1975); vol. 288, cols. 141-142 (17 February 1976).

19 ibid., vol. 278, cols. 343-350, (12 February 1975). See also University College Cork Press Release (1975), *An Analysis of the Dáil Eireann Debate on Third Level Education (February 1975) – Part 1: Some Statements by Dr. Garret FitzGerald.*

20 *Irish Independent*, 25 January 1975. Also *Dáil Debates*, vol. 288, col. 127 (17 February 1976). Keating himself confirmed that he was a member of the cabinet sub-committee which removed degree powers from NCEA. See *Seanad Debates*, vol. 94, col. 1466 (26 June 1980). Dr. FitzGerald appears to have played the major part in producing the detail of the December 1974 proposals (private information). See also FitzGerald, G. (1991), *All in a Life: An Autobiography*, Dublin: Gill and Macmillan, p. 306.

21 *Irish Times*, 14 January 1975.

22 *Education Times*, 19 December 1974.

23 *Dáil Debates,* vol. 277, cols. 715-727 (22 January 1975); vol. 278, cols. 71-103 (11 February 1975); cols. 321-358 (12 February 1975).

24 NCEA, *Second Report*, p. 50; NCEA, *Third Annual Report*, p. 17.

25 *Dáil Debates*. vol. 279, col. 2000 (17 April 1975); vol. 280, col. 785 (30 April 1975). See also *Irish Press*, 19 February 1975. The approach appears to have been made to University College Cork.

26 NCEA, *Third Annual Report*, p. 54.

27 National Institute for Higher Education Dublin, *Report of the Governing Body 1975-78*, p. 1; *Education Times*, 31 July 1975; *Irish Independent*, 19 December 1974, 13 March 1975; *Irish Times*, 7 February 1975; *Irish Press*, 11 March 1975.

28 *Irish Times*, 9 June 1975. NCEA, *Third Annual Report*, p. 55. A joint partnership agreement between TCD and the City of Dublin Vocational Educational Committee was published in April 1976 (Luce, *The First 400 Years*, p. 194). A full outline of the agreement and a discussion of its subsequent history is to be

found in Duff, Hegarty and Hussey, pp. 72-83.

29 *Irish Times*, 9 June 1975, 24 November 1975, 12 December 1975. *Evening Herald*, 1 December 1975.

30 *Irish Times*, 31 May 1975, 6 December 1975, 9 February 1976.

31 *Irish Independent*, 28 September 1975.

32 The point was made strongly by Dr Donal McCarthy, President, University College Cork, (*Irish Times*, 29 October 1975).

33 *Limerick Leader*, 5 November 1975.

34 NIHE Limerick, *Press Release*, 15 December 1975. While detailed evaluation of the degree programmes at NIHE was being conducted by UCC personnel, UCC itself was involved in discussions with UCG which resulted in a joint memorandum recommending full independent status for both the Cork and Galway colleges, with NIHE enjoying associate status of an independent Galway or Cork university.

35 *Irish Independent,* 18 February 1976. *Evening Herald*, 18 February 1976. Even worse was to follow some weeks later when a leaked NCEA assessors' report recommended the withholding of approval for the European Studies diploma and indicated unhappiness with the administrative systems diploma also. See *Sunday Independent,* 11 April 1976.

36 A UCC lecturer, who was involved in the evaluation and assessment process during this period, described to the author with some seriousness sitting in the NIHE staff canteen and feeling akin to a German officer in occupied Poland.

37 *Irish Times*, 26 February 1976, 12 March 1976.

38 *Sunday Independent*, 4 April 1976; *Irish Times*, 6 April 1976, 9 April 1976, 14 April 1976.

39 *Irish Press*, 14 May 1976; *Irish Times*, 4 August 1976.

40 *Irish Independent*, 14 January 1976. Although the term of office of the first Council expired on 15 February 1975, the minister in addressing it on that day requested the members to remain in office until their successors had been appointed. At around the same time the first chairman, J. C. Nagle, accepted an invitation to act as chairman of an EEC working party, and accordingly NCEA elected Noel Ó Maolcatha as acting chairman during his absence. Mr Ó Maolcatha continued in this capacity after Mr Nagle's resignation in July 1975.

41 *Dáil Debates*, vol. 288, cols. 125-157 (17 February 1976); cols. 334-366 (18 February 1976).

42 NCEA, *Third Annual Report*, p. 55; *Education Times*, 6 November 1975.

43 *Dáil Debates*, vol. 288, col. 130 (17 February 1976); vol. 290, col. 1298 (13 May 1976); vol. 293, col. 1161 (4 November 1976); vol. 294, col. 173 (17 November 1976).

44 *Irish Press*, 16 November 1976.

45 NCEA, *Fifth Annual Report*, p. 37. Richard Burke at this stage had resigned to take up the position of Irish EEC Commissioner.

46 *Irish Independent*, 8 October 1976.

47 *Irish Times*, 26 November 1976; *Dáil Debates*, vol. 298, col. 271 (24 March 1977); NCEA, *Fifth Annual Report*, p. 8.

48 HEA, *General Report 1974-1984*, pp. 66-67.

49 *Irish Press*, 2 August 1976.

50 *Dáil Debates*, vol. 293, col. 1159 (4 November 1976).

51 The working party was chaired by the minister. The members were Liam Ó Laidhin, Assistant Secretary, Department of Education, Seán Ó Conchobhair, Chairman, Higher Education Authority, James F Dukes, Secretary, Higher Education Authority, Professor Ian Howie, Vice-Provost, Trinity College Dublin, Rev Professor Enda McDonagh, Professor of Moral Theology, St Patrick's College Maynooth, Joseph P. McHale, Secretary-Bursar, UCD, Seamus Ó Cathail, Academic Secretary, UCG, and Professor Tadhg Ó Ciardha, Registrar, UCC. The meetings were also attended by the principal officer in charge of higher education in the Department of Education, Micheál Ó hOdhráin, and the author, who acted as recording secretary for the group.

52 *Dáil Debates*, vol. 293, col. 1159 (4 November 1976); vol. 294, col. 31 (16 November 1976).

53 Personal recollection of the author.

54 *Dáil Debates*, vol. 299, col. 645 (11 May 1977). Mr Barry also indicated on this occasion that, while the original intention was to have a comprehensive higher education Bill, he was toying with the idea of bringing in legislation for NCEA and the NIHEs separately.

55 A number of the proposals would have been very controversial had they ever appeared in a published Bill. For example, the draft heads made no provision for any direct representation on NCEA of any of the VECs, VEC colleges or Regional Technical Colleges, although such colleges accounted for the vast bulk of students likely to be recipients of the Council's awards. At one level, of course, this was merely an implementation of the spirit of the December 1974 proposals.

56 There were other long-term effects within individual universities. For example, the December 1974 decision effectively safeguarded the future of the Cork Dental Hospital.

57 By the end of 1977, degree awards were available to VEC students in architecture, construction economics, applied science, advanced business studies, advanced marketing and hotel and catering management. Human nutrition and dietetics followed in 1982, building services in 1983, environmental health in 1984 and music education in 1985. Medical laboratory science and management law followed subsequently. By 1989 over 500 DIT students per annum were being conferred from these courses. Luce refers to this as a type of 'merger' very different from that originally envisaged. (Luce, *The First 400 Years*, p. 195).

58 Dr FitzGerald concluded jokingly in his autobiography that 'three academics were perhaps too many'. FitzGerald, *All in a Life*, p. 306.

59 For example, the absence of VEC representation on the NCEA Council.

CHAPTER 8

1977-1980
A Period of Consolidation

The period from July 1977 to December 1980 can be judged in retrospect to have been the heyday of the binary system. That system received statutory backing, there was significant growth in student numbers and course development, major financial support came through the European Social Fund, and in 1980 the state's first White Paper on Education gave conceptual support to the activities of the previous decade.

The status of NCEA

Within a month of coming into office in July 1977 the new Fianna Fáil cabinet decided to restore degree powers to the National Council for Educational Awards.[1] In the following November the Minister for Education, John Wilson, announced that NCEA would be the degree-awarding authority for students successfully completing degree-level courses in the National Institutes for Higher Education, Thomond College of Education and the regional technical colleges.[2] Both NIHE Limerick and Thomond College of Education were already recognised colleges of the National University of Ireland. At its meeting of December 1977 the Senate of the National University of Ireland withdrew the recognition given to the two colleges in the previous year.[3] At its meeting of December 1977 NCEA decided to award degrees to the 1978 graduating class at both NIHE and Thomond College on the basis of the recognition already accorded to the two colleges by NUI.[4] Subsequently the Council decided to grant its awards on the basis of this recognition to all students already enrolled before November 1977.[5] The return to NCEA validation for the Limerick colleges was to be slow, if relatively smooth. The process of validation and evaluation which commenced in 1977-78 only began to apply with the graduate group of 1981.

Restoring the degree powers of NCEA was a priority with the government. By February 1978 a draft memorandum had been prepared for the government containing the heads of a bill for the statutory establishment of the Council. Both in content and in substance the heads were significantly different from those devised by the 1976 working party chaired by Richard Burke, and it would seem that the February 1978 document owed very little to that group.[6] The contents of the draft memorandum received wide, though informal, circulation among interested bodies during 1978 and further significant changes had been made by the time the draft legislation appeared for its first reading in the Dáil in November 1978. The restoration of degree powers to NCEA represented a very real political coup for some of those most closely associated with the Council. They had lobbied unsuccessfully for the retention of these powers during Mr Burke's term of office. While profoundly disagreeing with what he and his colleagues were planning, they had succeeded in avoiding being at odds with him publicly,[7] unlike the chief officers and the governing bodies of many of the other institutions of higher education. The question of degree powers for NCEA had been kept on the political agenda, and the Fianna Fáil opposition adopted the restoration of these powers as a policy it would implement, if and when it was returned to government. It duly delivered on this.

The members of the Council appointed by Mr Burke in 1976 remained in office until July 1980 and were largely in favour of the Council's having its degree powers restored.[8] There was no similar enthusiasm among them for preserving the planning and co-ordination role which Mr Burke had given to NCEA instead of its degree powers, and with the departure of the coalition government in 1977, the idea of substantial planning and co-ordination powers for NCEA was allowed to die.

While it was not to be afforded any significant role in planning and co-ordination by the Fianna Fáil government, NCEA was envisaged as the national awards body for virtually all of higher education outside the universities. There were some exceptions. No effort was made to reverse the *fait accompli* of the association of the colleges of teacher education with the universities.[9] Relationships which individual colleges had established, or begun to establish, with the universities arising out of the policy of the coalition government were not always reversed without difficulty. A case in point was that of the National College of Art and Design.

The College had been set up by statute in 1971 at the end of a tempestuous period, when it had come to be recognised increasingly that its status as an integral part of the Department of

Education was quite inappropriate.[10] With the appointment of a director, Jonah Jones, in 1974 the College began a period of growth. The aim of the director was to secure the same recognition, grants, mobility and postgraduate facilities as students elsewhere, and accordingly obtaining degree recognition was seen by him as a priority. With the withdrawal of degree powers from NCEA he recommended the college board to enter into an agreement with Trinity College Dublin. By late 1977 agreement had been reached.[11] Immediately following upon the announcement that NCEA would be the degree-awarding body for NIHE and Thomond College of Education, the minister was asked about the discussions between the College and TCD concerning validation. He responded that the question of degree awards in the case of the National College of Art and Design had yet to be determined.[12]

In January 1978 the board of the College decided to submit two courses to Trinity College Dublin, while the minister meanwhile made it clear that NCEA was the body which he would wish to see awarding degrees at the College.[13] He subsequently instructed the College to submit its degrees to NCEA.[14] Because the minister appointed the board, he was in a strong position with the National College of Art and Design. Indeed he was to make his displeasure at the College's resistance very clear subsequently. When the National Council for Educational Awards Bill came to be circulated in November 1978, the College was named as one of the national institutions to which the legislation would apply but, unlike other institutions so named, it did not have the power to nominate a member of the Council.[15] The College lobbied strongly to have such power and its case was taken up by the opposition.[16] Representation was conceded by the minister by the time the Bill reached its committee stage.[17]

If NCAD was unable to withstand ministerial pressure to come under the NCEA umbrella, the wishes of the minister could not prevail in all cases. An example of the limits to ministerial power was to be provided by the London-based and apparently inconsequential Institute of Medical Laboratory Sciences (IMLS). Even after the formation of the first *ad hoc* NCEA, awards to those studying to become medical laboratory technicians continued to be made by the Irish National Committee for Certificates and Diplomas in Medical Laboratory Sciences. This committee was administered by the Department of Education. In 1976 the then minister, Mr Burke, asked HEA for its advice on the report of a sub-committee on course restructuring in medical laboratory science. A joint committee of HEA and NCEA was set up to consider the report's proposals. It first met in December 1976 and reported in May 1977.[18] The committee recommended that awards in medical laboratory sciences should be incorporated into the NCEA national scheme, and that certificate and diploma courses should be restructured.[19]

In October 1977 the minister decided that NCEA would henceforth be the sole validating authority for medical laboratory sciences.[20] NCEA established a medical laboratory science committee which would report to its Board of Science and Paramedical Studies and take responsibility for awards to be made in 1978 and thereafter. External examiners were appointed early in 1978 and, unusually for it, NCEA decided to continue with the practice of having nationally-set examinations for medical laboratory science for 1978 and 1979, pending the validation of courses at the College of Technology, Kevin Street and the RTCs at Cork and Galway.[21] NCEA held discussions with the Department of Health on a number of issues arising from the design of the courses. Discussions were also commenced with the Institute of Medical Laboratory Sciences with a view to obtaining exemptions for NCEA award-holders from the academic requirements for appropriate grades of membership of the Institute. These grades directly influenced career and salary levels of medical laboratory technologists within the health service.

For a variety of reasons, among them the limited level of involvement which NCEA would concede to IMLS on NCEA's Board of Studies and assessment panels, the Institute refused to make any concessions towards granting exemptions to NCEA students. It withdrew recognition from the Kevin Street course as soon as it was transferred to NCEA for validation. Relations between the Institute and NCEA were never cordial, and reached a low ebb when the Chairman of NCEA, Dr Tom Walsh, played the green card at an NCEA press conference and spoke of the significance of the transfer of validation to NCEA and the importance of a sovereign state making its own awards and not being dependent on any external institution.[22] Further discussions between NCEA and IMLS got nowhere. Certificate and diploma awards were made in Kevin Street, Cork and Galway in 1978.[23] Certificate awards were made in Cork RTC in 1979. It was suggested to the minister, John Wilson, in the Dáil in May 1979 by a Cork deputy, Richard Barry, that he had permitted the Dublin

Institute of Technology to negotiate a separate agreement for recognition of its medical laboratory science examinations with IMLS outside NCEA, while denying similar permission to the RTCs at Cork and Galway. The minister, although he referred to ongoing discussion, did not deny the suggestion.[24]

The year 1979 saw the end of the road for NCEA as the awards body in medical laboratory science, and after a six-year hiatus the question of awards in medical laboratory sciences was to come back for further review to the joint committee of HEA and NCEA in 1983.[25] The Department continued to make the awards all through the following decade. A small British-based professional body with a significant trade union function had been able to defy the minister and force him to retain validating functions he wished to jettison. The IMLS battle was not however a 'stand-alone' affair, and the key to it lay in the fact that hitherto the only course recognised by the Institute was at a college of the City of Dublin Vocational Education Committee. The IMLS affair was a forerunner of a much larger battle in relation to the validating role of NCEA.

The City of Dublin Vocational Education Committee and the Dublin Institute of Technology

In March 1978 the minister, John Wilson, indicated that it was his policy that NCEA should be responsible for the award of degrees, diplomas and certificates in all non-university areas.[26] The one major body with whom he did not succeed in implementing that policy was the City of Dublin Vocational Education Committee. That Committee had an ambivalent relationship with NCEA almost from the time of the formation of the Council. By 1977 only two of the six third-level colleges of the VEC, the College of Technology, Bolton Street, and the Dublin College of Catering, Cathal Brugha Street, dealt with NCEA for the purposes of course validation and had students who were in receipt of NCEA awards at the completion of their courses. Even these relationships had their problems and in October 1977 the VEC was in disagreement with the Council on the question of the appointment of extern examiners, with the Committee (through its Chairman, Patrick Donegan) apparently refusing to accept that NCEA had powers to appoint examiners for the VEC colleges.[27]

If the Committee was ambivalent towards NCEA, it was positively hostile to the proposal to establish a National Institute for Higher Education at Ballymun, which at that time was still envisaged as absorbing all of the existing third-level work of the Committee. The Committee's response to the perceived threat to both the autonomy, and indeed the existence, of its third-level activities was to attempt to build on the links which it had established with Trinity College Dublin for the purposes of degree awards. A joint liaison council, which had been established between the two bodies, produced an elaborate scheme which included proposals for the design and teaching of joint courses, the sharing of staff appointments and interchange of teaching duties, the shared use of premises and equipment, and co-operation in library facilities, computers and in careers and appointment services.[28] When the proposal came before the College Council at Trinity College, consideration of it was deferred.[29]

As it became clear that there would be no speedy solution provided by Trinity College, the City of Dublin Vocational Education Committee decided to rely on its own resources. In 1974 the Committee had produced a plan to merge its higher education colleges into a unified institution with a twenty-five member governing body.[30] There were elaborate arrangements for voting and non-voting members and it was suggested that the entity would in the long term come to have a high degree of autonomy. At its meeting of 25 May 1978 the Committee made an order establishing the Dublin Institute of Technology (DIT), the order to come into effect on 1 September 1978.[31] The governing body of the Institute was to be one of the Committee's special sub-committees. An academic council was established to monitor and co-ordinate the academic activities of the Institute, including examinations and other assessments, and to organise boards of studies for the assessment and validation of courses.[32] The principal of the College of Technology, Kevin Street, Hugh de Lacy, was appointed the first Director of the Institute.

The establishment of DIT was seen by some as a further attempt to put pressure on the Minister of Education with regard to the decisions on NIHE Dublin. On paper at least it was an attempt to give an academic coherence to the Committee's third-level activity that would have some kind of parallel to what both NCEA and NIHE Dublin could offer. It came at a time when the minister and the Committee were already playing a cat-and-mouse game. Shortly before the announcement that DIT was being established, the minister had circulated the draft NCEA Bill. The one significant omission from the draft heads was any reference to the Dublin VEC colleges. On the other hand NIHE Dublin figured prominently in the draft Bill. When the Bill itself came to be published in November 1978, no reference was made to DIT or its constituent colleges.

Both of the main Dáil opposition speakers attempted to explore the mind of the minister with regard to DIT and City of Dublin VEC, and the relationship of both to NCEA. In his first contribution to the debate on the NCEA bill in 1978 the Fine Gael spokesman, Edward Collins, observed that there was no explicit statement in the bill that NCEA would have the sole right to award degrees, diplomas and certificates in colleges with which it was associated, and that there was no limitation on the right of a college to seek recognition for its courses from one of the universities.[33] This was, of course, central to the issue of whether DIT colleges could continue their relationship with Trinity College, and Mr Collins asked for a ministerial statement on the matter. When the debate was resumed in February 1979, Mr Collins suggested that the minister had lacked the courage to sort out the Dublin question for the long term and referred to the obvious friction between the Committee and the minister.[34] Deputy John Horgan, Labour Party spokesman, referred to the Dublin problem as having two components, the fact that the VEC colleges were refusing to submit courses to NCEA in all but a few cases, and that some of the institutions were submitting courses to a university for validation. His view was that it was impossible for the minister, within currently accepted definitions of university autonomy, to prevent any university from recognising any course it chose, whether or not it was submitted by an institution designated under the NCEA Bill.[35] He suggested that the minister had the power to hinder the Committee/university relationship by refusing to recognise the courses for grant purposes.

The minister did not address the issue of the Dublin colleges until under question at the Committee Stage of the Bill in April 1979. As Deputy Collins had observed, relations between himself and the City of Dublin VEC were indeed poor.[36] There were two main bones of contention between the minister and the Committee in relation to third-level education. One, to be examined shortly, related to a decision to proceed with the National Institute for Higher Education in Ballymun. The second referred to the NCEA Bill and the minister's expressed desire that the Council should be the awards body for all non-university education. It was already clear that the Committee was unenthusiastic about the Bill. The Committee chairman, Mr Donegan, had taken advantage of a conferring ceremony at the College of Technology, Bolton Street, to criticise it. He was particularly critical of NCEA's involvement in examinations and its advisory powers with regard to the financing of courses, and he launched a general attack on the foisting of external interference on colleges which wished to exercise academic responsibility and which had already demonstrated appropriate competence.[37]

When the minister eventually came to be explicit about the position of the Dublin colleges under the NCEA Bill, it emerged that it was his intention that there would be no interference with existing colleges, that there was nothing in the bill to prevent the colleges continuing to have recognition from universities, or for a designated college having its courses validated by a body other than NCEA.[38] The point had been conceded. The minister was not in a position to compel the Dublin colleges to submit their courses to NCEA and he was not going to attempt to do so. The minister did include the individual colleges of the Dublin Institute of Technology (but significantly not the Institute itself) among those colleges to which the NCEA Act applied when he came to make a designation order in establishing the Council in 1980.[39] Effectively the Act provided a facility for colleges to submit courses to NCEA if they so chose, but the minister did not attempt to prevent the VEC from dealing with Trinity College.

For NCEA this was something of a setback because there was now a precedent which others could follow. The Dublin Institute of Technology and its individual colleges took care to ensure that, where NCEA awards were received by students, the existence of Institute or VEC awards was not lost sight of. At each conferring involving NCEA, students went to the rostrum twice, first to receive an Institute award and then to receive the national certificate or diploma from an NCEA representative. The symbolic victory and the degree of independence achieved by the Committee and the Institute was not allowed to be forgotten. The significance of all this was doubtless lost on most students as they made two trips to the rostrum on conferring day. As far as NCEA was concerned, the Committee's victory was to have effects that were to prove more than symbolic in the long term.

The National Council for Educational Awards Act

Almost eight years elapsed between the initial establishment of NCEA and the passing of the National Council for Educational

Awards Act 1979 through the houses of the Oireachtas. During that time the Council had two *ad hoc* incarnations, and the eventual parameters within which it was required to operate were significantly different from both its previous remits. Under the Act it had the general function of promoting, co-ordinating and developing technical, industrial, scientific, technological and commercial education, and education in art and design, provided outside the universities, whether professional, vocational or technical, and it also had a function in encouraging and promoting liberal education.[40] It was to give effect to these responsibilities through the approval of courses in designated non-university institutions and the granting and conferring of degrees, diplomas, certificates and other educational awards. In so doing it had to be satisfied that the standards of courses of study and examinations corresponded to, or were analogous to, any relevant standards for the time being in force in universities.[41] The Council was composed of a chairman, director and twenty-three members. Specific provisions were made for the appointment of members recommended by the NIHEs, Thomond College of Education, the National College of Art and Design, the universities, and staff and students of institutions to which the Act applied. Nine of the twenty-three were nominated by the government on the recommendation of the Minister for Education. While the general tenor of the Act was closer to the remit of the first *ad hoc* NCEA than the second, there was one particularly important difference. The first *ad hoc* Council could consider submissions from literally any third-level institution that approached it. The Act only applied to those colleges that were named in the Act or designated by the minister.[42]

The Bill and the Act made it clear that NCEA no longer held any function in planning. It was left with two minor legacies in this area. It had, for the purpose of promoting awards, the ability to co-ordinate any two or more courses of study in designated institutions, and it could advise the minister through the Higher Education Authority in relation to the cost of providing, financing or modifying a course of study.[43] This was a tiny role compared to the potential for involvement in resource allocation contained in the Burke terms of reference. Even these limited roles drew opposition and adverse comment from both Edward Collins and John Horgan, the opposition education spokesmen, during the committee stage of the debate.[44] The other principal areas of concern for the opposition were the facility in the Bill which allowed the Council to set examinations,[45] and what were seen as excessive powers given to the director under the Act.[46]

A body such as NCEA was always going to have to cope with many centrifugal forces. This was the inevitable outcome of having to deal with institutions which did not necessarily see NCEA's interests as coterminous with theirs. In that context the actual composition of the Council was crucially important and, as has already been indicated, the Council was segmented into various representational groups with ten of the twenty-five members nominated directly by the Minister for Education, who, in making these nominations, had to take into account the extent to which industry, agriculture, fisheries, commerce, any of the professions, and the management, staff and students of institutions to which the Act applied, needed representation on the Council.[47] The minister himself amended the Bill to allow specific representation from the National College of Art and Design. Deputy Collins was of the view that the representation of three from the DIT and RTC sector was unfair and inadequate, and attempted to improve that shortfall.[48]

It was never going to be possible to satisfy all the potential constituencies. A crucial question was the extent to which the Council was meant to be representational. In introducing the second stage of the Bill Mr Wilson had stated that the allegiance of the members of the Council was to the Council, and that they were not there to promote the particular demands of their nominating institutions.[49] Nevertheless, as Deputy Horgan pointed out, he was attempting to have it both ways, because he had elsewhere indicated that his concern was that the provisions of the Bill would make for a well-balanced and competent council representative of the main areas of professional and academic activities involved.[50]

As Horgan pointed out, this was significantly different from how this issue had been handled when setting up the Higher Education Authority. The terms of reference of the *ad hoc* HEA envisaged that, even where appointees were staff members of colleges under the purview of the Authority, they did not represent the institutions from which they came and were so instructed by the minister of the day in his inaugural statement. The Act establishing the Authority stipulated that 'the members of an tÚdarás shall have a chairman and not more than eighteen ordinary members of whom at least seven shall be academic members and at least seven shall be other than academic members'.[51] It will be recalled that the Commission on Higher Education, in recommending the establishment of a permanent Commission for Higher Education, had recommended that none of its nine members be drawn from any of the institutions which came within its scope.[52] The higher education system had come a long way from such political idealism and detachment in the twelve years since that recommendation had been published.

What Mr Wilson was dealing with was a highly politicised system with some very sophisticated lobbying groups. Those working with or for the National Council for Educational Awards, both in its *ad hoc* and its statutory incarnations, realised quickly that they were operating in a highly political environment. That is not to deny that there was a great deal of solid achievement in the areas of quality assurance, course and curriculum development, detailed course evaluation and the establishment and acceptance of high professional standards in most areas coming within the Council's purview. Nevertheless the representational principle inherent in the constitution of all of the three models (including the statutory model) of NCEA's governing council ensured that potential conflicts of interest were never far from the surface of its deliberations. NCEA's approach to handling this problem at an early stage in its statutory existence eventually went a considerable way to determining how long it would have a central role as the cement of a binary system.

The Act required the Council to be satisfied that the standard, in general, of courses of study and examinations in institutions to which the Act applied should correspond with, or be analogous to, any relevant standards for the time being in force in universities. Section 9 of the Act permitted the Council to establish boards of studies to perform some of its functions. The boards of studies in making recommendations in relation to the standard required or proposed for admission to a course, or for the conferring, granting or giving of a degree, diploma, certificate or other educational award, were required to have regard to any corresponding standard required by a university in the state and not to recommend a lower standard.[53]

Given the attitude towards universities displayed at various times in the previous decade by many of those associated with the new institutions, it was to be expected that there would be some dissatisfaction with this latter provision. This was given expression in the Dáil by Edward Collins who made three different attempts to have these references changed. His argument was that many of the courses in the technological colleges had no university parallels, and that most of them related to the 'technological professions' and that comparability with standards in universities was out of place in the Bill.[54] Deputy Horgan felt that the references to university standards flew in the face of everything that the minister was trying to do with the Bill.[55] His suggestion was that the Bill refer to standards in force in the discipline or to internationally applicable standards. The minister, John Wilson, appealed *inter alia* to the fact that there was a similar reference in the charter of NCEA's kindred UK body, the Council for National Academic Awards, and stated that the whole purpose of referring to university standards was to indicate that what the Council was offering (and what the legislature wanted) was not a second class award, but one equal to that of a university. It did not mean importing a 'university ethos' into the colleges.[56] The use of the word university, in relation to standards, was a reference to something which was a known standard of excellence in our society.[57] The problem, which was, of course, to rear its head sooner than might have been expected in 1979, was that if all the activity in an institution was of university standard, why should it not be called a university?

Both the Bill and the debate on the Act, particularly in the Dáil, went a considerable way to clarifying the likely contours of the binary system, the circumscribed role which NCEA would have within it, and the huge area of discretion which would remain with the minister and the Department of Education. Deputy Horgan observed that there was no specific reference to third-level institutions and third-level education as such, and he thought that the Bill might be deemed to be flexible enough to allow NCEA to extend its activities downwards into second level.[58] Deputy Collins returned a number of times to the desirability of giving NCEA a role in apprenticeship education.[59] Minister Wilson made it clear that 'where we have technical education at third-level, and where courses are accepted for certificate and diploma awards, that is technician and higher technician courses, NCEA has a role'.[60] NCEA was not intended to have any involvement below technician level and that policy did not change subsequently.

The Act also set limits to where NCEA could operate institutionally. Section 1 of the Act set out the institutions to which the Act referred, namely An Coláiste Ealaíne is Deartha (the National College of Art and Design), the National Institute for Higher Education Limerick, the National Institute for Higher Education

Dublin, Thomond College of Education, any Regional Technical College and any institution specified in an order made under Section 20 of the Act. Deputy Horgan had referred to the desirability of an institution well away from the technological area having the ability to submit courses to NCEA, and cited the Irish School of Ecumenics.[61] He heard encouraging noises in response from the minister, but when designation orders came to be made in August 1980, the Irish School of Ecumenics did not figure. Five private colleges, which already had run courses carrying approval from the *ad hoc* NCEA, were included. The other ten designated colleges were all public sector institutions.[62] Any college subsequently wishing to submit a course to NCEA had to go through what was liable to be a lengthy bureaucratic process. This process was ultimately controlled by the Department of Education and the entire procedure proved in time to be something which would weaken NCEA's standing and credibility.

The minister's commitment to the binary system emerged as being somewhat qualified. As he saw it, the technological area was young and growing, though needing 'time to build up its muscle' and in danger of being smothered by the traditional third-level institutions.[63] He also indicated at the time of the Committee Stage of the NCEA Bill that he saw Thomond College, NIHE Limerick, and the teacher education colleges developing into a technological university by the end of the century.[64]

A much more significant point was also clarified during the debate on the Bill, namely whether NCEA was to have monopoly powers with regard to degree awards in the non-university sector. From early in his time as minister Mr Wilson had indicated that his policy was that NCEA should be responsible for all awards in the non-university sector. The City of Dublin Vocational Education Committee successfully resisted the minister on this point when he conceded during the Committee Stage that there was nothing in the Bill which would prevent the Dublin VEC colleges from continuing to obtain recognition from the universities. Accordingly NCEA did not have a monopoly. It was therefore only a matter of time before an institution other than the Dublin colleges exploited this reality even further. The statute which was intended to copperfasten the binary system in effect ensured that such a system could never be watertight.

To be or not to be? – The National Institute for Higher Education Dublin

If the City of Dublin VEC succeeded in besting the minister on its relationship with NCEA, it did not enjoy the same success with regard to the other, and for it perhaps more crucial, issue of the National Institute for Higher Education. The concept of a National Institute for Higher Education Dublin first surfaced in the statement of December 1974. From the outset it met with the opposition of the City of Dublin Vocational Education Committee, which understandably resented any proposal which would deprive it of those of its activities with the highest perceived quality and prestige. Opposition to the NIHE idea was not however total within the VEC.[65]

The first governing body of the Institute was appointed directly by the government on the nomination of the minister, and included representation from trade unions, agriculture, business, industry and education.[66] The governing body, along with its Limerick counterpart, held its first meeting at the behest of the minister on 19 June 1975.[67] Its general function was *inter alia* to plan, in consultation with the Department of Education and the Higher Education Authority, the specific form of the Institute to be established, the appropriate staffing arrangements and the type of courses to be made available. It also had the task of entering into discussions with the City of Dublin VEC concerning the transfer of existing third-level courses in the Committee's colleges to NIHE, and to enter into discussions with one or other or both of the Dublin universities concerning degree validation.[68] The governing body had to elect a chairman from among its number and, as already noted, at its second meeting Patrick Donegan, a trade union official and Chairman of the City of Dublin VEC, was duly elected. Dr Liam Ó Maolcatha, an inspector in the Department of Education, had been seconded as acting Director of the Institute early in 1975.

Progress with regard to the development of the Institute was slow. The governing body experienced protracted difficulty in obtaining sanction for secretarial staff and premises of any kind.[69] Two committees of the governing body established in October 1975 saw their primary goal as the progress of discussion with the City of Dublin VEC regarding course transfer. This was not to be an easy task. The initial approach on the topic was made eventually in February 1976. A meeting between representatives of the two sides took place in April 1976. In June 1976 it was agreed that both sides would establish a liaison committee to progress matters. Mr Donegan was included among the NIHE representatives. When the City of Dublin VEC came to nominate its members in the following October, he was also nominated for membership of that group. When the two groups met, the NIHE group presented a list of courses which it felt should be involved in the transfer. No further discussion took place over the summer or autumn of 1976. More than a year had passed and it was clear that no progress was being made between the two bodies. At this stage the minister intervened and, shortly before his departure to Brussels, established a small working party on higher technological education in the Dublin area chaired by Dr Tom Walsh, NCEA Chairman, with representation from both the VEC and the NIHE governing body. The committee reported in just over one month on the apportionment of academic activity, courses and buildings, the transfer of staff, a governing structure for the VEC colleges and their relationship to the new institution.[70]

The working party may have reported quickly, but there was now a new minister, Peter Barry, and he told the Dáil at the end of March 1977 that he had had no discussions on the report with any of the interested parties.[71] This hiatus allowed the VEC to string along the NIHE governing body even further, although it had conceded that the location of courses at professional (degree level) and craft level was not in question, since they would divide naturally into the NIHE and VEC institutions respectively. In April 1977 the NIHE governing body proposed the transfer of a marketing or business studies course to the Institute.[72] The response from the Committee was in the negative, and at that stage it had become clear that no progress by negotiation could now be made by the governing body.

Shortly before he departed to Brussels, Mr Burke made what in retrospect was probably the most crucial decision in that he sanctioned the appointment of Dr Daniel O'Hare as the first Director of the Institute. Had he stalled on that, as there was intense pressure on him to do,[73] it is quite conceivable that NIHE would never have come into existence. There was now in post an experienced and energetic educator and administrator whose full-time job it was to ensure that the Institute became something more than a toothless planning body.[74] Dr O'Hare took up the post in March 1977. The coalition government went out of office after the election of June 1977. The next crucial question was whether

Fianna Fáil's policy would encompass the development of an institution which had been invented in a set of proposals against which the party had waged relentless opposition for two-and-a-half years.

If the City of Dublin VEC hoped that the new minister would kill NIHE, it was to be disappointed. Mr Wilson let it be known fairly quickly that he was proceeding with the idea.[75] In December 1977 the governing body produced a detailed plan for the future of the Institute which pointedly refrained both from any reference to a then current proposal to build a college of commerce at Ballymun as the first phase of the Institute, or to the transfer of existing courses from the City of Dublin VEC. By early 1978 the Teachers' Union of Ireland, the main union representing the teaching staff at the colleges of City of Dublin VEC, had come around to accepting the notion of the National Institute, and it was also clear that Dr O'Hare was openly trying to do something to break the logjam.[76] He was quoted as saying that it was always intended that the VEC should continue a third-level operation in Dublin, and that there was scope for both bodies, and that with the need for places in Dublin, it would be possible for NIHE to provide new courses without the VEC having to give up anything.[77] At that stage his hopes were that the Institute would open in 1980 with business studies students. The Society of College Lecturers, a group representing lecturers in the VEC colleges, continued to support the NIHE concept, because in the words of its spokesman, Neil Gillespie, the archaic academic structures in the VEC colleges had the effect of excluding the majority of third-level teaching staff from any meaningful participation in decision-making.[78]

In the early part of 1978 the minister was clearly uncertain about the nature and the extent of the activity to be made available at the new Institute. In April, asked whether it was proposed to proceed with a college of technology in Ballymun, he could only answer that the matter was still under consideration and that a final decision was not expected for some time.[79] In May the VEC established the Dublin Institute of Technology, as already indicated, and at the very least this action can be interpreted as the Committee's establishing a body which could be either a rival or a substitute for NIHE. In June the report of the NIHE governing body was published together with the proposals contained in its long-term physical development plan submitted to the minister and the Higher Education Authority. The plan had a price tag of thirty-three million pounds, it envisaged that the construction of a college of commerce would commence before the end of 1978, and that the Institute would build up to a complement of five thousand students within five years.[80] The Institute proposals also worked on the assumption that there would be no transfer of courses from the VEC.

During summer 1978 there was no progress in discussions between the Institute and the Committee. The Committee's acting chief executive officer, John McKay, eventually told the liaison committee in November that the VEC was refusing to transfer courses to NIHE.[81] Immediately the minister confirmed to the Dáil that it was intended to transfer higher level courses from DIT to NIHE Dublin.[82] Shortly afterwards he set up another body to arrange the transfer.[83] The VEC refused to nominate anybody to that committee, and told the minister that it was unwilling to transfer any courses.[84] The refusal was made at one of the very rare meetings between the minister and the Committee. A document presented to the minister queried the need for NIHE and indicated that the VEC colleges, while needing capital development, had facilities the replacement value of which was thirty million pounds. The document referred to the recognition achieved abroad by the VEC courses, cited the example of Massachusetts Institute of Technology to ridicule the idea that a local authority was an inappropriate body to control a national institution, and suggested that some of the VEC second-level educational plant could be used for third-level enrolment in the short term.

After this meeting and submission it apparently became impossible for the redoubtable Mr Donegan to continue to ride two such fractious horses simultaneously, and he resigned as Chairman of the NIHE Governing Body.[85] Clearly Mr Wilson now had a serious fight on his hands. To a great extent he was to be rescued by the National Institute. It is evident that some of the forces within the governing body decided that progress was possible only by ignoring the VEC issue, and by assuming that there would be no transfer of courses.[86] In that vein the Institute had submitted a document to NCEA on its proposals for a first suite of programmes.[87] In July 1979 the Institute announced its plans for initial recruitment of staff for commencement in 1980. It is worth noting that none of the staff recruited in the first eighteen months came from a college of the City of Dublin VEC, a pattern which was to continue. Refurbishment of the Albert College was planned to begin in the autumn of 1979 when the UCD Faculty of Agriculture would have finally vacated the building.[88] At this stage the Institute was committed to the Ballymun site. The governing body had not been unanimously happy with it and had investigated other options, including a site on the western perimeter of the city which was bigger and seemed to have more potential for development as a single site. Final decisions on these matters were effectively taken out of the governing body's hands by the minister and his officials.[89]

By March 1980 the Institute was in a position to advertise for students for its first six degree programmes in business studies, accounting and finance, computer applications, communication studies, analytical science and electronic engineering.[90] The Institute had also hoped to have a distance study unit in operation at an early stage, but this was put in temporary cold storage for financial reasons.[91] In April 1980 the Minister for Education turned the first sod at the campus.[92] In November the Institute opened its doors to its first two hundred and thirty students. At a press conference on the occasion the director, Dr O'Hare, said that its role would be 'unashamedly applied and technological, directing its attention to the needs of industry, business and agriculture'.[93]

So almost six years after its establishment had been heralded, the Institute came into existence. It had not taken, in spite of the efforts of ministers Burke and Wilson, any degree or other work from the City of Dublin VEC and no staff had been transferred. To that extent the VEC had won a major victory. On the other hand its very existence was a defeat for those on the Committee who had attempted to prevent its ever opening its doors. A whole new area of non-university third-level education would grow in Dublin outside the control of the VEC and in premises that had originally been earmarked for the Committee. The main loser over the period had been the school-leavers in the Dublin area, who were less well served for third-level technological education than their contemporaries elsewhere in the country.[94] In 1980 Dublin's NIHE was a small, though well-planned, organisation. For the foreseeable future its destiny was likely to be significantly influenced by its more famous sister institution in the Mid-West, the National Institute for Higher Education Limerick.

NIHE Limerick – The *Soi Disant* University?

Very few institutions can have welcomed the result of the 1977 general election more than the National Institute for Higher Education Limerick. For almost two years it had rarely been out of the newspaper headlines for long. It was at odds in a major way with the Minister for Education and with the colleges of the National University of Ireland. By any standards it had been a traumatic period for the Institute. Years afterwards the director, Dr Walsh, described the aftermath of NUI recognition as a process of slow strangulation.[95] In the same address he stated that a combination of academic and political energies had been brought to bear with such intensity that the emerging university in Limerick came close to collapse in that period, and that the activities of three well-intentioned, but inept, members of government coincided with the focused energies of vested academic and religious interests that took advantage of an opportunity when Limerick was most vulnerable, the year its first graduates were due to be conferred.

In retrospect it can at least be said that the Cosgrave government showed a perhaps unwitting cruelty in sending the Institute and Dr Walsh to NUI (and specifically to his *alma mater*, University College Cork) to seek validation, when for the previous five years he had excoriated those institutions for their snobbery, irrelevance and academic self-importance. NUI had never asked to have Dr Walsh and his college as a part of its responsibility but, when they were so included, some of the faculty at UCC would have been less than human had they not felt tempted to take Dr Walsh and, by extension, his Institute down a peg or two. There appears no strong evidence, apart from Dr Walsh's personal testimony, that they succumbed to the temptation. While there was difference of views about the rationale for, and standards of, NIHE courses, the case for NUI malevolence as of now is not proven.[96]

What is clear is that at no stage during the period of the Cosgrave coalition government were the embers of university ambitions in Limerick quenched entirely. As already noted, Mr Burke had given them encouragement in his first six months as minister. The December 1974 decisions had left open the possibility of Limerick's being an autonomous degree-awarding body should validation by existing university institutions prove an impossibility. The NIHE governing body duly marked the first anniversary of the December 1974 proposals by proposing to the minister that he establish a university in Limerick, given the evidence of the unsatisfactory nature of the NUI link.

NIHE had no further success on that score with Mr Burke, but an institution with such well-honed political skills was unlikely to pass up the opportunity presented by a general election to seek some commitment from prominent local politicians. And so in June 1977 Desmond O'Malley, the Fianna Fáil front bencher in the East Limerick constituency, was telling staff and students that his party would allow the Institute to develop to the stage where it would award its own degrees.[97] Not to be outdone, and in spite of the events of the previous two years, the Minister for the Gaeltacht, Tom O'Donnell, also running for re-election in East Limerick, was quoted as saying that the coalition government was pledged to the evolution of a university in the city at 'some time in the future'.[98] Meanwhile the NIHE Parents' Action Committee had joined student representatives in urging the next government to take NIHE out from under the control of NUI, and all candidates in East Limerick had been contacted in writing to solicit support for that undertaking.[99] The issue of a university for Limerick was not going to be allowed to die easily.

The restoration of degree powers to NCEA meant that NIHE would return to dealing with it for validation of degree programmes. At the time of announcing this reversal of the coalition government's policy the new minister, John Wilson, foresaw NCEA acting as an umbrella under which the National Institutes for Higher Education in Dublin and Limerick could develop into technological universities. Wilson envisaged this as a long-term development likely to occur some time before the end of the century.[100]

The clouds had clearly lifted in Limerick. In July 1977 Dr Walsh, fresh from doing battle with NUI and the Minister for Education, was returning to his recurring themes of aligning higher education with manpower requirements and the over-supply of graduates from the arts, law, teaching and the social sciences.[101] By a piquant anomaly the first and last conferring of NUI degrees at the Institute took place in July 1977. While the first graduates had finished at NIHE in 1976, understandably no conferring had taken place in that year because, in the circumstances, the vexed issue of NUI validation could have called forth student demonstrations. One hundred and twenty-four graduates were conferred by NUI and twenty-five NCEA diplomas were awarded on the same occasion. Dr Walsh took the opportunity to attack the NUI matriculation examination. Referring to the recent history of relations, he added that in the Institute they had intentionally broken well-established academic rules and that, while they regretted having upset many of their academic associates, they remained unrepentant.[102]

That the NUI relationship had left a very sour taste among some of the principal actors at NIHE could not be doubted. Dr Walsh returned to the theme again in September 1977 when he attacked the entry requirements of the NUI engineering schools as being academically inappropriate and socially discriminatory. He pointedly praised the TCD/City of Dublin VEC relationship as being one where a sense of equal partnership permeated, unlike the feudal lord and vassal relationship which they had experienced in Limerick.[103] The curtain finally came down on this rancorous liaison in December 1977 when the NUI Senate formally withdrew the recognition of the Institute.[104]

No major problems were anticipated in relations with NCEA, which on the surface at least had been cordial. There always had been NIHE representation on the Council itself.[105] NIHE personnel were to be found on most NCEA boards of studies and panels of assessors, while many others acted as extern examiners.[106] There could be no complaint of feudal relationships there. Moreover the thrust of NCEA's activities with such a strong technological and commercial flavour was very congenial to the rationale and self-perception of NIHE. Nevertheless a strong NCEA was likely to be an obstacle to NIHE's ambitions for university status sooner rather than later. The NIHE approach therefore was largely to downplay the involvement of NCEA in any marketing of NIHE. A perusal of *NIHE News*, an Institute newsletter which began to appear on a regular basis from September 1979 onwards, would suggest that NCEA was an almost invisible and marginal presence as far as the Institute was concerned. The marketing technique appeared to involve a process suggesting that NIHE was already a technological university and that it was only a matter of time before this reality was formally recognised.[107] Even at that stage it was quite clear that NIHE was not going to worry unduly about legal niceties when it came to portraying the Institute as a university-type institution. Time was to show how fruitful this approach would be.

Whatever one's views of Dr Walsh's performance as a publicist for NIHE, one has to acknowledge his extraordinary achievement in this period in galvanising almost total support for his Institute (and he tended to be its personification) among the staff, the students and all local opinion in the mid-west region. He also succeeded in achieving similar support from the students' union and the Union of Students in Ireland, although his own regular forays into prescribing for sundry ills of the nation indicated that his political and social views were at a different end of the ideological spectrum from those of the majority of USI leaders in the period. Dr Walsh was almost a decade in advance of political fashion in his articulation of what subsequently came to be regarded as free market opinions. In the same period USI had among its presidents future left-wing politicians like Pat Rabbitte and Éamon Gilmore, yet he retained USI's support all during the 1970s. One cannot imagine a university president escaping their ire had any of them expressed similar sentiments on divers matters such as student loans.

With the ending of the virtual state of siege and the dissipation of the siege mentality, some of the unresolved internal problems within NIHE finally came to the surface in 1978. NIHE had been funded directly by the Department of Education until December 1976, when it was designated under the Higher Education Authority Act.[108] Nevertheless the Department of Education still retained a strong involvement and NIHE did not enjoy the same level of financial autonomy as other HEA-funded institutions such as the universities.[109] Two industrial disputes, one involving academic staff and the other technicians, began late in 1977.[110] These disputes ran right through into the summer of 1978, and the ban on assessment and the marking of examinations had meant that students had no assessment results over a period of almost nine months.[111] The staff eventually agreed to mark the examination papers of final-year degree and diploma students shortly before the date for final examination boards.[112] Behind all this was the reality that an institution with over one hundred academic staff had no pension scheme nor promotion structure. In addition, staff were complaining about the workload placed on them by the Institute's continuous assessment system, while extra loads of administrative and public relations work which were expected of them in turn impeded further study and research work.[113]

While the staff at NIHE Limerick never subsequently showed the same level of militancy as, for example, their counterparts in the VEC colleges, it took a number of years before the staff structures of the Institute were finally established, and the events of late 1977 and early 1978 were an indication of some of the price exacted by the turmoil of the previous two-and-a-half years. As in so many institutions in the Irish public sector, the penchant for the *ad hoc* eventually led to trouble at NIHE also. In fairness both to NIHE and to Dr Walsh, it has to be said that the *ad hoc* component was supplied almost exclusively by the Department of Education and its political masters.

From its first intake of 113 in 1972, the Institute had grown to a full-time student body of 680 by the academic year 1975-76 and this had more than doubled to 1484 full-time undergraduates by 1980-81. The Institute enrolled its first 25 part-time students in 1976 and by 1980 it had 321. It had 110 full-time and 15 part-time postgraduates by 1980-81. Of the 1,484 full-time undergraduates, about 55 per cent (819) were in engineering and science, just over 30 per cent (453) were in business studies, with under 15 per cent (212) taking European studies, the humanities component of the Institute.[114] Of the 539 new entrants to the Institute in 1980, three quarters (404) were male, the engineering bias within NIHE being reflected in the low take-up of that discipline by women. Almost 31 per cent of the new entrants were the offspring of farmers, higher than any of the university colleges, and well above the range of 23 per cent for third-level education at large. About 30 per cent (154) of the new students came from County Limerick and 39 per cent (207) from the four counties bordering Limerick. It had entrants from every county in the Republic, but its regional composition was not markedly different from the university colleges.[115]

By 1980 NIHE Limerick had established a high profile for itself nationally, and in general it had managed to thrive on its adversity in the middle of the decade. By 1977 it was getting 2,400 applications for its 360 places.[116] A number of features distinguished it from other third-level colleges, features to which the director regularly called attention.[117] One was co-operative education, the requirement for periods of industrial placement on all degree programmes, described by Dr Walsh as 'a dynamic American technique'. A second was the modular credit system of course organisation. In theory this was to allow the students flexibility in choosing modules in the degree. In reality the menu from which students could choose was quite restricted. This, allied to the Institute's almost religious commitment to continuous assessment, meant in essence that the programmes were distinguished by short discrete modules and a course or programme structure which was fragmented compared to all other degree courses in the state, which normally worked on a system of terminal examinations. Other factors differentiating the Institute were its emphasis on teaching methods and curricula stressing the practical application of theoretical knowledge, and a recruitment policy which targeted staffs' industrial experience as much as their academic credentials. NIHE was also a highly capitalised institution with some of the most modern equipment of any college in the country.

In 1980 it admitted 260 full-time undergraduate students into its engineering programme. UCD, the largest of the university engineering schools, admitted 180.[118] NIHE was already on its way to becoming for a period the largest engineering school in the country, and the type of technological flagship so dear to its director's heart. Unlike its sister institute in Dublin, which from its inception in 1980 never ran any sub-degree programmes (whether full-time or part-time), NIHE Limerick had a sizeable number of diploma students and for a few years ran a certificate programme in data processing.[119] When the first NCEA conferring of both degrees and diplomas at NIHE took place in 1978, the Council awarded 111 national diplomas and 115 degrees.[120] The subsequent growth was, of course, almost exclusively at degree level, but right through the following decade, NIHE Limerick maintained a commitment to offering national diploma programmes.[121]

On the same campus as NIHE, and indeed within yards of it, was another third-level institution of similar age with a not dissimilar tempestuous childhood. The decision to build the National College of Physical Education and to locate it in Limerick was taken in 1970, the year in which the NIHE Planning Board was established.[122] In October 1973 it was announced that it would be expanded into an institute for the preparation of teachers of other subjects such as woodwork and metalwork, who at that time were educated in a range of courses under the aegis of different vocational education committees.[123] The National College of Physical Education and the College of Education for Teachers of Specialist Subjects, as it came to be called, were eventually given one governing body and the entire entity was renamed Thomond College of Education.[124] The unusual circumstances of its first NCEA degree awards have already been alluded to, but, in line with the prevailing policy of Mr Burke as minister, the governing body applied for and received NUI recognition in November 1976.[125]

While the director and governing body of the college may have been more muted than their NIHE counterparts as far as the coalition government proposals were concerned, the same could not be said of the student body which was, over a number of years, more recalcitrant than its peer group at NIHE. No conferring of degrees took place in 1976 because the graduates refused to accept a degree of Bachelor of Education from the National University of Ireland, a decision which was to cause many of them problems with their salaries in the following year.[126] Even by late October 1977 no decision had been taken on who would make the award to the 1977 cohort, and the impasse was broken only when NUI threatened to award the degrees *in absentia*, whereat the governing body agreed to a conferring and the graduates accepted their degrees under protest.[127]

The students showed a similar militancy in June 1980 in refusing to accept a terminal examination at the end of the second year of the degree programme, and the ensuing boycott of classes and concomitant demonstrations lasted until the following November.[128] As a small institution with an intake of 128 and a student body of 316 in 1980, Thomond College of Education seemed a likely candidate for merger with NIHE, if ever a university came to be designated. The minister, John Wilson, thought so too. During the Dáil debate on the Bill establishing the college on a statutory basis, he recalled his vision of the complex at Limerick involving a technological university with NIHE, Thomond College and Mary Immaculate College of Education involved in the development.[129] Whether at that juncture the governors, staff and students at Thomond College of Education would have been quite so enthusiastic about any embrace into the bosom of the brash elder brother on the Plassey campus is a moot point.

Legislation for the national institutes and Thomond College of Education

The Acts establishing the two national institutes were identical in their constitution, while there were minor variations to the Thomond College Act in recognition of its essential difference as a teacher education college.[130] The striking element in all three statutes was the degree of control which the ministers and the Department of Education wished to retain for themselves.[131]

During the debate on the Bill for NIHE Limerick, Deputy Edward Collins went to some length to compare the NUI charters and the autonomy of its colleges on matters like appointments with what was envisaged for NIHE.[132] Deputy Horgan commented that, while ostensibly they were legislating for the establishment of a new national institution, in reality they were in danger of creating something more like a glorified community school.[133]

Arguably the most perceptive observation on the governing structures of the new colleges was that made by the Chancellor of the National University of Ireland, Senator T.K. Whitaker, when, in the Senate debate on the National Institute for Higher Education Limerick Bill, he commented that the Bill treated NIHE Limerick as if it were a state corporation rather than a pioneering third-level institution.[134] This comment was especially apposite in the case of the Institute. Anybody dealing with it on a regular basis, with comparable experience of both universities and RTCs, quickly realised that it had the qualities of a modern aggressive corporation with corporate goals, marketing flair and a penchant for public relations, and with a hierarchy and non-collegiate culture that did not have to worry about awkward independent entities such as faculties and departments.[135] In this corporate culture Dr Walsh (and indeed Dr O'Hare at NIHE Dublin) had therefore more time and space to concentrate on corporate goals in the following decade, and time was to prove that they were well up to the job. Their legislation certainly permitted them to be chiefs rather than chairmen. A governing body of twenty-five, which contained only four members of staff and two students,[136] was less likely to provide the directors with the kind of problems or surprises which could occasionally detain their counterparts occupying the posts of university president or provost.

There was one stipulation in the Acts for both NIHE Limerick and NIHE Dublin which had potential for problems in the long term. The first function of both institutes in accordance with Section 4 of their respective Acts was 'to provide degree level courses, diploma level courses and certificate level courses and such other courses, including post-graduate courses, as may seem appropriate to the Governing Body'. The Interpretation Section of the Act[137] made it clear that a degree level course meant a course of study leading to the award of a degree by the National Council for Educational Awards. Diploma level and certificate level courses had similarly restricted meanings. In other words the NIHEs could make no awards of their own. NCEA had a monopoly in this area.

In the succeeding decade the NIHEs did not attempt to exploit the inequity of this provision. On one occasion only was NCEA caused any immediate problem by this requirement. In 1984 it was necessary to create somewhat hurriedly an award called 'NCEA Diploma in Continuing Education (Small Business Management)' to cater for twenty-three students of small business taking a course run at the Regional Management Centre located on the campus at NIHE Limerick.[138] This was a new type of award for which no prior criteria had been set down by NCEA, and indeed it was closer to adult than to technician education. Given, as has already been seen, that the minister could not enforce such a restriction on the Dublin VEC colleges, there was an inherent unfairness, if not indeed illogicality, in placing such a restriction on the NIHEs. The fact that the two institutions did not subsequently make hay with this anomaly would tend to indicate that they had their eyes on an altogether bigger prize from an early stage, and were not going to provoke an unnecessary quarrel in the short term with whoever happened to be Minister for Education.

The European Social Fund and the VEC sector

For the VEC sector, and the regional technical colleges in particular, by far the most important development in the late 1970s was the gradual introduction of funding of students through the European Social Fund. From the time of Ireland's entry into the European Economic Community in January 1973 assistance through the Social Fund had been high on the list of priorities of a number of Irish organisations, both in the state and the private sector.[139] In 1973 alone there were twenty-two applications to the European Social Fund seeking £5,250,000 in assistance.[140] In that year Ireland succeeded in obtaining 5.4 per cent of the entire fund, a proportion which had risen to over 8 per cent by 1977.[141] From the beginning the biggest beneficiary of the Fund in Ireland was AnCO, the Industrial Training Authority.[142]

In June 1975 the EEC Council decided to make a special Social Fund provision to facilitate the employment, and the geographical and professional mobility, of young people under twenty-five years of age. In December 1975 the Minister for Education, Richard Burke, informed the Dáil that three Irish schemes were under consideration. One was an IDA-sponsored scheme for the training of surplus apprentices, another was an off-the-job training scheme for unemployed school leavers, while the third, from the Department of Education, covered the training of young persons in four areas. The areas concerned were pre-employment courses, secretarial courses, courses for technician-level skills and one- year foundation courses for young persons wishing to pursue careers as accountants and administrators.[143]

One of the schemes, that for middle-level technicians, had in fact already commenced. Advertisements offering assistance for twenty places on a technician-type course had appeared in the newspapers in the summer of 1975, and the first students were admitted to the regional technical colleges in the autumn of 1975.[144] The students were selected through the National Manpower Service. No fees were payable by the students. There was a training allowance of £8.30 per week and no means test applied to the students concerned.[145] The introduction of the scheme to the colleges was gradual over a number of years and very low-key.[146] It is doubtful whether, in the early years of this financial assistance, the majority of school leavers, their parents or, in some instances, even guidance counsellors were aware of the existence of these courses. There were understandable reasons for the low-key and stealthy approach.

EEC regulations at that time permitted funding only of training, not of education. John Wilson as minister, on one of the rare occasions when these grants came to be mentioned in public (invariably because they had been alluded to by the opposition in the Oireachtas) emphasised that these were grants for training, and suggested to the Fine Gael spokesman, Edward Collins, that, as Chairman of Waterford Regional Technical College, he would be aware of the delicate nuances involved, and that they should not want to upset any flow of funds by referring to the grants as 'educational scholarships or educational subventions'.[147]

Wilson's predecessor, Peter Barry, had likewise been coy when under question from Wilson himself when the latter was opposition spokesman for Fianna Fáil. While allowing that 199 grant-aided courses were being conducted in the academic year 1976-77, Barry claimed that they were 'not really part of the structures of formal education in the narrow sense', but were intended by the EEC to act as retraining for people who had become redundant. He added that the courses were 'not in themselves certification courses' and that terminal examinations and certification were not really associated with them.[148] Strictly speaking this was true, but less than frank in its elucidation of the realities. Fictions were being resorted to. What could be sold to NCEA as lamb in the form of a course for technicians could be presented as mutton to the relevant EEC officials, if there were tacked on extra hours of 'instruction' (not teaching) in technical matters in which students were not examined and no formal certificates were available other than certificates of attendance. In the early years colleges normally concealed such realities from NCEA committees, NCEA's visiting panels of assessors and its extern examiners, while the officials of the Department of Education obligingly preserved NCEA (and in the period 1975-77 its ostensible planning and co-ordination powers) from any serious contact with, or knowledge of, the financial arrangements reached with Brussels.

The fact that Ireland had such a particularly large slice of the Social Fund, and the abnormal reticence of successive ministers for Education in claiming any credit for what had been successfully extracted from Brussels, are good indicators of the extent to which the Irish negotiators were pioneers in extending the boundaries of the European Social Fund (ESF). In 1979 there were 1,958 students obtaining assistance in middle-level technician courses,[149] and in the same year assistance under ESF overtook the state's expenditure on VEC scholarships.[150] By 1982 there were 3,065 students in receipt of grants.[151] By that point the existence of ESF funding was openly recognised and admitted, and had come to be extended beyond the initial areas of engineering and science. ESF grants however were still a preserve of the VEC colleges and university courses were not eligible.[152] By 1984 the coalition government's blue-print, *Building on Reality*, mentioned up to 12,000 students on ESF courses in 1984-85.[153]

By 1980 it had become obvious that, provided the European Community and the European Social Fund continued to subvent technician courses of the kind which it had supported from 1975 onwards, the Irish government and the Department of Education were happy to see an increasing amount of money devoted to courses of that type. The really substantial expansion of the scheme of ESF support was to come in the middle years of the ensuing decade and by 1990, the education system (with even the universities obtaining a share) would absorb a far larger proportion of ESF funding than would the various training agencies under the aegis of the Department of Labour.[154] What became clear also in retrospect was that Irish administrators, backed by ministers, made an undeclared choice in the latter half of the 1970s to use European Community financial assistance to alter the pattern of supply in higher education, and direct it primarily to short-cycle higher education. So thorough was the transformation that, from having a tiny short-cycle sector before 1970, by 1981 internationally Ireland had, after the Netherlands, the largest proportion of third-level students taking sub-degree courses.[155] The quiet introduction of ESF funding in 1975 had played a major role in that transformation.

The growth of the system

Between 1970 and 1980 twelve new publicly-funded third-level teaching institutions were launched in the Republic of Ireland. Another, the National College of Art and Design, had been put on a statutory basis, reorganised and given national status. The National Council for Educational Awards had been established to give a coherent national framework and status to the awards in the new institutions. By the year 1980 the new system finally appeared to have taken shape.

Growth in student numbers is indicated in Appendix 1.[156] It will be evident from the table that over the period from 1970 to 1980 the full-time student body in the sector had increased by 145 per cent. In the same period full-time students in the universities grew by 21 per cent.

The overall figures mask a very significant trend. While the number of students at university comprised 55 per cent of all full-time third-level students in 1980, new entrants to the non-university sector in the same year were actually greater than the number of new undergraduates. In 1980 there were 5,513 new full-time entrants to universities, 1,175 to colleges of education and 6,672 to the technological sector.[157] The new entrants to the technological sector[158] comprised half of all new full-time third-level entrants.[159] Although the main growth was in the colleges operating under NCEA auspices, the growth of art and design courses at regional technical colleges and other VEC colleges from 1975 onwards meant that the proportion of awards made to students of engineering and science dropped. By 1980, 39 per cent of all NCEA awards were in engineering and construction studies, while 20 per cent were in science and paramedical studies.[160] Just over a quarter of all NCEA awards in 1980 went to students of business and social studies, although this understated the proportion of business studies students in the sector, as the DIT colleges (College of Commerce Rathmines and College of Marketing and Design) and Limerick Technical College did not submit their business courses for NCEA approval, and Regional Technical

Colleges (except for those at Galway, Dundalk and Tralee) made significant full-time provision for courses leading to the examinations of professional bodies, primarily in accountancy. The 15 per cent in the humanities (363 NCEA awards in 1980) were mainly composed of students of art and design, with a sprinkling of students from physical education, philosophical studies and childcare.[161] There was a massive vocational component in both course provision and the awards pattern, and John Wilson had no need for his expressed fear of an explosion in liberal arts.[162]

Part-time provision in the new vocational institutions varied. In general terms neither NIHE Limerick nor any of the RTCs had as high a proportion of part-time students as the City of Dublin VEC colleges.[163] In 1978-79 the DIT colleges (excepting the College of Music) had 3,178 full-time students and an estimated 14,282 part-time. The RTCs were reckoned to have just over 10,000 part-time students as against 4,848 full-time. Only Cork RTC with 3,139 part-time students compared to 884 full-time had a ratio of part-time students to full-time which was greater than 2:1. Of the nine regional technical colleges Cork was the largest in size, followed by Galway (831 full-time, 1,516 part-time) and Waterford (628 full-time and 1,026 part-time). The smallest at Tralee had 184 full-time and 294 part-time students.[164] For the 4,945 full-time students in regional technical colleges in 1979-80 there were 890 full-time lecturers, indicating an altogether more generous teacher-student ratio than existed in universities.[165] This point is illustrated by Table 4,[166] where the situation in Cork is taken as indicative of the national picture.

TABLE 4: Comparative figures for students, teaching staff and administrative staff at University College Cork and Cork Regional Technical College, 1978

	Students		Teaching Staff		Admin Staff
	Full-time	Part-time	Full-time	Part-time	
UCC	4261	732	204	69	202
CORK RTC	776	1967	164	124	22

The teaching staff ratios were altogether more generous at the regional technical colleges. By contrast the minimum of administrative backup was provided there. This was, and has continued to be, a feature of those colleges. Given the size and level of complexity to which some of the colleges had grown by 1980 (not to mention in subsequent years), their administrative infrastructure was minimal. It was noteworthy that such under-resourced administrative facilities did not generate a spate of litigation among dissatisfied or misinformed students.

The new system of higher vocational and technological education was unashamedly geared towards the workplace, but during the first decade relatively little research was conducted as to how effective it was in actually meeting the needs of industry, and relatively little on how well the output of graduates and award-holders actually met the demands of the marketplace towards which the system was intended to direct them. From 1979 onwards, during the period of conferring in autumn and winter, NCEA surveyed its award recipients for information on their destinations immediately after graduation. The 1980 survey (with an 85 per cent response rate) indicated that 50 per cent of all graduates went into full-time employment, 7.5 per cent into part-time employment and over 30 per cent to further study. This left 11.5 per cent still seeking employment some months after completing examinations. The comparable figure for 1979 was 6 per cent, and for 1981 13.25 per cent.[167] The Council conducted one survey on a cohort of award recipients of five years' standing, the award holders in engineering and construction studies of 1979.[168] Less than 6 per cent of the respondents were unemployed at the time, with students from electrical and electronics engineering faring better than those in construction studies, and in civil and mechanical engineering. More than half the group had gone on to further study of some kind, about one quarter had worked abroad for some period, although only 8 per cent were abroad at the time of the survey. Thirty-nine per cent of the respondents were in manufacturing industry, 17 per cent in the construction industry with another 10 per cent in consultancy. The evidence from the surveys was in line with studies conducted later in the decade in showing that those completing third-level vocational courses in general fared well in the marketplace.

Because of the way the colleges of the City of Dublin Vocational Education Committee and Limerick Technical College (subsequently re-christened Limerick College of Art, Commerce and Technology and eventually in 1998 to become Limerick Institute of Technology) were funded, it is not possible to calculate exactly how much was spent on higher technical and vocational education during the period from 1970 to 1980.[169] State recurrent expenditure on the universities in 1970-71 amounted to £5,824,000 rising to £17,962,200 in 1975 and £44,329,500 in 1980. In 1970-71 expenditure on the technological sector, excluding the Dublin and Limerick VEC, was £386,000, rising to £5,655,810 in 1975 and £19,351,900 in 1980. In the five-year period from 1975 to 1980, while university recurrent expenditure had increased by 247 per cent, expenditure on the vocational sector had gone up by 342 per cent.[170]

Detailed breakdown of grants per student in different third-level institutions was not available, but estimates were furnished from time to time by the Minister for Education in reply to Dáil questions. Table 5 gives one estimate of costs per student in 1980.[171]

TABLE 5: Costs per student at various third-level colleges, 1980

University College, Dublin	£1,614
University College, Cork	£1,616
University College, Galway	£1,680
NIHE, Limerick	£1,531
National College of Art & Design	£2,275
Thomond College of Education	£4,640
Teacher Education Colleges	£1,786
Regional Technical Colleges	£1,405

It must be assumed that in this breakdown all exchequer costs (including grants and scholarships) are covered. It would appear however that the subsidy from the European Community for the training grants for RTC students is not included. If it were, the cost of RTC students from all public funds would have been greater. In 1979-80 there were 1,931 students in receipt of EC grants (mainly in regional technical colleges) and in 1980-81 that number had risen to 3,069 (about 28 per cent of all students in the third-level VEC sector).[172] As will be clear from the above figures, supplied via the Department of Education, the cost of educating students at regional technical colleges was reckoned as lower overall than educating university students. It was only slightly so, and it must be concluded that the decision increasingly to support this type of education at third-level as a matter of public policy was not one based on cost, but on other ideas discussed elsewhere.

By 1980, as illustrated in Table 6, grant and scholarship

provision was proportionately twice as high for students in the vocational/technological sector as it was for university students.[173]

TABLE 6: Grant and scholarship numbers and costs at third-level, 1979-80 and 1980-81

	1979-80		**1980-81**	
	Number	Cost	Number	Cost
Higher Education Grants	5,219	£3,666,155	5,021	£3,812,608
VEC Scholarships	1,686	£902,058	1,762	£953,375
EEC Training Grants	1,931	£1,158,137	3,069	£1,709,485

In 1979-80 there were 25,646 degree students in the relevant HEA-funded institutions and the 5,219 grants covered 20.75 per cent of that student body. VEC scholarships or EEC grants numbering 3,167 covered 8,882 students (or 40.72 per cent of the student body).[174] In 1980-81 there were 26,256 students at the HEA-funded colleges and 10,910 in the vocational/technological sector. The proportion in receipt of scholarships and grants in the two sectors was 19.1 per cent and 44.3 per cent. The main reason for the enormous disparity was not the social composition of the two sectors, but rather the fact that EEC grants, unlike the Higher Education grants and the VEC scholarships, were not means-tested.

As noted, the only new institutions to open in the latter half of the decade were the National Institute for Higher Education Dublin in 1980, and Tralee Regional Technical College, which was an upgrading of an existing second-level college, and which was designated a Regional Technical College in 1977.[175] Other regions of the country were attracted to the possiblity of having a regional technical college. John Wilson, when opposition spokesman on education, had floated the idea of a college in Cavan.[176] After the designation of Tralee, the next centre to argue its case was Castlebar.[177] Mr Wilson as minister told the Dáil in December 1978 that there were no plans for a third-level college in Mayo.[178] Next out of the blocks was Thurles where a very sophisticated case was built up by the VEC of Tipperary (North Riding) spearheaded by the chief executive officer, Luke Murtagh.[179] Bray also entered the fray after Thurles.[180] Its appearance had to be understood in the context of a recently published study on higher education in Dublin.[181] The report prepared for the Higher Education Authority recommended the provision of at least four new colleges in Tallaght, Dún Laoghaire/Shankill/Bray, Blanchardstown and in the suburbs north of the city, to meet the needs of Dublin's growing population. The report found it difficult to compare overall student participation rates between Dublin and the country as a whole. It was only when one of the authors, Dr Patrick Clancy, was commissioned by the Higher Education Authority to conduct a national survey of participation in higher education that it became clear that Dublin and its neighbours were among the counties at the bottom of the league table for rates of admission to higher education.[182]

The 1980 White Paper declared that four new regional technical colleges would be provided in the Greater Dublin area.[183] This did not happen. The National Institute for Higher Education Dublin was to be the last new public sector third-level institution to open for over a decade. The process of consolidation was under way. In that sense 1980 marked the end of the development phase. It was also the year which saw the end of a legislative flurry which crystallised the non-university third-level sector for a period at least. In addition it saw the Department of Education declare its thoughts in an unprecedented way through a White Paper. A system was now in place, and it was possible to be clear on the legislation and the ideas with which the Department of Education sought to underpin it.

The White Paper on Educational Development

The White Paper on Educational Development[184] published in December 1980 was unique in that, for the first time in the fifty-six years since the establishment of the Department of Education, a comprehensive statement from the Minister for Education on the entire spectrum of education in the state had been issued. It emerged because it had been a commitment in the Fianna Fáil manifesto at the time of the 1977 general election.[185] One of its fifteen chapters was devoted to third-level education.[186] It was scarcely the most impressive part of the document.

Almost one third of the entire chapter was taken up with a largely historical description of the origins of the National Museum, the National Gallery and the National College of Art and Design. Nevertheless, allowing for such padding, there was an insight into the thought processes of the official mind on the arrangements nationally for third-level education. There was once again a commitment to dissolve the National University of Ireland and to establish its constituent colleges as independent universities, a committee to review the operations of the RTCs in the light of their original purposes was proposed, four new regional technical colleges for the Dublin region were promised, the desirability of greater diversification in the range of course options within educational institutions was raised for consideration, a limited building programme was outlined, and a quite lengthy discussion on student support proposed amending existing schemes to encourage the study of technical drawing, mathematics, and scientific and agricultural subjects at Leaving Certificate in the hope of increasing the intake into scientific and technological courses at third-level.

Apart from these issues, the most notable aspects of the White Paper were its repeated emphasis on technology, its projections for future student numbers and its general tone. In the second paragraph of the chapter on third-level education the White Paper referred to the contribution made by third-level education institutions towards meeting the requirements of an expanding economy for highly-qualified manpower. It went on to say that, given the constraints on public expenditure, it was essential to ensure that, where the government had identified priority objectives for third-level education, available funds would be applied to meet these priorities. It was indicated that the government would examine the funding arrangements for third-level education, including the HEA Act, to ensure priority of allocation of resources for such identified areas of national development.[187]

The paper saw the main developments in higher education over the previous fifteen years as having been in technology, and added that further emphasis on technology was called for, with particular regard to engineering, manufacturing technology, electronics and computer technology.[188] It proposed, subject to the availability of resources, to undertake significant expansion of engineering education in all regions, at both graduate and technician level, and also to continue the enlargement of business studies already in train.[189] Provisions were also envisaged to ensure that there was no shortage of teachers at second and third level in science and technology subjects. Given that it was also proposed to improve the student support schemes to steer applicants towards these courses, there could be no doubting the Department's renewed emphasis on technology.

The White Paper contained projections on student numbers for the coming decade across all levels of education. The language used in the chapter on third-level education implied a commitment to subsequent development in science, technology and business studies. It therefore came as a surprise to turn to the projections for the year 1990-91.[190] Whereas in the previous fifteen years third-level numbers had almost doubled (from 20,700 students in 1965-66 to 38,800 in 1980-81), it was officially reckoned that in the following decade there would be growth of less than one-third in student numbers (from 38,800 to 51,000 in 1990-91). Moreover the projections implied that the regional technical colleges, apart from the four proposed in Dublin, had reached steady state. With respect to the following decade, of the 12,200 extra places envisaged, 5,200 were projected for the universities, 2,800 for the two NIHEs and, according to the text, 3,000 were to be filled by four Dublin RTCs. Hence the other nine RTCs would increase by a mere 1,000 students in ten years. Yet no mention was made of this brake on their development. Indeed the text seemed to imply the opposite, which suggested that the statisticians and the administrators drafting the policy had not been in serious communication with each other. In the event, of course, it was to be the statisticians who proved to be short of the mark.[191] By 1990-91 the number of full-time students in third-level education had risen to 69,988,[192] an increase of 80 per cent rather than the projected 30 per cent.

Finally the language and the tone of the White Paper were illuminating. White Papers in Irish public administration traditionally deal with problem areas where change may be required and, more particularly, where administrative reorganisation affecting subordinate bodies is planned by the parent department. This White Paper on the surface was no different. NUI was going to be restructured and the RTCs were to have four wise persons look at their activities. The most bizarre passage came in the second paragraph of the chapter. As has been seen, the document mentioned ensuring that priority in allocating resources should go to identified priority areas. It concluded by saying that the Minister for Education would direct the attention of the Higher Education Authority to the need for ensuring that 'funds made available by the government for particular projects should be appropriated accordingly'.[193]

At this juncture it is difficult to know what HEA had done to deserve such gratuitous insult, which appeared to suggest, if not misappropriation, at least misdirection of state funds. It had a good record in planning and projecting insofar as its own institutions were concerned.[194] There was no evidence that it was a force in opposing the government's technological emphasis, or that the universities were digging in their heels on this issue either.[195] Indeed the opposite was indicated by HEA's involvement with the Industrial Development Authority (through the Manpower Consultative Committee) in developing engineering and computer-related courses in 1979/80 across the third-level sector.[196] It is possible that not even the opening of departmental archives will explain this particular reference, and it may be that it affords nothing more than a good insight into the time-worn methods employed by civil servants to control state-sponsored or state-funded bodies.[197] Perhaps the obvious meaning is the correct one. Higher education was, at the end of 1980, primarily about technology, and it was the intention that the power of the purse would be used to ensure that this would continue to be the case.

The powers behind the throne

During the 1970s higher education in Ireland took a significant change in direction. By 1980 the state had a well-developed and quite coherent 'binary system' of higher education. What had been undertaken in the period was a relatively successful experiment in social engineering. One very important group in this entire process can be overlooked. This group comprises the civil servants who were involved with the policy at various stages.

The entire initiative owed a great deal to the arrival of interventionist ministers in the 1960s, particularly Hillery and O'Malley. But it was also assisted by the change in the way senior civil servants, such as Seán O'Connor, came to view their own role and became influential figures in promoting the new policy. O'Connor was in many ways an untypical civil servant in that he deliberately involved himself in public debate on policy, and in the process attracted a good deal of controversy. There were other senior civil servants who played a major role, possibly more significant roles than either O'Connor or any of the others, Tarlach Ó Raifeartaigh, Sean MacGearailt, Doiminic Ó Laoghaire and Liam Ó Laidhin, who occupied the position of secretary between 1966 and 1980. It is, for example, widely believed that the credit for obtaining so much finance for technician education through the European Social Fund was due almost entirely to Dr Finbarr O'Callaghan who, as assistant chief inspector and subsequently as assistant secretary in the 1970s, had a major influence on these events. In addition Micheál Ó hOdhráin, principal officer with responsibility for higher education from 1966 to 1978, and his successor for the following six years, Paddy Moloney, played very significant roles in the development of higher education policy.

Any public policy initiative must rely to a very considerable extent on the commitment and ability of the senior civil service. This will be recognised within the service itself, but it is rarely emphasised outside. The view that the civil service is nothing more than a conduit through which the policies of political masters are given effect is, in many instances, as misleading as the opposing belief that politicians are nothing more than the puppets of the civil service. The reality usually lies somewhere quite distant from either of these two opposite poles. The civil servants are important. They influence events. Sometimes their commitment to implementing a policy eventually gives them something resembling a personal agenda. The outsider rarely knows. In the Irish tradition civil servants have been scrupulous about respecting the requirements imposed upon them by the Official Secrets Act.[198] Evidence as to the contribution of civil servants therefore remains largely anecdotal.[199] Indeed there is no guarantee that archival material will shed much light on the distinctive contribution of individual civil servants. History is liable to ascribe achievements to ministers or other politicians, to forceful individuals like Dr Edward Walsh, or to the board members or executives[200] of bodies like HEA or NCEA. Judging purely on anecdotal evidence, it seems that Dr Finbarr O'Callaghan was by far the most influential figure, if not in crafting, at least in promoting non-university higher education in the period from 1966 to 1980.

Notes

1 *Irish Times*, 30 July 1977.

2 ibid., 19 November 1977.

3 *Irish Press*, 16 December 1977. The minister had asked NCEA to take full cognisance of the collaboration which had already operated between NUI and the two colleges with regard to those due to graduate in 1978 and subsequently.

4 NCEA, *Sixth Annual Report*, p. 7.

5 NCEA, *Seventh Report*, p. 7.

6 Department of Education, *Draft Memorandum for the Government, Feabhra 1978*.

7 They even managed to retain quite friendly relations on a personal basis. The Chairman of NCEA, Dr Tom Walsh, and the director, Pádraig Mac Diarmada,

appear to have been two people who maintained good relations with the minister, while working closely with the Fianna Fáil opposition to attempt to retain NCEA's degree powers.

8 Only one-third of the Council was appointed directly by the minister. The other two-thirds were nominated by the governing bodies of the two NIHEs. Principals and directors of colleges, whose futures it was originally intended the Council should plan and co-ordinate, were well represented and they were in a strong position to neutralise any ambitions which NCEA entertained in this area, particularly after the change of government in 1977.

9 Neither was any attempt made to remove the relatively recent status of recognised college of the National University of Ireland achieved by the Royal College of Surgeons in Ireland.

10 See, for example, the recommendations of the Commission on Higher Education, *Commission Report*, pp. 314-324. For a comprehensive coverage of the ongoing crisis at the National College of Art and Design, see Turpin, *A School of Art in Dublin*, pp. 415-558.

11 *Hibernia*, 19 June 1980; Turpin, pp. 596-599.

12 *Dáil Debates*, vol. 301, col. 1348 (22 November 1977).

13 *Irish Independent*, 16 January 1978. See also *Dáil Debates*, vol. 306, col. 921-924 (11 May 1978).

14 *Cork Examiner*, 1 February 1978.

15 *Irish Press*, 24 November 1978; *Dáil Debates*, vol. 310, col. 475 (30 November 1978).

16 *Dáil Debates*, vol. 310, cols. 532-3 (30 November 1978); vol. 311, cols. 1217, 1237 (14 February 1979).

17 *Dáil Debates*, vol. 313, cols. 1589-1599 (26 April 1979).

18 HEA, *General Report 1974-1984*, p. 55.

19 NCEA, *Fifth Annual Report*, p. 8.

20 *Irish Independent*, 26 October 1977.

21 NCEA, *Sixth Annual Report*, p. 9.

22 *Irish Times*, 10 May 1978. Dr Walsh was here giving a rare public airing to a belief held by a small number of those involved with the Council that NCEA should take over the validation and examination activities of all professional bodies, particularly those with headquarters outside Ireland. The poor relationship between NCEA and IMLS seems also to have been fuelled by a strong personality clash between NCEA Director, Pádraig MacDiarmada, and the key activist for IMLS in the Republic of Ireland, Seán Hanratty.

23 NCEA, *Sixth Annual Report*, pp. 36-38.

24 *Dáil Debates*, vol. 313, col. 1749 (1 May 1979).

25 HEA, *General Report 1974-1984*, p. 55.

26 *Dáil Debates*, vol. 304, col. 765 (2 March 1978). The statement was in reply to a question from Deputy Edward Collins as to whether he intended that NCEA would in future be responsible for the degree aspect of a diploma course in applied science at the College of Technology, Kevin Street.

27 *Irish Independent*, 3 October 1977. About the same time the Committee decided not to submit any more courses to NCEA for validation. See *Irish Times*, 21 December 1978.

28 *Irish Independent*, 1 February 1978.

29 *Irish Times*, 2 February 1978. For a summary of the relationship between Dublin Institute of Technology and Trinity College Dublin, see Luce, *The First 400 Years*, pp. 194-195.
30 *Irish Independent*, 29 April 1978. For the establishment of the Institute see Duff, Hegarty and Hussey, pp. 36-43.
31 *Dáil Debates*, vol. 310, col. 1051 (7 December 1978).
32 *Education: Special DIT Issue*, (Dublin: Poolbeg Press), Special Issue, August and October 1986, p. 6.
33 *Dáil Debates*, vol. 310, cols. 543-544 (30 November 1978).
34 ibid., vol. 311, cols. 1214-1215 (14 February 1979).
35 ibid., cols. 1233-1234.
36 So poor were the relations that, in his first three years in office, he apparently met the Committee on just one occasion (*Irish Press*, 27 June 1980).
37 *Irish Independent*, 21 December 1978.
38 *Dáil Debates*, vol. 313, col. 1000 (3 April 1979).
39 *Statutory Instrument*, No. 252 of 1980.
40 *National Council for Educational Awards Act 1979*, Section 3(i).
41 ibid., Section 3(2)b.
42 ibid., Section 1.
43 ibid., Section 3(2)(d)(ii), and 3(2)(e).
44 *Dáil Debates*, vol. 313, cols. 1517-1524 (25 April 1979); cols. 1568-1578 (26 April 1979).
45 This was a power which the *ad hoc* Council had exercised on just one occasion, in relation to medical laboratory science in 1979. It was never subsequently used. Deputy Collins was particularly opposed to this provision, and saw it as leaving open the possibility of a most unwelcome involvement by NCEA in colleges (Dáil Debates. vol. 311. cols. 1213-1214, 14 February 1979).
46 Deputies Collins and Horgan were strongly opposed to the naming of the director, Pádraig MacDiarmada, as the first director of the statutory Council. MacDiarmada's name was removed by the minister at Committee Stage. They were also opposed to the director's being a member of the Council, and pushed this issue to a vote, the only occasion in the entire debate where this happened (*Dáil Debates*, vol. 316, col. 161, 17 October 1979)
47 *NCEA Act*, Section 5(2).
48 *Dáil Debates*, vol. 313, col. 1600 (26 April 1979).
49 ibid., vol. 310, col. 474 (30 November 1978).
50 ibid., vol. 311, col. 1237 (14 February 1979).
51 *HEA Act*, Schedule. Section 2.
52 *Commission Report*, vol. 1, p. 477.
53 *NCEA Act*, Section 9(4).
54 *Dáil Debates*, vol. 313, col. 1503 (25 April 1979).
55 ibid., col. 1505.
56 ibid., col. 1508.
57 ibid., vol. 316, col. 151 (17 October 1979).
58 ibid., vol. 311, col. 1228 (14 February 1979).
59 ibid., vol. 316, cols. 1229-1230 (8 November 1979); vol. 313, cols 1004-1010 (3 April 1979).
60 ibid., col. 1010.

61 vol. 311, col. 1228 (14 February 1979); vol. 313, col. 1001 (3 April 1979).

62 The five private colleges were All Hallows College, Dublin; Holy Cross College, Clonliffe; St Patrick's College, Thurles; Holy Ghost College, Kimmage Manor; and the College of Industrial Relations, Dublin. The public sector colleges designated were five DIT colleges at Bolton Street, Kevin Street, Rathmines, Cathal Brugha Street and Parnell Square; Crawford Municipal School of Art, Cork; Dún Laoghaire School of Art and Design; Limerick Technical College; the Institute of Public Administration and Shannon College of Hotel Management. (NCEA, *Eighth Report*, pp. 6-7).

63 *Dáil Debates*, vol. 311, col. 1241 (14 February 1979).

64 ibid., vol. 313, col. 1575 (26 April 1979).

65 The Society of College Lecturers, an unofficial but influential forum for lecturers within the Committee's colleges, did not share the Committee's antipathy to the establishment of the new Institute. Society of College Lecturers, *Policy Document on NIHE Dublin*, 9 July 1975, passim.

66 *Dáil Debates*, vol. 279, col. 2040 (17 April 1975).

67 *Irish Press*, 11 June 1975.

68 NIHE Dublin, *Report of Governing Body*, p. 1.

69 ibid, p. 12.

70 *Dáil Debates*, vol. 298, col. 371 (24 March 1977); NIHE, Dublin, *Report of Governing Body*, p. 15.

71 NIHE Dublin, *Report of Governing Body*, p. 9.

72 The Governing Body had just learned that World Bank money was available to develop a 'Commerce Building'.

73 Personal information.

74 A perusal of the Report of the Governing Body for the period from 1975 to 1978 makes it clear just how powerless it actually was. The document in its understated way is as damning an indictment of what can pass as public administration Irish-style as it is possible to find.

75 *Dáil Debates*, vol. 301, col. 889 (15 November 1977).

76 *Irish Times*, 23 February 1978.

77 ibid.

78 ibid., 8 March 1978.

79 *Dáil Debates*, vol. 305, col. 59 (5 April 1978).

80 *Irish Independent*, 14 June 1978. The list of degree courses quoted at the time proved to be precisely those with which the Institute would eventually commence in 1980.

81 ibid., 17 November 1978.

82 *Dáil Debates*, vol. 310, cols. 1051-52 (7 December 1978). Also col. 791 (6 December 1978). The minister's reply of 7 December could be interpreted as his intending to transfer all higher-level courses to Ballymun.

83 *Irish Times*, 21 December 1978.

84 *Irish Independent*, 19 January 1979.

85 ibid., 13 January 1979; *Irish Press*, 14 February 1979.

86 It would appear that the minister himself dropped the idea of course transfer in January 1979. *Business and Finance*, 6 November 1980

87 National Institute for Higher Education Dublin (1978), *The Planning and Accreditation of the Institute's Courses*.

88 *Irish Times*, 4 July 1979.
89 NIHE Dublin, *Report of Governing Body*, p. 14.
90 *Irish Independent*, 28 March 1980.
91 ibid. See also *Sunday Press*, 16 March 1980.
92 *Irish Times*, 2 April 1980.
93 ibid., 11 November 1980.
94 In the year in which the Institute opened it emerged that County Dublin had one of the lowest participation rates in higher education in the entire country.
95 Walsh, E.M.(1990), 'Two Ideas of a University Contrasted', paper to seminar at University College, Cork, 16 November 1990. See also *Irish Times*, 17 November 1990, 19 November 1990.
96 The 'inept' politicians, to whom Dr Walsh referred, appear to have been Richard Burke, Garret FitzGerald and Justin Keating. The vehemence of his attack on fellow academics was noteworthy. Outside the ritual combat of politics it is unusual for such strong bitterness to be so publicly aired in relation to fellow-participants in the upper echelons of Irish public life. It is all the more striking in Dr Walsh's case, in that his achievements are well recognised and he is personally a man of considerable charm and graciousness. The author could find little evidence of NUI malevolence, while aware of an informed view that in this period Dr Walsh was treated shabbily and vindictively by NUI and UCC.
97 *Irish Times*, 4 June 1977.
98 *Irish Independent*, 11 June 1977.
99 ibid., 13 June 1977.
100 ibid., 1 August 1977.
101 *Irish Times*, 14 July 1977.
102 *Evening Herald*, 18 July 1977; *Irish Times*, 19 July 1977.
103 *Irish Times*, 8 September 1977.
104 *Irish Press*, 16 December 1977. The withdrawal of recognition from Thomond College of Education was completed at the same time.
105 Dr Walsh's eighteen years of unbroken membership of the Council from 1972 to 1990 was longer than that of any of the other original members of the first *ad hoc* Council.
106 NCEA, *Annual Reports 1972-80*, passim.
107 See, for example, McGinn. J., 'The Technological University', *Business and Finance*, June 1979. McGinn was the newly appointed Director of Co-operative Education. The uninitiated outsider on reading this article would have concluded that NIHE had already reached the status and designation of university. See also, Walsh, E.M., 'Towards a Technological University – The Year Reviewed', *NIHE News*, no. 6, September 1980.
108 HEA, *General Report 1974-84*, p. 9.
109 The author could judge this from his own observations as a staff member with the Authority at that time.
110 *Irish Independent*, 18 January 1978.
111 *Irish Times*, 7 June 1978. This was all the more serious at NIHE, as it relied on continuous assessment for grading purposes to a far greater extent than any other third-level institution in Ireland.
112 ibid., 27 June 1978.

113 *Limerick Chronicle*, 8 July 1978.
114 Higher Education Authority, *Accounts 1980 and Student Statistics 1981/82*, pp. 21, 23, 25, 33.
115 Clancy, P. (1982), *Participation in Higher Education: A National Survey*, Dublin: Higher Education Authority, pp. 15, 21, 69, 77, 78.
116 *Irish Times*, 20 October 1977.
117 For example, *Limerick Chronicle*, 14 July 1977, 20 August 1977.
118 Clancy, *1982 Participation Survey*, p. 60.
119 NCEA, *Annual Reports 1972-1980*, passim.
120 NCEA, *Sixth Annual Report*, p. 36.
121 In 1987, 86 sub-degree awards were made as against 472 degrees. A certain amount of non-degree work was apparently shouldered by the Regional Management Centre (subsequently retitled the Plassey Management and Technology Centre) on the same campus. The Centre was put into receivership, and subsequently into liquidation, in circumstances embarrassing for the University in August 1995.
122 *Dáil Debates*, vol. 248, col. 1926 (23 July 1970); vol. 259, col. 1569 (15 March 1972).
123 ibid., vol. 268, cols. 401-404 (23 October 1973).
124 ibid., vol. 286, cols. 926-936 (4 December 1975).
125 ibid., vol. 294, col. 173 (17 November 1976).
126 *Irish Times*, 20 October 1977.
127 *Irish Independent*, 29 October 1977. Also, *Irish Times*, 11 November 1977.
128 *Irish Press*, 19 November 1980.
129 *Dáil Debates*, vol. 324, col. 306 (12 November 1980).
130 *National Institute for Higher Education Limerick Act 1980*.
National Institute for Higher Education Dublin Act 1980. (This was identical in form to that for NIHE Limerick).
Thomond College of Education Act 1980.
131 This was perhaps to be expected. The Department's first foray into legislation for many years came in 1971 with An Coláiste Ealaíne is Deartha Act 1971 setting up NCAD on a statutory basis. It had been severely criticised at the time for attempting to maintain a tight measure of control on a third-level college. See particularly the contribution of Garret FitzGerald, *Dáil Debates*, vol. 256, col. 771 (2 November 1971).
132 ibid., vol. 319, cols. 1498-1506 (17 April 1980).
133 ibid. col. 1514. See also *Seanad Debates*, vol. 94, col. 1474 (26 June 1980), col. 1555 (2 July 1980).
134 ibid., vol. 94, col. 1541 (2 July 1980).
135 Or the local VEC in the case of regional technical college principals.
136 *National Institute for Higher Education Limerick Act 1980*, Section 5.
137 ibid., Section 1.
138 NCEA, *Eleventh Report*, p. 44; *NCEA Directory of Approved Courses in Higher Education, 1987*, p. 29.
139 For details of the first applications by eight Irish organisations in 1973, *see Dáil Debates*, vol. 267, cols. 195-96 (4 July 1973). The Commissioner for Social Affairs was the first Irish Commissioner, Dr Patrick Hillery.
140 *Dáil Debates*, vol. 270, col. 938 (19 February 1974).

141 ibid. vol. 302, col. 1271 (13 December 1977). For details of the amounts spent by the Fund in Ireland during the first five years of Irish membership of the Community, see *Dáil Debates*, vol. 308, col. 393-4, (17 October 1978).

142 ibid., vol. 255, col. 785 (4 November 1975); vol. 286, cols. 1002-3 (4 December 1975); vol. 302, col. 1271 (13 December 1977); vol. 328, cols. 336-346 (26 March 1981).

143 Ibid., vol. 286, col. 1004 (4 December 1975).

144 Maurice N. Hennessy, 'Regional Colleges and the EEC Plan', *Cork Examiner*, 10 August 1975.

145 *Dáil Debates*, vol. 296, col. 427 (27 January 1977).

146 So low-key and undocumented was the introduction of ESF funding to the Regional Technical Colleges that a 1981 ESRI study of the financing of third-level education showed no awareness of any kind that courses at regional technical colleges had been subvented handsomely by the Fund over the previous six years. See Barlow A.C. (1981), *The Financing of Third-Level Education*, Dublin: Economic and Social Research Institute.

147 *Dáil Debates*, vol. 309, col. 628 (9 November 1978).

148 ibid., vol. 297, col. 613 (2 March 1977).

149 ibid., vol. 314, col. 479 (10 May 1979).

150 ibid., vol. 324, col. 11 (11 November 1980). The big breakthrough in amounts available from the European Social Fund came in 1984. The minister concerned, Gemma Hussey, attended at the end of the process and, not having been a TD much less a spokesman on education before 1982, was able to wonder why no Education minister had come over and done the same before then. She clearly had never learnt of the coup that had been achieved less than a decade previously. Hussey, G. (1990), *At the Cutting Edge, Cabinet Diaries 1982-87*, Dublin: Gill and Macmillan, p. 101.

151 *Dáil Debates*, vol. 334, col. 972 (12 May 1982).

152 ibid., vol. 337, col. 2046 (13 July 1982).

153 *Building on Reality 1985-7* (1984), Dublin: Stationery Office, p. 93. By 1986 over 88% of all new entrants to full-time courses at regional technical colleges were in receipt of ESF grants. See Clancy, *Who Goes to College?*, p. 28.

154 *Irish Times*, 31 May 1991.

155 UNESCO, Statistical Yearbook 1985, quoted in Clancy, P. (1989), 'The Evolution of Policy in Third-Level Education' in D.G. Mulcahy and D. O'Sullivan (eds)., *Irish Educational Policy: Process and Substance*, Dublin: Institute of Public Administration, p. 120.

156 The figures in the table are compiled from the *Statistical Reports (Tuarascáil Staitistiúil)* of the Department of Education for the period concerned. The figures for Vocational/Technological appear to comprise the City of Dublin VEC Colleges and Limerick Technical College. In 1972-73 and 1973-74 they also include NIHE Limerick. The figures for HEA-assisted colleges appear to comprise NIHE Limerick, the National College of Art and Design from 1977/78 onwards and NIHE Dublin in 1980-81. They do not include NCPE/ Thomond College of Education which features under Teacher Education and for which the figures were as follows: 1974/75: 279; 1975/76: 277; 1976/77: 249; 1977/78: 213; 1978/79: 360; 1979/80: 355. Due to unexplained changes in the format of the reports it is not possible to explain fully the variations in the category of 'Other'.

157 An Roinn Oideachais, *Tuarascáil Staitistiúil 1980-81*, p. 2. Clancy, *1980 Participation Survey*, pp. 10-11.

158 The definition of the sector is as in Clancy, *Participation Survey*. It should be noted that Clancy's study of new entrants excludes a small number of institutions included in the Department of Education statistics.

159 This trend was to continue right into the next decade. By 1986, 59 per cent of the new entrants were to the technological sector (Clancy, *Who Goes to College?*, p. 13). The subsequent six-year period saw a reversal of the trend, with the technological sector enrolling 11,840 new entrants (47 per cent), just 83 (0.3 per cent) more than the university sector in 1992 (Clancy, *Access to College*, p. 30).

160 NCEA, *Eighth Report*, p. 27.

161 ibid., pp. 25, 31.

162 *Dáil Debates*, vol. 313, col. 1008 (3 February 1979).

163 ibid., vol. 314, cols. 1057-1058 (22 May 1979). Similar details are not available for later years.

164 ibid. Details for 1978-79 are included in Appendix 2. For comparable figures for university colleges, see HEA, *Accounts 1978 and Student Statistics 1978/79*, pp. 48-58.

165 *Dáil Debates*, vol. 320, col. 665 (2 May 1980).

166 ibid., vol. 309, col. 465 (8 November 1978). Details of full-time staff numbers for the RTC system for the period are not available. Figures have been supplied for 1993/94 for all full-time staff. *Dáil Debates*, vol. 449, col. 1823 (28 February 1995). (Athlone – 177, Carlow – 161, Cork – 402, Dundalk – 187, Galway – 272, Letterkenny – 146, Limerick – 190, Sligo – 164, Tallaght – 120, Tralee – 150, Waterford – 240, DIT – 1094).

167 National Council for Educational Awards (1981), *A Report of a Survey of NCEA Award Recipients*, Dublin: National Council for Educational Awards.

168 National Council for Educational Awards (1985), *The Career Development of Engineering and Construction Studies Award Recipients*, Dublin: National Council for Educational Awards. This survey had a response rate of 57 per cent, 446 out of 768 questionnaires circulated.

169 The colleges of the VECs in the cities of Dublin and Limerick had until 1993 to compete for resources with second-level schools within their own VEC scheme. The details of their recurrent allocations were not published.

170 The figures for recurrent grants for the two sectors have been compiled from the Books of Estimates for the years 1971-72, 1976 and 1981. It should be noted that the estimates switched to a calendar year basis in 1974. Previously the Exchequer's financial year operated from April to March. The switch was achieved by a nine month financial year from April to December 1974. The figures for the university sector comprise the National University of Ireland, UCD, UCC, UCG, TCD, St Patrick's College Maynooth, the Royal College of Surgeons in Ireland and in 1970-71 and 1975 the College of Pharmacy. The third-level work of the last institution was absorbed into Trinity College Dublin, in 1976. The figures for the vocational sector comprise the RTCs and NIHE (1970-71, 1975 and 1980). The figures for the three years mainly take into account voted expenditure on the colleges channelled through either the Department of Education or the Higher Education Authority. The figures for

these years do not include capital grants, nor do they include subventions via higher education grants, nor in the case of UCD and UCC do they include grants from the Department of Agriculture to students of agriculture, dairy science and veterinary medicine.

171 *Dáil Debates*, vol. 337, col. 91 (29 June 1982). These figures are not easily reconciled with figures published in 1995 by the Higher Education Authority, see Higher Education Authority (1995), *Interim Report of the Steering Committee's Technical Working Group*, Table 2.4, p. 47. These would indicate that the recurrent cost for a student in 1980 in a university was £4,190 and for a student in RTCs/DIT £4,900.

172 *Tuarascáil Staitistiúil 1980-81*, p. 60.; ibid., 1979-80, p. 107.

173 ibid.

174 In calculating the students at HEA-funded institutions the numbers for Thomond College of Education (245 in 1979/80 and 316 in 1980/81) have been deducted from the totals. A small number of students in Regional Technical Colleges were in receipt of higher education grants. It is reckoned that these were at least set off by the students in receipt of VEC scholarships at NIHE and NCAD.

175 *Dáil Debates*, vol. 302, col. 953 (7 December 1977). The upgrading was finally achieved in the aftermath of the 1977 General Election during the campaign for which the Town of Tralee VEC had successfully elicited the support of both the Taoiseach, Liam Cosgrave, and the leader of the opposition, Jack Lynch. The Committee was informed of the enhancement of status before the coalition government went out of office.

176 ibid., vol. 271, col. 370 (20 March 1974).

177 *Evening Herald*, 30 September 1978; *Western Journal*, 22 September 1978, 22 January 1979; *Western People*, 14 July 1979.

178 *Dáil Debates*, vol. 310, col. 791 (6 December 1978). An 'outcentre' of Galway Regional Technical College was eventually established in Castlebar and the first students enrolled in the autumn of 1994.

179 *Nenagh Guardian*, 30 June 1979; *Clonmel Nationalist*, 14 December 1979; *Tipperary Star*, 8 January 1980; *Irish Press*, 18 March 1980. See also *Dáil Debates*, vol. 317, col. 1215 (6 December 1979); vol. 325, col. 1675 (17 December 1980). By 1990 the proposal had been adapted by the local action group to become one for a regional development institute (*Dáil Debates*, vol. 309, cols. 1082-1088 – 8 May 1990). The proposal was sanctioned in December 1994 by the caretaker Minister for Education, Michael Smith, and confirmed by the rainbow coalition government in January 1995, at the same time as the decision to build a regional technical college in Dún Laoghaire (*Irish Times*, 26 July 1995).

180 *Irish Times*, 11 December 1979. *Wicklow People*, 28 December 1979.

181 Clancy, P. and Benson, C. (1979), *Higher Education in Dublin: A Study of Some Emerging Needs*, Dublin: Higher Education Authority.

182 Clancy, *Participation Survey*, p. 36.

183 *White Paper on Educational Development* (1980), Dublin: Stationery Office, p. 84.

184 *White Paper on Educational Development*. Prl 9373.

185 ibid., p. iv.

186 ibid., pp. 70-79.

187 ibid., p. 70.

188 ibid., p. 75.

189 ibid., p. 76.

190 ibid., pp. 2-3. In considering options the Department had available to it a range of projections based on different assumptions prepared by the Higher Education Authority. In the event the Department went for an altogether lower figure than that recommended by HEA (HEA, *General Report 1974-84*, pp. 92-95). The projections had been published, see Sheehan, J. (1978), *Future Enrolments in Third-Level Education*, Dublin: Higher Education Authority.

191 This is not a point that is obvious merely with hindsight. The author referred to this issue shortly after the publication of the White Paper. See White, A. (1981), 'Higher Technological Education in the 1970s', *Irish Educational Studies*, pp. 319-320.

192 Higher Education Authority (1994), *Reports, Accounts and Student Statistics 1990/91 and 1991/92,* Dublin: Higher Education Authority, p. 19.

193 *White Paper*, p. 70.

194 Indeed it was considerably better at projecting student numbers than the Department was to prove itself in the White Paper. In its 1974 Progress Report the HEA projected the full-time university population in 1979/80 at 24,214 (HEA, *Progress Report*, pp. 21-24). The actual outturn was 22,937.

195 On the contrary. During the decade from 1974 to 1983 growth in student numbers in HEA-funded institutions almost exactly mirrored that of the other side of the binary divide, with the large increase in student numbers coming in engineering, science and commerce.

196 This could, of course, partially explain a level of resentment among some civil servants. Basically, with the (perhaps innocent) co-operation of IDA, the Department of Education had to an extent been bypassed by the Manpower Consultative Committee, and the institutions in the technological field had been approached through HEA. The significance of this point is raised in the following chapter.

197 It has been suggested to the author that official displeasure was provoked by HEA's decision to provide capital funding for engineering education at Trinity College Dublin, thereby reversing one further decision of December 1974.

198 Seán O'Connor respected this ethos also, in spite of his liking for public controversy. The author can recall him, as Chairman of the Higher Education Authority, declining a radio interview for the simple reason that he was worried about acquiring the reputation for being a readily accessible 'civil service gasbag'. In drafting his reflective study *A Troubled Sky*, he spent many hours in the UCD library documenting events, mainly through Dáil reports, of which he had direct knowledge and on which he also had strong views. He would not leave himself open to the charge that he had abused his undertakings in relation to official secrets. (Conversation with author, February 1986.)

199 It used to remain anecdotal for at least a generation. This has changed only slightly with the passing of the Freedom of Information Act 1997.

200 Most notably James F. Dukes, the first Secretary of HEA, his successor, John Hayden, and Pádraig MacDiarmada, Director of the National Council for Educational Awards from 1973 to 1996.

CHAPTER 9

The Universities Come in from the Cold

One of the most striking aspects of the change of direction in Irish higher education in the period from 1960 to 1980 was that the push towards meeting manpower needs and the requirements of a rapidly industrialising society came almost entirely from within the education sector. There is no evidence of prodding from elsewhere within the state. There was no parallel interest or demand among those devising or implementing industrial policy, nor among the spokesmen for industry itself.[1] It has already been noted that OECD had observed that Irish industry in the early 1960s did not appear to be concerned about the absence of technicians, and that the Steering Committee on Technical Education suggested that, if there was no demand by industry for trained personnel, then it had to be stimulated by the educational sector. With very few exceptions that gap was to continue until the end of the 1970s. The establishment of the Department of Labour in 1966 was to accentuate the pattern of minimal interaction between the decision-makers in education and those charged with industrial development.[2]

Up to the middle 1960s an important role was envisaged for the Department of Education and the VEC sector in planning for Ireland's new industrial future. The *Second Programme for Economic Expansion*,[3] *Investment in Education*, the OECD report on the training of technicians and the reports of the National Industrial and Economic Council all envisaged the education system contributing, not alone to economic and industrial development, but even in such areas as manpower forecasting. The creation of the Department of Labour and, more particularly, of the Industrial Training Authority (AnCO) in 1967 changed the focus.[4] The Taoiseach, Seán Lemass, speaking on the debate on the Bill establishing the Department, referred to the considerable psychological and other advantages in having all major matters relating to manpower under one ministry.[5] With the establishment of AnCO and its subsequent dramatic growth from 1967 onwards the provision of trained manpower for industry tended to be viewed as its bailiwick. It was much easier for incoming foreign industry to deal with a single body like AnCO on matters of training and labour force skills than to liaise with one of thirty-eight VECs which had no similar clear-cut brief. The same applied to the Industrial Development Authority (IDA) in putting together any grants package involving the training of a workforce. The Authority was eventually to come to play a major role in bridging industrial and educational policy.

IDA was established in 1949. In 1969 legislation reconstituting it led to a major upgrading of that body under a very dynamic managing director, Michael Killeen. It virtually took over responsibility, not just for the implementation, but almost for the making, of industrial policy.[6] The emphasis on foreign investment which emerged from 1958 onwards became even more marked.

The early reports of the statutory IDA illustrate how the emphasis in its work of enticing foreign industries was on physical, rather than skilled, assets. At that point IDA did not place any importance on human capital. In dealing with industrial training its emphasis was very traditional.[7] In 1971 it felt that the most satisfactory long-term solution to the problem of skilled labour shortage in Ireland was to step up the intake into apprenticeship in the industrial trades and to shorten the period of apprenticeship through more intensive training arrangements, and it noted with approval AnCO's reviewing of the apprenticeship systems to bring them more into line with the needs of modern Irish industry.[8]

The advent of the regional technical colleges and the first technician output from them merited noting by IDA in 1972,[9] but even in the mid-1970s the planning of additional provision to meet the training needs of technicians and other skilled workers was a matter for consultation with the Confederation of Irish Industry and the Irish Congress of Trade Unions, and co-operation with AnCO and the National Manpower Service.[10] The educational authorities scarcely figured. During the period of the Authority's hegemony in industrial policy there was very little contact between it and the education sector. The vocational sector of higher education had taken on board the notion that it must be responsive to the needs of an industrialising society, but the industrial planners were not cognisant of what was happening in the education system. The liaison with those concerned with the skills of the workforce was largely confined to those involved with industrial training. There were indeed public representatives, like Barry Desmond, who were concerned that the national approach to industrial training was too narrow and short-term.[11] But there was no forum for the issues to be thrashed out between the two sides. What was happening was that the higher education system was very much influenced by what had become industrial and economic policy, but there was no reciprocal influence. The concept of human capital took some considerable time to find its way into official policy on Irish industrial development. However IDA was results-driven to a degree unusual among Irish state bodies, and it had a research and planning arm which was looking at long-term trends.[12] If working through the cumbersome structures of the 'social partners' was likely to impede the job-creation process, IDA had the inventiveness to circumvent such formidable obstacles.

By the time the Authority came to launch its industrial plan for the period 1978-82 its strategy was to shift Irish industry into products with higher added value, based on good quality and design and aimed at specialist market niches using well-planned professional marketing. The strategy was intended to 'capitalise on the strengths of the country, such as the high level of education, where we have an advantage over third-world countries'.[13] This was a crucial step. For the first time a significant institution from outside the education sector was about to take seriously, and exploit the efforts of, those in the education world who, inspired primarily by ideas originating with OECD, had established an alternative approach to higher education.[14] From 1978 onwards the annual reports of the Authority began to record its involvement with the Manpower Consultative Committee, its liaison with the Higher Education Authority and the provision of needed courses at universities and regional technical colleges.[15] By 1981 the report was describing IDA's links with colleges,[16] and by the mid 1980s travellers through airports saw large IDA advertisements with smiling groups of Irish graduates whom high-tech companies were encouraged to recruit. The IDA pragmatists, in their battle to attract footloose foreign investment, were prepared to harness skill and talent wherever it could be found, and in the process it cut through the prejudices about universities to be found among some in the VEC system and the Department of Education.

The first major sign of change came in 1978 with the formation of the Manpower Consultative Committee. The Committee was the initial forum for dialogue between IDA and the education system.

Under the chairmanship of the Minister for Labour, Gene Fitzgerald, it met for the first time in December 1978.[17] Its terms of reference were to advise the government on the role of manpower policy in meeting economic and social objectives. Its initial concentration was on occupational shortages. The Committee quickly identified a number of areas of skills shortage,[18] and it noted *inter alia* a large imbalance in the supply of engineering and computer personnel.[19] The shortages identified, and the IDA estimates of job creation over the following four years, suggested a serious obstacle to the attainment of government targets. While many of the shortages identified were in areas which were within the purview of AnCO (sewing machinists, bricklayers, fitters and welders), shortages of electrical and electronic engineers and technicians, mechanical and production engineers, chemical technologists, computer programmers and systems analysts were not. If these shortfalls were to be tackled it was to the educators, not the trainers, that the Committee would have to turn.

The Manpower Consultative Committee asked the Higher Education Authority to meet it early in 1979. The Authority was further asked to consult with all higher education institutions and to consider whether an urgent programme of expansion could be prepared to alleviate existing shortages and increase output to meet projected demand from 1983 onwards. A programme was prepared quickly. For institutions not designated under the HEA Act, it was highly unusual to be approached by the Authority with a request to make proposals for course expansion. Some of them did not actually respond to the HEA initiative and accordingly missed out on the allocation of funds and courses.[20] Four university colleges, NIHE Limerick, six regional technical colleges, Limerick Technical College and three of the colleges of the Dublin Institute of Technology were included in the programme which received government approval in May 1979. The programme enhanced intakes into twenty-two existing courses, brought additional options to five others, and introduced thirty new courses and fifteen short-term conversion courses for graduates.[21]

The programme resulted in a sharp increase in the output of graduates in electronic and mechanical engineering and in computer science. Output of engineering graduates increased by 40 per cent between 1978 and 1983, while the output from computer science increased tenfold in the same period. From 1979 onwards the higher education system and its output came to loom much larger in the thinking of the Industrial Development

Authority. Arising out of the same process the Confederation of Irish Industry established its own manpower policy committee and both its director general, Liam Connellan, and its recently appointed director of economic policy, Con Power, the former Principal of Sligo Regional Technical College, became prominent lobbyists and spokesmen on different aspects of the relationship between industry and the educational system.[22] The initial impact of this was to reinforce the emphasis on the vocational within the higher education system and also to introduce more earmarked money.[23]

The involvement of IDA with universities through the Manpower Consultative Committee (MCC) from 1978 onwards was a vital turning point in how universities came to be perceived. The funding which arose out of the MCC programme was very helpful to some of the universities,[24] and the Hardiman report in 1987 commented that the programme had underlined the commitment of the university sector to technological education and its readiness to respond quickly and flexibly.[25] The growth areas for students in institutions funded by HEA were engineering and business studies. In March 1981 there were 2,382 full-time undergraduate students in commerce/business studies and 2,891 in engineering. Ten years later the comparative figures were 4,291 and 4,373.[26] The university pattern was mirroring what was happening in the sub-degree system with NCEA and DIT awards. IDA had brought the universities into the mainstream of economic and industrial planning.

There was another reason why universities were back in the mainstream. Antipathy to the arts degree, and what it was deemed to stand for, finally began to decline in the 1980s. The talking down of the arts degree had had its effects in various ways over the years. The President of UCD, Dr Tom Murphy, was able to tell a conference organised by HEA in 1984 that, of the 1,045 students admitted to the Faculty of Arts in his university in 1983-84, only eight would have attained a place in the Faculty of Medicine.[27] Not merely were able students avoiding arts type courses, but professions and major recruiters of graduates were displaying a similar preference for vocationally relevant studies. For example, the pattern of entry among Irish chartered accountants was highly dependent on business studies graduates in contrast to the broad spectrum drawn upon for similar recruitment in Britain.[28]

The antipathy to the arts degree was always capable of surfacing anew. In 1984, for example, Charles Haughey, leader of the opposition, indicated that he would be ruthless about cutting some of the liberal arts courses in universities. He felt that the main urge in third-level education should to be towards science, technology, research and development.[29] Education spokesmen in 1990s were still capable of recycling the battle-cries of the 1970s with little adaptation.[30] Moreover Dr Edward Walsh was always ready to keep this particular pot boiling. As late as 1990 he delivered an outspoken attack on the perceived values of liberal education, when, in a vigorous diatribe at a John Henry Newman Centenary Symposium in UCC, he virtually labelled Newman (of all people) a sectarian bigot.[31] This quixotic tilt at one of the most seminal thinkers on university education laid bare both the paradox and the weakness of the Walsh position.

By the time Dr Walsh made this *cri de coeur* he was President of the newly-established University of Limerick. One cannot but admire the extent of his personal achievement within a twenty year span of taking a greenfield site, building it into an enormous third-level campus, and also achieving for it the title and status of university, all against considerable opposition on many fronts. This was added to by the major achievement of the Foundation Building, providing Limerick and the university with a concert hall of international quality, with funds raised by private sponsorship in accordance with Dr Walsh's own philosophy.[32] Nevertheless part of Dr Walsh's appeal over many years had been that of the self-proclaimed outsider,[33] which allowed him to maintain a role as an attacker of the universities. His championing of technology had something of the same quality. Part of the success of the tactic was that it tapped into an anti-intellectual and philistine undertow in Irish life.[34] Such populist language was all the more potent because it came from a key figure within higher education itself. Attacks on the university ethos became harder to sustain once he himself became a university president. In addition the transformation of the University of Limerick was completed in 1991 with the enactment of the University of Limerick (Dissolution of Thomond College) Bill.[35] The adjacent teacher education college, which twenty years previously some senior civil servants had fought vigorously to keep independent of NIHE, was now absorbed into the new university.[36] This injected into the university a swathe of faculty with qualifications and backgrounds different from what NIHE with its technological thrust had traditionally recruited. Dr Walsh in some sense was making his peace with the arts, while in Dublin his counterpart, Dr O'Hare, was about to engage in discussions with St Patrick's College, Drumcondra, another institution of teacher education.

While the emphasis on the vocational remained extremely strong, the 1980s nevertheless saw the first signs of a reversal of the trend. Some members of the academic community were prepared, not only to question the Walsh orthodoxy, but to defend the values under attack.[37] Two ministers, Gemma Hussey and Mary O'Rourke, and a number of Dáil deputies indicated that the support for better technological education need not be accompanied by an onslaught on the values represented by the arts and humanities.[38] If some of those charged with developing educational policy had weakened slightly in their commitment to making technological and vocational requirements the overriding priorities in higher education, new proponents of this approach began to emerge among those involved in formulating industrial policy. This became clear from some events surrounding the 1991 Culliton Report.

An Industrial Policy Review Group, chaired by industrialist and banker Jim Culliton, was established in 1990 to review and make recommendations on industrial policy.[39] One of the nine chapters of its report was devoted to 'Education, Enterprise and Technology.' The recommendations in this section were largely based on a commissioned study on *Industrial Training in Ireland* prepared by academic and consultant, Dr Frank Roche, and economist, Paul Tansey.[40] The nub of their argument was that skills and workforce quality would become increasingly important as a differentiating factor in national competitive advantage. To bring this about a higher priority was required for the acquisition of useable and marketable skills by the community as a whole, and particularly by the education system. That system was seen as exhibiting a strong academic bias, even within its specifically vocational segment.

The report recommended developing a parallel stream of non-academic vocationally-orientated education at second-level, commanding widespread recognition and support. Where previously education had been driven by increasing participation rates at progressively higher levels of educational attainment, the emphasis now needed to switch to a greater search for economic efficiency, measured in terms of the education sector's contribution to industry needs. These arguments were adopted almost *in toto* in the Review Group's Report, which called for a major effort to reverse the trend of recent years and to place a new emphasis on vocational and technological training.[41] It appeared as if the authors of the documents were not fully aware of what had been happening in Irish education in the previous twenty years.

The Culliton vision could no longer expect a smooth ride and it came under attack from various quarters. One of the first, and most unlikely, was a speaker at the annual conference of the Irish Management Institute, Professor Liam Fahy of the Boston University School of Management, who declared that the call for greater emphasis on technical and vocational training at second-level was precisely what Ireland did not need. What it needed rather were people who were broadly educated and then acquired a technical expertise.[42]

A more significant attack on the Culliton Report came from someone who, almost a generation previously, had been a major critic of the academic bias of the Irish education system, the former Taoiseach, Garret FitzGerald. In the Dáil debate on the Culliton Report he launched an attack on those portions of the report dealing with education.[43] He found the tone of the report basically unsympathetic to education in its proper sense, and felt that its simplistic view confused education and training. Above all he set out to argue that the oft-repeated statement in the Roche/Tansey report that the education system had become progressively more academic was demonstrable nonsense, citing and quantifying the decline in the study of subjects such as history and geography as against some of the more vocational subjects, particularly business organisation and accounting.[44] Like Professor Fahy he too had direct experience of foreign industry locating in Ireland, and adverted to the fact that, for most incoming industrialists, an educated workforce was more attractive than one that was narrowly trained.

Had the Culliton Report appeared ten years earlier, it is indeed likely that it would have had a major influence on the education sector. Its conclusions were taken up in the 1992 Green Paper *Education for a Changing World.* While showing considerable respect for the findings of Culliton and paying homage to the nurturing of an enterprise culture, the Green Paper, instead of the Culliton prescription of a separate non-academic vocational stream, proposed to build on and expand the range of vocational options within the existing Leaving Certificate programme.[45] There was still much of the pragmatic and the utilitarian in the Green Paper's approach to higher education, and Dr FitzGerald, in a valedictory Dáil speech, expressed his concern at the extent to which the Green Paper treated the higher education system as if it were a business and nothing else.[46] The teeth of Culliton had by now been drawn and crude utilitarian arguments promoting the narrowly technical over the academic had ceased to have the same force. When the 1995 White Paper on Education came to be published, the utilitarian focus was further diluted.[47]

A contrasting approach to Culliton was discernible in the 1996 strategy document produced by Forfás, the policy advisory and co-ordination board for industrial development, science and technology in Ireland.[48] There was none of the academic/technical dualism which had been resurrected by Tansey and Roche. The Forfás document regarded the skills and creativity of the workforce as the main determinant of the competitiveness of the enterprise sector and saw fundamental changes occurring in the nature of skills requirements. According to Forfás the key general skills required in the future would include a) managerial and social, b) communication, presentation and writing, c) foreign language competence, d) problem solving and synthesis, e) learning abilities and memory training, f) teaching, g) broad science and computer literacy, h) understanding of business organisation and economic principles and i) appreciation of design.[49] It also indicated that with increasing internationalisation the need for foreign language competence would become more vitally important, and it foresaw potential shortages with regard to education for software development and languages. The report was indicative of how much the education system had become central to the success of the state's industrial policy and it was also apparent that the latter policy had come around to playing to the strengths of the country's education system rather than highlighting or bemoaning its weaknesses.

The establishment in the late 1960s of a system of higher education outside the universities was driven by a conviction that higher education and industrial needs required closer alignment and that this task could not be left to the universities. A binary system was developed which in the early years aspired to a close co-ordination of education and the country's manpower requirements. By the mid-1990s some of these assumptions had been undermined. A quantitative analysis, contained in the *Interim Report of the Steering Committee's Technical Working Group*, a working group established by the Higher Education Authority, could casually observe that the group did not 'consider it realistic, as a basis for determining future higher education needs, to seek to correlate closely the output of the sector with labour market needs. So far as we are aware, such an exercise does not form a part of higher education policy in any developed economy.'[50] This was a far cry from the thought processes of those who initiated or invented the binary system in Ireland. It was not just the rehabilitation of the universities by the Industrial Development Authority which had partially undermined that vision. The rationale for the binary system had also been dented by the upgrading of the two National Institutes to university status in 1989. The significance of this issue is examined in the next chapter after a consideration of other trends in higher education to the end of the millennium.

Growth and ongoing issues

Higher education grew throughout the period from the 1960s to the end of the century. Appendix 1 shows the numbers in full-time third-level education in the period from 1965 to 1998. The numbers had grown by a factor of six and had shown growth in every year. The smallest increases were in 1978 (1 per cent) and 1967 (1.9 per cent), the largest in 1965 (13.77 per cent) and 1993 (10 per cent). In the five-year periods from 1969 the percentage growth was: 1969-73: 31.6; 1974-78: 28.6; 1979-83: 29.3; 1984-88: 24.6; 1989-93: 41.7; 1994-98: 33.3.

The numbers in higher education grew consistently over a generation. The trend was in line with what was happening elsewhere in Europe.[51] A striking feature was that Irish third-level students were significantly younger than their European counterparts. In the early 1990s the median age of new entrants to higher education in Ireland was 18.6 years, as compared to a mean of 20.5 years for OECD countries in general. Eighty per cent of Irish new entrants were under 19.4 years, while the corresponding figure for OECD countries was 24.3 years.[52]

The proportion of the full-time student body enrolled at university remained remarkably consistent at 55.3 per cent in 1980, 54.2 per cent in 1990 and 54 per cent in 1997.[53] The technological sector accounted for 26 per cent of the student body in 1980, 39 per cent in 1990 and 37 per cent in 1997. A different pattern was apparent with new entries. Because so many of the programmes in the technological sector were short-cycle (i.e. of two years' duration) there was a faster throughput in these colleges. In 1980,

41 per cent of new entrants were at university and about 50 per cent in the technological colleges. By 1992 these proportions were virtually identical at 46.6 per cent (11,757 entrants to universities) and 46.9 per cent (11,840 entrants to the technological sector).[54]

One of the striking developments was in female participation. In 1965-66 females had accounted for 28 per cent of the state's university students, by 1980-81 this had jumped to 43 per cent and by 1997-98 it had reached 56 per cent.[55] In the technological sector, because of the huge majority of male students in engineering and technology disciplines, males outnumbered females, although by 1997 the proportion of females in the technological colleges had reached 47 per cent.

Numbers of postgraduate students as a percentage of total enrolments declined from 16 per cent in 1975 to 12 per cent in 1985, but had increased again to 16 per cent by 1994. If numbers in the Higher Diploma in Education (a mandatory qualification for graduates wishing to join the state register of secondary school teachers) were excluded, the numbers show an increase from 8 per cent in 1975 to 9 per cent in 1985 and 14 per cent in 1994.[56]

The distribution of disciplines across the university system remained relatively stable during the period from the mid-1960s to the mid-1990s. The most significant changes were the increase in business studies from 8 per cent of total enrolments in 1965 to 13 per cent in 1980 and 16 per cent in 1992, whereas medicine and dentistry had decreased from 17 per cent in 1965 to 9 per cent in 1992.[57] A similar pattern was apparent in the technological sector, as indicated by NCEA awards. In 1980 about 40 per cent of NCEA awards were in engineering, 25 per cent in business studies, 20 per cent in science and 15 per cent in humanities. The proportion of awards in business studies grew consistently. By 1988 it had overtaken engineering as the largest area for NCEA awards. By 1997 (when NCEA celebrated its silver jubilee) almost 44 per cent of NCEA awards were in business studies, 22 per cent were in science, 15 per cent in humanities and engineering was down to just over 20 per cent.[58] OECD figures on relative participation in degree courses by field of study in the early nineties showed Ireland ahead of other OECD countries in the percentages taking degrees in human sciences (mainly arts and social sciences) and in natural and physical science.

TABLE 7: Participation in degree courses by field of study: Ireland and OECD[59]

Subject	% Total Degrees in Subject Category Ireland	OECD Mean
Human Sciences	45.8	37.7
Law and Business	16.8	22.3
Natural and Physical Science	19.2	12.7
Engineering and Architecture	12.4	14.7
Medical Science	5.8	11.7
TOTALS	**100**	**100**

Another trend was the proliferation of specialised options at both undergraduate degree and national diploma level across all disciplines. Some of these were of an interdisciplinary nature such as the combining of languages with law, computing and marketing.[60]

All through the period from the 1970s to the late 1990s provision of higher education was largely concentrated on full-time students. Ongoing data on part-time provision is scanty, but in 1992 it was reckoned that there were about 24,000 students availing of higher education on a part-time basis, 60.3 per cent (14,398) in the RTC/DIT sector, 28.8 per cent (6,872) in universities and about 10 per cent elsewhere. The bulk of the provision was at evenings and weekends, about 90 per cent of those attending were at work, 85 per cent of students were under the age of forty, and most of the study was undertaken for career-related and professional updating reasons. Fifty-eight per cent of students were on certificate or diploma, 25 per cent were at undergraduate and 12 per cent at postgraduate level. One-third of the participants were in business, 20 per cent in engineering and 13 per cent in computing. Of these students, 10.5 percent availed of distance education and 3.2 per cent of correspondence education.[61]

Higher education during the period of its expansion made very limited provision for mature students. For many years the high levels of dependency, brought about by a high birth rate and a high level of emigration, created pressure on public finances where the young took priority. An almost constant labour force surplus meant that labour force supply was never seen as a problem, so there was no priority for retraining or upgrading the skills of the existing labour force.[62] The HEA-sponsored studies by Professor Patrick Clancy of new entrants to third-level showed that the proportions of students over 21 years of age on entry in 1980, 1986 and 1992 were 5 per cent, 2.8 per cent and 4 per cent. The percentage of all full-time students aged 23 years or over was 16.6 per cent in 1996/97, an increase from 13.8 per cent in 1992/93. A 1997 census showed that 5.4 per cent of all full-time students were mature students of 23 years or over. These represented 25 per cent of all mature students. The other 75 per cent were part-time and made up the vast bulk (80 per cent) of all part-time higher education students.

The first signs of a shift in state attitudes and interest in the area began to emerge in the mid-1990s when the dramatic upturn in the Irish economy led eventually to an emerging skills shortage. This in turn began to concentrate minds on the provision for lifelong learning and the underdeveloped potential of mature students. In 1995 the Report of the HEA's Steering Committee on the Future Development of Higher Education recommended that the intake of mature students in publicly-funded institutions should rise from the then current 3.7 per cent of total intake to about 15 per cent by the year 2010.[63]

The growth in full-time numbers was itself a reflection of increased participation in second-level education. About 20 per cent of the age cohort had completed the Leaving Certificate in 1965. This had risen to 80 per cent by 1995.[64] The vast majority of school-leavers went into some form of post-secondary education and training. The proportion of the age cohort entering higher education had increased consistently from 20 per cent in 1980, to 25 per cent in 1986, 36 per cent in 1992 and 46 per cent in 1998.[65] Almost as many again were in further education in the state on post-Leaving Certificate courses, in full-time courses in private colleges, agricultural colleges, nurse training, and in apprenticeship training programmes sponsored by FÁS, CERT or the Farm Apprenticeship Board.[66] In 1994 it was reckoned that about 3 per cent of school leavers went to study or train abroad, mainly in higher education in Britain and Northern Ireland.[67] In 1994 about 25 per cent of school-leavers went straight to the labour market. This number had declined to about 20 per cent some years later, but thereafter it tended to remain at about 80 per cent.

There remained considerable and persistent regional variation in participation in higher education. The three studies conducted by Professor Clancy on new entrants to third-level in 1980, 1986 and 1992 indicated that Western counties had the highest admission rates with the lowest entry found in Ulster and Leinster.

Galway had the highest rate of admission with 46 per cent of the age cohort enrolled in higher education. Kerry, Clare, Mayo, Leitrim, Sligo and Roscommon all had admission rates in excess of forty per cent. Laois, Offaly, Kilkenny, Monaghan, Waterford and Dublin had the lowest rates of entry. An analysis of Dublin revealed a huge variability by district. Parts of south County Dublin had admission rates in excess of 50 per cent, while one inner city district had an admission rate of 5 per cent.[68]

The relatively low participation rate in Dublin had been identified as early as 1980, when the White Paper had indicated that four regional technical colleges would be built in Dublin. Both the absence of an effective regional lobby and the various budgetary constraints visited upon capital spending in education in the 1980s meant that it was 1992 before a Regional Technical College opened in Tallaght, 1997 in Dún Laoghaire and 1999 in the case of Blanchardstown. The Castlebar campus of what was to become the Galway-Mayo Institute of Technology received its first students in 1994, while the Tipperary Rural and Business Development Institute, with campuses in Thurles and Clonmel, took in its first students in September 1999. The rationale of the latter institute was to develop innovative means of supporting rural economic development and foster a decentralised small to medium sized (SME) enterprise culture.[69]

One of the concerns of those running third-level institutions, as the value of third-level education and its contribution to regional development came to be widely and publicly accepted, was the pressure for more new institutions. The 1995 Steering Committee Report recommended consideration for franchising outreach centres, and enhancing the provision of distance education to facilitate those residing at some distance from a third-level institution. In 1995-96 about 1,500 students were attending certified courses in off-campus sites of higher education institutions, 600 of these being full-time. Provision was available at centres such as Cavan, Carlow, Kilkenny, Wexford, Ballina and Carrick-on-Shannon, with further initiatives expected in centres such as Skibbereen, Navan and Naas.[70] In October 1996 the Minister for Education, Niamh Bhreathnach, requested HEA to review the conduct of outreach centres. A technical working group was established, and its report in 1999 supported local initiatives leading to the establishment of a limited number of 'mixed mode' outreach centres of education, planned in partnership with a core higher education institution. Typically each centre would have a critical mass of approximately 800 students covering higher and further education. How this issue will be dealt with in the future is bound up with how the Department of Education and Science develops an approach at national level both to open and distance learning, and how information and communications technology is utilised within Irish higher education.[71]

The 1980s saw a growth in one year post-Leaving Certificate (plc) courses, which eventually came to characterise what was increasingly identified as the 'further education' sector. A significant part of the initial growth in plc courses occurred in the Dublin area, not least because of the lack of sub-degree places arising from the absence of technician provision other than at Dublin Institute of Technology. By the year 2000 there were about 25,000 plc places available in the state.[72] The co-ordination of this sector with the much larger higher education sector was one of the reasons adduced for the introduction of a new national qualifications structure discussed in the next chapter.

Within the Irish universities, dropout or failure to complete was a contentious issue. A HEA study of entry to higher education in the academic year 1989/90 showed, for the universities, a low level of non-completion by international standards at about 19 per cent overall.[73] A study of first year students at three Institutes of Technology (Carlow, Dundalk and Tralee) in 1996-97 showed an average non-completion rate among first year students of 37 per cent. The principal reason given by students themselves for leaving was the desire to pursue a different career. Almost all of those who left were pursuing other occupational and educational goals.[74]

A significant reduction in inequality occurred during the period from 1980 to 1992. The participation ratios in higher education for the four highest socio-economic groups declined from 2.56 in 1980 to 2.14 in 1986 and 1.84 in 1992. In the same period the five lower socio-economic groups rose from 0.39 in 1980 to 0.43 in 1986 and 0.63 in 1992. The more prestigious the sector and field of study the greater the social inequality in participation levels. Within the university sector the higher professional category was strongly represented within architecture, medicine and law, while semi-skilled and unskilled manual groups had their highest postgraduate representation in education and social science. The degree of inequality in entry was significantly less in the institutes of technology, where all of the manual socio-economic groups had their highest representation.

The first set of findings from the study for HEA of the 1998 cohort suggested a slowing in the reduction of inequality since 1992. Whereas in 1980 the six best represented and least represented groups sent respectively thirty-five and eight per cent to higher education, by 1998 the corresponding percentages were sixty-two and thirty.[75] The odds had improved although the percentage gap had increased. The authors observed that relative inequalities between classes were likely to change only when demand for advanced schooling from the privileged classes was saturated, and concluded that the policy of increasing the number of places at third level has the potential to further reduce inequality in higher education.

A major policy objective specified in the 1995 White Paper was the promotion of equality and the combating of disadvantage and social exclusion. The report of the 1995 Steering Committee recommended *inter alia* links between third-level and disadvantaged second-level schools, a pool of reserved places for students from disadvantaged backgrounds with priority attention for schools and students in identifiable deprived urban areas.[76] The 1992 legislation for Regional Technical Colleges, the 1997 Universities Act and the 1998 Education Act all enshrine the promotion of equality and gender equity.[77] Certain areas have had particular attention, most notably the access for, and participation of, students with disabilities.[78] Between 1996 and 1999 HEA provided funding worth over £2 million to the universities to develop targeted schemes to increase the participation of students from disadvantaged backgrounds. During the 1990s all universities set up programmes to improve access to third level among pupils in disadvantaged schools or areas. The success of the schemes has been variable and the number of students covered by them relatively small.[79]

As noted, female participation in higher education expanded throughout the 1980s and 1990s. Technology remained the most sex-typed field of study where the 15 per cent of female entrants in 1986 had increased to just 17 per cent by 1992.[80] The growth in female participation at third level was not reflected in the emergence of women at the forefront or leadership of the academic community. A 1987 HEA study showed that women accounted for only 14.5 per cent of all full-time academic staff in universities, and only 5.5 per cent of those in the senior grades. The situation was reckoned to be virtually the same in the technological sector.[81] The Committee recommended a programme for positive action. The 1997 Universities Act made the promotion of gender balance and equality of opportunity an objective of universities. Nevertheless a survey conducted by the *Irish Independent* in June 2000 showed that there were only 23 female professors working in the seven Irish universities in the state, and that of the 1,235 professors, associate professors and senior lecturers in the universities, only 169 (13 per cent) were women.[82]

The student expansion of the 1980s was not accompanied by a parallel increase in teaching staff. This was due mainly to a squeeze on budget allocations and a period of real wage cost increases. Between 1980 and 1993, staff student ratios in the university sector went from 16:1 to 22:1, while in the extra-university sector they went from 9:1 to 14:1.[83] In the year 2000 the university staff student ratio was reckoned to be 19:1.[84]

The O'Malley merger proposals of 1967, the HEA report on the Reorganisation of Higher Education and the December 1974 proposals had all stressed the importance of a Conference of Irish Universities. It was not until 1990 that the Conference of Heads of Irish Universities (CHIU) was formed. Increasingly the Conference became a commentator on some of the macro-issues effecting universities, such as the research capacity of universities and the case for extra investment in university infrastructure as part of the National Plan 2000-2006.[85] The Conference of University Rectors in Ireland (CRI) was established in 1992 as an organisation of the heads of the nine universities in the island of Ireland. It became involved in staff and student exchange, and in 2000 agreed to direct its activities over the following five years to economic regeneration, cultural literacy, tolerance and the sharing of information and resources.[86] Irish university heads were very much involved in the counterpart European body, the Conference of Rectors, Presidents and Vice Chancellors of European Universities (CRE).[87] The Council of Directors of Institutes of Technology was formed in 1993 with a secretariat and management services office located in Tralee. Its aim was to provide technical and legal support to Institutes and their management teams. These developments could be viewed as a maturing of the system of higher education.

While research had always been a central part of the work of the Irish universities, and while the block grant to universities had been regarded as including provision for both teaching and research, it had never been a major priority of state funding. The

Report of the Commission on Higher Education in 1967 had a clearcut and quantifiable recommendation in relation to staffing ratios, but it had nothing similar regarding research.[88] It accepted that academic staff should be enabled to spend at least fifty per cent of their working year on research and private study. It also felt that new ways should be developed for the organisation of research within the university,[89] and that research was the hallmark of the university. However, not least because of its composition, which included senior representation from existing research institutes, the Commission took the line that it was neither its remit nor its intention to develop a national policy for research.[90] Developing the research component of the Irish third-level sector was not a major priority of the Higher Education Authority in its early years.[91]

This began to change in the early 1990s. A management consultancy group was commissioned by HEA to carry out a comparative international assessment of the funding, organisation and management of university research. It was also requested to provide the data and analysis on which a documented case for additional research funding in the university sector in Ireland could be developed.[92] The consultants (the Circa Group), who conducted fieldwork in ten countries and interviewed a number of international scientists (all Nobel prizewinners), considered that against a background of chronic underfunding it was remarkable that the Irish universities had managed to improve both their research output and their contribution to industry and services in Ireland. It was evident that the sector had been sustained and stimulated by a mix of EU funding and private industrial and service sector contracting. Considering the scientific, social, cultural and economic contributions of university research, it was apparent from their analysis that there was something seriously amiss with policy towards the support of higher education research in Ireland. Of the main constituents of national science and technology policy, this one was more out of line with EU norms and practices than any other.

The group reckoned that the direction of university research in Ireland owed more to EU research policy and private sector influence than to national science policy and that it tended to react to, and be motivated by, whatever funding opportunities were available. It was opportunistic rather than strategic in its approach. The lack of an adequate funding base was partly the reason.[93] The report observed that internationally universities are judged on their research output more than any other factor, and that their international prestige (and competitiveness) depends on their research achievements. The report also showed that Irish universities lagged behind their European counterparts in planning, reporting and accountability, co-ordination, quality care and quality assessment.[94] This message finally came to be acted upon in a major way at the end of the 1990s.[95]

The late 1980s were a period of retrenchment in public expenditure in Ireland. Between 1985 and 1990 government expenditure on education as a percentage of gross domestic product (GDP) declined from 6.1 per cent to 5.3 per cent. On the other hand expenditure on higher education as a percentage of total government expenditure continued to grow throughout the 1980s and early 1990s, from 18.1 per cent in 1980 to 19 per cent in 1985, 21.4 per cent in 1990 and 24 per cent in 1993.[96] For universities state grants as a percentage of total operating budgets declined from 86 per cent in 1980 to 62 per cent in 1993. The decline was counterbalanced by an increase in fee income which rose from a level of 12 per cent in 1980 to 33 per cent in 1993.[97] This process was to be reversed by the decision to abolish fees for full-time undergraduate students in 1995. Academic staff-student ratios, as noted, increased from 16:1 in 1980 to about 22:1 in 1993. For the RTCs and DIT government expenditure on students declined by 57 per cent between 1980 and 1993. The major reduction took place between 1980 and 1985 when numbers in the colleges doubled. Academic staff student ratios in the RTC/DIT sector went from 9:1 in 1980 to 14:1 in 1993. The unit costs for students in the university and RTC/DIT sectors over the period were reckoned as follows:[98]

TABLE 8: Unit costs by sector

	1980	1985	1990	1993
Universities	£4,190	£3,990	£4,300	£4,140
RTC/DIT	£4,900	£3,950	£3,890	£3,720

More than anything else the change in relative units costs between the universities and the technological sector indicated the extent to which the universities had come in from the cold.

The level of demand for higher education continued to be underestimated by the central planners. The extreme caution of the Department of Education in the 1980 White Paper has already been noted. In 1995 the Report of the Steering Committee on the Future Development of Higher Education recommended an increase of 6,000 in enrolments by the year 2000. The Department of Finance representative on the Steering Committee was unable to agree to this proposal, and reckoned that only half of this increase was necessary.[99] In the event the universities exceeded the target, although the Institutes of Technology fell short.

There is clearly a limit to the growth of higher education in Ireland, but it has not yet been reached. The number of births in Ireland reached a peak of over 74,000 in 1980 and declined steadily to just under 48,000 in 1994. This reduced dramatically the age cohort of students of school leaving age between the years 1998 and 2015. It was reckoned to decline by 14 per cent between 1997 and 2004 and by 25 per cent between 1997 and 2015.[100] An increased participation rate was seen as one compensatory factor, as were an increase of 9 per cent in the birth rate between 1994 and 1997, and a likely growth in net immigration. Third-level institutions, particularly the universities, remained generally bullish about growth prospects, but in the late 1990s some of the Institutes of Technology began to face the prospect of minimum growth. There is no longer competition for entry to many technician courses, including those in high skill areas. All minimally qualified applicants are admitted. For some of the Institutes of Technology this could pose a serious challenge. It was still too early in the year 2000 to say when this would begin to bite in individual colleges and how it might force a restructuring within them.[101]

Notes

1 The Department of Industry and Commerce in the early 1960s was certainly not thinking in these terms. See, for example, Horgan, *Lemass*, pp. 215-217. Garret FitzGerald writing on this period recalled

> ... Seán Lemass, having left Industry and Commerce to become Taoiseach, had quite rightly swung away from a policy of protectionism towards free trade, but because he had left the Department, his former civil servants did not adapt at all to this change of direction and found it difficult to think in free trade terms. Consequently the whole thrust of the CIO (Committee on Industrial Reorganisation), and to a lesser extent the NIEC (National Industrial and Economic Council), was an educational one in which the Department of Finance, the unions, and then FUE and CII continued to educate Industry and Commerce towards free trade... However the task was not an easy one because the Industry and Commerce people were very hostile to the whole idea.

FitzGerald, G. (1992), 'How Others View Us – Political Views' in B. Chubb (ed.), *FIE – Federation of Irish Employers 1942-1992*, Dublin: Gill and Macmillan, pp. 112-113. The publication, marking the golden jubilee of the Federation, makes no mention of educational issues. Neither is any mention to be found in a similar publication on fifty years of the Confederation of Irish Industry. See O'Hagan, J.W. and Foley, G.J. (1982), *The Confederation of Irish Industry: The First Fifty Years 1932-1982*, Dublin: Confederation of Irish Industry. It was well into the 1970s before the Irish management of the multinationals operating in the country began to assume office in, and to have major influence on, the representative bodies of the industrial and commercial sector.

2 This happened in spite of the way in which NCEA, NIHE and some of the regional technical colleges involved individual industrialists in their activities. In one sense there was nothing surprising about this. It was only in the 1970s in many countries that the higher education system began to be widely envisaged as a preparation for employment in the private sector of industry and commerce as distinct from the public service generally. See Neave, *On the Edge of the Abyss*, pp. 139-147. Neave saw the emergence of forms of higher education geared to the non-protected labour market as one of the most important trends of the 1970s.

3 *Second Programme*, pp. 193, 206.

4 For a short description of the background to the establishment of the Department of Labour, see *Dáil Debates*, vol. 224, cols. 1794-1805 (20 October 1966). See also Ó Cearbhaill, T. (1992), 'How Others Saw Us' in Chubb, *FIE*, pp. 135-139.

5 ibid., vol. 223, col. 1289 (23 June 1966).

6 For an analysis of the Authority's role during this period see Lee, J.J. (1989), *Ireland 1912-85, Politics and Society,* Cambridge: Cambridge University Press, pp. 473-474, 530-540. For an insider's view of the evolution and operation of the Authority over the period from 1969 to 1999, see MacSharry R. and White P.A. (2000), *The Making of the Celtic Tiger: The Inside Story of Ireland's Boom Economy*, Cork: Mercier Press, pp. 183-355. The crucial role played by the Industrial Development Authority in eventually becoming the bridge between industrial and education policy is discussed later in this chapter.

7 Industrial Development Authority, *Annual Reports 1969-70, 1970-71, 1971-72.*

8 Industrial Development Authority, *Annual Report 1970-71*, p. 7.

9 The early IDA reports afford ample evidence that the initial impetus for technician education came from within the education sector, and was not brought about in response to promptings by the Department of Industry and Commerce, the representatives of Irish industry or IDA. IDA was among the first of the bodies outside the education sector to appreciate the potential of the new emerging cadre of technicians, but it cannot in any way be said to have inspired them. A perusal of the IDA reports for the decade from 1969 to 1979 brings home the foresight of the arguments in the report of the Steering Committee on Technical Education.

10 Industrial Development Authority, *Annual Report 1973-74*, p. 3.

11 *Dáil Debates*, vol. 266, cols.1415-1419 (28 June 1973).

12 For an early statement of IDA's planned approach to attracting investment, see McLoughlin, R. J. (1972), 'The Industrial Development Process: An Overall

View', *Administration*, vol. 20, no. 1, pp. 27-36. Also McSharry and White, pp. 272-308. Industrial Development Authority, *Annual Report 1971-72*, p. 28.

13 Industrial Development Authority, *Industrial Plan 1978-82*, p. 5.

14 There were no significant precedents for this. It is true that, for example, the Second Programme for Economic Expansion had included a section on education but, as has been seen, the ideas were almost certainly derived inputs from civil servants in the Department of Education, and education was not central to the thrust of the Programme.

15 Industrial Development Authority, *Annual Report 1978*, p. 2. *Annual Report 1979*, p. 18.

16 Industrial Development Authority, *Annual Report 1981*, p. 23.

17 *Dáil Debates*, vol. 311, col. 1433 (15 February 1979).

18 ibid., col. 1431.

19 HEA, *General Report 1974-84*, p. 68.

20 Source confidential.

21 HEA, *General Report 1974-84*, p. 69.

22 *CII Newsletter*, vol. 29, no. 11 (8 August 1978); vol. 29, no. 18 (26 September 1978); vol. 30, no. 1 (21 November 1978); vol. 32, no. 1 (29 November 1979); vol. 32, no. 7 (7 January 1980); vol. 33, no. 3 (13 June 1981); vol. 34, no. 10 (3 February 1982).

23 *Dáil Debates*, vol. 317, col. 1767 (13 December 1979). The Higher Education Authority indicated that there was a serious shortfall of specific additional resources in 1980 and subsequent years for the development of the manpower courses. HEA, *General Report 1974-84*, p. 69.

24 The UCG Engineering Department, for example, doubled in size between 1979 and 1983, while engineering numbers at TCD increased by 45% in that period (Report of the International Study Group to the Minister for Education (1987), *Technological Education*, Dublin, p. 15).

25 ibid. p. 16.

26 HEA, *Accounts 1980 and Student Statistics 1980/81*, p. 28. HEA, *Report, Accounts (1991 and 1992*) and *Student Statistics 1990/91 and 1991/92*, p. 53.

27 Murphy,T. (1984), 'Higher Education – The Changing Scene' in A. T. McKenna (ed.), *Higher Education: Relevance and Future*, Dublin: Higher Education Authority, p. 18.

28 *Accountancy Ireland*, December 1994. The main explanation for this difference was that élite British universities, notably Oxford and Cambridge, did not go down the route of vocational specialisation.

29 *Irish Independent*, 7 December 1984.

30 See, for example, Deputy Jim Higgins, Fine Gael spokesman on education, *Dáil Debates*, vol. 415, col. 2265 (18 February 1992).

31 Walsh, *Two Ideas of a University Contrasted*. For a detailed critique of Dr Walsh's views on the merits of an arts degree, see Palmer, P. (1990) 'Apples, Arts, Amnesiacs and Emigrants: The University Connection', *The Irish Review*, vol. 8, pp. 14-18.

32 *Sunday Tribune*, 26 September 1993.

33 Many of his ideas were outside what might be termed the mainstream consensus. His championing of the idea of privatisation and applying market principles to higher education drew responses from the President of Ireland,

Mary Robinson (*Irish Times*, 27 June 1994) and from a former Secretary of the Department of Education and Chairman of the Higher Education Authority, Doiminic Ó Laoghaire, Ó Laoghaire, D. (1988), 'Privatisation in Irish Education', *Seirbhís Phoiblí,* vol. 1, pp. 40-44. Ó Laoghaire was a reticent civil service mandarin, rarely provoked on to the record in public debate.

34 This was, after all, the era in which the technical professionals of Dublin Corporation happily assisted in pouring concrete on the heritage of Wood Quay, while there were numerous equally suitable sites for new Corporation offices within walking distance.

35 *Dáil Debates*, vol. 409, cols. 613-696 (30 May 1991).

36 The other teacher education institution in Limerick, Mary Immaculate College of Education, was also to establish a relationship with the University in the same period.

37 *Irish Times*, 18 October 1982, 19 October 1987; Ó Faoláin, N. 'Utilitarianism and an Academic Ideal', *Irish Times*, 6 February 1989; O'Connor, F. Counter March, *UCD Alma Mater*, September 1993, pp. 26-27.

38 *Dáil Debates*, vol. 350, col. 1973 (24 May 1985); vol. 390, cols. 1370, 1393-94 (25 May 1989).

39 Industrial Policy Review Group (1992), *A Time for Change: Industrial Policy for the 1990s*, Dublin: Stationery Office, p. 17.

40 Roche, F. and Tansey, P. (1992), *Industrial Training in Ireland*, Dublin: Stationery Office.

41 *Industrial Policy Review Group*, pp. 53-54.

42 Fahy L., (1993) 'Global Change and the Implications for Irish Business', paper to the 40th National Management Conference.

43 *Dáil Debates*, vol. 417, col. 2186-2191 (27 March 1992).

44 For further illustration of FitzGerald's argument and for a breakdown of changes in subject participation in senior cycle between 1972/73 and 1988/89 see Lynch, *Education and the Paid Labour Market*, p. 15.

45 *Green Paper, 1992*, p. 102.

46 *Dáil Debates*, vol. 423, col. 1703 (6 October 1992).

47 *White Paper, 1995.*

48 Forfás (1996), *Shaping Our Future: A Strategy for Enterprise in Ireland in the 21st Century*, Dublin: Forfás. Forfás is a body created out of the implementation of the Culliton Report. The then existing IDA was split into two with the foreign investment activity remaining with the body which retained the initials IDA (the Industrial Development Authority had, in fact, become the Industrial Development Agency), while indigenous industry became the responsibility of Forbairt, subsequently restyled Enterprise Ireland. Forfás co-ordinates the operations of both.

49 *Shaping Our Future*, p. 153. This issue was also dealt with in Neave, *Shifting Sands*, pp. 8-10. He notes that in a European context the main area of disagreement between industry and higher education appears to lie in the degree of job-specific skills to be incorporated into higher education courses, given that skills thought relevant today may be of historic interest tomorrow. He adds that the main concern of many firms at the cutting edge of high technology is that the skills required are general, rather than specific – ability to analyse, to communicate and to adapt to change (p. 9).

50 HEA, *Technical Working Group*, p. 51.

51 See, for example, Higher Education Authority (1995), *Interim Report of the Steering Committee's Technical Working Group*, p. 26. This indicates that between 1950 and 1990 higher education enrolments had risen by a factor of 11, similar to Germany and Greece among EU countries, and ahead of France, Netherlands, Spain and Britain.

52 *Report of Review Committee on Post Secondary Education and Training Places (1999)*, Dublin: Higher Education Authority, p. 24. See also Clancy, *Access to College*, pp. 41-43.

53 University enrolment had dropped as low as 46 per cent by 1987, but the designation of the two NIHEs as universities increased the proportion of university students upwards again.

54 Clancy, *Who Goes to College?* p. 52. Clancy, *Access to College*, p. 30. These figures are significantly different from those in the 1995 Report of the Technical Working Group, p. 25. The discrepancy of 11 per cent may be explained by the fact that Clancy's figures are for 'new entrants,' while the Technical Working Group may be calculating the number of first year students (although Table 1.2 of its report refers to 'First-Time Entrants').

55 *Committee on Places 1999*, p. 29.

56 *Report of the Steering Committee on the Future Development of Higher Education* (1995), Dublin: Higher Education Authority, p. 36.

57 ibid, p. 37.

58 NCEA, *Twenty-Fourth Annual Report 1997*, p. 37.

59 *Steering Committee*, p. 38.

60 The diversification within disciplines can be seen in both the annual reports of the National Council for Educational Awards and in the Directory of Courses published regularly by NCEA from 1979 onwards. The diversification across the entire third-level spectrum can be seen over the years in the various supplements produced annually by the national newspapers as an aid to students in choosing course options via the Central Applications Office. See, for example, *Irish Times*, 16 August 2000.

61 *Technical Working Group*, pp. 147-157. These figures relate to the year 1992 and cover education aimed at a recognised third-level qualification. They exclude courses which would come under the broad definition of adult or continuation education. See Appendix 3 for contrast of 1978/79 and 1993/94.

62 Clancy, P. (1999), 'Participation of Mature Students in Higher Education in Ireland' in T. Fleming, T. Collins and J. Coolahan (eds.), *Higher Education: the Challenge of Lifelong Learning*, Maynooth: Centre for Educational Policy Studies, NUI Maynooth, p. 29.

63 *Steering Committee*, p. 60.

64 *Committee on Places 1999*, pp. 28, 51.

65 *Steering Committee*, p. 114. Clancy, P. and Wall, J. (2000), *Social Background of Higher Education Entrants*, Dublin: Higher Education Authority, p. 63.

66 *Technical Working Group*, p. 80.

67 This figure dropped substantially from nearly 3,900 in 1997 to 2,900 in 1998, due mainly to the reintroduction of tuition fees for university education in the UK, a move in the opposite direction to that of Niamh Bhreathnach in the Republic a few years earlier (*Committee on Places 1999*, p. 32). By the year

2000 the figure had dropped to just over 2,000 (*Irish Times*, 26 September 2000).

68 Clancy, *Access to College*, pp. 158-159.

69 *Steering Committee*, p. 72; *Irish Times*, 8 April 2000.

70 *Technical Working Group on the Review of Outreach Centres of Higher Education Institutes: Final Review Report* (1999), Dublin: Higher Education Authority, p. vii-ix. This group was chaired by Professor Noel Mulcahy, who thirty years previously had chaired the Steering Committee on Technical Education.

71 *Report on Symposium on Open and Distance Learning (2000),* Dublin: Higher Education Authority. This report looks at some of the issues facing Ireland in relation to open and distance learning, including the issue of Ireland's role in virtual or internet-based education. Of particular interest was the declaration of the Chairman of the Higher Education Authority, Dr Don Thornhill, that he was not a believer in the so-called 'rationalisation of facilities' argument, and believed that monopolies in education do not serve the public interest (*Symposium*, p. 15).

72 *Irish Times*, 24 April 2000.

73 *Technical Working Group*, p. 21.

74 *Irish Times*, 23 March 2000, 24 April 2000. *Irish Independent*, 14 April 2000. For a concise summary of the issues in relation to the Institutes of Technology, see proceedings from '*Staying Power*': *A Colloquium on Increasing Retention Rates in Higher Education (2000)*, Dublin: National Centre for Guidance in Education, the Department of Education and Science, especially pp. 27-31, 51-56. See also *Irish Times*, 26 September 2000.

75 Clancy, *Access to College*, p. 154. Clancy and Wall, p. 68.

76 *Steering Committee*, p. 77.

77 For background on students from disadvantaged backgrounds, see *Commission on the Points System, Final Report and Recommendations* (1999), Dublin: Stationery Office, pp. 99, 129-143. For an international approach prepared for an Irish audience, see Skilbeck, M. (2000), *Access and Equity in Higher Education: An International Perspective on Issues and Strategies*, Dublin: Higher Education Authority.

78 See, for example, Committee on Access and Participation of Students with Disabilities in Higher Education: *Report to Higher Education Authority* (n.d. 1996?). A major part of this Committee's work was to establish the factual situation in regard to students with disabilities in Irish higher education institutions.

79 For a summary of provision on access programmes to universities and the institutes of technology, see *Irish Times*, 17 October 2000.

80 Clancy, *Access to College*, p. 170.

81 *Women Academics in Ireland (1987)*, Dublin: Higher Education Authority, p. 28.

82 *Irish Independent*, 12 June 2000.

83 *Steering Committee*, p. 26.

84 *Irish Times*, 27 June 2000. The Conference of Heads of Irish Universities in a document published in early 2000 referred to the current ratio as being 22:1.

85 *Guaranteeing Future Growth: University Research and Education, Investment Priority, National Plan 2000-2006*, Dublin: Conference of Heads of Irish

Universities. *Technology Foresight and the University Sector (2000),* Dublin: Conference of Heads of Irish Universities.

86 *Conference of Universities Rectors in Ireland – Background (2000),* CRI handout.

87 On the internationalisation of Irish higher education, see Coolahan, J. (1997), 'Third-level Education in Ireland: Change and Development' in F. Ó Muirceartaigh (ed.), *Ireland in the Coming Times: Essays to Celebrate T. K. Whitaker's 80 Years,* Dublin: Institute of Public Administration, pp. 207-209.

88 For its recommendation on research see *Commission Report,* pp. 628-637. For its views on staffing ratios, see pp. 585-603. The Commission concluded that the then current staff ratio in Irish universities was about 1:18 and that it should be improved to 1:12 by 1975. No such improvement occurred.

89 ibid, pp. 378, 596, 637.

90 Two of the most prominent members of the Commission were Dr Thomas Walsh, the Director of An Foras Talúntais (the Agricultural Institute, which largely dominated agricultural research in Ireland from the 1950s to the 1980s) and Dr Martin Cranley, Director of the Institute for Industrial Research and Standards. The period from 1940 to 1961 saw the establishment of a number of independent research organisations outside the Irish universities – the Dublin Institute for Advanced Studies, the Institute for Industrial Research and Standards, the Agricultural Institute (An Foras Talúntais) and the Economic and Social Research Institute. The Commission took the view that no particular form of research organisation is valid for all purposes, and that the independent research institute in certain cases may be the most appropriate organisation for research. (*Commission Report,* p. 378). For the Commission's views on the role of research and the universities, see pp. 345-380 and 605-638.

91 It does not figure, for example, in the Authority's own publication describing its activities up to 1984.

92 Circa Group Europe (1996), *A Comparative International Assessment of the Organisation, Management and Funding of University Research in Ireland and Europe,* Dublin: Higher Education Authority, p. i.

93 ibid, p. iii.

94 ibid, p. 224.

95 See below, Chapter 12.

96 *Technical Working Group,* p. 44.

97 ibid., p. 37. The fees virtually doubled in real price terms between 1980 and 1993 (ibid., p. 39.)

98 ibid., p. 47.

99 *Steering Committee,* p. 17.

100 *Committee on Places 1999,* p. 11. See also Clancy, P. (2000), 'Participation of Mature Students in Higher Education in Ireland' in Fleming et al, *The Challenges of Lifelong Learning,* pp. 29-44.

101 For an aspect of this debate see Conference of Heads of Irish Universities, *Guaranteeing Future Growth,* pp. 26-30. CHIU takes issue with the ESRI Report 'National Investment Priorities for 2000-2006.' A more sombre warning about prospects for Institutes of Technology was given in September 2000 by a report from the Department of Education and Science's Skills Initiative Unit

'Institutes of Technology and the New Economy'. It envisaged a drop in the number of full-time students in the Institutes (*Irish Times*, 19 September 2000). Almost simultaneously a report prepared for the Council of Directors of Institutes of Technology predicted that the drop in available students would make it difficult for colleges, especially Institutes of Technology, to maintain or expand current numbers (*Irish Times*, 9 October 2000).

CHAPTER 10

'The Centre Cannot Hold'

With the publication of the 1980 White Paper and the completion of the legislation governing the two national institutes and Thomond College of Education at the end of 1980, it appeared that the higher education system, after a decade of development and, at times, turmoil, was about to enter a period of further and quiet consolidation. The only long-standing piece of unfinished business was legislation to restructure, if not abolish, the National University of Ireland, and perhaps also amending legislation in relation to the University of Dublin.[1] The major decisions had apparently been made to copperfasten the binary approach. The National Council for Educational Awards existed in statutory form with degree-awarding powers, a near-monopoly on the awarding of degrees outside the universities and a remit confined to academic matters. The two national institutes for Higher Education, Thomond College of Education and the National College of Art and Design were governed by individual statutes, and had a role which was national rather than regional in scope. There were also the City of Dublin VEC and the City of Limerick VEC colleges,[2] and the regional technical colleges which operated formally under the Vocational Education Act 1930.

The assumption that the new structure had crystallised proved to be false. It firstly underestimated both the impatience and the political and lobbying skills of the Director of the National Institute for Higher Education Limerick, Dr Edward Walsh. As in the previous twelve years, the Limerick issue was to be a major determinant of the development of higher education in the 1980s. The progress of the relationship between NIHE and the National Council for Educational Awards provided an illuminating example of the long-term difficulties of pursuing a 'binary policy' within the political structures of the Republic of Ireland.

NCEA and NIHE Limerick

As has already been noted, Dr Walsh and the Institute in its corporate communications policy had begun to portray NIHE as a university-type institution long before it had obtained that status by statute.[3] At the time of the debate on the National Institute for Higher Education Limerick Bill in 1980, the then Minister for Education, John Wilson, envisaged NIHE becoming a technological university in due course, with Thomond College of Education and Mary Immaculate College of Education both involved in the development.[4] He had added that he hoped to live long enough to see that happening. Dr Walsh was still a relatively young man and did not seem to be content to leave that achievement to one of his successors. He was helped in achieving his goal by NCEA, which was not very astute in trying to keep either Dr Walsh or his colleague, Dr O'Hare of NIHE Dublin, identified with, or loyal to, the Council.

Although both the chairman and the director of NCEA were occasionally given to referring to the two NIHEs as the jewels in the NCEA crown,[5] both NIHE directors were excluded from the inner circle of NCEA decision-making. When the statutory Council was established in 1980, it apportioned its work among three committees, Course Recognition, Development, and Finance and Standing. The last-named was the main locus of decision-making within NCEA and heads of educational institutions were noticeably absent from it after the establishment of the statutory Council in July 1980.[6] The Course Recognition Committee was the body that considered all recommendations from the various boards of studies for the approval of courses. This was a very busy committee in the early days of the statutory Council,[7] and from its decisions had to be inferred many of the educational and academic policies of the Council since, as in the case of the second *ad hoc* Council of 1976, there was no academic or academic policy committee. The Course Recognition Committee between 1980 and 1982 consisted of the chairpersons of the ten boards of studies. Two of the principals of colleges in the VEC sector, who were Council members, chaired boards of studies and were *ipso facto* on this committee, but here likewise the two NIHE directors were excluded.

The NIHE directors had to be content with a seat on the Development Committee. Had there been any concept of NCEA as an ideas forum or an intellectual think-tank for the non-university third-level system, this committee could perhaps have had a forward-looking and influential role. The spirit informing the Committee's birth was more of a nostalgic hankering after the days of planning and co-ordination of the second *ad hoc* Council, and this Council committee was in reality nothing more than a toothless talkshop which was poorly attended and met fitfully. The Council reorganised its activities in 1982. At this stage the NIHE directors were promoted to the Course Recognition Committee, but neither joined one of the VEC sector principals on the Finance and Standing Committee.[8] Assuming that the inner circle of decision-makers on the NCEA Council wanted the NIHEs to remain part of the NCEA network for the medium term, it is difficult to understand how they could have been so foolish and short-sighted as to sideline these able and proud men in this fashion,[9] especially as it was no secret that they yearned for autonomy for their institutions.

The lobbying and public relations activity involved in nudging NIHE Limerick towards university status progressed over a number of years. A small indicator occurred during the summer of 1982 when the Director of the Institute, a position and title enshrined in the 1980 Act, was retitled 'President'.[10] In contrast to the high profile lobbying and self-publicity of the 1970s the campaigning on the issue of university status was more targeted and low-key during the first half of the 1980s. But there can be little doubt that it was always there. The lobby for the elevation of NIHE Dublin existed simultaneously and, while to an extent it operated in the slipstream of Limerick, it was also effective and relentless until it achieved its aims. [11]

The Hardiman Report

The campaign of the NIHEs achieved its major breakthrough with the appointment in November 1986 of the International Study Group chaired by T.P. Hardiman.[12] The terms of reference of the Study Group included examining the arrangements for the provision of third-level technological education outside the universities, and examining the case for the establishment of a technological university with NIHE Limerick and NIHE Dublin as constituent colleges. The Group convened on forty-seven occasions, visited seventeen third-level institutions, regulatory and academic bodies, met twenty-four representative groups in the course of its work, and produced a report within ten months.[13] The report concluded that the National Institutes for Higher Education in Dublin and Limerick should be self-accrediting, and should be established as independent universities – NIHE Limerick having the title of University of Limerick, and NIHE Dublin that of Dublin City University or the University of Leinster. It was also recommended that the title 'technological universities' should not be used.[14] The group considered that academic considerations were central to the examination of the case for university status,[15] and concluded that the two NIHEs were sufficiently scholarly to merit that status. As to the appropriateness of the title of university, the group felt that there was no satisfactory answer to the question of what comprised the essential nature of a university, and that there was little to be gained in attempting to impose a universally applicable definition.[16]

One of the most influential voices in putting the case for the two NIHEs had been the Confederation of Irish Industry (CII), which made a submission to the Study Group.[17] Here the cultivation of links with industry by both NIHEs now proved particularly fruitful. The President of CII in 1987, Dermot Whelan, was also Deputy Chairman of the Governing Body of NIHE Limerick, while two of his immediate predecessors were Terence Larkin, Chairman of the Governing Body of NIHE Dublin, and Tom Hardiman, Chairman of the International Study Group. CII was subsequently one of the main forces pressing to ensure that the findings of the Study Group did not gather too much dust in Marlborough Street.[18]

Legislation followed in the life of the twenty-fifth Dáil, but only just. The bills for the two new universities were the last piece of legislative business to be taken on 25 May 1989 before the Dáil was dissolved for a general election.[19] The minister, Mary O'Rourke, described herself as acting on the Hardiman group's unambiguous findings that the two bodies clearly operated at university level, and that the bill would convey to the international community Ireland's seriousness regarding industrial and business development.[20] The legislation was in the form of a minor amendment to the two 1980 Acts to change the titles of the institutes to universities, and those of the directors to presidents, to confer the power to award degrees, diplomas and certificates on the new universities, to amplify the definition of their functions, to give the governing bodies the authority to extend the functions of the universities with the approval of the Minister for Education, and to extend the functions of the academic councils to make recommendations to the governing bodies on the conferring of degrees, diplomas and certificates. The former Taoiseach, Garret FitzGerald, during the Dáil debate suggested that such minimal amending legislation left them with an inappropriate structure in that all the members of the governing body were appointed by the government, something which he felt had no precedent in these islands or the United States, and could lead to credibility problems with regard to the independence of these colleges. [21]

There was a certain irony in the legislation, particularly in the case of Limerick. As already indicated,[22] the binary approach had been invented partly as a result of Limerick's call for a university. At the time it was claimed that what Limerick would get would be something important which the country needed, and which the universities could not deliver. In that spirit Dr Walsh had been appointed and for many years he had attacked the supposedly outdated and élitist views of the universities, while at the same time retaining the aspiration to achieve the 'brand image'.[23] Given his robust comments on universities in the years before Limerick joined their ranks, it was not altogether surprising to find that there were still painful wounds from his erstwhile jousts with some of his new peers.[24]

There was a further element of irony in the Dublin situation. Here was an institution that was a mere decade in existence, whose creation and location had arisen from proposals of the City of Dublin Vocational Education Committee, and which was now an independent university with no federal or other bond, unlike the older universities. The campaign for the legislation had provided a fascinating insight into how a complex and elusive policy, such as the binary approach,[25] could be deflected in the Irish political system by a well-crafted lobby built around a single manageable issue. It also provided a headline for others to follow.

The RTCs and independence

While the declared ambition of the NIHEs might have indicated that they could unsettle the binary approach, the regional technical colleges would have looked less likely to pose a problem. However friction in that sector became apparent almost as soon as NCEA was established statutorily. It has already been noted that the NIHEs were not represented on NCEA's Finance and Standing Committee.[26] Moreover, although three VEC sector colleges were represented on the Council by their principals – the College of Technology, Bolton Street, and the RTCs in Cork and Dundalk – none of this trio sat on that Committee. The VEC sector was represented there by the chairman of the Irish Vocational Education Association, Jack McCann, and the only VEC chief executive officer on the Council, Robert Buckley. This was not the most promising start for what should have been a body concerning itself primarily with matters academic. Worse was to follow.

Over many years the assistant registrars, the staff members in the NCEA who worked as secretaries to boards of studies and who organised and co-ordinated the key validation and assessment work of the Council, met regularly (roughly each term) with the heads of the appropriate schools at the colleges involved with NCEA. This was a sensible management arrangement. The practice stopped almost as soon as the Council became statutory. It soon became apparent that this was due to a trial of strength between the chief executive officers of the parent VECs and the principals of the colleges. At that point the CEOs and the IVEA had the upper hand, as the Finance and Standing Committee appointments had presaged, and they insisted that assistant registrars should more properly meet with college principals than with school heads. (As a corollary, only CEOs, not RTC principals, should meet with the NCEA director). Over three years were to elapse before the meetings of assistant registrars and school heads were to recommence on a regular basis. Once again NCEA was damaged by becoming embroiled in a political battle that should have been none of its business.

What the battle also showed was that, unless chief executive officers and college principals were very sensible or pragmatic, there were difficulties in fitting expanding third-level colleges, which were increasingly contemplating degree work, into an administrative framework devised fifty years earlier for a lower and quite different level of education. Third-level institutions have a very strong urge towards autonomy, and time was to prove that the college principals, having lost that initial skirmish, would eventually win out.

The issue which the principals were to enlist most successfully in their battle was that of research and consultancy. This was an issue first raised through the National Board for Science and Technology. Its 1980 Science Budget had commented on national policy in relation to science and technology in higher education, and had seen *inter alia* the absence of research and consultancy in the technological colleges as a major deficiency.[27] The Steering Committee of the Association of Vocational Education Colleges, an umbrella body for the third-level VEC colleges, took up the issue and set up a working party following its 1982 annual conference. The working party's report recommended that research and consultancy should form an integral element of third-level teaching activity in vocational colleges, that each college should establish a management framework to foster them, and among a number of practical recommendations was one for the establishment of companies limited by guarantee within colleges to administer such work.[28] These concepts were novel in the context of VECs and did not always fit comfortably into the *weltanschaung* of some VEC committee members.[29]

In her 1984 estimates speech the minister, Gemma Hussey, proposed introducing a more flexible system which would allow RTCs to make a greater research and development contribution in their regions.[30] The 1985 Green Paper *Partners in Education – Serving Community Needs* considered that the actual work of the colleges had grown and changed considerably from the original RTC concept, and that it was no longer valid that their administration should be undertaken by the VECs but, rather, that they should be more closely related to the rest of the third-level area,[31] and operate with far more autonomy than heretofore.[32] It was clear that these proposals had backing from the Department of Education against both the chief executive officers and local politicians. The issue of governance of RTCs and the DIT was taken up by the Hardiman study group, which strongly recommended that statutory provision be made to allow RTCs to operate with more autonomy, and recommended the establishment of Dublin Institute of Technology on a statutory basis.[33] No further development in this area took place under either Gemma Hussey or Patrick Cooney, her successor in 1986-87.

Shortly after becoming Minister for Education in 1987, Mary O'Rourke, indicated that she did not see a necessity to make any radical alterations to RTC structures.[34] This was in keeping with her own liking for the link between an RTC and the local VEC, having cut her own political teeth through involvement with Athlone RTC and County Westmeath VEC. Nevertheless it was to be Mrs O'Rourke who, in 1991, was to introduce the bills dealing with regional technical colleges and the Dublin Institute of Technology which, in her own words, would be 'the key to greater autonomy, to self-governance and to improved and more effective interaction with business and industry'.[35] The bills aimed to retain the RTCs and the DIT within the VEC structure while establishing them as self-governing institutions.

The bills ran into considerable cross-party criticism in the Dáil.[36] The most significant critic was perhaps Deputy Noel Dempsey, shortly to become government chief whip, who challenged 'the viewpoint pushed by some people within the Department and within the colleges, most notably the principals, that the present governing and administrative structures have inhibited growth and expansion'.[37] He considered that the Bills pandered to the wishes of a small, but powerful, minority who saw an enhancement of their status in them and an opportunity to rid themselves of 'the shackles of local democratic control and accountability'. He believed also that this small minority was supported by highly-placed officials in the Department, who were anxious to regain control of the success story of higher education.[38] The bills were strongly opposed also by the Irish Vocational Education Association.[39] Given the level of opposition among politicians of all parties to the two Bills, the surprising thing is that they came through the Oireachtas. The three ministers concerned – Mary O'Rourke, Noel Davern and Séamus Brennan – were involved in a tight balancing act, and one opposition spokesman, Brian O'Shea, went so far as to suggest that the 'good sense of the former ministers, O'Rourke and Davern, had prevented the Department of Education from getting the Bill it wanted.'[40]

The potential problems associated with local political involvement survived under the new dispensation, as was demonstrated by events which unfolded in the summer of 1993 at Letterkenny Regional Technical College. When a court case involving the College, the newly-appointed secretary/financial controller of the College and the minister, and a second action, involving the students' union and the governing body, followed each other in quick succession, the minister, Niamh Bhreathnach, using Section 20 of the Regional Technical Colleges Act 1992, appointed Dr Miriam Hederman O'Brien to act as an inspector of various matters concerning the college.[41] The publication of her report was followed by the resignation of the governing body chairman, the transfer of the college director to another position and the appointment of a commissioner to manage the college.[42] The Regional Technical Colleges Act had not been a panacea and the interplay of politician and college management could still be highly problematic.

NCEA and the decline of the binary system

With the NIHEs elevated in status and the main VEC colleges granted a greater degree of autonomy, the role of NCEA came under scrutiny. In the 1970s one of the reasons why so much financial and other support was given to developing the NIHEs and the Regional Technical Colleges had been a conviction that universities could not perform the requisite role in planning for the technical needs of an industrialising economy. Accordingly a vibrant technical sector was developed outside the universities, with outlets in every region. Some control nationally of its output and standards was thought to be required. It was felt unwise to leave this function to the individual colleges. The Department of Education could not credibly claim to be an independent arbiter of standards. Hence there was a need for an independent quality agent, which in turn led to the formation of the National Council for Educational Awards in 1972.

While it would always have been impossible for a body like NCEA to be made up totally of knowledgeable and committed people with no vested interest whatever in the Council's affiliate institutions, it can certainly be argued that both its *ad hoc* constitution of 1976 and its statutory composition of 1979 were such as to ensure that its independence would be hard won and difficult to retain. Because of its close involvement with the VEC sector it was always liable to become a rope in a tug-of-war between the centralising thrust of the Department of Education and the centrifugal tendencies of the vocational sector. That Department is not, and never has been, comfortable with having independent state-sponsored bodies operating under its aegis. Indeed it consistently refused to recognise them as such.[43] In so doing the Department was by no means unique, but its attitude was not something to strengthen the resolve of a body such as NCEA, which needed independence, and departmental acceptance of that independence, if it was to thrive.

In the 1980s, as in the previous decade, NCEA had its achievements. At an operational level its boards of studies, panels of assessors and teams of extern examiners made a genuine contribution to establishing and maintaining high standards throughout most of the colleges with which it was associated.[44] Where colleges were prepared to take NCEA's role seriously, high standards were developed and maintained. By 1992 NCEA had made 78,751 awards in its twenty-year existence, over 10,000 of these at degree and postgraduate level.[45] Its first masters degree was awarded in 1982, its first doctorates in 1985 and its first honorary degrees in 1987.[46]

Its award structure developed in flexibility to cater for distance education students at the Institute of Public Administration. It facilitated the use of 'outreach' centres, initially at Ballina. It began to allow for the certification of single subjects from 1983 onwards. By 1989 it had launched an award structure *Accumulation of Credits and Certification of Subjects* (ACCS) which allowed for the accumulation of credits which could be acquired in different institutions, possibly outside Ireland.[47] Moreover its validating process, which in 1980 was still entirely based on the evaluation of individual courses, had moved on to conducting programmatic reviews of schools and/or departments, and subsequently reviews of an entire college or designated institution.[48] It was capable of making unpopular decisions. Courses were turned down, or their launch postponed or subjected to onerous conditions. The main difference between the 1980s and what happened in the mid 1970s (and indeed what happened regularly with NCEA's UK counterpart, the Council for National Academic Awards) was that the adverse decisions did not get an airing in the national media.

Yet, in spite of all the achievements, NCEA proved to be very coy and unimaginative in relation to its own organisational development. Its staffing structure remained *ad hoc* in character long after it had acquired statutory recognition in 1980.[49] It was almost as if the Council never saw a long-term future for itself. Neither did it seem to know how to play to its own strengths. NCEA had all the state's art schools under its aegis, and from 1977 virtually all awards of any national consequence in the visual arts were made by it. This provided an opportunity for an annual exhibition of the best of the artistic talent at student level nationally in any given year. Such an exhibition was held in 1986 at the Guinness Hopstore,[50] but strangely was not pursued in subsequent years in spite of having such obvious cultural, and indeed public relations, possibilities. Unlike HEA, NCEA did not commission research into relevant facets of its activity,[51] although arguably, as an academic body, this was altogether more crucial to it than to HEA. At the top level there was a reluctance to engage in public debate on ideas.

Where the coyness and dearth of ideas became most striking was in NCEA's response to the Hardiman study group. It was quite clear that the two NIHEs, the two jewels, wished to become detached from the crown. This had important implications for NCEA in the long run. It would have been of interest to many involved with higher education to know how NCEA felt on this topic. As the 1987 Annual Report duly noted,[52] a detailed submission was made to the International Study Group. No hints were offered as to its contents, although by the time the NCEA annual report appeared, the Hardiman document was long since in the public domain.[53] There was no clue as to whether NCEA had any regrets, or any suggestions as to new possibilities or new directions for the binary policy of which it was a cornerstone.

While such stoicism has its own admirable quality, public policy nevertheless can be helped by occasional clarification or reiteration by the body charged with its implementation. NCEA's stance could be viewed as taking its own authority for granted. Its affiliated colleges however did not always do that. Many of its activities could, and had, come under challenge. From an early stage one of the most problematic areas for the statutory Council was the issue of degrees at regional technical colleges. Politically this was a highly-charged question. Because of the arms' length relationship between the Department and NCEA, a gap was waiting to be exploited by any entrepreneurial regional technical college. This role was filled initially by Cork RTC, which in 1980 enrolled students on four primary degree programmes without any prior warning to NCEA (and apparently without the knowledge of the Department either). The Council and the respective boards of studies came under immense pressure to approve the courses.[54] All of them were eventually approved, but the process did little for the Council's standing.

The fact that NCEA did not have a monopoly on degree awards in VEC colleges was another problem area, and had already been highlighted by the DIT colleges in their maintenance of the relationship with Trinity College.[55] This precedent was pushed a little further in 1986 when Limerick College of Art, Commerce and Technology (a VEC-controlled college and a designated college under the NCEA Act) negotiated recognition with London University for a degree of Bachelor of Science in Economics.[56] At this stage it was clear that NCEA would not only have to compete with Irish institutions for validation fees, but even with universities and polytechnics outside the state.

The next challenge to NCEA's position came from an unexpected source. A private college in Dublin, Accountancy and Business College, had for some years been exploring the possibility of becoming designated under Section 20 of the NCEA Act.[57] In the mid-1980s there was apparently a policy in operation which ensured that no additional private college would be designated under the Act.[58] The trade union movement, led by the Teachers' Union of Ireland, was reputed to have been opposed to giving any further recognition to private colleges. Eventually finding that there was no progress down that apparent cul-de-sac, the Director of the College approached Liverpool Polytechnic (subsequently to become John Moores University) with a view to obtaining a licence to run the polytechnic's business studies degree programme on a franchise basis. This application was successful. Piquancy was added by the fact that the degree was validated by the Council for National Academic Awards, the NCEA's original UK role model.[59] This anomaly would almost certainly never have arisen had all colleges the possibility of approaching NCEA directly without having to negotiate the politically-controlled hoop which was statutory designation. Section 20 had now boomeranged on its minders in the Department of Education and the VEC sector. There followed a rush wherein a number of private colleges were designated. The horse at this stage had well and truly bolted, and two of the other private colleges which would later come to enjoy the status of NCEA designation, Griffith College and Portobello College, had entered into similar degree franchise arrangements with the University of Ulster and the University of Glamorgan.[60]

Section 20 of the Act, having facilitated a range of extra-territorial choices for colleges, had not yet exhausted its baleful influence. NCEA designation in itself became something to which private colleges aspired, and which could figure in their publicity even if they had no course approved with NCEA. Designation took place only following a recommendation from NCEA, but with regard to this too NCEA could be pressurised politically.[61] While it had no role in assessing the financial health of any of these colleges, NCEA's standing and authority was not enhanced when one of them went into liquidation shortly after designation.[62]

NCEA could be argued to have had three purposes. It represented an aspect of higher education policy in that it was a major instrument of the binary policy; it gave standing and status to the new system of higher vocational education launched in the 1970s. Secondly it was a device to give national validity to courses in local institutions, whether publicly-funded or private. Thirdly it was an instrument of innovation in higher education in areas such as modularisation and credit accumulation. With the proliferation of possible validating and award agencies available to Irish colleges, a development which was explicitly recognised in the legislation both of the regional technical colleges and the Dublin Institute of Technology, a cornerstone of the binary policy disappeared.[63] NCEA became just one of a number of potential validating agencies which colleges could approach.

In 1991 the minister decided to establish the National Council for Vocational Awards (NCVA) to 'initiate a comprehensive system of certification for students on vocational training programmes outside the third-level system.'[64] The minister and the Department at that stage thought that the level of education covered by post-leaving certificate and vocational preparation courses was not such that it should involve NCEA. When the Green Paper on Education came to be published less than a year later, the policy had changed and it was proposed to establish a new statutory council, the Council for Educational and Vocational Awards, which would cover all aspects of vocational training (including apprenticeship), as well as taking over the role of NCEA in relation to non-university courses. [65]

With the publication of the White Paper, *Education – Charting our Future,* in April 1995 there was another change of direction and the main discussion of the NCEA's role was to be found in the chapter on further, as distinct from higher, education. The White Paper proposed the establishment of TEASTAS, the Irish National Certification Authority 'under the aegis of the Department of Education'. This body was to be responsible for 'the development, implementation, regulation and supervision of the certification of all non-university third-level programmes', and this encompassed responsibility for the plans, programmes and budgets of NCEA which (with NCVA) was to be reconstituted into a sub-board of TEASTAS.[66]

TEASTAS was duly established on an *ad hoc* basis in September 1995 as the authority with full responsibility for the development, implementation, regulation and supervision of certification of all non-university and third-level, and all further and continuation education and training programmes. It was destined not to see a statutory incarnation. NCEA's status was further and severely damaged in 1996 by the publication of portions of a leaked consultants' report on the Council compiled for the Higher Education Authority by the accountancy firm KPMG. This report referred to the Council as having lost both its sense of purpose and direction, and suggested that NCEA was neither an efficient nor a cost-effective body.[67] For NCEA this publication was effectively the kiss of death.

University legislation

The problems associated with the binary system had to take second place for some time when the attention of the minister, Niamh Bhreathnach, was directed to university matters.

The Commission on Higher Education had recommended comprehensive university legislation to dissolve NUI and restate the constitution of TCD. No such legislation followed either then or for another generation, although virtually every Minister for Education from Donogh O'Malley to Niamh Bhreathnach had it as a matter of policy.[68] The coolness of the Department of Education and Ministers for Education towards universities began to be mitigated somewhat in the 1980s. Many of those who had fought the battles of the 1960s and 1970s had retired and the new senior civil servants, if not themselves graduates (as an increasing number of them were), were liable to have offspring going through third-level and less likely accordingly to see it as strange, or possibly even hostile, territory. The old battles about mergers and legislation had been in cold storage for years. The 1993 report on the National Education Convention contrasted the apparent consensus between government and universities on the question of third-level education with the position of a decade earlier, when many in the universities were deeply suspicious of the government's intentions in respect of legislation.[69]

Relations between Niamh Bhreathnach and the universities began to deteriorate in the early stages of her term as Minister for Education. Two issues brought this to the fore: the attitude of the universities to the minister's plans to abolish university tuition fees and an ongoing campaign by various university colleges for additional resources.[70] Essentially both these matters related to the issue of university funding. During the 1980s there had been increasing reliance on fee income to fund university expansion, so that by 1993 fees constituted 33 per cent of total university income as against 12 per cent in 1990.[71] University presidents were understandably uncomfortable with the idea that tuition should be almost entirely funded by the taxpayer, as there is a well-established view that many senior personnel in the civil service believe that, where the taxpayers are paying the piper, they should call the tune on their behalf. The universities were also supportive of the view, expressed by politicians and others, that the proposal to abolish fees was socially regressive, that it did nothing for lower income groups but would be a windfall for the middle class, and that it put off tackling inequalities in the existing funding of higher education grants.[72]

Relations with the universities appear also to have deteriorated in the course of their campaign for better funding in the same 1994-95 period. The campaign was eventually to prove successful in that in September 1995 the minister announced the creation of 6,200 additional places in the university sector at a cost of £60 million. This state funding was to be supplemented by the universities raising half of the money from private sources.

It was against this background that draft university legislation emerged.[73] The process was initiated by a confidential discussion document on university legislation sent to university presidents. Among its proposals were the dissolution of the National University of Ireland and the creation of four new universities from UCD, UCC, UCG and Maynooth, changes in the governance of the universities, and increased powers for the minister and the Higher Education Authority over the finances and staffing of the universities. This confidential set of proposals was eventually, and inevitably, leaked to a newspaper, leading to a Dáil debate and some months of public discussion of university governance in which the misgivings of personnel at Trinity College Dublin received a first public airing.[74] The draft Universities Bill eventually emerged in July 1996, completing what the minister had described as a lengthy process of consultation and dialogue between the Department of Education and the interested parties.

The tone of the legislation was authoritarian and centralist. The mindset of the drafters was essentially little different from the 1960s and apparently had learnt very little from the consultation process of the previous two years. In the event the universities were to get a significantly different Act from what appeared in the bill at its first reading. They were helped by two things: the relatively late stage in the life of the Dáil at which the draft legislation appeared, and the king-making role which the six university senators happened to occupy in the Senate. Apart from the acts transforming the NIHEs into universities, Niamh Bhreathnach's bill was the first comprehensive draft legislation on universities in the history of the state.[75] As already noted, a similar project was undertaken during the ministry of Richard Burke in 1976, but it did not go beyond the status of heads of bills and never appeared in the Oireachtas as a draft bill, partly because Burke moved to Brussels. Unlike Burke, Niamh Bhreathnach served a full term and she seems to have been determined to leave a major piece of legislation behind her. She was over three-and-a-half years in office by the time the draft bill emerged. This is late in the life cycle of a Dáil, which gave her a time problem. She was to have an even bigger problem with the Senate.

Normally the Senate would not have posed such a problem. Under the Irish Constitution eleven of its sixty members are appointed by the Taoiseach of the day, and this invariably is sufficient to ensure a government majority. In practice the Senate has very little scope to assert its powers to block or delay legislation. The twenty-seventh parliament in the history of the state was however unique. During its life the state experienced the only change of government which was not brought about by a general election. Following the break-up of the Fianna Fáil-Labour coalition in November 1994, the 'rainbow coalition' of Fine Gael, Labour and Democratic Left took over in December 1994. Labour continued in government and Niamh Bhreathnach continued as Minister for Education.[76] The new government, not having had control of the Taoiseach's nominees to the Senate, did not have a Senate majority. Six of the sixty senators were elected by the graduates of Dublin University and the National University of Ireland, and in a hung Senate they held the balance of power. University legislation was of salient interest to them and their presence was to have a major role in modifying the draft legislation.[77]

The opposition from the universities became evident from September 1996 onwards. First into the fray, and ominously for a Fine Gael-led government, was the former Taoiseach and now Chancellor of the National University of Ireland, Garret FitzGerald. In the first of two articles in the *Irish Times* he outlined the previously unheralded discrimination against academic representation in governing authorities, and identified a number of items within the bill which were particularly discriminatory in the case of the existing NUI university colleges. His second article was altogether stronger and referred to relevant sections of the bill 'which, between them proposed to hand over effective *de facto* control of our universities to the government-appointed Higher Education Authority'. These included provisions for issuing strategic development plans, annual reports, and detailed and evaluative material in prescribed form on the performance of a university. Further important constraints were on the universities' freedom to determine how their budgets would be spent and the power of HEA to send in someone to examine a university's books, if it did not like the annual returns relating to staffing. The universities could not borrow without the consent of both the Ministers for Education and Finance, and HEA could issue guidelines dealing with the proportion of the budget to be applied to different activities, and also on matters relating to the numbers and grades of employees. If the universities failed to comply, HEA could report the matter to the minister who would publish any such report in *Iris Oifigiúil*.

FitzGerald wondered 'how our Oireachtas came to be presented with such an extraordinarily authoritarian, indeed Thatcherite, Bill – a measure profoundly contrary to, and openly dismissive of, our highly successful university system?' He suggested that the impetus for the proposed dramatic extension of HEA's powers was almost certainly bureaucratic rather than political, and that the full implications of university autonomy had not been grasped at political level. He further suggested that with a general election due it was not the moment for the government to allow pressures from within the administrative system to embroil it in a quite unnecessary parliamentary row, which could be avoided by removing the discriminatory provisions against the NUI universities and the two unacceptable provisions for HEA guidelines.[78]

Further opposition followed from the Council of Convocation of the National University,[79] the NUI Senate,[80] the Irish Federation of University Teachers,[81] the Fellows of TCD, [82] the UCG Governing Body,[83] and the Governing Body of UCC.[84] The most serious setback for the minister was a statement of 29 October which appeared as a notice in the national press on 30 October from the Higher Education Authority signed by its chairman and secretary.[85] The Authority had been stung by some of the comment on the role of HEA and its interaction with the universities.[86] The statement reviewed the role of HEA since 1968, and pointed out that 'the financially sound and responsive system of university education in the state was due in no small measure to the nature of the collaboration and the positive working relationship built up between the Authority and the colleges'. It went on to say that HEA had consistently asserted the importance of university autonomy, holding that a certain 'critical distance' between universities and the state was 'a vital component of our democratic life'. It added that the role of HEA, in accordance with its statutory functions, was to allocate between the universities, in accordance with clear objective criteria, such funds as were made available by the government and to ensure, in accordance with public financial policy, that deficits were not incurred. It saw the process as having worked well and added that HEA 'has not sought and would not wish that any change in this process would be reflected in the legislation'. This was a very significant intervention given the widespread belief in the universities that the increased interventionist role of HEA in the legislation was something for which it had lobbied. Shortly afterwards the Authority submitted fifty-six suggested amendments.[87] At this stage the minister was very much on the back foot, having already made clear that she intended to introduce amendments to the Bill.[88]

At the Committee Stage of the Bill the minister brought forward over one hundred amendments. These amendments, while ostensibly technical for the most part, had the effect of amending or removing what the universities had objected to, and there seem to have been political negotiations between the Department and the Conference of Heads of Irish Universities.[89] Had this not happened, it is conceivable that the minister would not have got her bill through the Oireachtas. The revised bill went through the Dáil and on to the Senate in March 1997. It went through the Senate in April, but only following a further intervention on behalf of Trinity College which led to an amendment on the composition of academic councils.[90] The order initiating the Act was signed on 13 June 1997 by minister Bhreathnach at St Patrick's College Maynooth, where it gave birth to the National University of Ireland Maynooth. The college, together with UCD, UCG and UCC became a constituent university of the National University of Ireland. The Act also allowed for a separate Private Members' Bill for the University of Dublin to define a new structure for the Board of Trinity College Dublin, which would allow outside representation on the Board of the College for the first time since 1592.[91]

Niamh Bhreathnach succeeded where so many of her predecessors had failed. New legislation was passed which brought about major changes in the constitutional arrangements for the Irish university system. The legislation set out the ground rules for the establishment and identity of universities, defined the objects and functions of universities and the laid down rules for their governance. It also set out the state's requirements for planning and evaluation, finance, property and reporting. The end product was broadly satisfactory to the universities. One of those closely involved, Senator Professor Joe Lee, wrote in the immediate aftermath that there were still dangers, in a worse case scenario, of an authoritarian state control lurking in the Act.[92]

In the early 1990s it did indeed look as if the old hostility to universities and their autonomy had declined in the upper reaches of Irish public administration and among politicians. The draft legislation which initially emerged suggested otherwise, and it became clear that there still existed a deep distrust of universities in those circles. Two of the commentators, Professor Joe Lee and John Walshe, suggested that it did not necessarily emanate from the Department of Education as much as from other sources, possibly the Department of Finance.[93] The Higher Education Authority had been set up as a 'buffer' between the state and the universities a generation previously. While it had fallen out of favour somewhat with the universities in the previous decade (seen by many as an executive arm of the Department of Education), at a time of potential crisis for the universities it certainly did act as such a buffer and gave strong support to the concept of university autonomy.

The universities play a significant role in all modern states, particularly in developed societies. They remain one of the most important vehicles of independent thought in any country. Their influence and power in Irish society can be underestimated until challenged. Trinity College saw off many attempts to change it in the nineteenth and early twentieth centuries. The two Dublin university colleges saw off the very formidable Donogh O'Malley and his attempt to merge them in 1967, and they saw off proposals spearheaded by Richard Burke, Garret FitzGerald and Justin Keating in the 1970s. Niamh Bhreathnach, in turn, received a mauling when she attempted heavy-handed reform with her legislation. One suspects that the universities are safe from similar legislative threat for at least a generation. Whether the basic mistrust abates is another matter.

The regional technical colleges become institutes of technology.

With the elevation of the two NIHEs to university status, the regional technical colleges had become the cornerstone of the non-university third-level sector. Shortly after the passing of the Regional Technical Colleges Act 1992 and the removal of the colleges from the supervision of vocational education committees they began to acquire their own corporate identity.[94] In 1995 a Steering Committee on the Future Development of Higher Education, set up by the Minister of Education under the aegis of HEA, issued a report in which it recommended that the regional technical colleges be redesignated regional institutes of technology to reflect their changed and still evolving role.[95] The minister agreed to consult the colleges on a change of title.[96] The colleges were not satisfied with a mere name change. They had produced a joint proposal for the establishment of an Irish Technological University (ITU) to validate RTC courses.[97] It was contended that, because the colleges had to operate in an international context, change was needed to ensure the international standing of their graduates' qualifications.[98] In addition, it was maintained that the change was required if the RTCs were to compete for the sizeable segment of the student population which was being wooed increasingly by the British university system. The RTCs also seemed to share a feeling that the standing of their awards was being devalued by the increasing growth of NCEA validation in private colleges. By 1995 the RTCs dwarfed the rest of the NCEA sector. Seventy-nine per cent (9,301) of NCEA's 11,917 awards in 1995 were at RTCs. NCEA made 1,775 awards at degree and postgraduate level of which 1,090 (61 per cent) were in RTCs.[99]

While they may have operated under one umbrella from 1993 onwards, the RTCs were, and remain, in many ways a disparate group. They vary in size, range of disciplines, undergraduate and postgraduate development, part-time provision, and levels of harmony on the industrial relations front. They also vary in management styles and in their relationship to the wider industrial, business and political culture of their regions. A lobby for change with relation to this sector could come from below as well as from above. Just as the original binary policy was deflected by a single-minded campaign for a university for Limerick, so a similar regional argument was to dominate the affairs of regional technical colleges during 1997.

The campaign for a university for Waterford dated from 1977.[100] A report commissioned for Waterford Chamber of Commerce in 1985 recommended the establishment of an institute of technology there. The argument of the proponents was that the South-East was losing out on economic development and on the ability to attract foreign inward investment through not having a university. The issue was referred to the Steering Committee on the Future Development of Higher Education, and both the Committee and its Technical Working Group, recommended that the status of the regional technical college be upgraded to a higher level technological institute combining a wide range of degree as well as diploma/certificate courses, on the lines of the Dublin Institute of Technology, but clearly with a narrower range of disciplines because of its considerably smaller size.[101] The report felt that issues of regional equity could be dealt with in other ways. It concluded that there was a case for an extended range of degree facilities in the South-East, which could be met by the upgrading of the regional technical college.

Following the publication of the report of the Steering Committee political pressure came on the government from Waterford Chamber of Commerce and Waterford University Action Group. In January 1997 the minister, Niamh Bhreathnach, announced that the college would be upgraded to become Waterford Institute of Technology.[102] While the decision was widely welcomed in Waterford, it quickly generated uproar in Cork. Cork Regional Technical College depicted the upgrading of Waterford RTC as a lowering of its own status. It received immediate support from students, local politicians and the business community.[103] Claims for enhanced status were soon afterwards reported from Dundalk,[104] Athlone,[105] Sligo,[106] Tralee[107] and Carlow[108]. The minister moved quickly to establish a high-level group to advise her on the technological sector,[109] and specifically to advise on the criteria which should be applied to the redesignation of a regional technical college, and the most appropriate means whereby institutions should be independently evaluated in relation to such criteria.[110] The group was chaired by Professor Devilla Donnelly of UCD. It reported to the minister in early May.

The report of the Committee recommended the upgrading of all eleven RTCs to institute of technology status under a new Irish National Institute of Technology (INIT), a legal successor to NCEA with respect to the RTC sector. INIT was to be responsible for national awards, but after a review process could devolve its authority to individual colleges or groups of co-operating colleges. The minister proceeded to implement the change of name for Waterford RTC immediately, but promised to change the names of all the others as well.[111] The Waterford college was extremely angry, as it saw the upgrading of every other college as effectively keeping it within the RTC sector and thus negating the effect of the upgrading. Meanwhile the President of the Students' Union at Cork RTC had been nominated to run as a candidate against the sitting Labour TD in Cork South Central, and may have had a role in bringing about his defeat in the general election of June 1997.

In mid-May Niamh Bhreathnach announced an international review team, also chaired by Professor Donnelly, to establish a process to delegate authority to Waterford Institute of Technology to make its own awards. Her successor, Micheál Martin, launched this group in July 1997. Only the Waterford and Cork colleges initially made submissions to this group requesting delegation of authority.[112] In November 1997 the minister announced the upgrading of the Cork college, and in January 1998 all the regional technical colleges were upgraded to institute of technology status.[113] In October 1998 the review group recommended that both the Cork and Waterford colleges should be given the right to award their own qualifications in all existing sub-degree courses, but left to a future review the determination as to whether they should award their own degrees.[114] The minister accepted the proposal, but it was at that point contingent on a new qualification structure which the minister was to introduce by statute. In April 2000 a similar decision was recorded with regard to the Sligo Institute of Technology, and the Galway-Mayo Institute of Technology some months later.[115] As of late 2000 none of the four colleges had been delegated the relevant awarding powers.

At the end of a process which had begun with a proposal to bring Waterford Regional Technical College to a status equivalent to Dublin Institute of Technology, the upshot was that each regional technical college had had a change of name, but the Waterford college had not been upgraded vis-a-vis the others. Effectively the RTC system, led by the Cork college, had prevented Waterford from becoming disengaged from what was to be reclassified as the institute of technology sector. The Cork college could muster far more political firepower than Waterford. It is possible, but unlikely, that the issue of regional disadvantage which lay behind the argument for an upgrading of Waterford will disappear. The Limerick claim in its final phase took thirty years to achieve a university. One suspects that, for an outcome like that of Limerick to be achieved, it will require a single-minded individual of the calibre of Dr Edward Walsh, who is prepared to combine a drive for a university for the South-East with a determination that the Waterford College should not be tied forever to a national system of institutes of technology. The legislation now in place will make that task even more difficult than it was for Limerick and Dr Walsh.

The status of Dublin Institute of Technology

The colleges of the City of Dublin Vocational Education Committee which comprised the Dublin Institute of Technology, were removed from the responsibility of the Committee at the same time as the RTCs were taken from under the wing of their own respective VECs. DIT was treated separately from the RTCs and was given its own statute. There were significant differences between DIT and the RTCs. While there were considerable structural similarities between the two Bills and subsequent Acts, the main difference was that there was no provision in the RTC Act for RTCs to make their own awards. DIT on the other hand could confer, grant or give diplomas, certificates or other awards.[116] It was also granted other functions which could include the conferring of degrees, postgraduate degrees and honorary awards, which under the act could be assigned by the Minister for Education.[117] Another significant difference was that the title of 'President' was given to the chief officer of the Institute, rather than 'Director' as in the RTCs. Provision was made for the appointment of a number of directors in DIT which made each of them answerable to the president.[118] At the time of the debate on the DIT Bill it was suggested that the Institute should have degree-awarding powers.[119] Responding to the debate in the Senate at the end of the legislative process, the minister, Séamus Brennan, indicated that the Institute would be given degree-awarding powers preferably within a period of twelve months.[120] It took a little longer than that. In December 1995, Niamh Bhreathnach appointed an international review team to review quality assurance procedures in the Institute. In its report the following year the group recommended that degree-awarding powers at undergraduate and postgraduate level be extended to the Institute from 1998/99 onwards. That in turn entailed the phasing-out of the relationship with TCD.[121] The group also recommended that the unique nature of DIT as a multi-level institution should be preserved and nurtured. Degree awarding powers were officially granted to the Institute in November 1997[122] to come into effect in 1998/99.

In the meantime the Institute had made a strong pitch for university status. Following the publication of the Universities Bill in the summer of 1996 it made a submission seeking inclusion in the Bill.[123] According to the Institute President, Dr Brendan Goldsmith, the international review group had viewed the Institute as a university in everything but name, and failure to recognise it as such would militate against its students and graduates, both internationally and in the job market at home and abroad.[124] The Institute conducted a strong campaign through its students and parents[125] and its case for university status was taken up by the Fianna Fáil opposition during the Dáil debates on the Universities Bill in late 1996 and early 1997.[126] While the minister announced that DIT would achieve degree-awarding status as recommended by the International Review Group, she indicated that on the passing of the Act, she would request the government to avail of Section 9 of the Universities Act 1997 and appoint a body to advise the government on whether DIT should be established as a university.[127]

The commitment to set up the DIT Review Group was carried through by her successor, Micheál Martin, in July 1997 with the establishment of an international review group under the chairmanship of Dermot Nally, a former Secretary to the Government. That group reported in November 1998. The group looked at five possible options or scenarios: immediate university status, rejection of DIT's application, merger of DIT with an existing university, creation of a dual institution (i.e. one part dealing with degree and post-graduate work and the other with sub-degree work) and university status for DIT at a later date.[128] It came down in favour of the last option. It concluded that there were serious arguments against the immediate establishment of DIT as a university. These related to the maturity and cohesiveness of the Institute, the range and nature of postgraduate research provision, the qualifications and experience of academic staff and academic structures and conditions.[129] The group was anxious for DIT to develop and enhance its existing strong sub-degree and apprenticeship provision, and added that the DIT charter should appropriately reflect institutional commitment to the preservation and development of the multi-level nature of the Institute. The Group felt that the conditions it laid down for DIT to raise itself to university standard could be met within three to five years.[130]

Within three months of the presentation of the group's report to HEA, the Authority itself published its response. It accepted the finding of the Review Group that there were serious arguments against the establishment of DIT as a university and recommended accordingly against it.[131] It took issue with some of the other comments of the Review Group. The Group had recommended that DIT draw up targets for implementation with the consent of

HEA and that the Institute's progress towards these targets should be continually monitored by the Authority. HEA reckoned that this 'mentoring' role represented an inappropriate confusion of its functions and responsibilities, and felt that it would undermine the Authority's objectivity in making recommendations to government, as it was statutorily obliged to do. It added that a further review group would be required under Section 9 of the Universities Act 1997 before a decision on upgrading after the three to five year span envisaged by the Review Group.

The Review Group had also recommended that DIT become a designated institution under the Higher Education Authority Act 1971. The Authority, noting that the designation of institutes of technology under the Act was stated policy, was concerned to ensure that designation should not be construed as a stepping-stone to university status. The Authority's report effectively closed off university status for DIT for some years. Legislative development in 1999 made it look as if the elusive university status could be even more problematic for the Institute. For even if it achieves elevation to university status, it will now be caught by the provisions of Section 41 of the Qualifications (Education and Training) Act 1999, which will give it significantly less autonomy than any university established by or before the Universities Act 1997.

The Dublin Institute has a claim to be regarded as the flagship of the public sector side of the binary system. It is far and away the biggest of the public sector institutions with over 10,300 full-time and 10,000 part-time and apprentice students in the academic year 1996-97.[132] It offers a complete gamut of programmes from apprenticeship to PhD, something which both the International Review Group and the Higher Education Authority were anxious to maintain. If any institution is to be a bulwalk against academic drift or 'mission creep', DIT should be the exemplar. Yet, in fact, DIT, as in the days when it was a mere agglomeration of colleges of the City of Dublin Vocational Education Committee, has all the outer signs of an institution that is neither happy nor at ease with itself. Its industrial relations problems are severe.[133] When DIT achieved its independence from City of Dublin VEC at the end of 1992, one of the first objectives of its president and governing body was to introduce a faculty structure to supersede the administrative arrangement then based on six colleges and buildings scattered around Dublin's city centre.[134] Eight years later that faculty structure had not been implemented, not least because of trade union resistance. The primary cause of the Institute's problems has to be that the senior management and faculty do not have the requisite authority to manage the institution. They refer back to the Department of Education and Science for all major (and many minor) matters referring to industrial relations, buildings and capital development, and course development. DIT's facilities for students in relation to sport and various services are amongst the worst in the state.[135]

These issues bear upon the more strategic matters identified by the International Review Group. For university status to be met in the future that Group felt that academic structures and conditions providing comparable arrangements with those pertaining in existing universities needed to be introduced. In particular, 'flexibility comparable to university practice internationally must be obtained in relation to teaching contact hours, class sizes, access to laboratories outside office hours, and end of term closure dates'.[136] However matters like contact hours are governed entirely by negotiations with trade unions, and clearly the Department of Education and Science has, and will continue to have, considerable problems in negotiating with a trade union which has teaching members at both second and third-level and is both determined, and has the experience, to win traditional third-level privileges and payment rates for second-level teachers.[137] Tackling the issue of over-teaching is not within the exclusive powers of the management and decision-makers within DIT. The same applies to many other issues within the Institute.

Officially DIT does not wish to maintain its current position within the binary divide. It has the advantage, unlike other institutes of technology, that it can award its own degrees. It does not have university status; it is the only degree-awarding institution in the country which is in that position. In the long term the likelihood has to be that it will eventually achieve that status, if only to remove an obvious anomaly.

A new framework for qualifications

After many years of gestation the government in the person of Micheál Martin piloted the Qualifications (Education and Training) Bill 1999 speedily through the Dáil and Senate in the summer of 1999. The Act established the National Qualifications Authority, the Further Education and Training Awards Council, and the Higher Education and Training Awards Council and dissolved the National

Council for Educational Awards.[138] It also included extra provisions in relation to the institutes of technology, the Dublin Institute of Technology and the universities. It further introduced certain sanctions in relation to provision of third-level education by purely private colleges.[139] Essentially the Higher Education and Training Awards Council replaced NCEA, although Section 24 would suggest that it is purely geared to institutes of technology and some other unspecified establishments governed by statute. At one level it gives potentially more autonomy to colleges in that it envisages processes which will allow the delegation of the granting of awards to individual institutions.[140] The Further Education and Training Awards Council essentially absorbed the work of the National Council for Vocational Awards and effectively the existing awards activity of FÁS,[141] CERT,[142] TEAGASC[143] and Bórd Iascaigh Mhara.[144]

In introducing the Bill the minister, Micheál Martin, stated that 'all international experience shows that we must be vigilant to ensure that we are genuinely providing flexible and appropriate opportunities and are protecting the quality of qualifications'. The Bill was based on the 'four pillars of access, transfer, progression and quality'.[145] He went on to refer to the work of the Dearing Review in Britain which, he indicated, had concluded that academic drift and official neglect had seriously damaged Britain's competitiveness.[146] He concluded that the new arrangement would enable institutes to aspire to university status without impeding or downgrading the value of the work they had done to date.[147] In short a major consideration of the minister and the Department of Education and Science was to protect technician and other sub-degree activity currently conducted in institutes of technology. An important question here is whether this approach is likely to succeed.

The provisions of the 1999 Act, particularly Part V and Part VI, together with Section 9 of the Universities Act 1997, have introduced the prospect of two types of university in the Republic of Ireland – autonomous and non-autonomous. It is relatively clear that the Department of Education and Science has concluded that the process of establishing new Irish universities has not necessarily been completed. If so, the process in future will be considerably more complex than it was in the 1980s when the Hardiman Committee emancipated the two NIHEs. That Committee did not attempt to analyse the nature of universities or establish criteria. Essentially it took a pragmatic businessman's approach to a question of branding and marketing. The 1997 Universities Act, particularly in Part III, has addressed this issue, while the Nally Review Group (which considered the application of DIT for university status) gave substantial thought to international criteria for the granting of university status.[148] The new process would suggest that any future applicants for university status will have to go through somewhat more rigorous hoops than was required of the NIHEs.[149] Where in the future institutions achieve university status, it is difficult to believe that they will in the long term accept a significantly lower degree of autonomy than their older counterparts. Third-level institutions appear to have an inherent aspiration for as great a degree of autonomy as can be achieved. But as long as the 1999 qualifications legislation exists, any autonomy achieved will be severely constrained.

A second question is how long the new arrangement of having three quality assurance bodies can survive. A country the size of Ireland does not need three state organisations to perform the function of quality assurance in higher and further education. If looked at purely in bureaucratic terms, the new arrangements introduced by the 1999 Act may make sense; they can certainly be represented as the honourable outcome of a long-standing turf war between the Department of Education and Science and the Department of Enterprise, Trade and Employment (and their predecessors of different nomenclature),[150] a declaration of the primacy of education over training or of lifelong learning over the quick training fix.[151] In the author's view all of this could and should have been achieved while retaining a single body, the National Council for Educational Awards. If NCEA's statute was not wide enough to achieve what was required, it should have been amended rather than devalue the 150,000 awards made by that body between 1972 and 1999, some at the level of doctorate. In most modern societies degrees are normally associated with universities only. In the 1970s for various policy reasons the Irish state decided to set up an organisation outside the universities with power to award degrees. Degrees acquire recognition over time. In that they resemble brands. The casual manner in which the NCEA degree designation was abandoned by the Irish state bodes ill for its successor body and the likely status to be earned by its degrees. It is ironic that a Fianna Fáil administration should have been prepared to abolish the organisation so unceremoniously, a predecessor having gone to such lengths to preserve it from the Cosgrave government's decisions of 1974. NCEA had no publicly vocal defenders within Fianna Fáil when the various centrifugal forces of Irish vocational education and training wished to dismember it.

At first sight the replacements do not seem to be more flexible. The fact that these new bodies still had not been launched almost eighteen months after being legally established, and that both NCEA and NCVA limped along under a stay of execution, did not indicate any great sense of vision, urgency or excitement in regard to this initiative.[152] It is unlikely that on their own these three organisations will, over a generation, save the binary system. Its survival depends on the Department of Education and Science and on the teachers' unions, in this case the Teachers' Union of Ireland. In a society that is rapidly changing and which is in many ways a microcosm of globalisation, they represent two conservative forces which still retain real power in Irish life. The fate of the Dublin Institute of Technology, and whichever of the other institutes of technology (most likely Waterford) next presents itself for university status, will finally determine whether the Department and the unions can preserve the binary system which both clearly want to retain.

Notes

1 From 1966 to 1996 every Minister for Education, who lasted any length of time in the position, committed himself or herself to introducing amending legislation. A comprehensive universities Bill finally appeared in July 1996 and Niamh Bhreathnach was eventually to see legislation through the Oireachtas in 1997.

2 The title 'Dublin Institute of Technology', covering the six third-level colleges operated under the aegis of the City of Dublin Vocational Education Committee, which had been adopted by the Committee in May 1978, received formal ministerial recognition from minister John Boland in December 1981. *Dáil Debates*, vol. 331, col. 1006 (3 December 1981).

3 The approach adopted by Dr Walsh and others in referring to NIHE Limerick as a university is not open to a subsequent generation. It has been outlawed by Section 52 of the Universities Act 1997, which forbids the use of the term 'university' to describe an educational establishment or faculty without the approval of the minister.

4 *Dáil Debates*, vol. 321, col. 321 (21 May 1980). ibid., vol. 374, col. 306 (12 November 1980).

5 At one conferring they were referred to as 'the twin pinnacles on the pyramid', an unusual architectural concept.

6 NCEA, *Eighth Report*, p. 16.

7 This was the period when the NIHEs and RTCs started new courses in computing, electronics and mechanical drawing following the initiative of the Manpower Consultative Committee.
8 NCEA, *Tenth Report*, p. 16.
9 Dr Walsh was a member of the NCEA Council from 1972 to 1989, and the author heard him observe as late as 1987 that in fifteen years on the Council he had never chaired a meeting.
10 The position of director was created by Section 7 of the National Institute for Higher Education Limerick Act 1980 and its functions were set out in the Second Schedule to the Act. The change is reflected in the *NIHE News*. In the issue of April 1982 Dr Walsh is referred to as the director, while in the July 1982 issue he is referred to as the president. It is understood that the decision to make the change was made by the governing body.
11 See, for example, the comments of Deputies George Bermingham, *Dáil Debates*, vol. 390, col. 1277 (27 May 1989) and Michael Barrett (ibid., col. 1383).
12 Report of the International Study Group to the Minister for Education, (1987), *Technological Education*, Dublin.
13 ibid., p. 1.
14 ibid., p. 3.
15 ibid., p. 28.
16 ibid., pp. 30-31. Since the Committee was not interested in such philosophical issues, the problem virtually boiled down to a decision on whether the institutions deserved a specific prestige brand name.
17 *CII News*, vol. 47, no. 14, 18 August 1987; *Irish Times*, 11 August 1987.
18 Private information.
19 *Dáil Debates*, vol. 390, cols. 1262-1279, 1357-1410 (25 May 1989).
20 ibid., vols. 1268-1269.
21 ibid., cols. 1357-1358. This issue surfaced briefly following appointment of the governing bodies of both universities made by a subsequent Minister for Education, Séamus Brennan. The appointments, made during a post-election transition period, did not emerge in public until about six weeks after they had taken place. *Irish Times*, 24 December 1992.
22 Supra, Chapter 4.
23 One of the strongest arguments put to the Hardiman Group by the Confederation of Irish Industry submission was that there were 'problems of image which required time and effort to counteract, the main problem revolving around the question posed by international business as to whether an NIHE was a university or not'. (*CII News*, 18 August 1987).
24 Walsh, *Two Ideas of a University Contrasted.* Also *Irish Times*, 19 November 1990.
25 The essence of the binary policy was that there had to be a range of publicly-funded institutions of higher education which would be responsive to government policy objectives, unlike the autonomous universities which were not so readily amenable.
26 Moreover two of the nominees on the Council from NUI Colleges were members of that Committee, which only served to rub salt in the NIHE wounds.
27 National Board for Science and Technology, *Science Budget 1980.*

28 AVEC Working Party on Research and Consultancy (n.d.), *Report on Research and Consultancy in VEC Colleges*, pp. 10-11.
29 One RTC principal told the author at the time that some sceptical VEC members, at home with issues such as apprenticeship education, saw proposals of this nature as a device for 'getting nixers for lecturers'.
30 *Dáil Debates*, vol. 350, col. 1976 (24 May 1984).
31 *Green Paper 1985*, p. 16.
32 ibid., p. 20.
33 *Technological Education*, p. 40.
34 *Dáil Debates*, vol. 373, col. 2088 (16 June 1987).
35 ibid., vol. 412, col. 265 (5 November 1991).
36 See, for instance, the speeches of Deputy Brian O'Shea (Labour), *Dáil Debates*, vol. 412, cols. 632-635 (7 November 1991); Tomás MacGiolla (Workers' Party) cols. 642-646; Neil Blaney (Independent) col. 673; Éamon Gilmore (Democratic Left), vol. 413, cols. 556-558 (21 November 1991); Dinny McGinley (Fine Gael), col. 570; Fergus O'Brien (Fine Gael), col. 574; Noel Dempsey (Fianna Fáil) cols. 686-690.
37 ibid., vol. 413, col. 686 (21 November 1991).
38 ibid., col. 690.
39 ibid., col. 646; also vol. 421, col. 2015 (1 July 1992).
40 ibid., vol. 420, col. 1500 (4 June 1992).
41 Hederman O'Brien, M. (1994), *Report to Niamh Bhreathnach TD, Minister for Education, under Section 20 of the Regional Technical Colleges Act 1992 on Letterkenny Regional Technical College*, Dublin: Stationery Office.
42 *Irish Times*, 22 October 1994; *Irish Independent*, 28 October 1994; *Irish Times*, 29 October 1994; *Irish Times*, 1 November 1994. Niamh Bhreathnach had become Minister for Education in January 1993, the first member of the Labour Party to occupy the portfolio.
43 There had been numerous occasions where, virtually alone of government departments, the Department of Education has parried questions about state-sponsored bodies under its aegis by refusing to admit that it had any. For example, *Dáil Debates*, vol. 305, col. 541 (12 April 1978); vol. 310, col. 520 (30 November 1978); vol. 337, col. 866 (2 July 1982). The author put this point to a former Secretary of the Department, Doiminic Ó Laoghaire, who insisted that only commercial or trading bodies merited the title of state-sponsored, and not purely administrative organisations such as NCEA or HEA. Other departments did not take this approach to Dáil questions on the topic.
44 *Full-Time Courses in VEC Colleges – Report of a Committee established to examine Third-Level Courses which lead to awards of NCEA and other bodies outside the Universities*, September 1989, p. 44. (This internal Department of Education document, prepared by a Committee chaired by the Secretary of the Department, was generally known as the Lindsay Report).
45 NCEA, *Nineteenth Report*, p. 20.
46 NCEA, *Annual Reports*, passim.
47 NCEA, *Sixteenth Report*, p. 7.
48 NCEA, *Fourteenth Report*, p. 5.
49 Annual reports from 1980 onwards keep referring to the matter, but NCEA never managed to progress the issue. For almost a quarter of a century NCEA had the

Gilbertian situation that, while at any one time there were up to eight officials with the title of assistant registrar, there was never a staff member sporting the title of registrar.

50 NCEA, *Fifteenth Report*, p. 6. In 1996 the National College of Art and Design became a recognised college of the National University of Ireland.

51 It did initiate, and subsequently participated with HEA in, an annual survey of the first destination of its award-holders in each academic year.

52 NCEA, *Fourteenth Report*, p. 6.

53 The *Sixteenth Report* in 1989 did advert to the departure of the two NIHEs, wished them well for future success and welcomed the confirmation of the high standards at the NIHEs by the international team.

54 *Dáil Debates*, vol. 346, cols. 151-152 (22 November 1983).

55 See above Chapter 8, Footnote 38.

56 *Limerick Leader*, 13 September 1986. See also *Irish Times*, 26 October 1993. Subsequently the degree tuition was provided by Limerick Senior College, a VEC college which was not even an NCEA-designated institution.

57 Personal knowledge of the author who was approached on the issue by the college, while acting as Assistant Registrar with NCEA. The college changed its name to Dublin Business School in 1996.

58 The views of council members of NCEA from public sector third-level colleges in the vocational and technological sector towards private colleges ranged from ambivalence to hostility. Several institutions, most notably the College of Industrial Relations and a number of seminaries, had been associated with NCEA from early in its *ad hoc* phase. While there were some key individuals on the Council who would have been lukewarm about having such colleges designated under Section 20 of the Act, there was in general a tolerance at least, of the involvement of these long-standing not-for-profit institutions with NCEA. There was an altogether more negative, and even hostile, attitude towards a number of private colleges which began to flourish in Dublin in the 1980s and whose *raison d'etre* was unashamedly commercial. Educationists from the public sector did not take kindly to education being treated as a commodity as distinct from a public service. Ironically the Dublin colleges flourished partly because of the absence of public sector provision of the kind recommended in the Benson and Clancy report of 1979. Likewise the initial growth of post-Leaving Certificate courses was primarily a phenomenon of the Dublin region, where provision of technician and sub-degree third-level education had fallen behind the rest of the country.

59 *Irish Times*, 8 August 1991.

60 *Sunday Business Post*, 17 October 1993; *Irish Times*, 6 December 1994.

61 *Irish Times*, 24 January 1995. The institution concerned was Newman College in Dublin.

62 ibid.

63 *Regional Technical Colleges Act 1992*, section 5(1)(b). *Dublin Institute of Technology Act 1992*, section 5(1)(c).

64 *Dáil Debates*, vol. 420, col. 1643 (5 June 1992).

65 Green Paper, (1992), *Education for a Changing Ireland*, Dublin: Stationery Office, pp. 115, 199-200.

66 *1995 White Paper*, p. 83. The retention of TEASTAS 'under the aegis of the

Department of Education' represented a bureaucratic victory, as there was apparently a real possibility of such a body incorporating the work of FÁS and coming within the responsibility of the Department of Enterprise and Employment.

67 *Irish Independent*, 29/30 August 1996. *Irish Times*, 30 August 1996. The NCEA Director, Pádraig Mac Diarmada, had tendered his resignation in July 1996.

68 It had petered out with the end of the debate over the merger of the two Dublin university colleges, but re-emerged with the Burke proposals of December 1974, the Programme for Action in Education 1984-87, the 1992 Green Paper and again in the 1995 White Paper.

69 Coolahan, J. (ed.) (1994), *Report of the National Education Convention*, Dublin: National Education Convention Secretariat, p. 26.

70 These issues are comprehensively dealt with in Walshe, J. (1999), *A New Partnership in Education: From Consultation to Legislation in the Nineties*, Dublin: Institute of Public Administration, pp. 124-131.

71 *Steering Committee Technical Working Group*, p. 47.

72 The proposal, which was linked to the abolition of income tax relief for covenants, was brought forward by the minister during the life of the Fianna Fáil/Labour administration of 1992-94, and was eventually implemented during the life of the 'Rainbow Coalition' of 1994-97. It might initially have appeared to have the potential political appeal of the free secondary education scheme introduced by Donogh O'Malley in 1967. This was not to prove to be the case, and the initiative was not sufficient to save the minister's seat in Dún Laoghaire in the 1997 general election.

73 Walshe, *A New Partnership in Education*, pp. 131-156. Again this provides a very useful summary of the issues surrounding the introduction and progress of the university legislation.

74 On this occasion, as on so many others in the previous twenty-five years, the leak came through John Walshe, the education correspondent of the *Irish Independent*. Here the leak seems to have landed in his lap from a source within the university system; in many other instances stories on ongoing classified issues came via Mr Walshe's own investigative nose. Hitherto, and certainly prior to the passing of the freedom of information legislation, educational politics has been characterised by behind-the-scenes lobbying and off-the-record briefing of journalists.

75 There were a number of minor acts dealing with the National University of Ireland in the period from 1922 to 1960, in 1926, 1929, 1934, 1940 and 1960 (*Commission on Higher Education*, pp. 469-470).

76 She was out of office for a month, when Labour resigned from government in November 1994.

77 Two of them, Professor Joseph Lee and Dr David Norris, were full-time academics at University College Cork and Trinity College Dublin respectively.

78 Garret FitzGerald, *Irish Times*, 23-24 September 1996.

79 ibid., 21 October 1996.

80 ibid., 24 October 1996.

81 ibid., 25 October 1996.

82 ibid., 31 October 1996.

83 ibid., 5 November 1996.

84 Walshe, *A New Partnership*, p. 145.
85 *Irish Times*, 30 October 1996.
86 Most notably, it would appear, an article in the *Sunday Independent* by Professor Ronan Fanning, a UCD historian. (Walshe, *A New Partnership*, p. 147.)
87 *Irish Independent*, 11 November 1996.
88 *Irish Times*, 23 October 1996. Not all the universities were critical of the Bill. The minister received statements of support from the presidents of the University of Limerick and Dublin City University, and also from St Patrick's College Maynooth, which was about to become an independent university. The organisational opposition at all times came from the NUI, UCD, UCC, UCG and Trinity College.
89 Walshe, *A New Partnership*, p. 150.
90 *Irish Times*, 25 April 1997.
91 The enabling legislation had still not been passed in September 2000. A private Bill sent to the Oireachtas by the Board of Trinity College was withdrawn following a ruling from the university Visitors which ordered the authorities to rehold a ballot of TCD's fellows and scholars following certain irregularities. *Irish Times*, 27 December 1996; *Sunday Tribune*, 4 January 1997.
92 J. Lee, *Sunday Tribune*, 27 April 1997.
93 There was at the time a suggestion that Niamh Bhreathnach, who qualified as a teacher at the Froebel College in Dublin and was not a university graduate, was a minister who was particularly unsympathetic to universities. This was certainly believed at the highest level within the universities (private information).
94 As already noted, the colleges set up their own directorate in 1993, with a full-time secretariat headed by Joseph McGarry, who was seconded from the position of Head of Business and Social Studies at Tralee Regional Technical College.
95 Steering Committee on the Future of Higher Education, (1995), *Report of the Steering Committee on the Future of Higher Education*, Dublin: Higher Education Authority, p. 33.
96 *Irish Times*, 2 March 1996.
97 ibid., 23 April 1996.
98 This was an echo of the argument put forward by the then NIHEs a decade previously.
99 NCEA, *Annual Report* 1995. Just under 15 per cent of NCEA's awards for 1995 were at primary degree and postgraduate level.
100 *Irish Times*, 28 January 1997.
101 For a discussion of the Waterford case for a university, *Interim Report of the Steering Committee's Technical Working Group*, pp. 98-101; *Report of Steering Committee*, pp. 29-31, *Dáil Debates*, vol. 372, col. 956 (5 May 1987); vol. 404, col. 2286 (12 February 1991).
102 *Irish Times*, 19 January 1997. It subsequently emerged that the Taoiseach, John Bruton, had put pressure on the minister for a change in status. While leaving the exact timing to her, he had made clear also that he wanted the decision taken before a visit to Waterford in late January. *Irish Independent*, 27 January 1997.

103 *Irish Times*, 23 January 1997.
104 *Irish Independent*, 24 January 1997.
105 ibid., 27 January 1997.
106 ibid.
107 *Irish Times*, 31 January 1997.
108 ibid., 11 February 1997.
109 ibid., 31 January 1997.
110 Unpublished Report of High-Level Group to advise on the Technological Sector, May 1997, p. 11.
111 *Irish Independent*, 15 May 1997.
112 *Irish Times*, 28 October 1997. Submissions were subsequently made by the Galway/Mayo and Sligo Institutes of Technology.
113 ibid., 29 January 1998.
114 ibid., 15 October 1998.
115 *Irish Times*, 21 April 2000.
116 Dublin Institute of Technology Act 1992, Section 5.1(b). For a discussion of the Act and its progress through the Oireachtas see Duff, Hegarty and Hussey, pp. 84-98.
117 ibid, section 5.2(a).
118 ibid, section 10.
119 *Dáil* Debates, vol. 412, col. 628 (7 November 1991 – Theresa Ahearn); vol. 413, col. 968 (26 November 1991 – Jim Higgins); vol. 421, cols. 2267-2269 (1 July 1992 – Jim Higgins, Brian O'Shea); cols. 891-893 (23 June 1992 – Jim Higgins); cols. 2274-2276 (1 July 1992 – Tomás MacGiolla).
120 *Seanad Debates*, vol. 133, col. 1914 (10 July 1992).
121 For a summary of the Group's findings, see *Report of the International Review Group to the Higher Education Authority (1998)*, p. 17.
122 *Irish Independent*, 5 November 1997.
123 *Dáil Debates*, vol. 479 (no. 2), col. 541, 14 May 1997.
124 *Irish Times*, 28 November 1996.
125 *Irish Times*, 20 December 1996.
126 See, for example, Máire Geoghegan Quinn, *Dáil Debates*, vol. 472, col. 1174, (10 December 1996), Micheál Martin, vol. 476, cols. 459-460, (12 March 1997).
127 *Dáil Debates*, vol. 479, col. 542 (14 May 1997).
128 *International Review Group*, pp. 35-37.
129 ibid., p. 35.
130 ibid., p. 41.
131 Higher Education Authority (1999), *Recommendations of the Higher Education Authority to Government in accordance with the terms of Section 9 of the Universities Act 1997 covering the application by DIT for establishment as a University*, Dublin: Higher Education Authority, p. 11.
132 The exact numbers were 10,343 full-time, 7,081 part-time and 2,912 apprentice students (*International Review Group*, pp. 14-15). In 1996-97 the numbers for Cork RTC, the biggest of the then RTC sector were quoted as 4,600 full-time and 3,000 part-time (with an additional 2,000 students at the School of Music and 1,800 apprenticeship students), *Irish Times*, 4 November 1997.
133 In private this is a matter with which many staff are unhappy and has had a significant effect on morale.

134 *Irish Times*, 17 September 1996, 3 March 1998, 20 October 1998.
135 See, for example, *Irish Times*, 7 December 1999. Inevitably perhaps the students were about to pursue industrial and strike action to protest against the long-fingering of any improvement in this area over so many years. The promise of the availability of the old Grangegorman psychiatric hospital may in time provide DIT with adequate campus facilities.
136 *International Review Group*, p. 39.
137 The Teachers' Union of Ireland represents virtually all lecturing staff at Institutes of Technology. Since the foundation of the RTCs in the early 1970s it has been a constant complaint of many lecturing staff, though rarely aired publicly or on the record, that the second-level tail has wagged the third-level dog within ITs (or RTCs), and that as a result the Department of Education and Science regularly applied second-level norms to these colleges. As there are now no second-level activities in any of the institutes of technology, this ought to become less of a problem.
138 Qualifications (Education and Training) Act 1999.
139 These were regarded as particularly onerous by the colleges concerned, and looked on by some as reflecting a determination on the part of the Department of Education and Science to virtually squeeze them out of the market altogether (private information). See also *Irish Independent*, 13 May 1999. Certainly Section 24 of the Act and the Bill appeared to be designed to have that effect.
140 Qualifications Act 1999, Section 29. It should be noted that, although the Act was passed in the summer of 1999, it had still not been implemented in the latter half of the year 2000. It would appear that a group had been established at the Department of Education and Science with a view to implementation in the summer of 2000. (*Faisnéis*, Newsletter of the National Council for Educational Awards, December 1999).
141 FÁS hitherto dealt *inter alia* with the certification of industrial apprenticeship.
142 A body similar to FÁS for the hotel, catering and tourism industry which had its own National Tourism Certification Board.
143 The Agriculture and Food Development Authority which provides research, advisory and training services for the agricultural sector.
144 The Irish Sea Fisheries Board which provides inter alia training services to the fishing industry.
145 *Dáil Debates*, vol. 504, col. 1278 (18 May 1999).
146 ibid., col. 1279.
147 ibid., col. 1279.
148 *International Review Group*, pp. 67-75.
149 This is not to suggest that the outcome in the 1980s would have been any different in the case of the NIHEs. Both had their eye on university status virtually from their inception.
150 The Department of Education became the Department of Education and Science in 1997.
151 See *Irish Independent*, 16 January 1997, 18 December 1997, 19 October 1998.
152 While the Act formally established the three new bodies, it needed a ministerial commencement order to bring them into existence. This had not been signed by late October 2000. The legislative process in the Oireachtas was speedy; the same cannot be said for the subsequent implementation.

CHAPTER 11

Some International Comparisons

From the 1960s onwards most developed countries expanded their provision of higher education. The new order replaced the narrowly-based university systems which had developed in many countries in the first half of the century. The increased demand for higher, or university level, education was the initial factor driving the change. The growing demand for a labour force with a wider range of skills was a second. While the reshaping took diverse forms and happened at varying paces and different times, it was a general phenomenon across Europe and the developed world.[1]

Ireland's tenfold growth in student numbers (10.7) in the forty year period 1955-94 was just at the European average (10.7), comparable to France (10.7), Germany (10.6) and Sweden (10.4). Britain was slightly higher at a growth of 12.1, the same as Italy.[2]

Arising out of these developments a number of new concepts emerged to describe and explain phenomena which had begun to take shape in the 1960s. Among the most influential, all developed during the 1970s, were those of 'élite, mass and universal higher education', 'short cycle higher education', 'academic drift', and 'binary systems'.[3] They can serve to give a comparative context to higher education in Ireland.

From élite to mass higher education

Ireland today has a system of universal higher education, three decades after the first such system developed in the United States. The American sociologist, Martin Trow, defined élite systems as those which enrol up to 15 per cent of the age group, mass systems as those enrolling between 15 and 40 per cent, and universal systems as those which enrol more than 40 per cent.[4] The numbers attending higher education in the Republic of Ireland for the years from 1964 to 1998 are included at Appendix 1. In 1995 80 per cent of the age cohort was reckoned to have completed Leaving Certificate. Of that relevant age cohort 50 per cent was estimated to have proceeded to higher and further education.[5] In

1996 it was estimated that 62 per cent of those leaving school proceeded to full-time post-secondary education.[6] The government-appointed group which arrived at these estimates reckoned that this latter figure would have increased to 70 per cent by 2004. Ireland had entered what Trow defined as universal higher education.[7]

The investment in third-level education over a generation has put Ireland at one of the highest levels of third-level attainment among OECD countries. In 1995 only six countries – Canada, US, Belgium, Norway, Korea and Sweden – had a higher level of third-level attainment among the population between the ages of twenty-five and thirty-four.[8]

Table 9 refers to the percentage of people with higher education qualifications in EU countries in 1996 and 1997. In 1996 Ireland ranked first for the percentage of 25, 26 and 27 year olds who held higher education qualifications.[9]

TABLE 9: Percentage of population with higher education qualifications 1996 and 1997

Age	Ireland		EU Average		Ireland's Ranking	
	1996	1997	1996	1997	1996	1997
25	38.6	36.2	19.0	20.4	1	1
26	35.8	34.6	20.0	21.4	1	3
27	35.6	34.4	21.0	21.6	1	2
28	31.0	33.6	20.9	21.6	2	2
29	30.5	31.3	21.5	21.8		2
30	28.9	31.1	21.6	22.5	3	2
31	28.8	29.0	21.5	22.0	3	4
32	27.7	28.3	21.4	21.9	4	3
33	28.1	27.7	20.9	21.6	3	3
34	26.0	25.8	20.8	22.0	4	7
25-34	31.2	31.2	20.9	21.7	2	2

Appendix 4 shows the Irish participation rate on entry to third-level education among twenty-one OECD countries. The Irish figure of 39.9 per cent was just below the median for the states concerned and put Ireland ahead of countries such as Australia, Norway, the United Kingdom, New Zealand, Austria and Switzerland. The only countries with a higher proportion of their age cohort in non-university higher education are Sweden, Japan, Belgium and Norway.[10]

The 1970s and 1980s constituted the period of major growth for the non-university system in Ireland. In the fifteen years between 1972-73 and 1988-89, while full-time student numbers in Irish universities grew by only 34 per cent, those in the non-university technological sector grew by 431 per cent. With the upgrading of the NIHEs to university status in 1989 the pattern changed and growth in university numbers actually outstripped the non-university technological sector; the universities' full-time student body grew by 87 per cent in the six years 1988-94 as against 66 per cent in the vocational/technological sector.[11] Even allowing for the trends in recent years, the proportion of Irish students in non-university higher education is still exceptional in terms of developed countries.

Public educational expenditure as a percentage of total public expenditure in 1992 was 13.7 per cent. This put Ireland above an OECD average of 12 per cent.[12] Public expenditure on tertiary education was 3.2 per cent of all public expenditure against an OECD mean of 2.8 per cent. In terms of the developed world Ireland puts a relatively high premium on education, and within that Ireland has placed a special emphasis on higher education. In the typical percentage distribution of education expenditures in OECD, about 22 per cent tends to go on third-level education.[13] In Ireland this figure is 24 per cent. Only 8.8 per cent of all educational enrolments in Ireland are at third-level compared to an OECD mean of 12.5 per cent. Ireland has a ratio of expenditure to enrolment of 2.8, the highest of a total of 17 OECD countries for which such figures were available in 1995, and for which the OECD mean was 1.8, at which level both Canada and the United States were to be found.[14] The relative amount spent on third-level students vis-à-vis those at primary level varies enormously among countries ranging from between 145 to 160 per cent in Italy, Sweden and Austria to over 300 per cent in the United Kingdom, the Netherlands, Japan and Switzerland. Here again Ireland tops a list of 16 OECD countries with a relative spend of 410 per cent per student at third level vis-à-vis students at primary level. The figure for the United States was 212 per cent.[15] Of twelve OECD countries surveyed in 1998, the increase in expenditure from both public and private sources to third-level educational institutes between 1990 and 1995 was highest in Ireland at 42 per cent. The next highest was Australia at 39 per cent.[16]

Throughout the 1990s there was by international standards a very strong continuing commitment to higher education among most Irish decision-makers and planners. Figures produced by OECD (published in 2000 and reproduced at Appendix 5) showed that on an index of change in expenditure on tertiary education between 1990 and 1996 in eighteen countries Ireland was significantly ahead of all others. Higher education is still viewed by the state as a form of investment rather than of consumption. It is seen as having a role in supporting economic development,[17] and Irish governments appear content for the present to underwrite social demand for higher education.[18]

The policy advisory body, the Higher Education Authority, has prepared projections that would allow the number of new entrants to higher education to grow by 23 per cent in the period from 1994 to 2011, which would then see over 52 per cent of the age cohort entering higher (as distinct from further) education. By 1997-98 enrolment in the university sector was ahead of Steering Committee projections by 5 per cent, while that in the institutes of technology was lower than projected by almost 4 per cent giving an overall enrolment at 102,500 which was 1 per cent ahead of projections. The decision to abolish all third-level fees for full-time students, the planned building programme, particularly in the university sector, and the increased commitment to research demonstrate the continuing perceived importance of higher education and its ability to retain popular political support. There is every reason to believe that the growth in 'universal' provision is likely to continue well into the coming decade. Such a development will have long-term implications for the inherited structure of Irish higher education.

The binary system, Irish-style

To cater for the explosion in demand for higher education in developed countries during the 1960s two main strategies were adopted. Existing universities were expanded and new ones created, or else greater emphasis was placed on less traditional or alternative forms of higher education. The latter was the route chosen in Ireland. It was in one sense surprising that Ireland should have gone in that direction. A contrast has been drawn between two generic types of higher education systems in 'Atlantic' and 'Mediterranean' Europe.[19] 'Atlantic' Europe has more examples of dual or binary systems, whereas the university has remained dominant in 'Mediterranean' Europe.[20] It is argued that the contrast can be explained by differences in industrialisation.

Because the industrial revolution came sooner and was more intense in 'Atlantic' Europe, those industrial economies stimulated the development of non-traditional and non-university higher education. Non-industrialised countries had less need to develop elaborate systems of technical education. Italy, Portugal, Greece and Spain[21] had higher education systems where universities still predominated.

Ireland, although geographically an 'Atlantic' country in European terms, was non-industrialised and entered the 1960s with a higher education system which had more in common with 'Mediterranean' than with 'Atlantic' Europe. For a variety of domestic reasons[22] and under the influence of a number of ideas which became current through increasing contact with the Organisation for Economic Co-operation and Development during the 1950s and 1960s, the decision-makers in Irish education decided to take an initiative to build an infrastructure of higher vocational and technological education virtually *ab ovo*.[23] In essence a political decision was taken that the expansion of higher education would happen largely outside the universities. The initial development was of a scheme of short-cycle higher education in a national system of two-year certificates and three-year diplomas.

According to the acknowledged authority on the subject, Dorothea Furth, three models existed for 'short-cycle higher education'. The first was the multipurpose model to be found in community colleges in the United States. The second was the specialised model which existed, for example, in the French *Instituts Universitaires de Technologie* (IUTs), the German *Fachhochschulen*, the regional colleges in Norway and the higher vocational institutions in the Netherlands. The third was the binary model which was exemplified by the United Kingdom.[24] While the initial conception of the RTCs put them in a category akin to the specialised model, the fashion in which some of the new Irish institutions drew on British influences[25] suggests that it is more valid to categorise the Irish system of higher education that grew up in the 1970s as belonging to the binary model.[26]

While British models had an influence on the incipient Irish system in the late 1960s and early 1970s, there were nonetheless significant differences in approach and the use of British models was very eclectic. The polytechnics in Britain had a broad disciplinary range, whereas even in the two flagship Irish institutions, the NIHEs, the base was narrow. The polytechnics offered graduate programmes and their study periods and qualifications did not substantially differ from those of universities. The non-university technological system in Ireland was some years in existence before any graduate awards were made and graduate programmes tended initially to be of a conversion nature.[27] The British polytechnics had a strong research ethos, whereas only NIHE Dublin took this approach at an early stage of its existence.[28] Another difference was that the National Council for Educational Awards, although modelled even in its operating structure on CNAA in Britain, started with sub-degree work and was never, unlike its role model, confined to degree work. The NIHEs were closest in concept to the British polytechnics and they achieved university status three years in advance of their British peers.

The main component of the alternative Irish system was the complex of regional technical colleges and these had more in common with non-university institutions developed in Germany, France, the Netherlands and Norway. The characteristics of those colleges have been identified as a) the provision of course programmes of shorter duration than at universities, b) the practical orientation of curricula, c) responsiveness to industry and business, d) limited ranges of subjects mostly in engineering and business studies, e) little, or only applied, research and f) heavy teaching loads for faculty.[29] Such a definition is fully appropriate to the Irish regional technical colleges.

Academic drift

The Irish alternative, or non-university, third-level system relatively quickly demonstrated the phenomenon of 'academic drift', a term coined in 1974 by the English academics, Tyrrell Burgess and John Pratt.[30] As defined by them it consisted of a tendency among British polytechnics to dispense with part-time sub-degree-level students, the better to concentrate on full-time degree-level candidates. The trends showed that the polytechnics, rather than seeking to integrate part-time with full-time study programmes and retaining the original practice of admitting new types of students who qualified in different ways from their university counterparts, were in fact striving to copy the university model. While the polytechnics were more successful than universities in catering for socially disadvantaged and educationally under-represented groups in society, this had become less important than the task of seeking academic respectability along the lines associated with a university mode of study. One commentator concluded as early as 1982 that in terms of the structure of their courses, length of study and distribution of fields of study, the polytechnics had to all intents and purposes become universities in everything but name;[31] they acquired that status in 1992.

Academic drift has not been exclusively a British phenomenon. The same phenomenon had been observed in the French IUTs and the Norwegian Regional Colleges as early as the 1970s.[32] An identical tendency to seek to upgrade their functions has been attributed to the German *Fachhochschulen*.[33] One writer, Claudius Gellert refers to academic drift as an undesirable tendency of tertiary institutions with lower prestige to become like universities, one which signifies above all a predominance of the research paradigm in institutions of higher learning.

There are conflicting views as to how to counteract academic drift. For Gellert the best way to guarantee protection is to maintain separate administrative identities for non-university institutions and to encourage an ethos favouring such separation. The English writer, Guy Neave, on the other hand, has argued that this is pointless. He observed that whether the policy involved was based on a 'binary' or 'multipurpose' relationship between the university and the non-university sector, internal pressures distorted the original notions on which the policies were founded, and there was a tendency to move towards 'university' norms and practices. In his view the assumptions underlining non-integrated or alternative forms of higher education (such as the distinction between academic and vocational education, the belief that alternative forms of higher education could supply shortages of skilled manpower in very particular areas, or that it was possible to 'match' skills in education with those required in the occupational structure) were founded on faulty premises. In his opinion all systems of higher education display a dynamic towards integration.[34] In that view academic drift is a phenomenon to be both expected and welcomed.

Academic drift, Irish style, shared two of the characteristics referred to above. Firstly, there was a considerable decline in part-time provision in the vocational and technological sector.[35] Between the academic years 1978-79 and 1993-94, while the full-time student body of the RTC/DIT colleges more than quadrupled, the number of part-time students halved. The universities in the meantime increased their proportion of part-time students.[36] The decline in part-time student provision did not represent a departure from any explicit brief that obliged the colleges to cater for that clientele, nor was there any evidence of concern among politicians or decision-makers at this trend. This drift in the vocational/technological sector merely reflected the extent to which all forms of higher education have been seen, especially by the decision-makers, as an immediate extension of second-level schooling. The Irish state in the past has consistently discriminated against those who did not proceed to third-level immediately after completing second-level. This pattern had its most dramatic expression in the decision to abolish the fees for all undergraduate degree work in publicly supported institutions,[37] a concession which did not extend to part-time students for some years.

The second characteristic, the upward movement towards university norms and practices, has been very clear and very strong in Ireland. It has been illustrated how the two National Institutes for Higher Education very quickly achieved university status, having been originally conceived as the flagship institutions for the new technological and vocational sector. The way in which a lobby for a university at Limerick was able to harness wide-ranging political support for the project eventually made it impossible for any technocratic rationale to stand in its way. The same process began in the Institutes of Technology. The 1995 White Paper saw them as primarily short-cycle institutions, but no strong intent was declared to keep them that way. While NCEA was successful in introducing large numbers of personnel from business and the professions into the alternative sector of higher education whether as assessors, examiners or academic policy makers, the colleges remained primarily academic institutions. The pattern of quality control applied by NCEA, especially in relation to examinations, was a mirror image of the university system. The NCEA's Act required university standards in all degree work. Once RTCs (later to become ITs) embarked on degree work in any volume, achievement in that area became a major, if informal, benchmark within the RTC/IT system.[38] All the evidence would suggest that the level of degree work in ITs will continue to grow and that their ambitions will be towards joining the university ranks. With the passing of the Universities Act and the Qualifications Act it would appear that the decision-makers accept that this is the likely dynamic. Essentially they plan to retain the binary system Irish-style by having two types of university, autonomous and non- autonomous.[39]

Britain and Australia were two societies which developed binary systems. Australia effectively abolished its binary system in

1987, while Britain did so in 1992.[40] That Ireland has not followed suit is explicable largely because of the central role of the state in higher education, as in so many other aspects of Irish life.

The state and higher education

In a series of articles on trends in European higher education over the period 1975 to 1995, the British journalist and academic, Guy Neave, identified three developments – one economic, one administrative and one politico-philosophical – which were pattern-moulding forces for higher education.[41]

The first reflected the quickening pace of cross-national exchange. The European dimension in higher education policy saw the assumption by Brussels of an increasingly large role in the tactical, strategic and administrative concerns of higher education. Change was symbolised in ventures such as the European Community Course Credit Transfer System or student exchange programmes such as ERASMUS and COMETT. Ireland participated widely and enthusiastically in these schemes both at university and non-university level. The European dimension in Irish non-university higher education had been a feature since the formative stage of the expanded Irish system. The contribution of the European Social Fund had been central to the growth of that sector, with support also forthcoming from the European Structural Fund.[42] A major outcome of this was that mainland Europe came to be perceived as a possible employment destination for Irish students in a way that would not have occurred to a previous generation whose ambitions were contained within the English-speaking world.

The second major change noted by Neave was the strengthening of the regional level of administration and a transfer of specific responsibilities from centre to region which could be detected in France, Norway, Sweden, Britain and Spain. This was not a phenomenon which was in any way replicated in Ireland. The main thrust, if anything, was in the opposite direction. This was reflected in the removal of the Dublin Institute of Technology and the regional technical colleges from the responsibility of the vocational education committees to a position where they acquired independent management boards and were funded directly by the Department of Education and Science. In terms of administration, Ireland has remained one of the most centralised of European countries.[43]

The third major change posited by Neave is at the level of political philosophy. According to him the decade 1985-1995 saw widespread reinterpretation of the place of governments in the affairs of nations. The growing influence of economic liberals, and their dissatisfaction with a model of higher education increasingly perceived as an extension of the welfare state, had major effects on the way in which higher education came to be portrayed by influential commentators. What was previously regarded as public service was cast in a new light as a state monopoly. Because monopolies are exercised in the interests of cabals rather than of the citizen, they were represented as self-serving, inefficient, irresponsible and antipathetic to free competition. Despite all that was said about the drive towards quality, enterprise, efficiency and accountability and despite the attention lavished on devising new operating procedures, Neave insisted that this revolution in institutional efficiency was driven by the political process. The reconstruction of Europe's higher education systems, in both East and West, around the dominant precept of the 'market' represented a watershed in political philosophy applied to higher education, every bit as important as the debate which taxed higher education in the early 1960s, and which had to do with exploiting the reservoirs of untapped talent in a nation. The decision then to expand higher education was no less political but rested on the dual optimism of the educability of the younger generation and the willingness of the community to devote the resources to achieve it.

If one accepts this analysis as an accurate summary of what happened in the mainstream of higher education in Europe in the 1980s and 1990s, then Ireland has to be judged to be outside that mainstream. Higher education has not come to be looked upon as a form of social welfare; it is still seen as an investment. The optimistic belief in its potential can be seen, for example, in the willingness of the government to have the state take on the responsibility for payment of fees by university students, a development which more than anything else has to be judged as running contrary to the principles and patterns outlined by Neave. The Irish higher education system has not become 'market-driven' in the way he describes, and there was not at the turn of the century any evidence of a changing intellectual climate that would facilitate such an outcome. Higher education is still primarily the state's business.

In a classic analysis of the forces of co-ordination in systems of higher education, the American writer Burton Clark, has identified three: the state, academic oligarchy and the market.[44] In Ireland the market is always one arbiter of what happens in higher education. Student choice, as expressed through a centralised applications apparatus for all of third-level education, is an aspect of this. The explicit attempt, analysed in this study, to link higher education with the labour market, which lay behind the establishment of the alternative system of higher education, is another. It has ensured that Irish higher education now has an explicitly vocational component which did not exist thirty years ago. While the change centred around the non-university sector, the universities themselves adapted to the vocational imperatives which had become part of the climate.[45]

The pecking order of student demand in third-level education is highly vocational. The most sought after categories of study in 1995 were actuarial studies, veterinary medicine, law with French, physiotherapy, pharmacy, commerce with French, architecture and radiography.[46] In 1999 they were medicine, law with French, law with German, pharmacy, actuarial and financial studies, dentistry, human genetics, veterinary medicine, psychology and (in the case of TCD) history and politics.[47] This was somewhat different from what Dr Edward Walsh excoriated in the universities a generation previously.[48] It may have been possible in the 1970s to draw a distinction between short-cycle higher education and the university on the basis of the 'utilitarian training' provided in the former and the 'fundamental knowledge generation and transmission' which characterised the latter. Insofar as it was ever valid, that distinction has been eroded in Ireland since the early 1980s. The Irish universities have been primarily teaching institutions with a very strong vocational thrust in most of their activity. Significantly, and in spite of all the promotional work of thirty years, engineering, technology and science still do not figure near the top of the pecking order.

In Ireland the interchange between higher education and the market is to a considerable extent mediated through the state. Bodies such as Forfás, or the Industrial Development Authority, have been more likely to influence or, at least, modify provision at third-level than organisations such as the Irish Business and Employers' Confederation (IBEC), trade associations or individual companies.[49] The views of IDA or Forfás, and their researches on trends in informatics, financial services or other apparently crucial areas in the labour and skills markets, have been more likely to lead to new course initiatives, or pump-priming by the Department of Education and Science or the Higher Education Authority, than any other force.

Accordingly the key relationship and the prime area for conflict may arise between the state and what Clark refers to as the academic oligarchy. The Irish state is extremely strong and is involved in many areas of economic life from which other European states have disengaged in the past twenty years.[50] Its involvement with higher education is considerable. The bulk of higher education funding comes from the state. The recurrent state grant had been declining as a proportion of income from 1980 to the mid 1990s, but it began to rise dramatically again with the decision of the government to abolish fees for full-time study at third-level.[51] Understandably this development was not welcomed by the third-level authorities, most notably the universities, both because of fears that the state would not in the long term make good the deficit which could arise through the change, and because of the increased leverage which the new relationship and increased dependency could confer upon the state. Relations between the state and third-level (and particularly between the state and universities) are less strained than they were in the 1970s, although the experience with the universities bill in 1996-97 showed that the potential for the relationship to turn sour remains. Government expenditure on higher education as a percentage of total government expenditure on education increased from 18.1 per cent in 1980 to 19 per cent in 1985 to 21.4 per cent in 1990 and to 24 per cent in 1993.[52] The real problems may come if, and when, third-level education begins to lose its existing share of public expenditure, or for whatever reason goes out of favour with politicians and consequently with bureaucrats and technocrats.

The range of sophisticated mechanisms available to the state to bend third-level institutions to its will is, on the face of it, formidable. Since 1992 HEA has been developing a new funding model which was introduced fully for the first time in 1995. The new arrangement represents a switch to formula funding whereby colleges are funded in relation to core budgets and targeted programmes. The model is designed to inaugurate a greater degree of financial accountability. The range of financial information now available to HEA is enormous, and includes the identification of the extent of variation in current cost between institutions for similar courses. A variety of reservations on the new funding system are to be found within the institutions designated under HEA, but the Authority would argue that the new model provides a sound basis for a realistic relationship between the state and universities which gives maximum devolution of authority and responsibility to the colleges, while ensuring accountability to the state for due performance.[53]

A further area of potential threat to the self-regulation and autonomy of third-level comes with the emphasis on quality assurance which was set out in the White Paper and incorporated into the universities legislation of 1997 and the qualifications legislation of 1999 covering the non-university higher education sector. Neave observed that by the early 1990s the issue of quality had taken on the dimensions of a universal concern, though he notes the contradiction (and saw something faintly contemptible) in the spectacle of governments insisting on higher education's delivering 'quality' at the very moment when those governments have resolutely engaged in modifying the quality of the framework within which higher education operates (asking for quality while being either unwilling or unable to uphold their side of the bargain).[54]

This development has been characterised as the rise of the evaluative state. One of its closest observers in Ireland has questioned whether it is inevitable that, as participation rates rise, the state must assume the dominant role in the policy process, whether the academic autonomy of the university must fall victim to the steering role of the state, and whether the cult of 'quality, efficiency and enterprise' necessarily demands that market criteria replace the values associated with the 'internal' model of university governance.[55]

While the unusually centralised nature of the Irish state might suggest an unfavourable answer to those concerns of universities and colleges, the trends are not as one-sided as might at first appear. The American academic, Clark Kerr, former President of the University of California at Berkeley and Chairman of the Carnegie Commission on Higher Education, noted that worldwide over the twenty-five year period from the early 1960s to the mid-1980s there was a huge attempt at planned change in higher education, and huge controversy over the attempted changes, but that the long-term results were few.[56] One of the main unsuccessful movers of change were governments acting in a partisan way and under pressure. Governments change, and even governments still in power have short attention spans regarding higher education and often little understanding of academic life. He notes that one must be impressed by the endurance and quiet power of the professoriate to get their way in the long run, and adds that this way at all times and in all places is nothing less than the preservation of the *status quo* in terms of structure and governance.

Neave likewise observes that higher education is a 'loosely coupled system' in which the linkages between government, administration and institutions are not straightforward, rational, or still less amenable to being directed to where political authorities would like. It has been characterised as a 'bottom-heavy' structure with a large number of 'veto points'. At every level within third-level institutions the potential exists to reinterpret, block or turn aside national policy directives.[57]

The Irish higher education system, although heavily dependent on the state for its funding, has shown itself able over a thirty-year period to deflect or seriously delay the wishes of government. In the 1970s the proposal to merge TCD and UCD was reversed, while the Burke proposals of December 1974 were largely neutered at the time. The two flagship teaching institutions of the non-university side of the binary system had succeeded in upgrading themselves to university status before the end of the 1980s. While the state has managed to refocus its approach to maintaining a binary system, the Dublin Institute of Technology and the other institutes of technology will almost certainly continue to strive for self-validation over the next decade and for longer, if necessary.

The university is an international institution with strong national roots. The patterns of academic organisation, many of the basic assumptions about the nature of universities and higher education, the pattern of study, and relations between students and faculty are common through many societies all around the world. Academic culture has common features worldwide. The university remains a primary centre of learning and a repository of accumulated wisdom. In what is increasingly a knowledge-based society, the university and higher education are likely to remain at the centre of economic and cultural development.[58] Although it is part of the public sector, the autonomous sector of higher education is not a state institution, and the international nature of the university has allowed it to retain a certain independence from its primary paymaster. There is another dimension. Mass higher education is qualitatively different from élite higher education, even if its roots and institutional forms are similar. The increase in student numbers has resulted in different types of programmes; more attention to the job market has meant different types of education and training, and the development of the concept of lifelong learning. But the trend towards mass higher education has been accompanied by an even more powerful trend towards what can be called disciplinary higher education.[59]

The explosion of knowledge and the fragmentation of disciplines, which begets sub-disciplines and subsets, has led to huge system complexity. For example, in history it is estimated that the output of literature in the two decades between 1960 and 1980 was equal to that which occurred between the time of the Greek historian Thucydides in the fourth century BC and the year 1960. There are no limits to such disciplinary expansion. Governments cannot keep up surveillance and they cannot effectively micro-manage something like this. Higher education has to develop its own ways of managing such complexity. Hence the growth in devolution and in decentralisation which Neave observed throughout Europe in the 1980s. Ireland has been out of step here. A highly centralised state has tried to retain as much control as possible. Almost certainly it is a doomed enterprise. As Burton Clark has pointed out, the great increase in system complexity is enough to drive modern systems of higher education towards decentralisation of formal control. The integrated and centralised model becomes so dysfunctional that even ministers themselves have come to the point of view that those in the field, at the institutions, are better positioned to know what is going on in the various corners of the system and to try to guide the flow of change.[60] They are in a better position to add value than are bureaucrats at the centre of the system.

The Irish system of higher education has strong European roots. It has a strong statist quality and unionisation is common in its ranks. It has been involved with, and benefited from, developments in higher education within the European Union over the past twenty years. Its dealings with markets are mediated through the state. There is no worthwhile market for private higher education. A small private sector which grew up in Dublin in the 1980s and early 1990s has been largely swamped by the growth of, and investment in publicly-funded higher education in the Dublin region during the 1990s. The new qualifications legislation may largely squeeze out what remains of this private market. Higher education as a profit-making activity is anathema in Ireland, not just to many trade unionists, but to academics and to politicians and bureaucrats as well. In that sense Irish higher education is altogether closer to European than to American models. (The British model, which initially influenced the development of higher education in Ireland, was European rather than American in its nature and has remained so, in spite of, and even because of, the onslaught it received during the Thatcher/Major era of Conservative rule from 1979 to 1997).

It is not inconceivable that higher education in Ireland could take on more of the complexion of its American counterpart in the foreseeable future. In the past decade Irish universities have begun to see the potential for augmenting state funding with private money. This was pioneered by Dr Walsh at Limerick. He particularly targeted both the Irish-American community and the multinationals in the United States. All other universities have followed suit, and state investment will increasingly look to be matched by private funding. Private funding will become even more important, if and when government funding of Irish education reaches a plateau, and the currently strong belief in the importance of developing human capital weakens among Irish politicians and bureaucrats. The influence of private industry and business will also be expanded as Irish universities increasingly become research-driven. Responsiveness to markets will then become even more important. Over the next decade there is likely to be intense competition among the Irish universities as to which of them becomes most outstanding at research. This process will almost certainly distance them even further from state supervision. The Department of Education and Science will increasingly find that it cannot exercise the kind of control of major research universities that is possible with primary or secondary schools.

American cultural styles have become more influential in Ireland in the past decade. The increased wealth owes much to the massive amount of American investment which has been attracted to the country over a generation. Whether that influence can eventually change the prevailing ethos in higher education from European to American will be one of the more interesting questions of the opening years of the new century.

Notes

1 Scott, P. (1995), *The Meanings of Mass Higher Education,* Buckingham: The Society for Research into Higher Education and Open University Press, p. 33. Scott maintains that the fundamental imperatives were the same everywhere and arose from the modernisation of society and the economy.

2 Eicher, J. C. (1998), 'The Costs and Financing of Education in Europe,' *European Journal of Education*, vol. 33, no. 1, p. 31.

3 Teichler, U. (1993), 'Structures of Higher Education Systems in Europe' in Gellert, *Higher Education in Europe*, pp. 23-36. The model of 'élite, mass and universal higher education' was developed by Martin Trow, 'short-cycle higher education' by OECD, 'academic drift' by the British academics, Tyrrell Burgess and John Pratt, and 'binary system' was given currency by the British politician, Anthony Crosland, although, as already noted, the expression was coined by his ministerial predecessor in the Department of Education and Science, Edward Boyle. Teichler distinguishes the 'binary system' as a model of an institutional type.

4 Quoted in Scott, *Mass Higher Education*, p. 2.

5 *Committee on Places 1999*, p. 51. Of an age cohort of 67,700 it was estimated that 29,200 entered higher and further education in Ireland, 2,400 went on to higher education in the United Kingdom and a further 2,000 were enrolled in higher education in private colleges in Ireland. The total transfer of 33,000 students indicated a transfer rate of 62 per cent of those who sat Leaving Certificate.

6 ibid. p. 54. Post secondary education was defined as publicly funded third- level in the state, third-level abroad, private colleges, post leaving certificate colleges (plcs which accounted for 12 per cent of school leavers), apprenticeship, non third-level nursing, agricultural training and CERT training.

7 ibid. p. 51. A number of writers would now regard all forms of post-secondary education as part of the unit which is mass higher education. Scott makes the point that, as American higher education includes the two-year community colleges in its participation index, it is necessary to include post-eighteen year old students in further education colleges elsewhere to secure a fair comparison with US figures (Scott, *Mass Higher Education*, p. 2).

8 *Committee on Places 1999*, p. 22. The figures have been drawn from the 1997 edition of the OECD publication, *Education at a Glance*.

9 ibid., p. 23. The statistics are compiled from the Eurostat Labour Force Survey 1996 and 1997.

10 The statistics, upon which Appendix 4 is based, omit Canada and the United States. Previous OECD indicators had placed both Canada and US with about half of their relevant age cohort as enrolling in non-university tertiary education. (OECD indicators for 1988, *Education at a Glance* (1992) p. 79.) Both Australia (34.3 per cent) and Netherlands (19.0 per cent) also had high rates for non-university entrants in 1988. In both cases the non-university higher education sector has since been absorbed into the university system.

11 It should, of course, be noted that university numbers were boosted by the addition of the NIHEs in 1988-89. Full-time university numbers increased from 27,448 in 1987-88 to 33,811 in 1988-89. However starting from the new line in 1988-89, growth in full-time student numbers over the subsequent five years at universities outpaced the technological sector by 55 per cent to 50 per cent. There is in addition a significant contrast between full-time student numbers and initial enrolment figures which follow another pattern. Short-cycle institutions by definition have a higher and quicker throughput. In 1992 of the 25,219 enrolments in third-level, 11,757 (46.7 per cent) were in the university sector

(Clancy, *Access to College*, p. 30). In August 1996, at the end of the first round of acceptances through the CAO/CAS, the national system of applications for university and non-university places, 16,471 students had accepted certificate and diploma places in the non-university sector and 16,027 had accepted places for degrees (*Irish Times*, 30 August 1996).

12 OECD, *Education at a Glance*, 1995, p. 122.

13 ibid., p. 95.

14 ibid., p. 98.

15 ibid., p. 99. No figure is available for Canada in the OECD table.

16 The increases elsewhere were Australia: 32 per cent, UK: 32 per cent, Spain: 31 per cent, France: 29 per cent, Finland: 23 per cent, Japan: 19 per cent, Canada: 9 per cent, Denmark: 9 per cent, Iceland: 9 per cent, Netherlands: 1 per cent, Hungary: 10 per cent (OECD, *Education at a Glance, OECD Indicators*, 1998, p. 85).

17 See, particularly, *Committee on Places 1999*, pp. 2-5, 12-18. The educational attainment of the populace is seen as a (and perhaps the) main source of industrial competitive advantage, and not only as a good, but a necessary, investment. See also, *Report of HEA Steering Committee*, pp. 52-56. Another significant indicator of belief in the connection is Forfás, *Shaping our Future*, pp. 160-162.

18 This has not been the usual experience of European countries. See, for example, Neave, G. (1985) 'Higher Education in a Period of Consolidation 1975-85', *European Journal of Education*, vol. 20, pp. 109-124. Neave states that one of the traits of the period 1975-85 in Europe was that in most countries, except for Italy, expenditure on higher education had dropped, and that the sector's 'ecological niche' in government expenditure was no longer as secure as had been thought. Ireland has never thought that way.

19 Scott, *Mass Higher Education*, p. 39. A reading of the various tables in OECD's publication *Education at a Glance* reinforces the validity of this distinction.

20 See Appendix 4.

21 The relative strengths of the non-university sector in these countries is analysed in a series of contributions in Gellert (ed.), *Higher Education in Europe*, pp. 72-121. See also the contribution on Italy by Moscati, R., in G. Neave and A. Van Vught (eds.) (1991), *Prometheus Bound: The Changing Relationship between Government and Higher Education in Western Europe*, Oxford: Pergamon Press, pp. 91-107.

22 Supra, Chapters 2 and 3.

23 While the decision-makers drew on British models, they did so eclectically and it cannot be said that the Irish initiative copied Britain. OECD was arguably a far more potent external influence, and the RTCs had no comparable British model.

24 Furth, D. (1992), 'Short-Cycle Higher Education: Europe', in Clark and Neave, *Encyclopedia of Higher Education*, vol. 2, p. 1218.

25 Most notably, the National Council for Educational Awards, but also the Limerick Institute (eventually to become the National Institute for Higher Education), in recommending which the Higher Education Authority drew on the model of the British polytechnics (Higher Education Authority, *A Council for National Awards*, p. 10). The authoritative outline of Irish higher education

within the specific context of a binary system is to be found in Clancy, P. (1993), 'Goal Enlargement and Differentiation: the Evolution of the Binary Higher Education System in Ireland', in Gellert, *Higher Education in Europe*, pp. 123-133.

26 Not all authorities are happy with the use of the terms 'short-cycle higher education' or 'binary system' as concepts for comparative analysis. Furth, for example, in the article referred to in footnote 24 (p. 1217) feels that the distinction between long-cycle university on the one hand and short-cycle/non-university on the other is no longer clear. She feels it more accurate to refer just to university and non-university. Even the latter distinction she sees as no longer clear, and suggests 'alternatives to universities' as a more useful concept. Séamus Ó Buachalla, writing on 'Ireland' in the volume on National Systems of Higher Education of the same encyclopedia (Clark & Neave, eds., *Encyclopedia of Higher Education*, Volume 1, pp. 334-343) suggests that accuracy and clarity would best be served by using the labels 'university' and 'non-university' to describe the sectors (p. 337). Nevertheless, the concept of binary system is used here, not merely because it has become an accepted part of the vocabulary, but because it seems to be explicit government policy to preserve the 'binary system'.

27 NCEA, *Annual Report* for 1981 and subsequent years, passim.

28 NIHE Limerick, even well into its second decade, did not emphasise research. Its encouragement to staff was to engage in industrial consulting in line with its Director's emphasis on closeness to the business world. The large effort which was put into continuous assessment was another factor which would have inhibited staff research.

29 Gellert, C. (1993), 'Academic Drift and the Blurring of Boundaries in Systems of Higher Education', *Higher Education in Europe*, vol. XVIII, no. 2, p. 80.

30 Burgess and Pratt, *The Polytechnics: A Report*, pp. 23-30.

31 Neave, *On the Edge of the Abyss*, p. 128.

32 Neave, G. (1983), 'The Dynamic of Integration in Non-integrated Systems of Higher Education in Western Europe', in Hermanns et al. *The Compleat University*, pp. 266-267.

33 Gellert, *Academic Drift*, pp. 80-81.

34 Neave, *Integration in Non-Integrated Systems*, pp. 269-276.

35 Appendix 4.

36 If one excludes from the reckoning the Dublin Institute of Technology, which grew out of City of Dublin VEC provision and which has always dwarfed the RTC colleges in terms of part-time provision, the university sector in 1993/94 had more part-time students than the regional technical colleges. For a discussion of the policy issues relating to part-time students see Clancy, *Access to College*, pp. 171-172.

37 *Dáil Reports*, vol. 448, no. 6. (8 February 1995). Also vol. 457, no. 2, cols. 253-255 (14 November 1995). *Sunday Independent*, 29 January 1995. See also *Irish Times*, 29 December 1995.

38 One should not under-estimate the importance of informal peer pressure. The author observed this most noticeably in the case of Dundalk RTC. From an early stage of dealing with the college at NCEA it became clear that on any criteria this was an institution that across the board had an efficient and professional

approach to its task. It was not a college from which one expected to encounter serious problems of either an academic or a quasi-political nature. One of the most obvious qualities was that there was from the top down a clear view of the college as fitting within a national brief to educate students to technician level. Dundalk RTC was slower than some other colleges with (from the perception of NCEA staff) more obvious quality problems to aspire to run degree programmes. It eventually followed the trend, but its sloth was informally regarded by many in the wider system as a qualitative blemish.

39 Section 41, Qualifications (Education and Training) Act 1999 read in conjunction with the Universities Act 1997, section 9.

40 For the British experience see Pratt, J. (1997), *The Polytechnic Experiment 1965-1992*, Buckingham: Society for Research into Higher Education and Open University Press, pp. 305-329. Also Pratt, J. (1992), 'Unification of Higher Education in Britain,' *European Journal of Education*, vol. 27, no. 1/2, pp. 29-44. Australia operated a binary policy for twenty years from the mid 1960s to the mid 1980s. There is a wealth of analysis available on why the binary approach was abandoned there. See particularly Williams, B. (1992), 'The Rise and Fall of the Binary System in Two Countries and the Consequences for Universities', *Studies in Higher Education,* vol. 3, pp. 281-293; Mahony, D. (1992), Establishing the University as the Sole Provider of Higher Education: The Australian Experience, *Studies in Higher Education,* vol. 2, pp. 219-236; Harman, G. (1991), 'Institutional Amalgamations and Abolition of the Binary System in Australia under John Dawkins', *Higher Education Quarterly*, vol. 45, no. 2, pp. 176-198. For a general overview of binary systems, see Davies, S. (1992), 'Binary Systems of Higher Education', in Clark and Neave, *Encyclopedia of Higher Education*, pp. 1066-1070.

41 Neave, G. (1995), 'On Living in Interesting Times: Higher Education in Western Europe 1985-1995,' *European Journal of Education*, vol. 30, no. 4.
Neave's other surveys, all to be found in the *European Journal of Education*, are:
- i) 'On the Edge of an Abyss: an overview of present developments in European higher education', vol. 17, no. 2, 1982, pp. 123-144.
- ii) 'Higher Education in a Period of Consolidation, 1975-1985', vol. 20, nos. 2-3, 1985, pp. 109-124.
- iii 'On Shifting Sands: changing priorities and perspectives in European higher education from 1984 to 1986', vol. 21, no. 1, 1986, pp. 7-24.
- iv) 'On Preparing for Markets: trends in higher education in Western Europe 1988-1990', vol. 25, no. 2, 1990, pp. 105-122.
- v) 'The Politics of Quality: developments in higher education in Western Europe 1992-1994', vol. 29, no. 2, 1994, pp. 115-133.

42 Osborne R. D. (1996), *Higher Education in Ireland: North and South*, London: Jessica Kingsley Publishers, p. 25.

43 For an indication of how it compares with other countries as regards centralisation of educational administration, see OECD – *Education at a Glance*, 1995, pp. 115-120.

44 Clark, B. R. (1983), *The Higher Education System: Academic Organisation in Cross-National Perspective,* Berkeley: University of California Press, pp. 136-181.

45 This point is developed in Clancy, *Goal Enlargement and Differentiation*, pp. 126-129.

46 *Irish Times*, 23 August 1995. These are subjects which all have a *numerus clausus* (i.e. a fixed number of available places).

47 *Irish Times*, 11 January 2000.

48 Ironically the most sought-after courses are in the Dublin university colleges. In a competitive market the students have gone for the old institutions with the well-recognised brand names which were the butt of Dr Walsh's criticisms in the 1970s. In 1995 Architecture at DIT was the only one of the 'top ten' courses offered outside TCD or UCD. This, of course, is partially a function of (and is partly distorted by) the relative underprovision of third-level education in Dublin, and partially a reflection of a reluctance on the part of Dubliners to move elsewhere in the country for higher study, a pattern not reflected elsewhere in Ireland. While the points system for rationing of places as operated in Irish higher education is a market mechanism, markets in higher education, as in all else, are rarely pure.

49 The skills shortages of the late 1990s did see individual multinationals begin to build relationships with institutes of technology. Moreover with the growth of national agreements including industry, various unions and other social partners, relations with industry increasingly are coming to be mediated through the Irish Business and Employers Confederation. Both IBEC and the Irish Congress of Trade Unions will provide nominees for the new bodies set up under the 1999 qualifications legislation.

50 For a somewhat polemic assessment of this topic, see Guiomard, C. (1995), *The Irish Disease and How to Cure it*, Dublin: Oak Tree Press, pp. 83-113.

51 The percentage share contributed by the state grant to institutions funded by the Higher Education Authority had dropped from 86 per cent in 1980 to 62 per cent in 1993 with a corresponding rise in fee income from 12 per cent to 33 per cent. In the RTCs and DIT the corresponding figures for state grants were 91 per cent and 80 per cent, with fee income rising from 9 per cent to 17 per cent. (Higher Education Authority, *Technical Working Party*, p. 42).

52 *HEA Technical Working Party*, p. 44. The growth in the market share of third-level is not surprising given the extent of the growth of the student population and the transition to a system of mass higher education.

53 For a useful summary of current HEA funding policy and operations see Osborne, *Higher Education in Ireland*, pp. 74-85.

54 Neave, *The Politics of Quality*, pp. 115-134.

55 Ó Buachalla, S. (1992), 'Self-Regulation and the Emergence of the Evaluative State: trends in higher education policy, 1987-1992;' *European Journal of Education*, vol. 27, nos. 1/2, p. 76.

56 Kerr, *A Critical Age in the University World*, pp. 183-193.

57 Neave, *On Shifting Sands*, p. 14.

58 For a development of this theme, see Altbach, P. G. (1998), 'Comparative Perspectives on Higher Education for the Twenty-first Century'; *Higher Education Policy*, vol. 11, pp. 347-356.

59 This theme is developed in Clark, B. R. (1997), 'Higher Education as a Self-guiding Society', *Tertiary Education and Management*, vol. 3, no. 2, pp. 91-99.

60 ibid., p. 94.

CHAPTER 12

A New Agenda?

Since the late 1980s Irish economic performance has been spectacular, not alone in international terms, but even more so bearing in mind Ireland's historical performance since the foundation of the state in 1922. In the ten years from 1987, Irish GNP expanded by about 70 per cent. In the same period the USA expanded by 27 per cent, the fifteen country EU by 24 per cent, and the United Kingdom by 20 per cent. After independence Ireland had a long-standing problem with low levels of job creation. By 1997 there were 23 per cent more jobs in the economy than in 1987. The comparable figures for USA, UK and EU were 17 per cent, 5 per cent and 3 per cent. In 1987 Irish GNP per capita had stood at 59 per cent of the European Union average, little changed from the position of 1960, when economic planning was first introduced. By 1997 GNP per capita stood at 88 per cent of the EU average.[1] With the continued growth over the following three years GNP per capita had converged on the EU norm and the Republic was apparently on its way to becoming one of the wealthier countries of the European Union, a remarkable transformation in less than half a generation.

A number of explanations have been offered for Ireland's performance. These include the fiscal stabilisation of the late 1980s, the importance of foreign investment, a shift in the balance of international trade, the partnership approach to incomes policy with its accompanying wage moderation and peaceful industrial relations, infrastructure inflows from the European Union, Ireland's strategic position as one of the only two English-speaking countries in the European Union, the role of convergence (where some lagging economies have opportunities to catch up on their neighbours by importing technology and capital), the peace process in Northern Ireland, and the role of education as a catalyst for enhanced labour force skills and productivity.[2] There is general agreement that Ireland's education provision has been one of the contributors to Ireland's newly acquired wealth, and one of the key factors in sparking off its unprecedented economic growth.

Ireland was perhaps well placed to profit from the advent of the 'knowledge society'.[3] A highly developed educational infrastructure had been put in place over a period of about one hundred and fifty years. It started with the national schools from 1831 onwards. Secondary education was slow to develop, and its general absence in the period prior to 1878 was one of the reasons attributable for the failure of the Queen's Colleges and of the Catholic University.[4] With the introduction of the Intermediate Education Act in 1879 the number of secondary schools began to grow, mainly under the aegis of the Catholic Church, and particularly through the work of religious orders. Because of the very influential role occupied by the Catholic Church in Irish society from the early nineteenth century to the 1970s, that Church's emphasis on the importance of education caused it to be highly valued in Irish society. The status of the teacher at both primary and secondary level was very high, and in a society which was economically stagnant, and in which religious vocations flourished, teaching attracted some of the country's finest brainpower, in turn adding to the already high status of the profession.[5]

The churches, particularly the Catholic Church, invested a great deal in education both in terms of manpower and finance. The hegemony of the Catholic Church in education was to come to a relatively abrupt end, mainly because vocations, not just to teaching orders, but to religious life generally, abruptly withered on the vine from the late 1960s onwards.[6] By that point the state itself, spurred on by the OECD-inspired findings in *Investment in Education*, was prepared to step in, most obviously with the scheme for free secondary education introduced by the minister, Donogh O'Malley, in 1967. Participation rates beyond the compulsory school leaving age (raised from fourteen to fifteen in 1972) rose dramatically. In 1964 a mere 36.8 per cent of sixteen year olds and 24.8 per cent of seventeen year olds remained in full-time education. The corresponding figures for 1994 were 93.6 per cent and 83.3 per cent.[7] Student numbers at second level schools had trebled in the period, while, as has been seen, numbers at third-level increased by a factor of six. The growth of higher education was fuelled by student demand.

Since the early 1960s public spending on education has doubled its share of the national income. Government spending on education increased from 3.1 per cent of GNP in 1961 to 6.5 per cent in 1993.[8] In that period Gross Domestic Product had more than trebled, so spending on Irish education took larger slices of a much larger cake. Education has continued to be viewed as a form of investment rather than consumption, and as a result education has been largely insulated from budgetary cutbacks. Within educational spending higher education has retained its proportion of public expenditure, again because it is viewed as an investment. As noted, Ireland in the 1990s has gone against the tide in mainland Europe, and has diverged even more from the approach in Britain.[9] The decision of Niamh Bhreathnach to abolish student fees for all full-time degrees in universities and public sector colleges meant that higher education was to be funded to an even greater extent from public funds, a reverse of current European trends, and a reassertion by the Irish state of the importance of a human capital approach to economic development.

With such huge levels of economic growth the age-old problem of unemployment had largely vanished,[10] and from 1997 onwards skill shortages manifest in the Irish economy became a real concern. In November 1997 the government launched a £250 million Education Technology Investment Fund, which was intended to modernise the infrastructure of third-level colleges, to develop new means of study to meet skill shortages, and to promote the innovation required to maintain and expand economic growth. Of the amount £80 million was for infrastructure at the institutes of technology, £30 million was for equipment renewal in universities and £60 million for new software courses and programmes.[11] Established around the same time was the Business and Training Partnership Fund and an Expert Group on Future Skills Needs which was charged with analysing future demand. This group provided its first report in June 1998 on software and hardware,[12] with a second report in December 1998.[13] The group particularly identified a skills shortfall with professionals and technicians in engineering and computer science. The current annual supply was over 6,000, but the report saw another 2,000 needed in each year between 1997 and 2003. It was to third-level that the state looked to meet this shortfall; universities and colleges were central to a new drive.[14]

The primary emphasis and concern of the state sector, and the Department of Education and Science,[15] has remained with science and technology. One of the biggest threats to continued growth in science and technology is a well-documented decline in interest in chemistry and physics subjects amongst second-level students,[16] a problem which is being compounded by the difficulty of attracting chemistry and physics graduates into second-level teaching.[17]

With participation rates in full-time higher and further education having climbed above 60 per cent, Ireland has advanced far into universal higher education. Policy on funding for higher education in Ireland has always been focused on school leavers. Third-level education was seen as an immediate follow-on to secondary schooling, and students who did not avail of it then had financial and other barriers put in the way of re-entry at a later point.[18] The extent and effect of this discrimination in Irish higher and further education finally came to be accepted by the state in the 1998 Green Paper, *Adult Education in an Era of Learning*.[19] It noted, drawing on OECD statistics, that of a group of twelve OECD countries, Ireland with 45 per cent had the lowest percentage population aged 25-64 with upper secondary education. By comparison USA had 85 per cent, and Germany 84 per cent.[20] Even more striking were further figures on the percentage distribution of first time new entrants to public and private third-level institutions by age group in 1995. Here again Ireland was in the bottom part of a league table of sixteen. Whereas on average 15.7 per cent of new university students were over the age of twenty-five, in Ireland this figure was 2.3 per cent.[21] One might have expected that the non-university sector (being overwhelmingly dominated by public sector colleges) would perform better than universities, but this was not the case. Only 1.1 per cent of new entrants to the non-university sector was over twenty-five years of age as against an average of 27.9 per cent across the sixteen countries.[22] Ireland's under-provision for mature students was only emulated by France and Greece. This is a very poor performance for a society which supports such a high level of higher education provision. The Green Paper observed that many of the other countries concerned have faced declines in the flow of young people into the labour force for some years, and are engaging in a systematic drive to invest in lifelong learning. The skill shortages which began to manifest themselves relatively quickly with Ireland's boom in the late 1990s finally drove the Irish state to examine similar approaches.

The main recommendations of the Green Paper were a national literacy programme, phased development of a back-to-education scheme for adults, increasing services to support access (such as childcare and guidance), a forum for practitioners of adult and continuing education, a representative National Adult Learning Council and local boards to plan needs and deploy resources. It also recommended that universities and institutes of technology introduce mature student quotas.[23] Virtually all of these figured when the follow-up White Paper was published in July 2000, with the addition of a Targeted Higher Education Mature Student Fund.[24] In the meantime the National Development Plan 2000-2006 was published in November 1999, and included £5.35 billion for education, with a commitment to literacy initiatives and expansion of second-chance and lifelong learning initiatives.[25] Simultaneously the Minister for Education and Science indicated that £194 million would be spent over a three-year period on a range of measures to tackle disadvantage. Some £30 million of this was to be devoted to third-level access, with a major expansion of college-based schemes aimed at increasing the number of disadvantaged students entering third-level.[26] The White Paper and the commitments contained in the National Development Plan mark a beginning, and perhaps have the potential to make the Irish system of higher education a truly universal one.

A further step in this direction was the establishment of a group to look *inter alia* at whether the abolition of fees for modular and part-time courses would increase the low level of participation by mature students in third-level education.[27] Issues of equality, discrimination and disadvantage could provide the focus for the Department of Education and Science for the early part of the new millennium, just as the social engineering project which involved the establishment of the national institutes and the regional technical colleges provided such a focus in higher education a generation previously. For such to happen there would necessarily have to be a substantial shift in the prioritising of resources, a shift that would also need an ongoing, and perhaps cross-party, political commitment.

There is one further, and relatively new, element which is liable to divert the decision-makers from a commitment to tackle matters of equality and the related issues of mature and second-chance students. That is the question of research. To date the primary commitment of Irish universities and the wider third-level sector has been to teaching rather than to research. The problems attendant on the advent of mass higher education elsewhere have not been a major problem in Ireland, because Irish universities had a level of resource that anticipated the conditions of mass and universal higher education. The country's largest university institution, University College Dublin, never enjoyed staff-student ratios that were remotely comparable to its British counterparts.[28] The Commission on Higher Education in 1967 concluded that the universities were understaffed and that 'the position must be remedied'.[29] This did not happen. Nonetheless the Irish third-level sector appears to have been successful in terms of educating a generation which had the knowledge base necessary for developing a thriving economy at the end of the millennium.

Eventually in the late 1990s, prodded by a number of reports including that of the Circa Group for the Higher Education Authority, the message concerning the importance of research began to be accepted. As noted, in November 1997 the government launched a £250 million Educational Technology Investment Fund. Included was £30 million for third-level equipment renewal grants and £15 million for research and technology development over a three year period.[30] A year later it announced a £180 million three-year investment programme for scientific and other research in universities and institutes of technology. The programme was to provide for government capital spending of £75 million, with £75 million in matching private funding to be raised by the colleges. On this occasion research in the humanities and social sciences was included. One third of the exchequer spending was to take the form of tax reliefs for corporate investment. Applications for funding were to go before a panel of seven leading international academics, four from the sciences and technology, and three from the humanities and social sciences.[31]

In July 1999 a total of £162 million was allotted under the first cycle of the programme to eleven third-level institutions. The largest sum, £24.5 million went to UCD for the Conway Institute for Biomolecular and Biomedical Research, a new Institute for the study of Social Change and a National Social Science Archive. All seven universities were among the recipients, in addition to the Royal College of Surgeons in Ireland, Athlone Institute of Technology, Dublin Institute of Technology and the Institute of Technology Carlow.[32]

The second cycle involving £65 million was launched in December 1999. Greater discretion was given in relation to the breakdown between capital and current expenditure. Inter-institutional co-operation was also encouraged. When the results were announced the largest sum, £27 million, went to a research partnership between UCD's Conway Institute and TCD's Institute of Molecular Medicine for a programme of biomolecular and biomedical research. Intense competition for research funding was bringing about partnership of a kind which Donogh O'Malley had attempted and failed to achieve thirty years earlier. Universities were being forced to identify their strengths, prioritise their research, and in some cases reject good research proposals simply because they failed to meet funding criteria.[33]

In the later months of 1999 a much bigger milk train began to appear on the horizon. In March 1998 Noel Treacy, the Minister for Science, Technology and Commerce had requested the Irish Council for Science, Technology and Innovation (ICSTI) to develop and undertake a Technology Foresight exercise in Ireland. It was envisaged that the outputs would provide the government with material for the preparation of a National Development Plan to be submitted to the EU Commission in the context of a forthcoming round of Structural Funds. The exercise focused on the knowledge needed to underpin innovation, growth and competitiveness in the Irish economy. ICSTI identified eight sectors for consideration: Chemicals and Pharmaceuticals, Information and Communication Technologies, Materials and Manufacturing Processes, Health and Life Sciences, National Resources (Agri-food, Marine, Forestry), Energy, Transport and Logistics, Construction and Infrastructure.[34] The time horizon for the exercise was set at 2015 and the exercise itself was completed in twelve months. The group concluded that there was a need for a substantial increase in natural capability in the niche areas of information and communication technologies and biotechnology. These sectors were identified as the engines of growth in the global economy, and the Irish economy needed to create a credible base of knowledge and activities in these key technologies.

The National Development Plan announced a £1.9 billion investment in research and development. The strategy was intended to deliver a message to international companies that Ireland took research seriously and would be a suitable base for their European research programmes. It was part of an overall plan to reposition Irish industry 'higher up the value chain'.[35] The investment was intended to bring Irish research and product development spending to about two per cent of GDP, close to the EU average, with about a quarter of the money going to colleges and university research departments.

Having accepted the ICSTI recommendation, the government established a Foresight Fund. An interesting battle then developed about the deployment of such massive resources. In November 1999 the Department of Enterprise Trade and Employment circulated a discussion document to all government departments on how to use the Foresight Fund. It made certain recommendations, including the establishment of two stand-alone institutes for biotechnology and computer research. A vigorous debate ensued in which both the Department of Education and Science and the Department of Health, and their related bodies, the Health Research Board and the Higher Education Authority, argued for the broadening and deepening of the quality of research done by third-level scientists. The newspapers became the fora for debate on the respective merits of the arguments.[36]

Fears were expressed that stand-alone institutes would attract the best university researchers, that they would duplicate the infrastructure already available at third-level and that world-class researchers would not be attracted to institutes with no track record. It was also argued that the international trend was against institutes, which could not foster the exchange of ideas and multidisciplinary cross-fertilisation which leads to discovery. The proponents of the stand-alone approach argued that Irish universities did not have sufficient researchers with an international reputation to achieve a world standard.

Eventually in March 2000, the Minister for Enterprise Trade and Employment, Mary Harney, launched the Foresight Research Foundation to oversee the spending of the £560 million Technology Foresight Fund.[37] An implementation group to advise on the Foundation's structures was established. An international competitive peer review process was to be used to identify suitable research initiatives. The Foundation would have the option to establish its own laboratories, if necessary, in order to achieve a world-class standard of research.

In the early 1990s Irish university academics would have regarded the scale of the financial commitment to research outlined by the state in two years between November 1997 and November 1999 as residing in the realm of fantasy. What it reflects is that Ireland in a relatively short time has become a wealthy European country and is still climbing. Higher education is, and has been, part of the engine of growth. As the country becomes wealthier and the higher education system expands, it will become more attractive to private and foreign investment.

Until relatively recently higher education in Ireland relied overwhelmingly on the public purse. During the 1980s a market for private education grew up in Dublin. The reason for this was that Dublin was one of the most poorly-served parts of the country for places in higher education.[38] This market began to contract in the 1990s with the establishment of the institutes of technology in Tallaght, Dún Laoghaire and Blanchardstown,[39] the discovery of DIT and the regional technical colleges by the Dublin middle-class when those colleges joined the national system of centralised third-level applications,[40] and most particularly through the decision to phase out tuition fees for full-time students in universities and institutes of technology. The qualifications legislation enacted in 1999 added further to the difficulties of private colleges,[41] and it seems unlikely that any of the existing private colleges will become major players in the Irish third-level sector.[42]

A difficult future for private education at the undergraduate end of higher education does not mean that private sector activity will not have a place at the upper or postgraduate end of the market. In 1999 it emerged that the Massachusetts Institute of Technology was in negotiation with the Irish government about establishing a £133 million technology campus in Dublin, which would be an advanced college for internet-related studies and would allow postgraduate students to grow their own experimental companies.[43] In January 2000 the family of businessman Tony Ryan approved plans to set up a £5 million academy to train entrepreneurs in management skills and advanced technology. The new institution is to have links with UCD and MIT.[44] Other successful Irish businessmen, such as Tony O'Reilly and Michael Smurfit and their associated companies, have been major benefactors of third-level education.

From the mid-1980s onwards the Irish universities had began a process of attracting private money, especially from the Irish-American expatriate and ethnic network. In 1997 it was revealed that four Irish universities between them had received £30 million from the philanthropic foundations of the reclusive Irish-Amercian, Charles (Chuck) Feeney.[45] The biggest recipient was the University of Limerick whose then president, Dr Edward Walsh, had pioneered the process of fund-raising for Irish universities in North America. Fund-raising of this kind is relatively new in Ireland, although it is virtually the defining activity of a university president in the United States, particularly in private universities. It is a process which is likely to grow, and with the increasing growth in wealth and in the number of Irish millionaires from new businesses, Irish universities are likely to benefit increasingly from this activity.

It seems reasonable to assume that the coming decades will see a significant growth in the research activity of Irish universities. It is also probable that this activity will be primarily concentrated in the existing seven universities. They are, in the process, likely to become a good deal wealthier, particularly as all of them seem to have well-developed alumni associations which may eventually provide valuable sources of income and endowment.

The growth in private funding over time is likely to change the relationship between the state and the university sector. It is unlikely that the percentage growth of funding for higher education from the exchequer will continue to grow indefinitely. At some point it has to reach a plateau, and eventually decrease. Where the state has positioned itself at that point is likely to be crucially significant for the future of Irish society. It is certain that the Irish taxpayer will not forever increase the amounts of money given to provide free tuition to all third-level full-time students, while at the same time bringing Ireland's research base up to, or even beyond, OECD and EU norms, and simultaneously supporting initiatives to address poverty and disadvantage.

While arguably the Irish state since the 1960s has been extremely successful in developing an education system to develop human capital as a motor for economic growth, it has been singularly unsuccessful in providing equality of opportunity or in spreading the benefits of education across the entire community. There remains an underclass one of whose defining characteristics is that it is dropping out of education early. As the state's own Green Paper on Adult Education admitted, even the rampantly capitalist market economy of the United States is altogether more successful and innovative in providing higher education for mature students. Ireland's neglect in this area has not made sense, even in economic terms, but it has taken a skills shortage in the Irish economy to highlight the issue.

Economic considerations have been the driving force of most of the state's commitment to, and investment in, Irish higher education in the past forty years. An initiative undertaken by the Department of Education in the 1960s was successful in making skilled manpower available to the Irish economy in the last years of the twentieth century. The huge growth in Irish GNP and the volume of wealth creation since the late 1980s would indicate that the investment has paid off and that the education system has effectively supported economic development. The primary thrust, whether at central government or at the level of the individual college, has been overwhelmingly economic. There is little evidence of a wider vision impelling the process.

The Irish state has perhaps a once-off opportunity during its current unprecedented period of economic growth to address the problem of inequality of access. For this to happen would require the Department of Education and Science to develop a new focus and a new social engineering project, similar to the manner in which it embraced and enhanced the drive for higher technical education in the 1960s. In so doing it would almost certainly have to be less concerned to control, as distinct from facilitating, developments in other parts of higher education. Whether it is capable of making such a strategic transition, or indeed whether the political process would permit it to do so, are matters on which the jury is currently out.

Notes

1 Barry, F. (1999), Basingstoke: 'Introduction,' in F. Barry (ed.), *Understanding Ireland's Economic Growth*, Basingstoke: Macmillan Press, p. 1. Figures from the state's Central Statistics Office (CSO) showed that Gross National Product grew by 8.1 per cent in 1998, and 7.8 per cent in 1999. *Irish Times*, 21 July 2000.

2 ibid, p. 1. Also Gray, A. W. (1997), 'Foreword: Irish Economic Challenges and International Perspectives' in A. W. Gray (ed.), *International Perspectives on the Irish Economy*, Dublin: INDECON Economic Consultants, pp. xvii-xxii; Tansey, P. (1997), *Ireland at Work: Economic Growth and the Labour Market 1987-1997*, Dublin: Oak Tree Press, pp. 249-255. According to OECD figures this had reached 92 per cent of the EU average in 1998, with the likelihood of catching up with the EU average within two to three years (Garret FitzGerald, *Irish Times*, 2 May 1998).

3 The prophet of the transition to the 'knowledge society' was the American sociologist, Daniel Bell. Bell, D. (1973), *The Coming of Post-Industrial Society*, New York: Basic Books. According to Bell 'knowledge' would replace energy (coal in the nineteenth century; oil and nuclear power in the twentieth) as the primary resource of the new kind of post-industrial society, just as energy replaced human labour in the earlier transition from pre-industrial to industrial society.

4 This point is made by a number of commentators from that period. See, for example, Kerr, D. A. (1982), *Peel, Priests and Politics*, Oxford: Clarendon Press, p. 355. It has been noted in relation to the problems with student numbers in the early years of Queen's College Galway, that there were a mere 700 students in classical schools in Connacht, the equivalent of one large secondary school today. O'Malley, L. (1999), 'Law' in Foley, *Queen's College to National University*, p. 82.

5 In its submission to the Commission on Higher Education, University College Cork indicated that 75 per cent of its arts graduates took the Higher Diploma in Education (UCC, *Submission to Commission on Higher Education*, p. 9, TCD

Manuscripts Library, Folder 5, File 7/42).

6 Given the central position occupied by the Catholic Church in the political, social and cultural (apart from the religious) life of the country, the dramatic collapse in religious vocations and the decline of so many of the religious orders and congregations from the late 1960s onwards is one of the most extraordinary social upheavals in Ireland in the second half of the twentieth century. It is also remarkable that such a significant phenomenon (to the author's knowledge) has not hitherto merited a single authoritative historical or sociological study.

7 Tansey, *Ireland at Work*, pp. 114-115.

8 ibid., pp. 117-118.

9 In July 1997 the newly-elected Labour government announced radical changes in the funding of higher education. These involved the abolition of maintenance grants for students and the introduction of fees for full-time first degree students, with the cost of the fees to be balanced by increased loans for student maintenance. For background to the decision see Williams, G. (1998), 'Current Debates on the Funding of Mass Higher Education in the United Kingdom,' *European Journal of Education*, vol. 33, no. 1, pp. 77-87.

10 As of July 2000 there still remained a level of 4.4 per cent unemployment, much of this concentrated among the long-term unemployed. The situation would be regarded as close to full employment in Irish terms. (*Irish Times*, 5 August 2000).

11 *Irish Times*, 7 November 1997.

12 *Business and Finance*, 25 June 1998.

13 *Irish Times*, 31 December 1998.

14 Ibid., 19 June 1998.

15 The Minister and Department of Education became known as the minister and the Department of Education and Science following a government decision of 30 September 1997.

16 The numbers of chemistry students at Leaving Certificate in 1997 had declined to 11 per cent from 21 per cent in 1987: the numbers taking physics had dropped to 14.5 per cent from 20 per cent in the same period, *Irish Times*, 3 November 1998. See also *Irish Times*, 1 December 1998, 5 October 1999, 22 November 1998, 8 February 2000, 27 March 2000, 16 May 2000, 23 May 2000; *Irish Independent* 12 March 1999, 12 September 1999 and 2 December 1999.

17 *Irish Independent*, 15 December 1998; *Irish Times*, 19 August 1999, 17 August 2000.

18 It was primarily because university and other third-level education was accepted as a follow-on to secondary schooling that it was politically possible for Niamh Bhreathnach to abolish tuition fees for full-time third-level only, while leaving them stand for part-time and postgraduate students and for mature students. The discriminatory nature of these proposals met with very little serious opposition.

19 Department of Education and Science (1998), *Green Paper: Adult Education in a Learning Era*, Dublin: Stationery Office.

20 *Green Paper*, p. 28. The figures from the twelve countries were, USA (85 per cent), Germany (84 per cent), Switzerland (82 per cent), Canada, Poland and UK (all 74 per cent), Sweden (72 per cent), Netherlands (60 per cent), New

Zealand (57 per cent), Austria (50 per cent), Belgium (49 per cent), Ireland (45 per cent).

21 *Green Paper*, p. 30. In Norway only 68.7 per cent of new entrants were twenty five years of age or under.

22 If one were to exclude the contribution of Dublin Institute of Technology, the largest provider of part-time and recurrent education in the entire higher education system, the performance by the public sector colleges is even poorer. This is all the more remarkable when one considers that a major rationale for the 'binary system' (as enunciated in Britain in the 1960s) was that it would provide for more diversity in higher education provision, and for groups who otherwise might be discriminated against. The situation in the Irish public sector colleges is testimony *inter alia* to the extent to which both the Department of Education and Science and the main teaching union, the Teachers' Union of Ireland, are forces of conservatism.

23 Colleges and universities had difficulties in meeting these. *Irish Times*, 12 October 1999; *Irish Independent*, 1 October 1999.

24 *Learning for Life: White Paper on Adult Education* (2000), Dublin: Stationery Office.

25 *Ireland: National Development Plan 2000-2006* (1999), Dublin: Stationery Office, pp. 83-114.

26 *Irish Times*, 16 November 1999.

27 *Irish Times*, 6 January 2000. This examination is to be carried out by the Expert Group on Future Skills Needs. This group, established in 1997, had previously examined skills shortages in the IT industry and in the pharmaceutical, food and construction industries.

28 Until it moved to Belfield, UCD had accommodation problems virtually from its foundation. McCartney: *UCD – A National Idea*, pp. 85-98, 117-127. Staff student ratios deteriorated significantly in the 1950s and 1960s (ibid., pp. 385-387). At one point it was calculated that the staff-student ratio in the Commerce Faculty was 1:146. There were, of course, other areas of the university whose ratios were much more generous. The Commission on Higher Education noted in the 1960s that in veterinary medicine, for example, there had been a real improvement in staffing ratios (*Commission Report*, p. 104).

29 *Commission Report*, p. 594.

30 *Irish Times*, 11 November 1997.

31 ibid., 20 November 1998, 1 December 1998.

32 HEA Brochure, *The Programme for Research in Third-Level Institutes 1999-2001*. The programme was managed by the Higher Education Authority on behalf of the Minister for Education and Science.

33 *Irish Times*, 6 May 2000, 23 May 2000, 25 July 2000.

34 Technology Foresight Ireland (1999), *An ICSTI Overview*, Dublin: Forfás, pp. 1-3.

35 *Irish Independent*, 16 November 1999.

36 See, for example, *Irish Times*, 24 January 2000, 31 January 2000, 15 February 2000, 25 February 2000, 29 February 2000, 6 March 2000, 11 April 2000.

37 *Irish Times*, 9 March 2000.

38 This was documented in the report produced for the Higher Education Authority in 1979 by Benson and Clancy, and the continuation of the process

was documented subsequently by Clancy's three studies for 1980, 1986 and 1992 on entry to third-level education.

39 Tallaght opened in 1992, Dún Laoghaire in 1997, and Blanchardstown in 1999. Benson and Clancy's report had identified these areas as meriting a regional technical college in 1979. They recommended a fourth such college in the North-East of Dublin. This has not to date been provided, although the government in December 1999 did announce its support for the relocation of the National College of Ireland (formerly the National College of Industrial Relations) to a site in Dublin's docklands (*Irish Independent*, 23 December 1999).

40 *Irish Independent*, 30 October 1998. In this context the data on the socio-economic status of new entrants to DIT, and the Institutes of Technology at Tallaght and Dún Laoghaire, in 1998 are most revealing. Clancy and Wall, p. 79.

41 For an insight into the difficulties faced by the private college sector see *Irish Independent*, 3 March 1998; *Irish Times*, 20 November 1997, 29 September 1998, 20 October 1999.

42 There has been a visceral dislike of private colleges among trade unionists and Department of Education officials, and indeed virtually all of those involved in third-level education, whether in university or public sector colleges. The fact that their courses were being validated by NCEA in increasing numbers was a factor in the Directors of Regional Technical Colleges wishing to form a consortium to issue their own awards as a reconstituted NCEA, whose awards they regarded as having been devalued by being readily available to private commercial colleges (*Irish Independent*, 27 January 1997).

43 *Irish Independent*, 24 June 1999. It emerged in March 2000 that over £50 million of the Technology Foresight Fund had been earmarked for the project known as MediaLab Europe, *Irish Times*, 9 March 2000.

44 *Irish Times*, 13 January 2000. The overall project had been co-ordinated by Dr Edward Walsh.

45 *Irish Times*, 24 January 1997.

APPENDIX 1

Numbers of full-time students in third-level education 1964-1997

	1964/65	**1965/66**	**1966/67**	**1967/68**	**1968/69**	**1969/70**	**1970/71**	**1971/72**	**1972/73**	**1973/74**
Universities	12,984	15,441	15,845	16,266	17,504	18,570	19,652	19,959	20,518	20,360
Vocational/Technological	852	1,007	1,067	1,202	1,449	1,704	2,128	2,447	2,707	2,907
RTC	–	–	–	–	–	–	194	590	1,214	1,600
Other	4,361	4,250	4,429	4,469	4,190	4,222	4,244	4,140	4,275	4,773
TOTAL	18,197	20,698	21,341	21,737	23,143	24,496	26,218	27,136	28,614	29,640
	1974/75	**1975/76**	**1976/77**	**1977/78**	**1978/79**	**1979/80**	**1980/81**	**1981/82**	**1982/83**	**1983/84**
Universities	20,711	21,317	21,921	22,776	22,885	22,937	23,205	23,908	24,533	25,249
Vocational/Technological	2,561	3,097	3,313	3,434	3,365	3,937	4,945	5,384	5,921	6,459
RTC	2,694	3,235	3,523	3,753	4,274	4,945	5,965	7,119	8,493	9,107
Other	5,023	5,499	6,290	6,835	6,632	7,071	7,813	8,130	8,727	8,999
TOTAL	30,989	33,148	35,047	36,798	37,156	38,890	41,928	44,541	47,674	49,814
	1984/85	**1985/86**	**1986/87**	**1987/88**	**1988/89**	**1989/90**	**1990/91**	**1991/92**	**1992/93**	**1993/94**
Universities	25,912	26,146	26,819	27,448	33,811	35,477	37,917	42,213	46,540	50,662
Vocational/Technological	7,306	7,814	8,105	8,416	9,382	9,956	10,470	11,745	9,834	10,713
RTC	9,885	11,139	11,376	12,411	13,886	15,353	16,801	17,903	22,364	23,960
Other	061	9,989	10,279	11,120	5,891	5,163	4,800	4,984	5,402	7,260
TOTAL	52,164	55,088	56,579	59,395	62,970	65,949	69,988	76,809	84,140	92,595

These figures are taken from the volumes of *Tuarascáil Staitistiúil* for the period. The figures appear to include NIHE Limerick and NIHE Dublin among the university totals for 1988-89. They became universities in 1989-90. The drop under Vocational/Technological in 1974-75 was due to the transfer of courses from the Crawford Municipal Institute to Cork RTC, that for 1992-93 by Limerick College of Art, Commerce and Technology becoming Limerick RTC. Teacher Education Colleges are included within universities from 1992/93 onwards. From 1993/94 onwards Vocational/Technological refers solely to Dublin Institute of Technology.

Appendix 1 – continued

Numbers of full-time students in third-level education 1964-1997

	1994/95	**1995/96**	**1996/97**	**1997/98**
Universities	52,760	55,142	57,389	60,562
Vocational/Technological	10,523	10,557	10,841	10,602
RTC	24,952	27,573	30,159	31,307
Other	8,446	9,390	9,112	9,711
TOTAL	96,681	102,662	107,501	112,182

APPENDIX 2

Student numbers (full-time and part-time) in technological sector in academic year 1978-1979.

Regional Technical Colleges		
	Full-Time	Part-Time
Regional Technical College, Athlone	375	719
Regional Technical College, Carlow	470	841
Regional Technical College, Cork	884	3,139
Regional Technical College, Dundalk	604	1,204
Regional Technical College, Galway	831	1,516
Regional Technical College, Letterkenny	365	N/A
Regional Technical College, Sligo	507	833
Regional Technical College, Tralee	184	294
Regional Technical College, Waterford	628	1,480
TOTAL	4,848	10,026
Colleges of Technology		
	Full-Time	Part-Time
College of Technology, Kevin Street	827	2,062
College of Technology, Bolton Street	1,033	5,074
College of Catering, Cathal Brugha Street	435	2,411
College of Commerce, Rathmines	462	3,468
College of Marketing & Design	421	1,267
TOTAL	3,178	14,282
	Full-Time	Part-Time
Thomond College of Education, Limerick	176	–
NIHE, Limerick	948	710

Note: No figures were available for Limerick Technical College.
Source: Dáil Debates, vol. 314, cols. 1056-57 (22 May 1979).

APPENDIX 3

Part-time student provision in 1978-79 and 1993-94

Regional Technical Colleges		
	1978-79	**1993-94**
Athlone RTC	719	214
Carlow RTC	841	350
Cork RTC	3,139	2,195
Dundalk RTC	1,204	282
Galway RTC	1,516	368
Letterkenny RTC	n/a	291
Limerick RTC	n/a	442
Sligo RTC	833	332
Tallaght RTC	n/a	583
Tralee RTC	294	110
Waterford RTC	1,480	838
Dun Laoghaire	n/a	48
Dublin Institute of Technology	14,282	7,262
TOTAL	24,308	13,315
University		
University College Dublin	935	2,113
University College Cork	710	876
University College Galway	182	486
Trinity College Dublin	756	1,850
Maynooth	6	481
University of Limerick (NIHEL)	199	952
Dublin City University (NIHED)	–	909
TOTAL	2,788	7,667

The figures for part-time students in the vocational/technological sector for 1978/79 are taken from *Dáil Debates,* vol. 314, cols. 1057-1058 (22 May 1979). Those for the university colleges are taken from *HEA Accounts 1978 and Student Statistics,* 1978/79, p. 21.

All statistics for 1993-94 are taken from *Dáil Debates*, vol. 461, col. 1838 (20 February 1996).

The figure of 199 for NIHE Limerick in 1978-79 is as per the HEA tables. The Dáil reply gave a figure of 710. University of Limerick is treated under 'University' in both years, although it did not become a university until 1989-90.

The response to the Dáil question in 1979 indicated that there was a small element of estimation in the part-time data for 1978-79.

For the record the full-time student numbers for 1978-79 and 1993-94 (in brackets) were: RTC/Vocational: 8,026 (34,673), University: 24,308 (52,300).

1978-79 full-time figures as per Dáil reply, 22 May 1979, HEA Student Statistics 1978/79, p. 15 and the Report of the Steering Committee on the Future Development of Higher Education, p. 105.

In the latter case the full-time university figures also include Royal College of Surgeons in Ireland and National College of Art and Design.

APPENDIX 4

Entry to tertiary education in 21 OECD countries, 1992 (Number of new entrants to full-time public and private tertiary education per 100 persons in the theoretical starting age, 1992)

	Total	**University**	**Non-University**
Japan	55.0	25.2	29.7
Denmark	52.8	41.5	11.2
Belgium	52.6	27.3	25.3
Sweden	52.0	14.7	37.3
Germany	49.0	33.0	16.0
France	48.0	30.6	17.3
Spain	43.3	43.3	–
Italy	41.7	41.3	0.4
Netherlands	40.1	40.1	–
Ireland	39.9	22.1	17.8
Australia	38.3	38.3	–
Norway	38.0	19.8	18.2
U.K.	36.9	26.6	10.3
New Zealand	36.7	24.9	11.8
Austria	34.1	27.9	6.2
Greece	29.3	15.9	13.4
Poland	28.8	19.7	9.2
Switzerland	28.2	15.2	13.0
Czech Republic	17.9	13.9	4.0
Hungary	15.0	8.7	6.3
Turkey	14.3	12.0	2.3
Mean	41.1	28.2	13.5

Source: *Education at a Glance – OECD Indicators*, OECD, 1995

APPENDIX 5

Index of change in expenditure on tertiary education between 1990 and 1996
(1990 = 100)

Australia:	132	Italy:	74
Austria:	128	Mexico:	92
Belgium (Fl.):	109	Netherlands:	97
Canada:	98	New Zealand:	107
Denmark:	113	Norway:	132
Finland:	128	Portugal:	147
France:	132	Spain:	140
Hungary:	56	Switzerland:	99
Ireland:	164	UK:	114

Source: *Education at a Glance 2000*, Paris: OECD, p. 58

Bibliography

1 Official Publications

An Cólaiste Ealaíne is Deartha Act 1971

Books of Estimates 1966-1999

Building on Reality 1985-87, Prl 2648 (1984)

Bunreacht na hEireann (Constitution of Ireland) (1937)

Commission on Accommodation Needs of the Constituent Colleges of the National University of Ireland, *Report*, Pr 5087 (1959)

Commission on Higher Education, *Summary and Report* (1967)

Commission on the Points System: *Final Report and Recommendations* (1999)

Dáil Debates 1959-1999

Department of Education, *Statistical Reports*, 1964-65 to 1997-98

Department of Education, *White Paper, Educational Development* (1980)

Department of Education, *Green Paper, Partners in Education* (1985)

Department of Education, *Green Paper, Education for a Changing Ireland* (1992)

Department of Education, *White Paper, Charting our Education Future* (1995)

Department of Education and Science, *Green Paper: Adult Education in a Learning Era* (1998)

Department of Education and Science, *Learning for Life: White Paper on Adult Education* (2000)

Dublin Institute of Technology Act 1992

Economic Development, Pr 4808 (1958)

Forfás, *Second Report of the Expert Group on Future Skill Needs* (1999)

Forfás, *Shaping Our Future: A Strategy for Enterprise in Ireland in the 21st Century* (1996)

Forfás, Technology Foresight Ireland, *An ICSTI Overview* (1999)

Hederman O'Brien, Miriam, *Report to Minister for Education on Letterkenny Regional Technical College* (1994)

Higher Education Authority Act 1971

Higher Education Authority, *A Council for National Awards and a College of Higher Education at Limerick* (1969)

Higher Education Authority, *First Report* (1969)
Higher Education Authority, *Report on Teacher Education* (1970)
Higher Education Authority, *Report on the Ballymun Project* (1972)
Higher Education Authority, *Report on University Reorganisation* (1972)
Higher Education Authority, *Progress Report* (1974)
Higher Education Authority, *General Report 1974-85* (1985)
Higher Education Authority, *Women Academics in Ireland* (1987)
Higher Education Authority, *Interim Report of the Steering Committee's Technical Working Group* (1995)
Higher Education Authority, *Report of the Steering Committee on the Future Development of Higher Education* (1995)
Higher Education Authority, *Accounts and Student Statistics* 1975 to 1995/96
Higher Education Authority, Committee on Access and Participation of Students with Disabilities in Higher Education: *Report to Higher Education Authority* (n.d. 1996?)
Higher Education Authority, *Recommendations of the Higher Education Authority to Government in accordance with the terms of Section 9 of the Universities Act, 1997 concerning the application by DIT for establishment as a University.* (1999)
Higher Education Authority, *Report of Review Committee on Post Secondary Education and Training Places* (1999)
Higher Education Authority, Technical Working Group on the Review of Outreach Centres of Higher Education Institutions: *Final Review Report* (1999)
Higher Education Authority, *Report on Symposium on Open and Distance Learning* (2000)
Industrial Development Authority, *Annual Reports 1969 to 1986*
Industrial Development Authority, *Industrial Plan 1978-82*
Industrial Policy Review Group, *A Time for Change: Industrial Policy for the 1990s* (1992)
Ireland: National Development Plan 2000-2006 (1999)
Local Authorities (Higher Education Grants) Act 1968
Local Authorities (Higher Education Grants) Act 1978
Minister for Education, *Statement Announcing Government Proposals in Relation to Higher Education* (1974)
National Board for Science and Technology, *Science Budget* (1980)
National Centre for Guidance in Education, the Department of Education and Science, *Staying Power: A Colloquium on Increasing Retention Rates in Higher Education* (2000)
National Council for Educational Awards Act 1979

National Council for Educational Awards, *Annual Reports*, 1972 to 1997

National Council for Educational Awards, *Directories of Approved Courses*, 1979, 1981, 1983, 1985, 1987, 1995, 1997, 2000

National Council for Educational Awards, *A Report of a Survey of NCEA Award Recipients* (1981)

National Council for Educational Awards, *The Career Development of Engineering and Construction Studies Award Recipients* (1985)

National Institute for Higher Education Limerick Act 1980

National Institute for Higher Education Dublin Act 1980

OECD Survey Team, *Investment in Education* (1965)

Organisation for Economic Co-operation and Development, *Training of Technicians in Ireland* (1964)

Organisation for Economic Co-operation and Development, *Reviews of National Policies for Education: Ireland* (1969)

Organisation for Economic Co-operation and Development, *Education at a Glance: OECD Indicators* (1995 to 2000)

Programme for Economic Expansion, Pr 4796 (1958)

Qualifications (Education & Training) Act 1999

Regional Technical Colleges Act 1992

Report of International Study Group to the Minister for Education, *Technological Education* (1987)

Review of the Application by the Dublin Institute of Technology for establishment as a University, *Report of the International Review Group to the Higher Education Authority* (November 1998)

Seanad Debates 1959-1999

Second Programme for Economic Expansion (1963)

Steering Committee on Technical Education, *Report to the Minister for Education on Regional Technical Colleges*, Prl 371 (1969)

Thomond College of Education Act 1980

United Kingdom, Committee on Higher Education appointed by the Prime Minister under the Chairmanship of Lord Robbins 1961-63, *Report* (1963)

United Kingdom, National Advisory Council on Education for Industry and Commerce, *Report of the Committee on Technician Courses and Examinations* (1969)

Universities Act 1997

Vocational Education Act 1930

2 Unpublished Material

Department of Education/Higher Education Authority, Papers relating to the Working Party on Legislation, September-November 1976

Department of Education, *Draft Memorandum from the Government Concerning Legislation for the National Council for Educational Awards*, February 1978

Department of Education, *Full-Time Courses in VEC Colleges – Report of a Committee Established to Examine Third Level Courses Which Lead to Awards of NCEA and Other Bodies Outside the Universities* [The Lindsay Report] (September 1989)

Dublin Institute of Technology, Self-Evaluation Study: Review of Quality Assurance Procedures in Dublin Institute of Technology (1996)

National Archives, *Department of Taoiseach*, Files 13258C, 13809B, 513962A, 513962B/1, 513962B/2, 5140108, 16289, 16735A, 16735B

National Council for Educational Awards, *Marks and Standards for Recognised Courses*, 1973 to 1987. *Schedules of Approved Courses*, 1981 to 1987

Report of the High-Level Group to Advise on the Technological Sector (Presented to the Minister for Education, Niamh Bhreathnach TD, 2 May 1997)

Trinity College Dublin, *Moody Papers on Commission on Higher Education, Minutes of Commission on Higher Education* (TCD Manuscripts Library)

3 Newspapers

Business and Finance
Clonmel Nationalist
Cork Examiner
Education
Education Times
Evening Echo
Evening Herald
Evening Press
Faisnéis
Hibernia
Irish Computer
Irish Independent
Limerick Chronicle
Limerick Leader
Limerick Weekly Echo
Nenagh Guardian
Seirbhís Poiblí
Sunday Business Post
Sunday Independent
Sunday Press
Sunday Tribune
Technology Ireland
Tipperary Star
Western Journal

Irish Press
Irish Times
Western People
Wicklow People

4. Journals

Administration
An Múinteoir Náisiúnta
Crane Bag
Economic and Social Review
Engineers Journal
European Journal of Education
Higher Education in Europe
Higher Education Quarterly
History
Irish Historical Studies
Irish Review
Journal of Education Policy
STEM
Studies
Studies in Higher Education
Tertiary Education and Management

5. Books

Andrews, C.S. (1982), *Man of No Property*, Cork: Mercier Press

Barlow A.C. (1981), *The Financing of Third-Level Education*, Dublin: Economic and Social Research Institute

Barry, F (ed.) (1999), *Understanding Ireland's Economic Growth*, Basingstoke: Macmillan Press.

Bell, D. (1973), *The Coming of Post-Industrial Society*, New York: Basic Books.

Bew, P. and Patterson, H. (1992), *Seán Lemass and the Making of Modern Ireland 1945-66*, Dublin: Gill and Macmillan

Bradley, R. J. A. (ed.) (1986), *Proceedings of NCEA/UNESCO International Symposium on Technician Training and Education*, Dublin: NCEA

Brown, T. (1982), *Ireland: A Social and Cultural History 1922-79*, London: Fontana Paperbacks

Calvocoressi, P. (1991), *World Politics since 1945*, London: Longman

Chubb, B. (ed.) (1992), *FIE – Federation of Irish Employers 1942-1992*, Dublin: Gill and Macmillan

Chubb, B. and Lynch, P. (eds.) (1969), *Economic Development – Planning*, Dublin: Institute of Public Administration

Clancy, P. (1982), *Participation in Higher Education: A National Survey*, Dublin: Higher Education Authority

Clancy, P. (1988), *Who Goes to College? A Second National Survey of Participation in Higher Education*, Dublin: Higher Education Authority

Clancy, P. (1995), *Access to College: Patterns of Continuity and Change*, Dublin: Higher Education Authority

Clancy, P. and Benson, C. (1979), *Higher Education in Dublin: A Study of Some Emerging Needs*, Dublin: Higher Education Authority

Clancy, P. and Wall, J. (2000), *Social Background of Higher Education Entrants*, Dublin: Higher Education Authority

Clark, B. R. (1983), *The Higher Education System: Academic Organisation in Cross-National Perspective,* Berkeley: University of California Press

Clark, B. R. and Neave, G. (eds.) (1992), *The Encyclopaedia of Higher Education,* Oxford: Pergamon Press

Coolahan, J. (1981), *Irish Education: Its History and Structure*, Dublin: Institute of Public Administration

Coolahan, J. (ed.) (1994), *Report of the National Education Convention*, Dublin: National Education Convention Secretariat

Corish, P.J. (1985), *The Irish Catholic Experience: A Historical Survey*, Dublin: Gill and Macmillan

Corish, P.J. (1995), *Maynooth College 1795-1995*, Dublin: Gill and Macmillan

Cronin, M. and Regan, J. M. (eds.) (2000), *Ireland: The Politics of Independence 1922-49*, Basingstoke: Macmillan Press

Cullen, L. M. (1983), *The Emergence of Modern Ireland 1600-1900*, Dublin: Gill and Macmillan

de Courcy, J. W. (1985), *A History of Engineering in Ireland*, Dublin: Institution of Engineers of Ireland

Duff, T., Hegarty J. and Hussey, M. (2000), *The Story of the Dublin Institute of Technology*, Dublin: Blackhall Publishing

Fanning, J.R. (1978), *The Irish Department of Finance 1922-58,* Dublin: Institute of Public Administration

FitzGerald, G. (1991), *All in a Life: An Autobiography,* Dublin: Gill and Macmillan

Fitzpatrick, J. and Kelly, J. (1985), *Perspectives on Irish Industry*, Dublin: Irish Management Institute

Fleetwood, J. F. (1983), *The History of Medicine in Ireland*, Dublin: The Skellig Press

Fleming, T., Collins, T. and Coolahan, J. (eds.) (1999), *Higher Education: The Challenge of Lifelong Learning*, Maynooth: Centre for Educational Policy Studies

Foley, T. (ed.) (1999), *From Queen's College to National University: Essays on the Academic History of QCG/UCG/NUI Galway*, Dublin: Four Courts Press

Gellert, C. (ed.) (1993), *Higher Education in Europe*, London: Jessica Kingsley Publishers

Goldthorpe, J.H. and Whelan, C.T. (eds.) (1992), *The Development of Industrial Society in Ireland*, Oxford: Oxford University Press

Graby, J. (1989), *150 Years of Architects in Ireland: The Royal Institute of the Architects of Ireland 1839-1989*, Dublin: RIAI and Eblana Editions

Gray, A. W. (ed.) (1997), *International Perspectives on the Irish Economy*, Dublin: Indecon Economic Consultants

Guiomard, C. (1995), *The Irish Disease and How to Cure it*, Dublin: Oak Tree Press

Gwynn, D. (1948), *O'Connell, Davis and the Colleges Bill*, Cork: Cork University Press

Harris, S. E. (ed.) (1964), *Economic Aspects of Higher Education,* Paris: Organisation for Economic Co-operation and Development

Hermanns, H., Teichler, U. and Wasser, H. (eds.) (1983), *The Compleat University: Break from Tradition in Germany, Sweden and the USA*, Cambridge, Mass.: Schenkman Publishing Company Inc

Hindley, R. (1990), *The Death of the Irish Language*, London: Routledge

Hoctor, D. (1971), *The Department's Story – A History of the Department of Agriculture*, Dublin: Institute of Public Administration

Hogan, D. (1986), *The Legal Profession in Ireland 1789-1922*, Dublin: Incorporated Law Society of Ireland

Holland, C. H. (ed.) (1991), *Trinity College Dublin and the Idea of a University*, Dublin: Trinity College Dublin Press

Horgan, J. (1997), Seán Lemass: *The Enigmatic Patriot*, Dublin: Gill and Macmillan

Hussey, G. (1990), *At the Cutting Edge, Cabinet Diaries 1982-87,* Dublin: Gill and Macmillan

Kennedy, K. A. and Dowling, B. R. (1975), *Economic Growth in Ireland – The Experience since 1947,* Dublin: Gill and Macmillan

Kerr, C. et al. (1979), *12 Systems of Higher Education: 6 Decisive Issues*, New York: International Council for Educational Development

Kerr, D. A. (1982), *Peel, Priests and Politics,* Oxford: Clarendon Press

Larkin, E. (1980), *The Making of the Roman Catholic Church in Ireland 1850-1860,* Chapel Hill: The University of North Carolina Press

Lee, J. (1973), *The Modernisation of Irish Society 1848-1918*, Dublin: Gill and Macmillan

Lee, J.J. (ed.) (1979), *Ireland 1945-70*, Dublin: Gill and Macmillan

Lee, J.J. (1989), *Ireland 1912-85, Politics and Society*, Cambridge: Cambridge University Press

Leonard, J. (1996), *A University for Kilkenny: Plans for a Royal College in the Seventeenth Century*, Dún Laoghaire: St Canice's Press

Luce, J. V. (1992), *Trinity College Dublin: The First 400 Years*, Dublin: Trinity College Dublin Press

Lyons, F.S.L. (1974), *Ireland Since The Famine*, London: Collins/ Fontana

MacSharry R. and White P.A. (2000), *The Making of the Celtic Tiger: The Inside Story of Ireland's Boom Economy*, Cork: Mercier Press

Maher, D.J. (1986), *The Tortuous Path – The Course of Ireland's Entry into the EEC 1948-73*, Dublin: Institute of Public Administration

McCarthy, J. F. (ed.) (1990), *Planning Ireland's Future: The Legacy of T. K. Whitaker*, Dublin: Glendale Press

McCartney, D. (1983), *The National University of Ireland and Éamon de Valera*, Dublin: The University Press of Ireland

McCartney, D. (1999), *UCD A National Idea: the History of University College Dublin*, Dublin: Gill and Macmillan

McDonagh, O. (1991), *O'Connell: The Life of Daniel O'Connell 1775-1847*, London: Weidenfeld and Nicholson

McDowell, R. B. (1997), *Crisis and Decline: The Fate of the Southern Unionists*, Dublin: Lilliput Press

McElligott, T. J. (1966), *Education in Ireland*, Dublin: Institute of Public Administration

McGrath, F. (1951), *Newman's University: Idea and Reality*, Dublin: Browne and Nolan

McGrath, F. (1979), *Education in Ancient and Medieval Ireland*, Dublin: Studies

McKenna, A. T. (ed.) (1984), *Higher Education: Relevance and Future*, Dublin: Higher Education Authority

McManus, F. (ed.) (1978), *The Years of the Great Test*, Cork: Mercier Press

McMillan, N. (2000), *Prometheus's Fire: A History of Scientific and Technological Education in Ireland*, Carlow: Tyndall Publications

McRedmond, L. (1990), *Thrown Amoung Strangers: John Henry Newman in Ireland*, Dublin: Veritas Publications

Meenan, F.O.C. (1987), *Cecilia Street: The Catholic University School of Medicine 1855-1931*, Dublin: Gill and Macmillan

Meenan, F.O.C. (1994), *St Vincent's Hospital 1834-1994: An Historical and Social Portrait*, Dublin: Gill and Macmillan

Meenan, J. (1990), *George O'Brien: A Biographical Memoir*, Dublin: Gill and Macmillan

Meenan, J. and Clarke, D. (1981), *The Royal Dublin Society 1731-1981*, Dublin: Gill and Macmillan

Moody, T.W. and Beckett, J.C. (1959), *Queen's Belfast 1845-1949: The History of a University*, London: Faber and Faber

Morrissey, T. J. (1983), *Towards a National University: William Delany S. J. 1835- 1924*, Dublin: Wolfhound Press

Mulcahy, D.G. and O'Sullivan, D. (eds.) (1989), *Irish Educational Policy: Process and Substance,* Dublin: Institute of Public Administration

Murphy, A. E. (ed.) (1984), *Economists and the Irish Economy from the Eighteenth Century to the Present Day*, Dublin: Irish Academic Press

Murphy, J.A. (1975), *Ireland in the Twentieth Century,* Dublin: Gill and Macmillan

Murphy J.A. (1995), *The College: A History of Queen's/University College Cork 1845-1995*, Cork: Cork University Press

Neave, G. and Van Vught, A. (eds.) (1991), *Prometheus Bound: The Changing Relationship between Government and Higher Education in Western Europe,* Oxford: Pergamon Press

Newman, J., Ward, C., and Ryan, L. (1971), *A Survey of Vocations in Ireland*, Dublin: Research and Development Unit

Ó Buachalla, S. (1988), *Education Policy in Twentieth Century Ireland*, Dublin: Wolfhound Press

Ó Cearbhaill, D. (ed.) (1984), Galway: *Town and Gown 1484-1984*, Dublin: Gill and Macmillan

O'Connor, S. (1986), *A Troubled Sky – Reflections on the Irish Educational Scene 1957-68,* Dublin: Educational Research Centre, St Patrick's College

Ó Grada, C. (ed.) (1994), *The Economic Development of Ireland Since 1870*, Aldershot: Edward Elgar Publishing Ltd

O'Hagan, J.W. and Foley, G.J. (1982), *The Confederation of Irish Industry: The First Fifty Years 1932-1982*, Dublin: Confederation of Irish Industry

O'Hagan, J.W. (ed.) (1984), *The Economy of Ireland – Policy and Performance,* Dublin: Irish Management Institute

O'Hara, B. (1993), *Regional Technical College Galway: The First 21 Years*, Galway: Regional Technical College

Ó Muircheartaigh, F. (ed.) (1997), *Ireland in the Coming Times: Essays to Celebrate T. K. Whitaker's 80 Years*, Dublin: Institute of Public Administration

Osborne R. D. (1996), *Higher Education in Ireland: North and South*, London: Jessica Kingsley Publishers

Pratt, J. (1997), *The Polytechnic Experiment 1965-1992*, Buckingham: Society for Research into Higher Education and Open University Press

Pratt, J. and Burgess, T. (1974), *The Polytechnics: A Report,* London: Pitman Publishing

Randles, E. (1975), *Post Primary Education in Ireland: 1957-70,* Dublin: Veritas Publications

Robinson, H. W. (1983), *A History of Accountants in Ireland*, Dublin: Institute of Chartered Accountants in Ireland

Roche, F. and Tansey, P. (1992), *Industrial Training in Ireland*, Dublin: Stationery Office

Rothery, S. (1991), *Ireland and the New Architecture 1900-1940*, Dublin: Lilliput Press

Rowe, D. (ed.) (1988), *The Irish Chartered Accountant: Centenary Essays 1888- 1988*, Dublin: Gill and Macmillan

Scanlan, P. (1991), *The Irish Nurse – A Study of Nursing in Ireland: History and Education 1718-1981*, Manorhamilton: Drumlin Publications

Scott, P. (1995), *The Meanings of Mass Higher Education,* Buckingham: The Society for Research into Higher Education and Open University Press

Sheehan, J. (1978), *Future Enrolments in Third-Level Education*, Dublin: Higher Education Authority

Silver, H. (1990*), A Higher Education: The Council for National Academic Awards and British Higher Education 1964-89,* Basingstoke: The Falmer Press

Skilbeck, M. (2000), *Access and Equity in Higher Education: An International Perspective on Issues and Strategies,* Dublin: Higher Education Authority

Teichler, U (1988), *Changing Patterns of the Higher Education System: The Experience of Three Decades*, London: Jessica Kingsley Publications

Turpin, J. (1995), *A school of art in Dublin since the Eighteenth Century: A History of the National College of Art and Design*, Dublin: Gill and Macmillan

Vaughan, W. E. (ed.) (1996) *A New History of Ireland, vol. vi, Ireland Under the Union II 1870-1921*, Oxford: Clarendon Press

Walker, M. (1993), *The Cold War,* London: Fourth Estate

Walsh, D. (1986), *The Party: Inside Fianna Fáil,* Dublin: Gill and Macmillan

Walshe, J. (1999), *A New Partnership in Education: From Consultation to Legislation in the Nineties*, Dublin: Institute of Public Administration

Whelan, B. (2000), *Ireland and the Marshall Plan 1947-1957,* Dublin: Four Courts Press

Whyte, J. H. (1980), *Church and State in Modern Ireland 1923-1979,* Dublin: Gill and Macmillan

Widdess, J. D. H. (1967), *The Royal College of Surgeons in Ireland and its Medical School 1784-1966*, Edinburgh: E &S Livingston

6 Articles and Theses

Akenson, D. H. (1996), 'Pre-university Education 1870-1921', in Vaughan, *Ireland under the Union 1870-1921*

Altbach, P. G. (1998), 'Comparative Perspectives on Higher Education for the Twenty-first Century'; *Higher Education Policy*, vol. 11

Barrett, C. and Sheehy, J. (1996), 'Visual Arts and Society 1850-1900', in Vaughan, *Ireland Under the Union*

Barry, F. (1999), 'Introduction', in F. Barry (ed.) *Understanding Ireland's Economic Growth*

Benson, C. (1991), 'Trinity College: A Bibliographical Essay', in C. H. Holland (ed.) *Trinity College Dublin and the Idea of a University*

Bradley, J. (1994), 'The Legacy of Economic Development: The Irish Economy 1960-1987', reproduced in C. Ó Grada (ed.) *The Economic Development of Ireland Since 1870*

Breathnach, E (1981), *A History of the Movement for Womens' Higher Education in Dublin 1860-1912,* Dublin: University College Dublin, unpublished MA thesis

Clancy, P. (1989), 'The Evolution of Policy in Third-Level Education', in D.G. Mulcahy and D. O'Sullivan (eds.) *Irish Educational Policy: Process and Substance*

Clancy, P. (1993), 'Goal Enlargement and Differentiation: the Evolution of the Binary Higher Education System in Ireland', in Gellert, *Higher Education in Europe*

Clancy, P. (1999), 'Participation of Mature Students in Higher Education in Ireland' in T. Fleming, T. Collins and J. Coolahan (eds.), *Higher Education: The Challenge of Lifelong Learning*

Clark, B. R. (1997), 'Higher Education as a Self-guiding Society', *Tertiary Education and Management*, vol. 3, no. 2

Cobban, A. B. (1992), 'Universities 1100-1500', in B. R. Clark and G. Neave (eds.), *The Encyclopaedia of Higher Education*

Collins, L. (1975), 'The Technician', *Engineers Journal,* vol. 28

Connellan, L. (1980), 'Trends to the Year 2000 – The Industrial Sector', *Ireland in the Year 2000,* An Foras Forbartha

Coolahan, J. (1989), 'The Fortunes of Education as a Subject of Study and Research in Ireland', *Irish Educational Studies*, vol. 1

Coolahan, J. (1997), 'Third-Level Education in Ireland: Change and Development', in F. Ó Muircheartaigh (ed.) *Ireland in the Coming Times: Essays to Celebrate T. K. Whitaker's 80 Years*

Davies, S. (1992), 'Binary Systems of Higher Education', in Clark and Neave, *Encyclopedia of Higher Education*

Dempsey, P. (2000), 'Trinity College and the New Political Order', in M. Cronin and J. M. Regan (eds.), *Ireland and the Politics of Independence 1922-49*

Eicher, J. C. (1998), 'The Costs and Financing of Education in Europe', *European Journal of Education*, vol. 33, no. 1

Fanning, J. R. (1990), 'The Genesis of Economic Development', in McCarthy, *Planning Ireland's Future Years*

Fanning, R. (1984), 'Economists and Government: Ireland 1922-52', in A. E. Murphy, *Economists and the Irish Economy from the Eighteenth Century to the Present Day*

FitzGerald, G. (1969), 'Grey, White and Blue', in B. Chubb and P. Lynch (eds.), *Economic Development – Planning*

FitzGerald, G. (1992), 'How Others View Us – Political Views', in B. Chubb (ed.), *FIE – Federation of Irish Employers 1942-1992*

Fleischmann, A. (1996), 'Music and Society 1850-1921', in Vaughan, *Ireland Under the Union*

Friis, H. (1964), 'Preface', in S. E. Harris (ed.), *Economic Aspects of Higher Education*

Furth, D. (1992), 'Short-Cycle Higher Education: Europe', in Clark and Neave, *Encyclopedia of Higher Education*, vol. 2

Gellert, C. (1993) 'Structures and Functional Differentiation: Remarks on Changing Paradigms of Tertiary Education in Europe', in C. Gellert (ed.) *Higher Education in Europe*

Gellert, C. (1993), 'Academic Drift and the Blurring of Boundaries in Systems of Higher Education', *Higher Education in Europe,* vol. XVIII, no. 2

Gray, A. W. (1997), 'Foreword: Irish Economic Challenges and International Perspectives', in A W. Gray (ed.) *International*

Perspectives on the Irish Economy

Griffith, J. P. (1887), 'Presidential Address', *Transactions of the Institution of Civil Engineers of Ireland,* vol. xix

Harman, G. (1991), 'Institutional Amalgamations and Abolition of the Binary System in Australia under John Dawkins', *Higher Education Quarterly,* vol. 45

Hogan, M. A. (1961), 'Presidential Address', *Transactions of the Institution of Civil Engineers of Ireland,* vol. 87

Jarrell, R. A. (1983), 'The Department of Science and Art and Control of Irish Science 1853-1905', *Irish Historical Studies,* vol. 23, no. 92

Kearney, P. J. (1975), *Towards a University: A Historical Account of the Campaigns to have a University Established in Limerick with Particular Reference to the Period 1838-1947,* NUI Galway Library (unpublished MA thesis)

Kelham, B. B. (1967), 'The Royal College of Science for Ireland (1867-1926)', *Studies,* vol. 56

Kennedy, K. A. (1992) , 'The Context of Economic Development', in J.H. Goldthorpe and C.T. Whelan (eds.), *The Development of Industrial Society in Ireland*

Kerr, C. (1987), 'A Critical Age in the University World: Accumulated Heritage versus Modern Imperatives'; *European Journal of Education,* vol. 22, no. 2

Lee, J. J. (1979), 'Seán Lemass', in Lee, *Ireland 1945-70*

Lydon, J. (1991), 'The silent sister: Trinity College and Catholic Ireland', in Holland, *The Idea of a University*

Lynch, K. (1992), 'Education and the Paid Labour Market', *Irish Educational Studies,* vol. 11

Mahony, D. (1992), 'Establishing the University as the Sole Provider of Higher Education: The Australian Experience', *Studies in Higher Education,* vol. 2

McCarthy, J. F. (1990), 'Whitaker and the 1958 Plan for Economic Development', in McCarthy, *Planning Ireland's Future*

McGeady, P. A. (1981), 'The Irish Veterinary College', in Meenan and Clarke, *Royal Dublin Society*

McLoughlin, R. J. (1972), 'The Industrial Development Process: An Overall View', *Administration,* vol. 20, no. 1

Mitchell, J. (1998), 'Queen's College, Galway 1845-1858: From Site to Structure'; *Journal of the Galway Archaeological and Historical Society,* vol. 50

Moody, T. W. (1958) 'The Irish University Question of the Nineteenth Century', *History,* vol. 43

Moscati, R. (1991), 'Italy' in Neave and Van Vught, *Prometheus Bound*

Murphy,T. (1984), 'Higher Education – The Changing Scene', in A. T. McKenna (ed.) *Higher Education: Relevance and Future*

Murray, J. P. (1999), 'Medicine', in T. Foley (ed.) *From Queen's College to National University: Essays on the Academic History of QCG/UCG/NUI Galway*

Neary, P. (1984), 'The Failure of Economic Nationalism', *The Crane Bag,* vol. 8, no. 1

Neave, G. (1982), 'On the Edge of the Abyss: An Overview of Recent Developments in European Higher Education', *European Journal of Education,* vol. 17, no. 2

Neave, G. (1983), 'The Dynamic of Integration in Non-integrated Systems of Higher Education in Western Europe', in Hermanns et al., *The Compleat University*

Neave, G. (1985) 'Higher Education in a Period of Consolidation 1975-85'; *European Journal of Education,* vol. 20

Neave. G. (1986), 'On Shifting Sands: changing priorities and perspectives in European higher education from 1984 to 1986', *European Journal of Education,* vol. 21

Neave, G. (1990), 'On Preparing for Markets: trends in higher education in Western Europe 1988-1990'; *European Journal of Education,* vol. 25, no. 2

Neave, G. (1994), 'The Politics of Quality: developments in higher education in Western Europe 1992-1994'; *European Journal of Education,* vol. 29

Neave, G. (1995), 'On Living in Interesting Times: Higher Education in Western Europe 1985-1995', *European Journal of Education,* vol. 30, no. 4.

Neusel, A. and Teichler, U. (1983) 'Comprehensive Universities – History, Implementation, Process and Prospects', in H. Hermanns, U. Teichler and H. Wasser (eds.), *The Compleat University: Break from Tradition in Germany, Sweden and the USA*

Nolan, S. (1984), 'Economic Growth', in J.W. O'Hagan (ed.) *The Economy of Ireland – Policy and Performance*

Ó Buachalla, S. (1984), 'Policy and Structural Development in Higher Education'; *European Journal of Education,* vol. 19, no. 2

Ó Buachalla, S. (1985), 'Church and State in Irish Education in this Century'; *European Journal of Education,* vol. 20, no. 4

Ó Buachalla, S. (1992), 'Self-Regulation and the Emergence of the

Evaluative State: trends in higher education policy, 1987-1992', *European Journal of Education*, vol. 27, nos. 1/2

Ó Buachalla, S. (1992). 'Ireland' in Clark and Neave, *Encyclopedia of Higher Education*.

Ó Cearbhaill, T. (1992), 'How Others Saw Us', in Chubb, *FIE*

Ó Cuiv, B. (1996) 'Irish Language and Literature', in Vaughan, *Ireland under the Union*

Ó hEocha, C. (1984), 'The Queen's College at Galway – Some Memories', in D. Ó Cearbhaill (ed.), *Galway: Town and Gown 1484-1984*

Ó Laoghaire, D. (1988), 'Privatisation in Irish Education'; *Seirbhís Phoiblí,* vol. 1

Ó Maolcatha, N. (1986), 'The Role of the Technician in Economic Development', in R. J. A. Bradley (ed.), *Proceedings of NCEA / UNESCO International Symposium on Technician Training and Education*

O'Connor, R. F. (1981), 'The Growing Demand for Catholic Education in the Eighteenth Century leading to the Establishment of St Patrick's, Maynooth 1795'; *Irish Educational Studies*, vol. 1

O'Connor, S. (1968), 'Post Primary Education: Now and in the Future'; *Studies,* vol. 57

O'Donnell, J. P. (1962), 'Manpower for Industry'; *Engineers Journal,* vol. 15

O'Donnell, J. P. (1963), 'Paris "Confrontation" Meeting on Irish Education: How the OECD Report was Prepared'; *Engineers' Journal*, vol. 16

O'Driscoll, F. (1985), 'Archbishop Walsh and St. Mary's University College, 1893-1908'; *Irish Educational Studies*, vol. 5, no. 2

O'Malley, L. (1999). 'Law' in Foley, *Queen's College to National University*

O'Regan, P. and Murphy, B. (1999), *Professionalisation in a Political Context: The origin and development of the accountancy profession in Ireland, 1884-1914* (paper delivered to Irish Accounting and Finance Association, UCC, May 1999)

O'Sullivan, D. (1992), 'Cultural Strangers and Educational Change: The OECD Report *Investment in Education* and Irish Education Policy'; *Journal of Education Policy,* vol. 7

O'Sullivan, D., (1992) 'Shaping Educational Debate: a case study and an interpretation', *Economic and Social Review*, vol. 23, no. 4

Palmer, P. (1990) 'Apples, Arts, Amnesiacs and Emigrants: The

University Connection', *The Irish Review,* vol. 8

Parkes, S. M. (1996), 'Higher Education 1793-1908', in W. E. Vaughan (ed.) *A New History of Ireland,* vol. vi

Pratt, J. (1992), 'Unification of Higher Education in Britain', *European Journal of Education,* vol. 27, no. 1/2

Quin, T. (1988) 'A centenarian renders his account', in D. Rowe (ed.) *The Irish Chartered Accountant: Centenary Essays 1888-1988*

Raftery, P. (1968), 'Presidential Address'; *Transactions of the Institution of Civil Engineers of Ireland,* vol. 94

Rau, E. (1993) 'Inertia and Resistance to Change of the Humboldtian University', in Gellert, *Higher Education in Europe*

Sheehan, J. (1979), 'Education and Society in Ireland 1945-70', in Lee, *Ireland 1945-70*

Teichler, U. (1993), 'Structures of Higher Education Systems in Europe', in Gellert, *Higher Education in Europe*

Vaizey, J. (n.d.) 'Introduction', *The Residual Factor and Economic Growth – Study Group in the Economics of Education*

Vaughan, W.E. (1991), 'Paying for the Christmas Dinner: the College's Income and Expenditure', in Holland, *The Idea of a University*

Walsh, B. M. (1979), 'Economic Growth and Development', in J.J. Lee (ed.), *Ireland 1945-70*

Walsh, E. (1974), 'The University Situation in Ireland Today', *University Education in Ireland* (IFUT)

Walsh, E. (1977), 'Education, Technology and Society', *STEM,* vol. 2

Walsh, E. (1980), 'Science, Technology and Education', *Ireland in the Year 2000: Proceedings of a Colloquy,* An Foras Forbartha

White, A. (1981), 'Higher Technological Education in the 1970s'; *Irish Educational Studies,* vol. 1

Williams, B. (1992), 'The Rise and Fall of the Binary System in Two Countries and the Consequences for Universities'; *Studies in Higher Education,* vol. 3

Williams, G. (1998), 'Current Debates on the Funding of Mass Higher Education in the United Kingdom', *European Journal of Education,* vol. 33, no. 1

7 Miscellaneous Publications

Albert Agricultural College, *Centenary Souvenir* 1838-1938

An Foras Forbartha, (1980), *Ireland in the Year 2000: Proceedings of a Colloquy*

Association of Vocational Educational Colleges (AVEC), (n.d.) AVEC Working Party on Research and Consultancy, *Report on Research and Consultancy in VEC Colleges*

CII News

Circa Group Europe (1996), *A Comparative International Assessment of the Organisation, Management and Funding of University Research in Ireland and Europe*, Dublin: Higher Education Authority

Coiste um Bheart Ollscoile Luimni (1961), *Submission from Limerick University Project Committee to the Commission on Higher Education*

Conference of Heads of Irish Universities (1999), *Guaranteeing Future Growth: University Research and Education, an Investment Priority – National Plan 2000-2006*

Conference of Heads of Irish Universities (2000), *Technology Foresight and the University Sector*

Fahy, L., 'Global Change and the Implications for Irish Business.' Paper to the Fortieth National Management Conference, April 1993

Fathers of the Society of Jesus (1930), *A Page of Irish History: Story of University College, Dublin 1883-1909*, Dublin: Talbot Press

Irish Federation of University Teachers. *Statement on Academic Freedom and University Autonomy*, 2 October 1971

Irish Federation of University Teachers (1974) *University Education in Ireland: Report of a Seminar, November 1973*

National Institute for Higher Education, Dublin, *Report of the Governing Body 1975-78*

National Institute for Higher Education, Dublin, *The Planning and Accreditation of the Institute's Courses*, December 1978

National Institute for Higher Education, Limerick. Prospectuses 1977-84

NIHE News

National University of Ireland, *Handbook* 1908-1932

Society of College Lecturers (at City of Dublin VEC Colleges), *Policy Document on NIHE Dublin*, July 1975

Steering Group in the Economics of Education, (n.d.), *The Residual Factor in Economic Growth*, Paris: Organisation for Economic Development

Standards and Routes to Registration – SARTOR (1997), London: Engineering Council

Transactions of the Institution of Civil Engineers of Ireland

UCD Alma Mater

Walsh, E. M., 'Two Ideas of a University Contrasted', Paper to seminar at University College, Cork, 16 November 1990

8 Interviews

de Lacy, Hugh. Former Principal, College of Technology, Kevin Street, Dublin, Member of the Higher Education Authority (1968-77), Member of the Governing Body, NIHE, Dublin (1975-80), Member of the National Council for Educational Awards (1976-80), Director, Dublin Institute of Technology (1978-85). Interview, 6 January 1988

Dukes, James F. Secretary, Higher Education Authority, 1966-1982. Interview, 17 November 1987

Grainger, Professor J.N.R. Member, Higher Education Authority (1968-1982), Member, National Council for Educational Awards (1972-76, 1980-85). Interview, 3 December 1987

McGlone, Jack. Acting Director, National Council for Educational Awards (1972-73). Interview, 1 December 1987

Ó Cathail, Séamus. Secretary, Commission on Higher Education (1960-67). Interview, 18 December 1987

O'Connor, Seán. Secretary, Department of Education (1973-75), Chairman, Higher Education Authority (1975-79). Interview, 8 February 1986

O'Donnell, John. Professor of Chemical Engineering, UCD (1953-1989). Member of Steering Committee on Technical Education (1966-67), Member of National Council for Educational Awards (1972-1985). Interview, 26 November 1986

Sheehan, Jeremiah P. Inspector, Department of Education (1959-1968), Secretary, Steering Committee on Technical Education (1966-67). Interview, 19 February 1989

Index

[The index denotes references in the main text, and does not cover those in footnotes]

A

Academical Institutions (Ireland) Act, 1845, 3
accountancy, 8–9, 16, 86, 166
Accountancy and Business College, 221–2
Accumulation of Credits and Certification of Subjects (ACCS), 220
Adelaide Hospital, 7
adult education, 53, 162, 195–6, 271–2
Adult Education in an Era of Learning (Green Paper), 271, 277
agricultural training, 10–11, 196
Agriculture, Department of, 88
Agriculture and Technical Instruction, Department of, 9, 10
Albert College, 152–3
Alexandra College, 5
AnCO, 53, 59, 162, 184–5, 187
Apothecaries Hall, 7
apprenticeships, 16, 34, 51, 59, 185, 196, 223
  and NCEA, 147
  in RTCs, 81
architecture, 10, 16, 91
art and design, 11–12, 165–6, 220
  arts courses, 15–16
  numbers in, 194–5
  value of, 106–7, 188–9, 190
Association of Certified and Corporate Accountants (ACCA), 9
Association of Chief Executive Officers, 83
Association of Vocational Education Colleges, Steering Committee, 216–17
Athlone, Co. Westmeath, 52
Athlone Institute of Technology, 273
Athlone RTC, 80, 84, 86, 217
  opens, 81
  upgraded, 231–2
Australia, 248, 249, 254–5
Austria, 248, 249

B

Ballina outreach centre, 220
Ballymun Project, 91, 102, 116, 118, 151, 153
Barry, Peter, 126, 128, 150, 163
Barry, Richard, 139–40
Belfast, 3, 12
Belgium, 248
Bhreathnach, Niamh, 48, 197, 218, 270
  and DIT, 233, 234
  RTCs upgraded, 231–2
  university legislation, 224–9
binary system, 102, 108–9, 173, 192–3
  attitude of state, 260

decline of, 218–23
heyday of, 136
international comparisons, 250–2, 254–5
NIHEL within, 211–13
problems of DIT, 235–6
proposals for change 1974, 113–32
quality assurance, 238–9
role of NCEA, 146, 147–8
in UK, 117, 118
birth rate, 203
Blanchardstown Institute of Technology, 197, 276
Blaney, Neil, 28–9, 54
Bolton Street College of Technology, 10, 16, 90–1, 92, 140, 143, 215
TCD links, 121–2
Bord Iascaigh Mhara, 237
Boston University School of Management, 191
Brennan, Seamus, 218, 233
Browne, Dr Noel, 106
Buckley, Robert, 215
Building on Reality, 164
Building Project Unit, 54
Burgess, Tyrrell, 252
Burke, Richard, 75, 85, 103, 137, 144, 153, 159, 225, 229, 260
ESF schemes, 162–3
higher education reorganisation, 131–2
higher education reorganisation, 1974, 113–27
and NIHEs, 150, 154–5
Working Party, 127–8
Business and Training Partnership Fund, 270
business studies, 9, 165

C

Canada, 248, 249
Carlow, 52
Carlow RTC, 80–1, 84, 198
management, 83
opens, 81–2
upgraded, 231–2
Carmichael School, 7
Carnegie Commission on Higher Education, 259
Carter, Professor C. F., 45, 50
Carty, Michael, 43
Carysfort College, 12
Castlebar, 197
Catholic Church, 269
Catholic University, 3–4, 5, 269
Cecilia Street Medical School, 4, 5, 6
CERT, 196, 237
Chartered Institute of Management Accountants (CIMA), 9
Chatham Row technical institute, 16
Christian Brothers Teacher Training College, 122
Church of Ireland Training College, 12
Circa Group, 201, 273
City of Dublin VEC (CDVEC), 16, 90–2, 102, 162, 211, 235
and Burke proposals, 116
and DIT, 140–3, 233
funding, 167–8
and NCEA, 122, 148
and NIHED, 149–53, 215
part-time courses, 166
TCD links, 130, 156
City of Limerick VEC, 211
civil war, 14, 15
Clancy, Professor Patrick, 170, 195–6, 196–7
Clare, County, 197
Clark, Burton, 257, 261
Clinton, Mark, 131
College of Commerce Rathmines, 90–1, 165

College of Science, 14
colleges of technology, 35, 80–1, 85, 101
Colley, George, 28–9, 43, 51, 52
Collins, Edward, 142, 144, 146–7, 160–1, 163
COMETT, 255
commercial education, 8–9, 15
Commission on Accommodation Needs, 41, 42
Commission on Higher Education, 31, 41–50, 146
  assumptions of, 44–6
  CDVEC submission, 91–2
  HEA recommended, 99, 100
  and Limerick, 66–7
  purpose and remit, 42–3
  reports, 46–7, 79, 96
  results, 47–50
  and research, 201–2
  reservations, 49–50
  and technical education, 55–7, 59–60, 86–7
  technological education, 105
  understaffing, 272–3
  university reorganisation, 224
Commissioners of National Education, 12
communications technology, 198
comprehensive system
  argument for, 117–20
  implementing, 120–2
  long-term effects, 129–32
  proposals for, 113–16
  Working Party on Higher Education, 127–9
Confederation of Irish Industry (CII), 108, 185, 188, 214
Conference of Heads of Irish Universities (CHIU), 200, 228
Conference of Rectors, Presidents and Vice Chancellors of European Universities (CRE), 200
Conference of University Rectors in Ireland (CRI), 200
Connellan, Liam, 108, 188
Conroy, Professor Richard, 107
Conservative Party, 262
Constitution of Ireland 1937, 28, 68, 226
Conway Institute for Biomolecular and Biomedical Research, UCD, 273
Cooney, Patrick, 217
co-operative education, 74, 158
Cork, 3, 52
Cork RTC, 86, 166
  degree programmes, 221
  medical laboratory science, 139, 140
  and NCEA, 215
  upgraded, 231–2
Cork School of Music, 12
Corr, J.G., 126
Corry, Martin, 106
Cosgrave, Liam, 113, 119, 239
Costello, Lt-General Michael J., 96
Council for Educational and Vocational Awards, 223
Council for National Academic Awards (UK), 56, 70, 87, 147, 220, 222, 252
Council for National Awards, 69, 87, 103
Council for Technological Education, 114, 119, 121
Council of Convocation of the National University, 227
Council of Directors of Institutes of Technology, 200
Crawford Municipal Technical Institute, 86
Crosland, Anthony, 117
Cullen, Paul, Archbishop of Armagh, 3
Culliton Report, 190–2
Cumann na nGaedheal, 14

Cumann na nInnealtóirí, 86–7

D

Dáil Éireann, 13, 17, 42, 43
  comprehensive system
    debates, 118–19, 120, 125, 128
  Culliton Report, 191–2
  grants, 99–100
  HEA debates, 103–4
  NCEA debates, 144–8
  NIHE debates, 160–2, 214–15
  RTC governance, 83–4, 217–18
  TCD-UCD merger, 96–7
  Universities Bill, 225–9
  universities discussed, 106–8
Davern, Noel, 218
de Lacy, Hugh, 87, 141
de Valera, Éamon, 13, 14, 27, 65–6, 68
Dearing Review, 237
decentralisation, 261
Delany, Fr William, SJ, 4
Democratic Left, 226
Dempsey, Noel, 217–18
dentistry, 7, 130
Desmond, Barry, 68, 186
distance education, 195, 197–8, 219
DIT Review Group, 233–6, 238
domestic economy, 16
Dominican order, 5
Donegan, Patrick, 116, 121, 122, 140
  chairs NIHED, 149–53
  and NCEA Bill, 142–3
Donnelly, Professor Dervilla, 231, 232
Dooge, Professor James, 107
dropout levels, 198, 277
Dublin, County, 197
Dublin City University (DCU), 214–15
Dublin College of Catering, Cathal Brugha Street, 16, 92, 140
Dublin Institute of Technology (DIT), 139–40, 188, 198, 231, 232, 237, 239, 260
  administration of, 255
  award agencies, 222–3
  and CDVEC, 139–43
  changed status, 233–6
  established, 141–2, 151
  faculty structure, 235–6
  funding, 203, 273
  and MCC, 187
  middle-class students, 276
  and NCEA, 144, 165
  and NIHED, 152
  self-government, 217–18
  TCD links, 221
Dublin Municipal School of Music, 12
Dukes, James F., 97, 104
Dun Laoghaire RTC, 197, 276
Dundalk, Co. Louth, 52
Dundalk RTC, 81, 84, 166, 198, 215
  upgraded, 231–2

E

Economic Co-operation Agency (ECA), 29, 30
Economic Development, 25
  economic policy, 25–6, 250
  and education, 26–9
First Programme for Economic Expansion, 25, 26
Foresight Fund, 274–5
skills shortages, 270, 271–2
Education, Department of, 11–12, 13, 14, 16–17, 41, 103–4, 186
  Ballymun Project, 91–2
  and Commission on Higher
    Education, 44–5, 49, 50
  Development Branch, 71
  and economic planning, 27–9

funding, 102, 109, 114
    ESF, 162–3
  and NCAD, 137–8
  and NCEA, 87–8, 89, 148, 219
  and NIHEs, 70–5, 149, 157
    legislation, 160–2
  and OECD, 29–31, 31–2
  and private colleges, 222
  relations with universities, 224–9
  role of civil servants, 173–4
  and RTCs, 59, 82, 84, 221
    governance, 217–18
    upgraded, 231–2
  TCD-UCD merger plan, 96–9
  and technical education, 33–6, 50–4
  and technological education, 70, 71–2
  White Paper 1980, 170–3, 203
  Working Party on Higher Education, 127–9
Education – Charting our Future (White Paper), 223
Education Act 1998, 199
Education and Science, Department of, 258, 270
  adult education, 271–2
  centralisation, 255, 262
  and distance learning, 198
  and DIT, 236
  Foresight Fund, 275
  primacy of education, 238
  Qualifications Bill, 236–9, 239
  social engineering, 277–8
Education for a Changing World (Green Paper), 191–2
Educational Technology Investment Fund, 270, 273
Elizabeth I, Queen, 1
engineering, 10, 15, 16, 156, 165
  in NIHEL, 159
  in TCD, 121–2
Enterprise, Trade and Employment, Department of, 238, 274–5
equality of access, 199, 272, 277–8
ERASMUS, 255
Erin Foods, 80, 81
European Community Course Credit Transfer System, 255
European Economic Community (EEC), 162
  funding, 163–4, 168, 169
European Recovery Programme, 29
European Social Fund (ESF), 173–4, 255
  and VECs, 162–5
European Structural Funds, 255, 274
European Union (EU), 201, 261, 268, 274
higher education policy, 255
Evening Herald, 116
Expert Group on Future Skills Needs, 270

F

Fahy, Professor Liam, 191
Farm Apprenticeship Board, 196
FÁS, 196, 237
Faulkner, Pádraig, 70–1, 80, 98, 106
  and HEA, 104
  and RTCs, 82, 84–5
  teacher training, 102–3
Federated Union of Employers (FUE), 83
Feeney, Charles (Chuck), 276
Fianna Fáil, 14, 15, 83, 98, 122, 125, 130, 163, 226, 234
  and education, 28–9
  and NCEA, 136–40, 238–9
  and NIHEs, 151, 155

White Paper 1980, 170–3
Finance, Department of, 14, 17, 27, 41, 203, 229
Fine Gael, 14, 102, 107, 116, 142, 226
FitzGerald, Dr Garret, 81, 102, 107, 126, 229
and comprehensive system, 118–19, 131
on Culliton Report, 191
and HEA, 103–4
on NIHEs, 214–15
Universities Bill, 226–7
Fitzgerald, Gene, 187
Foras Oideachais, An, 102
Foresight Research Foundation, 275
Forfás, 192, 257–8
France, 3, 44, 247, 251, 252, 253, 255, 271
Froebel College of Education, 122
funding, 41, 258–9
ESF, 164–5
fund-raising, 276–7
grants, 48, 225
private, 262, 276–7
public expenditure on, 202, 249–50, 269–70
research funding, 200–2
student grants, 168–9
Furth, Dorothea, 251
Further Education and Training Awards Council, 236, 237, 239
further education sector, 198

G

Gaelic League, 13
Galway, County, 197
Galway city, 3, 52
Galway RTC, 54, 85, 166
degree recognition, 125–6
medical laboratory science, 139, 140
Galway-Mayo Institute of Technology, 197, 232
Gellert, Claudius, 253
gender balance, 199–200
Germany, 44, 247, 251, 252, 253, 271
Gillespie, Neil, 151
Gilmore, Éamon, 157
Goldsmith, Dr Brendan, 233–4
graduate programmes, 252
Greece, 251, 271
Green Paper 1998, 271, 277
Green Paper, 1992, 191–2, 223
Green Paper, 1985, 217
Griffith College, 222
Guild of Barber Surgeons, 6

H

Hardiman, T.P., 213, 214
Hardiman Committee, 217, 237–8
and NCEA, 220–1
report, 188, 213–15
Harney, Mary, 275
Haughey, Charles J., 28–9, 108, 188–9
Hayes, Michael, 13
Health, Department of, 275
Health Research Board, 275
Hederman O'Brien, Dr Miriam, 218
Higher Diploma in Education, 13, 194
higher education, 1–2, 6–13. *see also* binary system; comprehensive system
for Catholics, 2–6
centralised, 255
disciplinary, 261
Dublin's needs, 169–70
female participation, 5, 8, 199–200
growth in, 165–70, 193–203, 202–3, 247
mass education, 247–50, 260–1

statistics, 79, 172, 247–8
and industrial policy, 184–93
international comparisons, 247–62
and the market, 256–8
and national prosperity, 268–70
off-campus sites, 197–8
participation rates, 198–9, 248
regional variations, 196–7
Qualifications Bill, 236–9
reorganisation proposals, 1974, 113–27
role of civil service, 173–4
role of the state, 255–62
technological ethos, 105–8
20th century, 13–17
Higher Education and Training Awards Council, 236, 237, 239
Higher Education Authority Act 1971, 157, 235
Higher Education Authority (HEA), 47, 48, 75, 128, 144, 200, 220
in 1980 White Paper, 171, 172–3
Ballymun Project, 91
and Burke proposals, 115
and comprehensive system, 119
and DIT status, 234–5
established, 99–105, 109
funding system, 258–9, 275
increased powers, 225, 226–7
inequality study, 199
and MCC, 186–8
Medical Laboratory Science, members of, 145–6
merger plan, 97–8
and NCEA, 87
and NIHEs, 69–71, 72, 74, 149, 151
projections, 250
relations with universities, 227–8, 229
reports
Dublin needs, 169–70
entrants, 195–6
future development, 196, 203
NCEA, 223
role and functions, 101–2
Steering Committee, 229–30
and teacher education, 102–3
and technological education, 105
Technical Working Group, 192–3, 197–8
Working Party, 127–9
Hillery, Dr Patrick, 27, 28–9, 33, 50, 57, 66, 96–7, 173
Commission on Higher Education, 41–2, 43
OECD survey, 31
and RTCs, 51
Honorable Society of King's Inns, 8
Horgan, John, 142, 144, 145, 147, 148, 161
Hussey, Gemma, 107, 190, 217
Hyland, William, 52

I

Industrial Development Authority (IDA), 162, 173, 193, 257–8
and training policy, 185–8
industrial education council, 92
industrial placements, 74
industrial policy
and education, 250–1
and higher education, 184–93
skills shortages, 196
Industrial Policy Review Group (Culliton Report), 190–2
Industrial Training Authority (AnCO), 59, 162, 184–5

Institute for the Study of Social Change, UCD, 273
Institute of Chartered Accountants in Ireland (ICAI), 9
Institute of Costs and Works Accountants (ICAW), 9
Institute of Medical Laboratory Sciences (IMLS), 138–40
Institute of Molecular Medicine, TCD, 273
Institute of Public Administration (IPA), 219
Institute of Technology Carlow, 273
Institutes of Technology, 203, 237. *see also* Regional Technical Colleges, 260, 276
  academic standards, 254
  established, 229–32
Institution of Civil Engineers of Ireland, 10
Institution of Engineers of Ireland, 86
Interim Report of the Steering Committee's Technical Working Group, 192–3
Intermediate Education Act 1879, 269
International Study Group. *see* Hardiman Committee
Investment in Education (OECD), 31–2, 36, 58, 184, 269
Irish Academy of Music, 12
Irish Business and Employers' Confederation (IBEC), 257
Irish Congress of Trade Unions (ICTU), 83, 185
Irish Council for Science, Technology and Innovation (ICSTI), 274
Irish Federation of University Teachers (IFUT), 87, 115, 227
Irish Folklore Commission, 48
Irish Independent, 116, 200
Irish language, 13, 28
Irish Management Institute (IMI), 52, 73, 122, 191
Irish National Certification Authority (TEASTAS), 223
Irish National Committee for Certificates and Diplomas in Medical Laboratory Sciences, 138–40
Irish School of Ecumenics, 148
Irish Technological University, 230
Irish Times, 98, 226–7
Irish Universities Act 1908, 6, 127
Irish Vocational Education Association (IVEA), 51, 54, 83–4, 218
  and NCEA, 215
Italy, 247, 249, 251

J

Japan, 248, 249
Jesuit order, 4, 5, 65
John Moores University, Liverpool, 222
John XXII, Pope, 1
Joint Clinical Medical Board, 128
Jones, Jonah, 138

K

Keating, Justin, 118–19, 131, 229
Kerr, Clark, 46, 259–60
Kerry, County, 197
Kevin Street College of Technology, 16, 90–1, 141
  medical laboratory science, 139–40
  TCD links, 121–2
Kilkenny, County, 197
Killeen, Michael, 185
Korea, 248
KPMG report, 223

L

Labour, Department of, 54, 164, 184
Labour Party, 108, 116, 142, 226, 231
Laois, County, 197
Larkin, Terence, 214
Leaving Certificate, 44, 48, 53, 171
  participation rates, 196
  in RTCs, 81, 82
  statistics, 247
  VEC scholarships, 84–5
  vocational options, 191
Ledwich School, 7
Lee, Professor Joe, 228–9
legal education, 8, 15
Leitrim, County, 197
Lemass, Seán, 27, 28, 29, 184
Leneghan, Joseph, 106
Lenihan, Brian, 28–9, 58, 102
  Ballymun institution, 91
  and HEA, 99–100, 101
  and NCEA, 87
  and NIHEL, 68, 69, 70, 72
  and RTCs, 80–1, 82, 83–4, 85
  TCD-UCD merger plan, 97–8
L'Estrange, Gerry, 83
Letterkenny, Co. Donegal, 52
Letterkenny RTC, 54, 85, 218
lifelong learning, 196
Limerick, 12, 43, 46, 52, 60. *see also* National Institute for Higher Education Limerick
  university lobby, 65–75, 87, 232, 254
Limerick College of Art, Commerce and Technology, 167–8, 221
Limerick Corporation, 66, 67
Limerick Institute of Technology, 167–8
Limerick Technical College, 165, 167–8, 187
Limerick University Project Committee, 66–7, 71
literacy programme, 271
Liverpool Polytechic, 222
Local Authorities (Higher Education Grants) Bill, 99–100, 107
London University, 16, 90, 221
Loreto order, 5
Louvain, 3
Lyddy, Margaret, 71
Lynch, Jack, 28–9, 33, 41, 43, 73
Lynch, Professor Patrick, 32
Lyons, Dr F.S.L., 115
Lyons, James, 71

M

McBride, Sean, 30
McCann, Jack, 83, 215
McCarthy, Charles, 52
MacDiarmada, Pádraig, 88
McDonagh, Thomas, 13
MacGearailt, Seán, 173
McGilligan, Patrick, 13
McGlone, Jack, 88
McKay, John, 152
MacNeill, Eoin, 13
McQuillan, Jack, 106
Magee College, Derry, 5, 66
Major, John, 262
Manpower Consultative Committee (MCC), 173, 186–8
manpower planning, 54, 184–6
Marshall Aid, 29, 30
Martin, Augustine, 107–8
Martin, Micheál, 232, 234, 236, 237
Mary Immaculate College of Education, 160, 212
Massachusetts Institute of Technology (MIT), 74, 152, 276

matriculation, 13, 44, 155–6
mature students, 195–6, 271–2, 277
Mayo, County, 197
medical laboratory science, 138–40
medical training, 4–5, 6–8, 15, 128
Mediterranean Regional Project, 30
military cadets, 48
modular credit system, 158–9
Moloney, Paddy, 174
Monaghan, County, 197
Muintir na Tire, 67
Mulcahy, Noel, 52, 107
Mulcahy, Richard, 28
Mungret College, 65
Murphy, Professor John A, 107
Murphy, Dr Tom, 188
Murtagh, Luke, 169
music training, 12

N

Nagle, J C, 88
Nally, Dermot, 234, 238
National Adult Learning Council, 271
National Board for Science and Technology (NBST), 216
National College of Art and Design (NCAD), 11–12, 12, 79, 170
  constitution, 48
  and NCEA, 144, 145, 147
  statutory basis, 165, 211
  TCD degrees, 137–8
National College of Physical Education, Limerick, 108, 120–1, 122–3, 125. *see also* Thomond College of Education (TCE)
National Council for Educational Awards Act 1978, 107–8, 138, 142–3, 143–8
National Council for Educational Awards (NCEA), 53, 56, 60, 113, 165, 188
  awards
    distribution of, 194
    number of, 219
    recipient surveys, 167
    RTCs, 215–18, 230
    sub-degree, 252
    types of, 165–6
  boards of studies, 88
  Burke proposals, 116, 125–6
  and CDVEC, 91–2, 139–43
  challenges to, 220–2
  and comprehensive system, 120–1, 130, 131
  Course Recognition Committee, 212, 213
  decline of binary system, 218–23
  degree powers lost, 114
  degree powers restored, 136–40
  Development Committee 212, 213
  developments in, 219–20
  dissolution, 236–7, 238, 239
  and ESF, 163–4
  established, 85, 108–9
  legislation, 143–8
  NIHED plans, 152
  and NIHEL, 73, 122–3, 211
  degrees, 155, 156, 159, 161–2
  quality control, 254
  representation on, 144
  role and functions, 86–90, 222–3
  staff, 220
  teacher training, 102–3
  VEC recognition, 122
  and Working Party on Higher Education, 128, 129
National Council for Vocational Awards (NCVA), 223, 237, 239

National Development Plan 2000-2006, 272
National Education Convention, 224
National Farmers' Association, 67
National Gallery of Ireland, 170
National Institute for Higher Education Dublin (NIHED), 114, 115, 128, 159, 169, 170, 189–90, 193, 237
  in 1980 White Paper, 172
  and CDVEC, 140–1, 142
  established, 126, 130, 149–53
  governing body, 121
  Hardiman Report, 213–15
  legislation, 160–2
  narrow base, 251–2
  and NCEA, 144, 147–8, 212, 220–1
  research, 252
  statutes, 211
  university status, 214–15, 218, 229, 254
  Working Party proposals, 129
National Institute for Higher Education Limerick (NIHEL), 56, 87, 102, 108, 153, 158–9, 193, 237
  in 1980 White Paper, 172
  and comprehensive system, 131
  degree courses, 72, 74
  established, 70–3, 212
  funding, 157
  governing body, 121
  Hardiman Report, 213–15
  legislation, 160–2
  and MCC, 187
  narrow base, 251–2
  and NCEA, 144, 147, 148, 211–13, 220–1
    degrees, 136, 138, 155, 156
  NUI links, 114–15, 122–5, 124–5
  numbers in, 158
  role of, 106
  staff structures, 157–8
  statutes, 211
  statutory arrangements, 113
  university status, 214–15, 218, 229, 254
    achieved, 189–90
    fight for, 132, 154–5
  Walsh as head, 73–5
  and Working Party on Higher Education, 128, 129
National Manpower Service, 163, 185
National Museum of Ireland, 170
National Plan 2000-2006, 200
National Qualifications Authority, 236, 239
National Social Science Archive, UCD, 273
National University of Ireland Maynooth, 228
National University of Ireland (NUI), 3, 5, 6, 7, 10, 11, 14, 65, 107, 224
  in 1980 White Paper, 171, 172
  business schools, 9
  charters, 160–1
  constituent universities, 228
  dissolution discussed, 126–7, 225–9
  Irish language, 13
  legislation, 13, 48
  and NIHEs, 115, 123–5, 154, 155–6
  pressure of numbers, 16–17, 41, 42
  recognised colleges, 136
  restructuring plans, 113–14, 211
  TCD-UCD merger plan, 96, 98
  and Thomond College, 160
  vocational, 15–16

Working Party on Higher Education proposals, 128
Neave, Guy, 253, 255, 256, 259, 260, 261
Netherlands, the, 165, 249, 251, 252
New Colleges, 60, 67
proposed, 46–7, 48, 49, 55–6
New Zealand, 248
Newman, John Henry, 3, 4, 44, 189
NIHE News, 156
NIHE Parents' Action Committee, 155
non-completion levels, 198, 277
Northern Ireland (NI), 9, 268
Norway, 248, 251, 252, 253, 255
NUI/TCD Agreement, 98
nursing, 7, 196

O

Ó Dálaigh, Cearbhall, 17, 42
Ó hÓdhráin, Micheál, 174
Ó Laidhin, Liam, 173
Ó Laoghaire, Doiminic, 173
Ó Maoláin, Tomás, 106
Ó Maolcatha, Dr Liam, 149
Ó Maolcatha, Noel, 125
Ó Raifeartaigh, Dr Tarlach, 97, 115, 173
O'Brien, Conor Cruise, 131
O'Callaghan, Dr Finbarr, 173–4
O'Connor, Seán, 29, 49, 52, 71, 173
O'Donnell, John, 52
O'Donnell, Tom, 155
O'Donovan, John, 101
Offaly, County, 197
Official Secrets Act, 174
O'Hare, Dr Daniel, 126, 153, 161, 189–90
and NCEA, 212
NIHED Director, 150–1
O'Kennedy, Michael, 106
O'Malley, Desmond, 155
O'Malley, Donogh, 28–9, 31–2, 48, 58, 113, 119, 173, 224, 229, 269, 273–4
and Commission on Higher Education, 43, 47
and Limerick university, 67–8
merger plan, 96–7, 99
and RTCs, 80, 82, 85
technical education, 51, 52
O'Reilly, Tony, 276
Organisation for Economic Co-operation and Development (OECD), 29–31, 46, 86, 105, 118, 186, 194, 248, 271
influence of, 251
reports, 58, 269
education, 31–2
technical education, 32–6, 184
Organisation for European Economic Co-operation (OEEC), 29–31
O'Rourke, Mary, 190, 214, 217, 218
O'Shea, Brian, 218
O'Sullivan, John Marcus, 13
outreach centres, 197–8, 220
Oxford, 1

P

Paris, 1, 3
Parnell Square technical institute, 16
Partners in Education - Serving Community Needs (Green Paper), 217
part-time courses, 166, 195
number of students, 253–4
Pearse, Pádraig, 13
penal laws, 3
Pharmaceutical Society, 7
pharmacy, 130
political philosophy, 256
polytechnics, 251–3

Portobello College, 222
Portugal, 251
postgraduate students, 194
post-Leaving Certificate courses (PLCs), 196, 198
Power, Con, 188
Pratt, John, 252
Presbyterians, 3, 5
private colleges, 148, 196, 221–2, 237, 261, 275–6
private funding, 262

Q

Qualifications (Education and Training) Act 1999, 235, 236–9, 254, 259, 261
quality assurance, 238–9, 259
Queen's Colleges, 3–5, 4, 10, 12, 65, 269
Queen's University Belfast, 6, 13
Queen's University in Ireland, 3, 5
Quinlan, Professor P. M., 104

R

Rabbitte, Pat, 157
Rasmussen, Dr Werner, 34
Rathmines Institute, 16
Regional Education Councils, 54, 82
Regional Management Centre, NIHEL, 162
Regional Technical Colleges Act 1992, 217–18, 229, 233
Regional Technical Colleges (RTCs), 35, 50–6, 102, 108, 131, 185, 199, 211
  in 1980 White Paper, 171, 172
  award agencies, 222–3
  and Burke proposals, 116
  central administration, 255
  degrees, 254
  development of, 79–86
  fight for autonomy, 215–18
  funding
    ESF, 162–5
  public expenditure on, 84, 203
  and higher education, 58–60
  influences on, 251, 252
  Institutes of Technology, 229–32
  Limerick site, 68, 71
  management of, 82–4
  and MCC, 187
  middle-class students, 276
  and NCEA, 144, 148, 165–6
  number of students, 85–6
  part-time courses, 166
  research and consultancy, 216–18
  self-government, 217–18
  staff ratios, 166–7
  Steering Committee report, 57–8
  syllabuses, 85, 89
religious orders, 79, 269
religious tests, 2
Report on University Reorganisation (HEA), 98, 200
research, 200–2, 252
  funding, 272–5, 277
  and RTCs, 216–18
Robbins Report, 43
Roche, Dr Frank, 190, 191, 192
Rome, 3
Roscommon, County, 197
Royal College of Physicians (RCPI), 6
Royal College of Science for Ireland, 9
Royal College of Surgeons in Ireland (RCSI), 4, 6–7, 8, 79, 107, 128, 273
Royal College of Veterinary Surgeons, 11
Royal Dublin Society (RDS), 8, 9, 10, 11–12
Royal Institute of Architects in Ireland (RIAI), 10

Royal University of Ireland, 5–6, 10, 56, 65
Royal Veterinary College of Ireland, 11
Russell, Ted, 66
Ryan, Tony, 276

S

St Mary's College of Physical Education Twickenham, 90, 120, 121
St Patrick's College Drumcondra, 12, 190
St Patrick's College Maynooth, 3, 65, 79
  and HEA, 101
  legislation, 225–9
  and NUI, 113, 126–7
  Working Party proposals, 128
Salamanca, 3
scholarships, 168–9
science, 15, 33, 165, 270
  research investment fund, 273
Science, Technology and Commerce, Minister for, 274
Science and Art, Department of, 11
Scientific and Technical Personnel, Committee for, 30
Seanad Éireann, 13, 104
  NIHE debates, 161
  Universities Bill, 226–9
  universities discussed, 106–8
Second Programme for Economic Expansion, 25, 27, 184
second-level education, 271
  and NCEA, 147
  participation rates, 196, 269
  and RTCs, 81–2
  social inequality, 199
seminaries, 79
Sheehan, Jeremiah, 52
Sisters of Mercy, 12
Sligo, County, 197
Sligo Institute of Technology, 232
Sligo RTC, 84, 86, 188, 231–2
Sligo town, 52
Smurfit, Michael, 276
social engineering, 277–8
social exclusion, 198–9
Society of College Lecturers, 151
Spain, 251, 255
staff
  appointments, 48
  DIT, 236
  ratios, 48, 166–7, 200
    male-female, 199–200
    understaffing, 272–3
  and research, 201–2
Steering Committee on Technical Education, 52–3, 70, 71, 91, 107, 184
  and Commission on Higher Education, 55–7, 59–60
  and higher education, 58–60
  report, 53–4, 57–8, 80
  and RTCs, 82, 85
  technician awards, 87
Steering Committee on the Future Development of Higher Education (HEA), 196, 203, 229–31
student exchanges, 255
student hostels, 48
students, 48
  age of, 193, 196
  degree course participation, 194–5
  female participation, 194
  part-time, 253–4
  variations in participation, 196–7
Studies, 29
Sugar Company, 80, 81
Sweden, 247, 248, 249, 255
Switzerland, 248, 249
Synod of Thurles 1850, 3

T

Tallaght RTC, 197, 276
Tansey, Paul, 190, 191, 192
Targeted Higher Education Mature Student Fund, 272
teacher education, 12–13, 49, 55, 71, 194
  degrees, 102–3
  and NIHEs, 189–90
  numbers in, 79
  university links, 103
Teachers' Union of Ireland (TUI), 151, 221–2, 239
TEAGASC, 237
TEASTAS, 223
technical education, 9–10, 16, 27, 82. *see also* Steering Committee on Technical Education
  curriculum, 35
  developments, 50–4
  needs of industry, 80–1
  OECD report, 32–6, 86
Technical Instruction Branch, 52
Technical Schools Leaving Certificate, 35, 50–1, 57
Technical Working Group (HEA), 230–1
technician training, 49, 51, 53
technological education, 46–7, 91–2, 148, 270
  in 1980 White Paper, 171–2
  academic drift, 252–5
  comparability to universities, 146–7
  Culliton Report, 190–2
  distribution of courses, 194
  emphasis on, 105–8
  growth in, 79, 165–70, 249
  and industrial policy, 184–93
  in NIHEL, 71, 74
  percentage of students, 193–4
  role of NCEA, 219
Technology Foresight Fund, 274, 275
Thatcher, Margaret, 262
theology, 114, 128
Thomond College of Education (TCE), 128, 136, 138, 189, 211, 212
  established, 159–60
  and NCEA, 144, 148
  Working Party on Higher Education proposals, 129
Thornley, Dr David, 104, 108
Timmons, Eugene, 106
Tipperary (North Riding) VEC, 169
Tipperary Rural and Business Development Institute, 197
trade certificates, 53
Training of Technicians in Ireland (OECD), 32–6, 58, 86
Tralee RTC, 166, 169, 198, 200, 231–2
Treacy, Noel, 274
Trinity College Dublin (TCD), 4, 6, 7, 10, 11, 15, 79, 224
  and Burke proposals, 115
  and CDVEC, 130, 141, 142
  charter, 2
  and comprehensive system, 121–2
  constitution, 48
  DIT links, 221, 233
  foundation, 1–2
  funding, 14–15, 273
  legislation, 211, 225
  Magee College links, 66
  medical training, 6, 8
  and NCAD, 137–8
  new Board structure, 228
  proportion of arts students, 15–16
  rationalisation with UCD, 126
  size of, 14
  UCD merger plan, 47, 69, 79, 96–9, 102, 119–20, 260
  VEC links, 121–2

Working Party proposals, 128
Trow, Martin, 247, 248
Tunney, James, 106

U

Union of Students in Ireland (USI), 116, 122, 157
United Kingdom (UK), 247, 248, 249, 255, 268
binary system, 254–5
higher education model, 262
influence of, 251–2
United States of America (USA), 44, 74, 215, 249, 268
adult education, 271
funding, 276
higher education models, 247, 248, 251, 262
universities, 96–9, 161, 172
accommodation crisis, 102
arts courses, 15–16, 106–7, 188–9, 194–5
autonomy of, 237–8, 260–1
Bhreathnach legislation, 224–9
British models, 44, 129
Burke proposals, 115
Culliton Report, 190–2
distribution of courses, 194
funding, 168, 224–5
fees abolished, 270, 276
private, 276–7
student grants, 169
tuition fees, 224–5
and HEA, 101, 104–5
and MCC, 186–8
and NCEA, 144, 146–7
numbers in, 193–4
Qualifications Bill, 237
research, 200–1, 272–5
role of, 43–5
status of NIHEs, 132, 213–14
and technological ethos, 105–8
and training colleges, 137–8
vocational studies, 257
Working Party on Higher Education proposals, 128
Universities Act 1997, 2, 199, 200, 234, 235, 238, 254, 259
amendments, 228
debates, 225–9, 233
University College Cork (UCC), 6, 11, 14, 66, 68, 75, 79, 104, 113
and Burke proposals, 115
independence proposed, 96
legislation, 225–9
medicine, 15
and NIHEL, 122–5, 154, 155–6
separation from NUI, 126–7
size of, 16–17
Working Party on Higher Education proposals, 128
University College Dublin (UCD), 4–6, 10–13, 52, 68, 79, 91, 108, 153, 159, 231, 276
arts students, 188
Folklore Commission, 48
and HEA, 101
legislation, 225–9
move to Belfield, 16–17, 41, 96–7
proposals for change, 1974, 113
rationalisation with TCD, 126
research, 272, 273
size of, 14
TCD merger plan, 47, 69, 79, 96–9, 102, 119–20, 260
University College Galway (UCG), 6, 48, 65, 68, 79, 88, 113
and Burke proposals, 115
and Galway RTC degree, 125–6
independence proposed, 96
Irish language, 13–14
legislation, 225–9
and NIHEL, 124–5
separation from NUI, 126–7

size of, 16–17
Working Party on Higher Education proposals, 128
University Development Committee, 17, 41, 42
University Grants Committee (UK), 41, 99
University of Dublin. *see* Trinity College Dublin
University of Glamorgan, 222
University of Limerick (UL), 189–90, 214–15, 262, 276
University of Limerick (Dissolution of Thomond College) Bill, 1991, 189
University of Ulster, 222

V

veterinary medicine, 130
Vincentian order, 12
vocational education, 16, 33, 59, 79, 223. *see also* Regional Technical Colleges
and manpower planning, 185–6
numbers in, 79
research and consultancy, 216–18
role of NCEA, 219
and RTCs, 81–2
Vocational Education Act 1930, 16, 32–3, 211
and RTCs, 82, 83–4
Vocational Education Committees (VECs), 80, 157. *see also* Regional Technical Colleges
Dublin, 90–2, 126
funding, 114, 162–5
and RTCs, 82–4, 114
scholarships, 84–5
Vocational Teachers' Association, 33, 51, 52

W

Walsh, Archbishop, 14
Walsh, Dr Edward, 71, 108, 174, 232, 257, 262
and Burke restructuring, 114–15
degree courses, 72
fund-raising, 276
head of NIHEL, 73–5
and NCEA, 211–13
and NUI, 124, 154, 155–6
role of, 156–7
and university status, 189–90, 215
Walsh, Dr Tom, 126, 139, 150
Walshe, John, 229
Waterford, 12, 52
university sought, 230–2
Waterford, County, 197
Waterford Institute of Technology, 231–2, 239
Waterford RTC, 81, 84, 86, 126, 163
Westmeath VEC, 217
Whelan, Dermot, 214
Whitaker, T.K., 25, 26, 27, 107, 161
White Paper 1995, 192, 199, 223, 259
White Paper 2000, 272
White Paper on Educational Development 1980, 170–3, 197, 203, 211
Wilson, John, 105, 108, 122, 160, 166, 169, 212
and CDVEC, 142–3
ESF funding, 163
and NCEA, 136–40, 144–8
and NIHEs, 151, 152–3, 155
Working Party on Higher Education, 126, 127–9